# The Refugee in International Law

# THE
# REFUGEE
# IN
# INTERNATIONAL
# LAW

GUY S. GOODWIN-GILL

CLARENDON PRESS · OXFORD
1983

Oxford University Press, Walton Street, Oxford OX2 6DP

London Glasgow New York Toronto
Delhi Bombay Calcutta Madras Karachi
Kuala Lumpur Singapore Hong Kong Tokyo
Nairobi Dar es Salaam Cape Town
Melbourne Auckland
and associated companies in
Beirut Berlin Ibadan Mexico City Nicosia

Oxford is a trade mark of Oxford University Press

Published in the United States
by Oxford University Press, New York

British Library Cataloguing in Publication Data

Goodwin-Gill, Guy S.
The refugee in international law.
1. Refugees—Legal status, laws, etc.
I. Title
341.48'6     JX4281
ISBN 0-19-825372-9

Library of Congress Cataloging in Publication Data
Goodwin-Gill, Guy S.
The refugee in international law.
Bibliography: p.
Includes index.
1. Refugees, Political—Legal status, laws, etc.
I. Title
JX4292.R4G66   1983      341.4'86      83-3946
ISBN 0-19-825372-9

Typeset by DMB (Typesetting), Oxford.
Printed in Great Britain
at the University Press, Oxford
by Eric Buckley
Printer to the University

# PREFACE

Refugees have been a continuous feature of international life in the present century. They were one of the first concerns of both the League of Nations and the United Nations, and over the last sixty years vast numbers have found the opportunity of a new life in countries of asylum and resettlement. Yet no end is in sight to the potential for future flows. The major inspiration for this book has come from my own involvement with the cases of many hundreds of refugees and asylum-seekers, in my capacity as a legal adviser in the Office of the United Nations High Commissioner for Refugees (UNHCR). Latterly, however, added impetus was given to the project by a growing sense of dissatisfaction with existing mechanisms and procedures, and the feeling that these and the commentaries on them have failed to develop and keep pace with the crucial issues, let alone with the dimensions of today's problems. At times it has seemed as if refugees are not only an apprehended, but also an accepted dimension to every conflict, whether resulting from external aggression or from radical, internal political and social upheavals.

The fact of flight across frontiers by those in fear for their lives or freedom neatly sets in opposition the sovereign self-interest of states and the apparently near-universal sentiments of concern which people feel for those deserving protection. Only since the beginning of this decade has attention begun to focus on what seems to me to be an essential premiss: that the situation of being a refugee is, and ought to be, a situation of exception; and on its corollary: that legal and political measures should be directed either to the avoidance of that situation, so that people may pursue their lives in peace, at home, and free from prejudice and persecution; or to its prompt resolution through voluntary repatriation.

Political realities, reported daily in the world's media, often make remote the attainment of this ideal; thus, refugee law and the protection of those who flee continue to occupy an essential place in any international regime professing concern for humanitarian issues. In the light of this dimension, I have attempted to describe the foundations and the framework of refugee law by concentrating on three core issues: the definition of refugees,

'asylum' for refugees, and the protection of refugees. My aim has
been to show that refugees are a class known to and defined by
general international law; that certain legal implications follow
from the existence of this class and of related principles (in particular, that states are bound not to return refugees to territories
where they may be persecuted or where their life or freedom may
be threatened); and that the international community, besides
being responsible in a general sense for finding solutions, also has
the necessary legal standing to protect refugees, for which purpose
it may be represented by UNHCR or by individual states. In pursuit of these objectives, I have examined the provisions and effectiveness of relevant treaties, state practice (especially in the face of
recent refugee crises), and the measures taken by states in their
municipal law and administrative arrangements to protect
refugees.

I hope that this book will serve not only as an authoritative
statement of the current law, but also as a pointer to the future,
as a basis for further enquiry and the development of appropriate
principles and solutions. Overall, the exceptional situation of the
refugee cannot be isolated from broader human rights issues. If so
much in the way of basic freedoms and standards of treatment can
be achieved for the refugee, then no less ought to be attainable on
behalf of every man, woman, and child who has not yet chosen
flight from their homeland.

Sydney                                                Guy S. Goodwin-Gill
December 1982

# ACKNOWLEDGEMENTS

This study has some of its origins in my research work leading to the degree of Doctor of Philosophy in the University of Oxford, part of which was published in 1978 as *International Law and the Movement of Persons between States*. Certain of the ideas were introduced, and others began to be elaborated, in an article published in volume 3 of the *Michigan Yearbook of International Legal Studies*. The greater part of the research and writing, however, was completed during 1981 and, wherever possible, has been updated in the light of developments throughout 1982.

The process whereby ideas have developed and matured necessarily owes much to the influence of those with whom I have worked, sparred, and disagreed over the last six years, too many to mention and thank by name. I am especially grateful, however, to Dr James Crawford, Reader in Law at the University of Adelaide and now of the Australian Law Reform Commission, and to Gervase Coles, Deputy Legal Adviser in the Australian Department of Foreign Affairs and now Chief, Conferences and Treaties Section, UNHCR. Both read substantial portions of the manuscript and offered much valued criticism and advice. The worth of my own practical experience has been heightened by my association with many government officials involved in refugee matters; it almost always seemed to me that we shared humanitarian objectives, even if our ideas about appropriate solutions to particular problems may have differed. I am pleased to have had the opportunity to work with Roy McDowall, of the United Kingdom Home Office; Ian Simington, Assistant Secretary, Refugees and International Branch of the Australian Department of Immigration and Ethnic Affairs and now Senior UNHCR Co-ordinator for South-East Asia; and John Hoyle, of the Australian Department of Foreign Affairs.

I owe a special debt to the members of Australia's Determination of Refugee Status Committee and its Secretariat, in particular, John Forster, for long its chairman and always a source of helpful advice; also Keith Baker, John Cleary, Peter Byrne, Sue Bromley, Greg Jones, Tony Greville, Barbara Phi, Peter Job, and Howard Porter. In New Zealand, too, I was pleased to be closely associated with the Inter-departmental Committee on Refugees, with its chairman, Bill Mansfield, Head of the Legal Division, Ministry of Foreign Affairs, and with Dell Higgie and Joan Wiltshire.

I received a great deal of practical help from colleagues in the United Nations Joint Office in Sydney. Gilberto Rizzo gave early encouragement before leaving as chief of that office to return to the United Nations Department of Public Information in New York. His successor, Dr Hugo Idoyaga, with many years field experience as a Representative for UNHCR, was a constant source of knowledge and assistance, while I am grateful also to my colleague in the resettlement area, Veronica Bull. The librarians of the United Nations Information Centre in Sydney, Pat Cook and Con Sarantis, willingly ferreted out many an obscure document, while Gayle Delaney and Nguyen Thi Thao gave patient help with typing. It will also be clear that much is owed to those colleagues in UNHCR Headquarters, Geneva, and in UNHCR offices throughout the world who were willing to share in a positive way their own views and experience. The opinions expressed here nevertheless remain my own, and are not necessarily held by the Office of the United Nations High Commissioner for Refugees.

Finally, it has been a pleasure once again to have had the benefit of the knowledge and courtesy of the staff of the Oxford University Press.

# CONTENTS

# PART IV    CONCLUSIONS

# ANNEXES

# TABLE OF TREATIES AND OTHER INTERNATIONAL INSTRUMENTS

# TABLE OF CASES

# SELECTED ABBREVIATIONS

| | |
|---|---|
| *AJIL* | American Journal of International Law |
| *AsylVfG* | *Asylverfahrensgesetz* (1982 Asylum Procedure Law of the Federal Republic of Germany) |
| *AuslG* | *Ausländergesetz* (1965 Aliens Law of the Federal Republic of Germany) |
| *BDIL* | *British Digest of International Law*, vols. 2b-7, London, 1965, 1967 (C. Parry, ed.) |
| *BGBl* | *Bundesgesetzblatt* (published laws of the Federal Republic of Germany and/or Austria) |
| *BVerwGE* | *Entscheidungen des Bundesverwaltungsgerichts* (decisions of the Federal Administrative Court of the Federal Republic of Germany) |
| *BVerfGE* | *Entscheidungen des Bundesverfassungsgerichts* (decisions of the Federal Constitutional Court of the Federal Republic of Germany) |
| CFR | Code of Federal Regulations (USA) |
| CTD | Convention Travel Document (issued under Article 28 of the 1951 Convention relating to the Status of Refugees) |
| D. Ct. | District Court (USA) |
| DORS Committee | Determination of Refugee Status Committee (Australia) |
| ECOSOC | Economic and Social Council of the United Nations |
| ETS | European Treaty Series |
| GA | United Nations General Assembly |
| Hackworth, *Digest* | G. H. Hackworth, *Digest of International Law*, 8 vols., Washington, 1940-4 |
| HC | House of Commons |
| HC Deb. | Parliamentary Debates, House of Commons, 5th series |
| HL Deb. | Parliamentary Debates, House of Lords, 5th series |
| ICJ | International Court of Justice |

| | |
|---|---|
| ICOR | Inter-departmental Committee on Refugees (New Zealand) |
| ILC | International Law Commission |
| ILO | International Labour Organization |
| ImmAR | Immigration Appeals Reports |
| IMCO | Intergovernmental Maritime Consultative Organization (renamed in 1982 as the International Maritime Organization (IMO)) |
| INA | Immigration and Nationality Act 1952 (USA) |
| INS | Immigration and Naturalization Service (USA) |
| IRO | International Refugee Organization |
| *JCRR* | *Jurisprudence de la Commission de Recours des Réfugiés* (France) |
| LN | League of Nations |
| LNTS | League of Nations Treaty Series |
| Moore, *Arbitrations* | John Bassett Moore, *History and digest of the international arbitrations to which the United States has been a party*, Washington, 1898. |
| Moore, *Digest* | John Bassett Moore, *Digest of International Law*, 8 vols., Washington, 1906. |
| OAS | Organization of American States |
| OAU | Organization of African Unity |
| OFPRA | *Office français de protection des réfugiés et apatrides* |
| OJ | Official Journal |
| PCIJ | Permanent Court of International Justice |
| RSAC | Refugee Status Advisory Committee (Canada) |
| UN | United Nations |
| UNDRO | Office of the United Nations Disaster Relief Co-ordinator |
| UNHCR | Office of the United Nations High Commissioner for Refugees |
| UNRRA | United Nations Relief and Rehabilitation Administration |
| UNRWA | United Nations Relief and Works Agency for Palestine Refugees in the Near East |
| UNTS | United Nations Treaty Series |
| *VerwRspr* | *Verwaltungsrechtssprechung in Deutschland* (collection of administrative law decisions) |
| Whiteman, *Digest* | Marjorie M. Whiteman, *Digest of International Law*, 15 vols., Washington, 1963-73. |

# PART ONE

REFUGEES

# Chapter I

# DEFINITION AND DESCRIPTION

## 1. Refugees

In this work, the word 'refugee' is used as a term of art, that is, a term having a content verifiable according to principles of general international law. In ordinary usage, it may enjoy a broader, looser meaning, signifying someone in flight, who seeks to escape conditions or personal circumstances found to be intolerable. The destination of the person fleeing is not relevant; the flight is to freedom, to safety. Likewise, the reasons dictating flight may be many; flight from oppression, from a threat to life or liberty, flight from prosecution; flight from deprivation, from grinding poverty; flight from war or civil strife; flight from the consequences of natural disasters, earthquake, flood, drought, famine. Implicit in the ordinary meaning of the word 'refugee' lies an assumption that the person concerned is worthy of being, and ought to be, assisted, and, if necessary, protected from the causes of flight. The 'fugitive' from justice, the person fleeing criminal prosecution for breach of the law in its ordinary and non-political aspect, is therefore often excepted from this category of refugees.[1] For the purposes of international law, states have limited the concept of the refugee as beneficiary of protection and assistance. For example, 'economic refugees'—the term is generally frowned upon—are not considered to come within the definition. The solution to their problem, perhaps, lies more within the province of international aid and development, rather than in the institution of asylum.

Defining refugees may appear an unworthy exercise in legalism and semantics, obstructing a prompt response to the needs of people in distress. States have nevertheless insisted on fairly restrictive criteria for identifying those who are to benefit from

[1] The Shorter Oxford English Dictionary defines a refugee as 'one who, owing to religious persecution or political troubles, seeks refuge in a foreign country; orig. applied to the French Huguenots who came to England after the revocation of the Edict of Nantes in 1685'. Refuge is in turn defined, *inter alia*, as 'shelter or protection from danger or trouble, succour sought by, or rendered to a person ... A place of safety or security; a shelter, asylum, stronghold'.

refugee status. For the victims of natural calamities,[2] the very fact of need may be the sufficient identifying factor, but for the victims of conditions or disasters with a human origin, additional factors are required. The purpose of any definition or description of the class of refugees is to facilitate, and to justify, aid and protection; moreover, in practice, satisfying the relevant criteria will indicate entitlement to the pertinent rights or benefits. In determining the content in international law of the class of refugees, therefore, the traditional sources—treaties and the practice of states—must be examined, with account taken also of the practice and procedures of the various bodies established by the international community to deal with the problems of refugees.

## 2. Refugees defined in international instruments 1922–46

In treaties and arrangements concluded under the auspices of the League of Nations, a group or category approach to the definition of refugees was adopted. That someone was (a) outside their country of origin and (b) without the protection of the government of that state, were sufficient and necessary conditions. A Russian refugee, for example, was defined in 1926 to include 'any person of Russian origin who does not enjoy or who no longer enjoys the protection of the Government of the Union of Socialist Soviet Republics and who has not acquired another nationality'.[3] In this instance, presence outside the country of origin was not explicitly required, but was implicit in the objectives of the

---

[2] By GA Res. 2816 (XXVI), 14 Dec. 1971, the Office of the Disaster Relief Co-ordinator was established with the UN, in recognition of the necessity 'to ensure prompt, effective and efficient response to a Government's need for assistance, at the time of a natural disaster or other disaster situation'. Cf. Brown, *Disaster Preparedness and the United Nations* (1979) 14-32; he cites (at 29) UN legal counsel opinion that the phrase 'other disaster situations' would ordinarily cover 'man-made disasters', but notes that this aspect was discounted in the Secretary-General's preliminary report (E/4994, 9) and that co-sponsors of Res. 2816 (XXVI) were not in agreement on the issue. See further UN doc. A/35/228, paras. 19-25 (1980), and the critical report of the Joint Inspection Unit: JIU/REP/80/11; UN doc. A/36/73 and Add. 1; also on special economic and disaster relief assistance, UN docs/ A/36/737 and Add. 1. In 1981, the General Assembly resolved to strengthen the capacity of the UN system to respond to natural disasters and other disaster situations: GA Res. 36/225, 17 Dec. 1981.

[3] Arrangement relating to the issue of identity certificates to Russian and Armenian refugees, 12 May 1926: 84 LNTS no. 2004. The definition of 'Armenian refugee' was to like effect: ibid. See also 'Assyrian, Assyro-Chaldean, and assimilated refugee' as defined in the arrangement of 30 June 1928: 89 LNTS no. 2006; art. 1, 1933 Convention relating to the international status of refugees, and reservations thereto: 159 LNTS no. 3663.

arrangements, namely, the issue of identity certificates for the purpose of travel and resettlement.[4]

A similar approach was adopted in 1936 arrangements in respect of those fleeing Germany,[5] which were later developed by Article 1 of the 1938 Convention, to cover:

(a) Persons possessing or having possessed German nationality and not possessing any other nationality who are proved not to enjoy, in law or fact, the protection of the German Government.

(b) Stateless persons not covered by previous conventions or agreements who have left German territory after being established therein and who are proved not to enjoy, in law or in fact, the protection of the German government.[6]

Article 1(2) excluded from the definition persons who left Germany for reasons of purely personal convenience.

At a meeting in Evian in the same year, participating states resolved to establish an inter-governmental committee with, as its primary objective, 'facilitating involuntary emigration from Germany (including Austria)'.[7] Included within the scope of the committee's activities were those who had yet to emigrate on account of their political opinions, religious beliefs, or racial origin, as well as those who had already left for those reasons and had not established themselves elsewhere.[8]

Commenting on definitions, Simpson observed in 1938 that all had certain inherent deficiences. He stressed the importance of keeping in view the 'essential quality' of the refugee as one 'who

---

[4] It was also provided that certificates should cease to be valid if the bearers returned to their country of origin; see form and wording of the certificate attached to the arrangement of 5 July 1922: 13 LNTS no. 355; Res. 9 of the arrangement of 30 June 1928: 89 LNTS no. 2005; certificate attached to the Convention concerning the status of refugees coming from Germany of 10 Feb. 1938: 192 LNTS no. 4461.

[5] Art. 1, provisional arrangement concerning the status of refugees coming from Germany, 4 July 1936: 171 LNTS no. 3952.

[6] 1938 Convention concerning the status of refugees coming from Germany: 191 LNTS no. 4461. The definition was subsequently extended to cover persons coming from Austria, following the *Anschluss*; see the additional protocol, 14 Sept. 1939: 198 LNTS no. 4634.

[7] See further below, ch. V. s. 3, on the scheme for 'orderly departure' from Vietnam. Speaking in 1979 to the Geneva Conference on Refugees and Displaced Persons in Southeast Asia, United States Vice-President Mondale characterized the 1938 Evian Conference as a failure. 'The civilized world', he said, 'hid in a cloak of legalism.' UN Press Release SG/REF/3, 21 July 1979, Take 2, p. 1.

[8] Para. 8, Resolution adopted by the Intergovernmental Meeting at Evian, 14 July 1938: LN OJ, 19th year, nos. 8-9: Aug.-Sept. 1938, 676-7. See also art. 1, agreement relating to the issue of travel documents to refugees who are the concern of the Inter-governmental Committee on Refugees, 15 Oct. 1946: 11 UNTS 73.

has sought refuge in a territory other than that in which he was formerly resident as a result of political events which rendered his continued residence in his former territory impossible or intolerable'.[9] This description is in turn something of an abstraction from what was known then about the 'political events' producing refugees. While the notion of the impossibility or intolerability of continued residence illustrates the problem of the refugee in broad strokes, after the Second World War stress was laid on more precise criteria. This is evident first in the constitution of the International Refugee Organization (IRO),[10] then in the Statute of the Office of the United Nations High Commissioner for Refugees (UNHCR), and finally in the provisions of the 1951 Convention relating to the Status of Refugees.

The constitution of the IRO, like many earlier instruments, specified certain categories to be assisted. 'Refugees' included victims of the Nazi, Fascist, or Quisling regimes which had opposed the United Nations, certain persons of Jewish origin, or foreigners or stateless persons who had been victims of Nazi persecution, as well as persons considered as refugees before the outbreak of the Second World War for reasons of race, religion, nationality, or political opinion. The IRO was also competent to assist 'displaced persons', including those deported or expelled from their own countries, some of whom had been sent to undertake forced labour.[11] In addition, the IRO Constitution included as refugees those unable or unwilling to avail themselves of the protection of the government of their country of nationality or former residence. It was expressly recognized that individuals might have 'valid objections' to returning to their country of origin, including 'persecution or fear based on reasonable grounds of persecution because of race, religion, nationality or political opinions,' and objections 'of a political nature judged by the [IRO] to be valid'.

## (3) Refugees for the Purposes of the United Nations

The Office of the United Nations High Commissioner for Refugees is the principal UN agency concerned with refugees; its

---

[9] Simpson, *Refugees—A Preliminary Report of a Survey* (1938), 1.

[10] A predecessor organization, the United Nations Relief and Rehabilitation Administration (UNRRA), was principally concerned with the repatriation of the millions displaced by the Nazi and Fascist regimes and by the effects of war. It was not authorized to resettle the displaced or to deal with refugees as such. Cf. Bethell, *The Last Secret* (1974); Tolstoy, *Victims of Yalta* (rev. ed. 1979).

[11] On the re-emergence of the term 'displaced persons' see further below, s. 3(2).

competence *ratione personae* is considered more fully below, but related developments within the UN have also affected the content of the refugee concept. Thus, Article 14 of the Universal Declaration of Human Rights declares: '(1) Everyone has the right to seek and to enjoy in other countries asylum from persecution. (2) This right may not be invoked in the case of prosecutions genuinely arising from non-political crimes or from acts contrary to the purposes and principles of the United Nations'. The relation of 'asylum'[12] to persecution is maintained in the 1967 Declaration on Territorial Asylum which also deals further with the circumstances in which 'the right to seek and to enjoy asylum' may not be invoked.[13] The bases for an international legal concept of the refugee must therefore be sought in treaties, in UN practice, and in the UNHCR Statute.

## (1) STATUTE OF THE UNITED NATIONS HIGH COMMISSIONER FOR REFUGEES (UNHCR)

UNHCR was established by the General Assembly to provide 'the necessary legal protection for refugees' and to seek 'permanent solutions for the problem of refugees'. According to its Statute, the work of the Office shall be of an entirely non-political character—it is to be 'humanitarian' and 'social' and to relate, as a rule, to groups and categories of refugees.[14]

The Statute first brings within UNHCR's competence refugees covered by various earlier treaties and arrangements. It next includes refugees resulting from events occurring before 1 January 1951, who are outside their country of origin[15] and unable or unwilling to avail themselves of its protection 'owing to a well-founded fear of being persecuted' or 'for reasons other than personal convenience'.[16] Finally, the Statute extends to:

Any other person who is outside the country of his nationality, or if he has no nationality, the country of his former habitual residence because he has or had well-founded fear of persecution by reason of his race, religion, nationality or political opinion and is unable or, because of

[12] See below, ch. V, s. 1.

[13] Art. 1(2). See annexe VI, and below, ch. III, s. 4.

[14] See annexe III.

[15] The phrase 'country of origin' is used for convenience here and throughout the text; it signifies, as appropriate, the refugee's country of nationality or, if he or she has no nationality, his or her country of former habitual residence.

[16] This latter provision would cover the situation of a person who, by reason of persecution already suffered, remains unwilling to return even though the circumstances which gave rise to his or her refugee status have ceased to exist. Cf. art. 1C(5), (6), 1951 Convention.

such fear, is unwilling to avail himself of the protection of the government of the country of his nationality, or, if he has no nationality, to return to the country of his former habitual residence.

This description is of universal application, containing neither temporal nor geographical limitations. The substantive or ideological criteria are nevertheless a significant restriction on the scope of refugees 'strictly so-called', who are required to establish a well-founded fear of persecution on the stated grounds.

The definition is of critical importance in determining who is entitled to the protection and assistance of the United Nations, for it is the lack of protection by their own government which distinguishes refugees from ordinary aliens. In attempting to make good this deficiency, the appropriate international bodies will aim generally to protect the refugee's basic human rights, including the right to life, liberty, and security of the person. Simultaneously, 'protection activities' may focus on specific issues peculiar to the refugee: for example, ensuring that no refugee is returned to a country in which he or she will be in danger; ensuring that every refugee is recognized as such, that asylum is granted, that expulsion is prevented, or that travel and identity documents are issued. Any intervention with state governments must therefore have a sound jurisdictional base.

## (2) DEVELOPMENT OF THE STATUTORY DEFINITION AND EXTENSION OF THE MANDATE

The UNHCR Statute, however, contains an apparent contradiction. On the one hand, it affirms that the work of the Office shall relate, as a rule, to groups and categories of refugees. On the other hand, it proposes a definition of the refugee which is essentially individualistic, requiring a case by case examination of subjective and objective elements. The escalation in refugee crises over the last 30 years has made it necessary to be flexible in the administration of UNHCR's mandate. In consequence, there has been a significant broadening of what may be termed the concept of 'refugees of concern to the international community'.

A major role in these developments has been played by the United Nations General Assembly and the Economic and Social Council, whose policy directions the High Commissioner is required to follow.[17] More recently, a similar influence has been exercised by the Executive Committee of the High Commis-

---

[17] Para. 3 of the Statute.

sioner's Programme. Established in 1957,[18] the Executive Committee's terms of reference include advising the High Commissioner, on request, in the exercise of the statutory functions; and advising on the appropriateness of providing international assistance through UNHCR in order to solve such specific refugee problems as may arise.

It was also in 1957 that the General Assembly first authorized the High Commissioner to assist refugees who did not come fully within the statutory definition.[19] The case involved large numbers of mainland Chinese in Hong Kong whose status as 'refugees' was complicated by the existence of two Chinas, each of which might have been called upon to exercise protection. Given the need for assistance, express authorization to the High Commissioner 'to use his good offices to encourage arrangements for contributions' was an effective, pragmatic solution.[20] Assistance to other specific groups was authorized in the years which followed.[21] Concurrently, the General Assembly developed the notion of the High Commissioner's 'good offices' as an umbrella idea under which to bring refugees who did not come within the competence, or 'immediate competence',[22] of the United Nations. The type of assistance which might be given was initially limited, often to the transmission of financial contributions, but that restriction was soon dropped.[23]

General Assembly resolutions are never consistent in their language, and their rationale, too, is often hidden. The nature of the activities in which UNHCR was involved, however, suggests that the class of refugees assisted were either clearly not within the Statute or else had not been specifically determined to be within the Statute. At the same time, the situations in question shared certain factors in common: the people in need (a) had crossed an international frontier, (b) as a result of conflicts, or radical political, social, or economic changes in their countries of origin. The very size of refugee problems in Africa in the 1960s made individual assessment of refugee status impractical, as did the absence

[18] GA Res. 1166 (XII), 26 Nov. 1957. There are now forty-one members of the Executive Committee, the latest addition being Namibia, represented by the UN Council for Namibia: Ecosoc Res. 1982/110, 19 Apr. 1982.

[19] GA Res. 1167(XII), 26 Nov. 1957. See also Res. 1784(XVII), 7 Dec. 1962.

[20] See Hambro, *The Problem of Chinese Refugees in Hong Kong* (1955), for background.

[21] For example, to Algerians fleeing to Tunisia and Morocco to escape the effects of the struggle for liberation: GA Resolutions 1286 (XIII), 5 Dec. 1958, 1389 (XVI), 20 Nov. 1959, 1500 (XV), 5 Dec. 1960, 1672(XVI), 18 Dec. 1961; and to Angolan refugees in the Congo: GA Res. 1671(XVI), 10 Dec. 1961.

[22] The term is employed but not defined in GA Res. 1499(XV), 5 Dec. 1960.

[23] Compare Resolutions 1167(XII) and 1784(XVII).

of appropriate machinery. Moreover, the pragmatic, rather than doctrinal, approach to the new problems was almost certainly influenced by factors such as the desire to avoid the imputation on newly independent states which is carried by every determination that a well-founded fear of persecution exists; and the feeling, not always made manifest, that while 'political conditions' had compelled the flight of the entire group in question, it might not be possible to establish a well-founded fear on an individual case-by-case basis. The 'group approach', by concentrating on the fact that those concerned are effectively without the protection of their own government, thus avoids the restrictions of the legal definition.[24]

More recently, the General Assembly has spoken of and unanimously commended the High Commissioner's activities on behalf of 'refugees and displaced persons of concern to his Office'. The reference to 'displaced persons' dates from 1975, when it was contemporaneous with UNHCR's first involvement in the Indo-China peninsula.[25] If the term was intended to cover groups, besides refugees, who had crossed international frontiers, then it may have been something of a misnomer. 'Displaced persons' had a special meaning in the constitution of the IRO, but had otherwise been commonly employed to describe those displaced *within* their own country, for example, by the effects of civil strife or natural disasters.[26]

Recent refugee crises illustrate both the development in the refugee definition and the problems which may arise in its application to large numbers of asylum-seekers. In the case of Indo-China, for example, it has been estimated that, since 1975, some one million people have left Kampuchea, Laos, and Vietnam.[27]

---

[24] Schnyder, 'Les aspects juridiques actuels du problème des réfugiés' Hague *Recueil* (1965-I) 339-450, at 426-43; Sadruddin Aga Khan, 'Legal Problems relating to refugees and displaced persons' Hague *Recueil* (1976-I) 287-352, at 306, 339-43.

[25] GA Res. 3455(XXX), 9 Dec. 1975.

[26] In 1977, the High Commissioner sought advice from the Executive Committee on the refugee/displaced person distinction, but no formal response was forthcoming. See further below, n. 35.

[27] A summary of the background is provided in UN doc. A/34/627, report of the Secretary-General on the meeting on refugees and displaced persons in South East Asia, Geneva, 20-1 July 1979, and subsequent developments. See also Osborne, 'The Indochinese Refugees: Causes and Effects' *International Affairs* 1980, 37-53; Grant, *The Boat People* (1980); Garcia Marquez, 'The Vietnam Wars' *Rolling Stone* May 1980; Turley, 'Hanoi's Domestic Dilemmas' *Problems of Communism* vol. 29 (1980) no. 4; Thayer, 'Dilemmas of Development in Vietnam' 75 *Current History* no. 442 (1978); id. 'Vietnam—Beleaguered Outpost of Socialism' 79 *Current History* no. 461 (1980); Foreign Language Press, Hanoi, *The Hoa in Vietnam* Dossiers I and II (1978); id. *Those who Leave* (1979); id. *With Firm Steps: Southern Vietnam since Liberation 1975-1977* (1978); 'Human Rights, War and Mass Exodus' *Transnational Perspectives* (1982) 34-8.

UNHCR had already become involved in the region, at the request of the governments concerned, and was promoting assistance programmes for those displaced by the effects of war within Laos and Vietnam.[28] With the turn of events in the spring of 1975, UNHCR was called upon to assist many who had left their countries of origin, in particular by securing asylum,[29] providing care and maintenance, and promoting resettlement; the Provisional Revolutionary Government in South Vietnam also requested UNHCR to promote voluntary repatriation.

Official documentation of the period reveals a reluctance to apply the term 'refugee' to those assisted by UNHCR. Reference is made, for example, to 'displaced persons from Indo-China outside their country of origin',[30] and to 'persons leaving the Indo-China peninsula in small boats'.[31] UNHCR's operations on behalf of such persons were never challenged on the basis that they might not fall within the mandate of the Office, and assistance and protection continued to be extended on the basis of a somewhat ambiguous resolution adopted by the General Assembly in December 1975.[32] The Executive Committee, however, began to employ more specific language in its annual conclusions. In 1976, it spoke of 'asylum-seekers' who had left their country in small boats,[33] and in 1977 referred expressly to the problems of refugees from Indo-China.[34]

[28] See the High Commissioner's statement to the 25th Session of the Executive Committee (1974): UN doc. A/AC. 96/511, annexe; report of the High Commissioner to the General Assembly (1975): E/5688, Add. 1, paras. 34-43. Such assistance was undertaken 'within the framework of [UNHCR's] "good offices" function', and 'on a purely humanitarian basis'.

[29] Already difficulties had been encountered in obtaining even temporary admission for those arriving by small boat or rescued at sea: UN doc. A/AC.96/516/Add. 1, para. 92.

[30] For example, in UN docs. A/AC.96/516/Add. 1; A/AC.96/INF.147; in the High Commissioner's report to the General Assembly (1976), reference is made to 'special operations within the framework of the High Commissioner's good offices function' and to 'displaced persons who face problems analogous to those of refugees': E/5853, paras. 170 ff.

[31] UN doc. A/AC.96/534, para. 57 (1976). References continued to be framed in terms of 'displaced persons' and 'boat people' through 1977 and 1978 (see E/5987, paras. 6, 185, 207, 212, 214; A/AC.96/553/Add. 1). In the latter year, however, official documents also began to use the composite 'refugees and displaced persons'; cf. the statement for those arriving by small boat or rescued at sea: UN doc. A/AC.96/516/Add. 1, para. 92.

[32] GA Res. 3455(XXX) on humanitarian assistance to the Indo-Chinese displaced persons.

[33] UN doc. A/AC.96/534, para. 87(f).

[34] UN doc. A/AC.96/549, para. 36(b). In 1980, the General Assembly referred to 'boat and land cases in South East Asia' as 'refugees': GA Res. 35/41, 25 Nov. 1980, para. 8.

In that year, the High Commissioner for Refugees also requested the Executive Committee to clarify the distinction between refugees and displaced persons. No formal advice was tendered, but there was considerable support for the view that refugees were those who had crossed an international frontier, whereas displaced persons had not.[35] This view still has its adherents,[36] but General Assembly resolutions indicate an extension of the High Commissioner's mandate from 'refugees strictly so-called' to include also a class of 'displaced persons' who have fled their countries of origin.[37] Apart from purely humanitarian considerations, this tendency indicates an awareness of the difficulty of determining in the case of a massive exodus that each and everyone has a well-founded fear of persecution in the sense of the UNHCR Statute. It may also suggest, although this is not obvious from the resolutions themselves, that something more general, such as lack of protection, should serve as the criterion for identifying persons 'of concern' to the High Commissioner.[38]

Lack of protection by the government of the country of origin is already an element in the statutory definition of the refugee. Given the impracticability of individual determinations in the case of large scale movements of asylum-seekers, that element acquires great significance. 'Protection' here implies both 'internal protection', in the sense of effective guarantees in matters such as life, liberty, and security of the person; and 'external protection', in the sense of diplomatic protection, including documentation of nationals abroad and recognition of the right of nationals to return. The 'right to return', in particular, is accep-

[35] See the High Commissioner's statement to the Executive Committee: A/AC.96/549, annexe, and for summary of the views of states: ibid., paras. 21, 26. For more detailed statements: A/AC.96/SR.284, paras. 13, 25 *bis*, 46; id. SR.287, paras. 26, 35; id. SR.288, paras. 30, 57; id. SR.291, para. 6. See also the High Commissioner's statement to the 31st Session of the Executive Committee (1980): UN doc. A/AC.96/588, annexe, 5.

[36] At the 1980 session of the Executive Committee, the representative for Turkey expressed the view that 'the time had come to ensure that UNHCR did not, by virtue of precedents, become a body which cared for anyone compelled for whatever reason to leave his country or even to move to a different area inside his country': A/AC.96/ SR.319, paras. 12-15.

[37] In 1973, the General Assembly requested the High Commissioner 'to continue his assistance *and protection* activities in favour of refugees within his mandate as well as for those to whom he extends his good offices or is called upon to assist in accordance with relevant resolutions of the General Assembly': GA Res. 3143(XXVIII) of 14 Dec. 1973. Res. 32/68, 8 Dec. 1977 continued UNHCR's mandate and noted 'the outstanding work ... performed ... in providing international *protection* to refugees and displaced persons ...' Res. 35/41, 25 Nov. 1980, refers to UNHCR's responsibilities 'for *protecting* and assisting refugees and displaced persons throughout the world'.

[38] Art. 2(7).

ted as a normal incident of nationality. In the case of those leaving Vietnam, however, that right has been subject to significant qualification. Although in 1975 the Provisional Revolutionary Government of South Vietnam requested UNHCR to promote voluntary repatriation, it stressed at the time that authorization to return fell within its sovereign rights and that each case would need to be examined separately.[39] That factor alone may justify protection and assistance by UNHCR, particularly where, in individual cases, further evidence is available of measures seriously affecting certain racial or social groups.

Although no objection was raised to UNHCR's activities on behalf of persons leaving Indo-China, challenges to the Office's competence have arisen with respect to other groups. In discussion of the High Commissioner's report in the Third Committee in 1979, for example, the representative of Afghanistan referred to UNHCR's 'assistance to fugitive insurgents in Pakistan'.[40] Recalling Article 1F of the 1951 Convention, he observed that assistance to those committing acts of aggression against Afghanistan contravened the UNHCR Statute, the 1951 Convention, and the UN Charter. The representative for Ethiopia, commenting on assistance in Somalia to Ethiopian refugees, considered that UNHCR's resources should not be 'over-extended to cover groups of people conveniently labelled as refugees who in most cases are either instruments of aggression and disruption or are nomadic groups on their seasonal movements...'[41]

Despite the protests of individual governments, the international community at large has not hitherto demurred when UNHCR has exercised its protection and assistance functions in cases of large-scale movements of asylum-seekers. This permits the conclusion that the class of persons within the mandate of, or of concern to, UNHCR includes: (1) those who, having left their country, can, on a case-by-case basis, be determined to have a well-founded fear of persecution on certain specified grounds; and (2) those often large groups or categories or persons who, likewise having crossed an international frontier, can be determined or presumed to be without, or unable to avail themselves of, the protection of the government of their state of origin. This is the broad meaning of the term 'refugee' for the purposes of the

---

[39] See statement by the observer for the Democratic Republic of Vietnam at the 26th Session of the Executive Committee (1975): UN doc. A/AC.96/521, para. 105.

[40] UN doc. A/C.3/34/SR.46, para. 58 f.

[41] Cf. GA Res. 35/180, 15 Dec. 1980 and GA Res. 36/153, 16 Dec. 1981, on assistance to refugees in Somalia: 'Human Rights, War and Mass Exodus', above n. 27, at 26-30.

United Nations, and this is the class which benefits from the principle of *non-refoulement* and from minimum standards of treatment. Beyond this minimum, however, both the obligations of states and the activities of UNHCR with regard to refugees in the broad sense may be limited to the provision of temporary refuge and material assistance, and the pursuit of voluntary repatriation. The refugee with a well-founded fear of persecution alone, perhaps, enjoys the full spectrum of protection and the expectation of a lasting solution in a country of asylum or resettlement.[42]

## 4. Refugees in the sense of the 1951 Convention and the 1967 Protocol Relating to the Status of Refuges

The states which acceded to or ratified the 1951 Convention agreed that the term 'refugee' should apply, first to any person considered a refugee under earlier international arrangements; and, secondly, to any person who, broadly speaking, qualifies as a refugee under the UNHCR Statute.[43] Originally, the definition, like the first part of that in the Statute, limited application of the Convention to the refugee who acquired such status 'as a result of events occurring before 1 January 1951'. An optional geographical limitation also permitted states, on ratification, to limit their obligations to refugees resulting from 'events occurring in Europe' prior to the critical date.[44] Finally, the substantive or ideological basis for the essential 'well-founded fear of persecution' differs slightly from that in the UNHCR Statute, by including the criterion 'membership of a particular social group' in addition to race, religion, nationality, or political opinion. The differences between the two definitions are due to amendments accepted by the Conference of Plenipotentiaries which adopted the final draft of the Convention.[45] The reference to 'membership of a particular social group', however, makes little practical difference in the respective areas of competence of UNHCR and states parties to the Convention. It can be seen as clarifying certain elements in the more traditional grounds for persecution—race, religion, or political opinion, and examples of persecution on social group grounds[46] will often prove, on closer examination, to have a

---

[42] Some reservations were expressed about the implications of an expanded refugee definition at the 32nd Session of the Executive Committee in 1981: UN doc. A/AC.96/601, para. 48. See further below.

[43] Art. 1A(2) of the Convention.

[44] Art. 1B.

[45] Cf. Grahl-Madsen, *The Status of Refugees in International Law* (1966) i.217.

[46] Ibid. 219-20.

political basis; thus, the group may be persecuted because the government considers it inherently disloyal and, rightly or wrongly, attributes dissident opinions to members of the group as a class.[47]

From the outset it was recognized that, given its various limitations, the Convention definition would not cover every refugee. The Conference of Plenipotentiaries therefore recommended in the Final Act that states should apply the Convention beyond its strictly contractual scope, to other refugees within their territory.[48] Many states relied upon this recommendation in the case of refugee crises precipitated by events after 1 January 1951, until the 1967 Protocol expressly removed that limitation.[49] It may still be invoked to support extension of the Convention to groups or individuals who do not fully satisfy the definitional requirements.[50]

Convention refugees are thus identifiable by their possession of four elemental characteristics: (1) they are outside their country of origin; (2) they are unable or unwilling to avail themselves of the protection of that country, or to return there; (3) such inability or unwillingness is attributable to a well-founded fear of being persecuted; and (4) the persecution feared is based on reasons of race, religion, nationality, membership of a particular social group, or political opinion.

## 5. Regional and related instruments

The 1951 Convention and the 1967 Protocol remain the principal international instruments benefitting refugees, and the definition which they offer has been expressly adopted in a variety of regional arrangements aimed at further improving the situation of recognized refugees.[51] That definition also forms the basis for Article 1 of the 1969 OAU Convention on Refugee Problems in Africa, though it has there been realistically extended to cover those compelled to leave their country of origin on account of external

[47] See further below, ch. II, s. 4(2).
[48] Recommendation E of the Final Act.
[49] See further below, ch. II, s. 4(2).
[50] Cf. declaration on territorial asylum adopted by the Committee of Ministers of the Council of Europe, 18 Nov. 1977, by which the right to grant asylum is reaffirmed in respect of Convention refugees 'as well as to any other person [member states] consider worthy of receiving asylum for humanitarian reasons'.
[51] See, for example, art. 1, 1980 European Agreement on Transfer of Responsibility for Refugees: ETS no. 107; art. 1, 1959 European Agreement on the Abolition of Visas for Refugees: ETS no. 31; art. 1(o), 1972 European Convention on Social Security: ETS no. 78. Cf. art. 1(d), EEC Regulation 1408/71: OJ no. L, 149/2.

aggression, occupation, foreign domination, or events seriously disturbing public order.[52] This expanded definition, which clearly matches the developments within the UN, has also been proposed as the criterion generally applicable in situations of mass influx, but care is required in calculating the precise legal implications.[53]

Latin America has long been familiar with the practice of diplomatic asylum[54] and with the concept of *asilado*. A treaty of 1889 acknowledged that 'political refugees shall be accorded an inviolable asylum',[55] while other agreements have dealt expressly with asylum granted in diplomatic premises or other protected areas.[56] The beneficiaries are usually described as being sought 'for political reasons' or 'for political offences', although the 1954 Caracas Convention on Territorial Asylum expressly refers to persons coming from a state 'in which they are persecuted for their beliefs, opinions, or political affiliations, or for acts which may be considered as political offences'.[57] Extradition is commonly the background to these regional agreements, for non-extradition of political offenders is clearly one part of the wider topic of asylum. Developments in the legal concept of the refugee have likewise had a corresponding influence on extradition arrangements. On the one hand, there has been a tendency to expand protection beyond the limitations which afflict the notion of political offence; on the other hand, international action to suppress the hijacking of aircraft, to counteract terrorism, and to protect diplomats, has imposed new limitations upon the class of those entitled to international protection.

## 6. Refugees in municipal law: some examples

The municipal law practice of non-extradition of political offenders is one of the antecedents to current principles protecting refugees from return to a state in which they may face persecu-

---

[52] See also the conclusions of the Executive Committee on the protection of asylum-seekers in situations of large-scale influx: UN doc. A/AC.96/601, para. 57(2)I, 1.

[53] See further below ch. V, s. 4.

[54] See further below ch. V, s. 1.

[55] See art. 16, 1889 Montevideo Treaty on International Penal Law: *OAS Official Records* OEA/Ser.X/1. Treaty Series 34; revised by the 1940 Montevideo Treaty on International Penal Law: ibid., art. 20 of which excludes extradition for 'political crimes'.

[56] See, for example, 1954 Caracas Convention on Diplomatic Asylum; text below, annexe X.

[57] Art. 2.

tion.[58] It remains doubtful whether the narrow principle of non-extradition of political offenders reflects a rule of international law despite its wide acceptance in municipal law, but apart from the extradition context, many states have nevertheless recognized that the refugee is someone worthy of protection and assistance. In some cases, the principle of asylum for refugees is expressly acknowledged in the constitution.[59] In others, ratification of the 1951 Convention and the 1967 Protocol may have direct effect in local law, while in still other cases, ratifying states may follow up their acceptance of international obligations by the enactment of specific refugee legislation or by the adoption of appropriate administrative procedures.

The Federal Republic of Germany, for example, has both constitutional and enacted law provisions benefitting refugees. The 1949 constitution prescribes that the politically persecuted enjoy the right of asylum,[60] and the 1982 Asylum Procedure Law provides that those recognized shall enjoy the status provided for by the 1951 Convention, as a minimum standard.[61] The Preamble to the 1958 Constitution of France acknowledges the principle of asylum, while a 1952 law establishing the *Office Français de Protection des Réfugiés et Apatrides (OFPRA)* declares that refugees within the competence of the *Office* shall include those within the mandate of UNHCR, as well as those within Article 1 of the 1951 Convention.[62]

The United States Refugee Act 1980 abandons the earlier ideologically and geographically based definition of refugees[63] in favour of that offered by the Convention and Protocol.[64] At the same time, it goes beyond those instruments by offering resettlement opportunities to those who might qualify as Convention refugees, save for the fact that they have not yet left their country

---

[58] Generally on this topic see Shearer, *Extradition in International Law* (1971) ch. 3; Epps, 'The Validity of the Political Offence Exception in Extradition Treaties in Anglo-American Jurisprudence' 20 *Harv. ILJ* (1979) 61; Goodwin-Gill, *International Law and the Movement of Persons between States* (1978) 142-6, 218-28.

[59] See, for example, the provisions listed in *A Select Bibliography on Territorial Asylum* (1977): UN doc. ST/GENEVA/LIB/SER.B/Ref.9, 68-74.

[60] Art. 16(2): *'Politisch Verfolgte geniessen Asylrecht'*.

[61] *Asylverfahrensgesetz (AsylVfG)*, art. 3.

[62] *Loi no. 52-893* of 25 July 1952, art. 2; see also *loi no. 70-107* of 25 Nov. 1970 authorizing accession to the 1967 Protocol.

[63] Refugees were limited to those fleeing from the Middle East or from Communist or Communist-dominated countries: Immigration and Nationality Act, s. 101(a) (42).

[64] Refugee Act 1980, s. 201; see further below, ch. VIII, s. 2(7).

of origin.[65] Canada similarly adopted the Convention definition in its 1976 Immigration Act,[66] where it serves both as a criterion for selection under admission programmes and as the basis for formal recognition of refugee status and the grant of asylum to those already in Canada.[67] In addition, Canadian law makes provision for the designation of other classes whose admission to Canada would be in keeping with humanitarian tradition.[68]

In other countries, the admission of refugees and special groups may be determined by the government in the exercise of broad discretionary powers. In Australia, for example, refugee policy declared in 1977 provides for the examination of claims to refugee status by persons in Australia and for resettlement opportunities to be offered to refugees in countries of first asylum and to 'people in refugee-type situations who do not fall strictly within the UNHCR mandate or within Convention definitions'.[69]

Although the Convention and Protocol are not formally incorporated in United Kingdom law, the rules adopted for implementation of the 1971 Immigration Act make express reference to the Convention definition in the context of applications for entry, for extensions of stay, and against deportation.[70] Switzerland has developed the Convention definition in its recent law on asylum, Article 3 of which declares:

[1]Sont des réfugiés les étrangers qui, dans leur pays d'origine ou le pays de leur dernière résidence, sont exposés à de sérieux préjudices ou craignent à juste titre de l'être en raison de leur race, de leur religion, de

[65] Ibid. This expanded category is dependent upon 'appropriate consultations' taking place between the President and Congress: ibid. and s. 207 (e). To describe as refugees those who have not actually fled is scarcely consonant with the ordinary meaning of the term. Cf. Fragomen, 'The Refugee: A Problem of Definition' 3 *Case W. Res. J. Int'l. L.* (1970) 45, at 57; he proposes a similarly misleading description.

[66] S. 2(1). The Act contains a statement of the objectives of Canadian immigration policy in s. 3, which includes the need 'to fulfil Canada's international legal obligations with respect to refugees and to uphold its humanitarian tradition with respect to the displaced and the persecuted'.

[67] Ss. 45-8, 70-1.

[68] S. 6(2). Three such classes were designated in 1978: Indo-Chinese (SOR/78-931), Latin Americans (SOR/78-932), and self-exiled persons (SOR/78-933). The classes in question are generally described by reference to their country of origin, as persons who are outside Canada and not still present in their country of origin, are unable or unwilling to return to their country, have not become permanently resettled, and are seeking resettlement in Canada.

[69] Ministerial statement of Refugee Policy and Mechanisms, *Parliamentary Debates*, 24 May 1977; see also statements on the Special Humanitarian Programme, ibid. 18 Nov. 1981, and on Refugee Policy, ibid. 16 Mar. 1982.

[70] *Statement of Changes in Immigration Rules*: HC 394, paras. 64, 87, 120, 138, 150 (20 Feb. 1980).

leur nationalité, de leur appartenance à un groupe social déterminé ou de leurs opinions politiques.

²Sont considérés notamment comme sérieux préjudices la mise en danger de la vie, de l'intégrité corporelle ou de la liberté, de même que les mesures qui entraînent une pression psychique insupportable.

³Sont également reconnus comme réfugiés, à moins que des circonstances particulières ne s'y opposent, les conjoints des réfugiés et leurs enfants mineurs.[71]

This far from comprehensive selection illustrates the extent to which certain states have translated their concern for the international problem of refugees into action on the municipal level. Immigration countries, such as Australia, Canada, and the United States, have incorporated the Convention definition, with occasional slight modifications, into their laws and policies. At the same time, they and other concerned states use that definition for the purposes of determining claims to asylum and/or refugee status which may be raised by persons physically present or arriving in their territory. A further notable feature is the tendency of states to take account also of the plight of others, not strictly refugees in the sense of the Convention, who have valid humanitarian reasons for being offered resettlement opportunities or protection. In Europe, for example, considerable discussion has focussed on the problems of so-called *de facto* refugees. Broadly, this group may comprise Convention refugees who, for a variety of reasons, are unable or unwilling to obtain recognition of their status[72] and others who, although not qualifying under the Convention, are unable or unwilling for reasons recognized as valid to return to their country of origin.[73]

## 7. Summary conclusions on the definition of the term 'refugee' for the purposes of general international law

Refugees within the mandate of UNHCR, and therefore eligible for protection and assistance, include not only those who can, on a case-by-case basis, be determined to have a well-founded fear of

---

[71] *Loi sur l'asile du 5 octobre 1979: FF 1979 II 977.*

[72] See Melander, *Problems emanating from Differences in Eligibility Practice in Europe* (1976) and *Refugees in Orbit* (1978).

[73] Weis, 'The Legal Aspects of the Problems of *de facto* Refugees' in *Problems of Refugees and Exiles in Europe* (1974). The notion of 'valid reasons' is expanded at 3-5 and would include (1) a person's reasonable belief that he or she would be prejudiced in the exercise of human rights, would suffer discrimination, or be compelled to act against conscience; and (2) war or warlike conditions, foreign or colonial occupation, or serious disturbance of public order in part or all of the person's country of origin.

*displaced persons also protected*

persecution on certain grounds (so-called 'statutory refugees'); but also other often large groups of persons who can be determined or presumed to be without, or unable to avail themselves of, the protection of the government of their state of origin (now often referred to as 'displaced persons'). In each case, it is essential that the persons in question should have crossed an international frontier and that, in the case of the latter group, the reasons for flight should be traceable to conflicts, or radical political, social, or economic changes in their own country. UNHCR may also assist persons displaced *within* their own countries and contribute to the rehabilitation and reintegration of returning refugees and 'externally' displaced persons.[74] The nature of such activities is exceptional and they are of limited relevance to the precise question of the international legal status of refugees.

On the basis of state and international organization practice, the above core of meaning represents the content of the term 'refugee' in general international law. Grey areas may nevertheless remain. The class of persons 'without, or unable to avail themselves of, the protection of the government of their state of origin' begs many questions. Moreover, it may be that the varying content of the term likewise imports varying legal consequences, so that the obligations of states in matters such as *non-refoulement*, non-rejection at the frontier, temporary refuge, and treatment of refugees after entry will depend upon the precise status of the particular class. It will be shown below, however, that the principle of *non-refoulement*, the foundation stone of international protection, applies to a broad class of refugees. Certain factual elements may be necessary before the principle is triggered—for example, mass movement to or across an international frontier and some evidence of relevant and valid reasons for flight, such as human rights violations in the country of origin—but it would hardly be permissible for a state to seek to avoid its obligations, either by declining to make a formal determination of refugee

---

[74] The facilitation of repatriation is a prescribed function of UNHCR (paras. 1 and 8(c) of the Statute). That this function should extend to a period after initial return, when technically the persons in question will have ceased to be refugees, was recognized by the General Assembly as early as 1961 (GA Res. 1672(XVI), 18 Dec. 1961: assistance to those repatriating to Algeria). This involvement has been maintained and expanded; see GA Resolutions 2789(XXVI), 6 Dec. 1971; 2958(XXVII), 12 Dec. 1972; 3143 (XXVIII), 14 Dec. 1973; 33/26, 29 Nov. 1978; 34/122, 14 Dec. 1979; 35/41, 25 Nov. 1980; see also the statement by the High Commissioner to the 31st Session of the Executive Committee (1980): UN doc. A/AC.96/588, annexe, 5.

status or by ignoring the development of the refugee concept in state and international organization practice.

Recent examples show that, while states are conscious of the potential threat to their own security which a massive influx may pose, none claims an absolute right to return a refugee, as such, to persecution. A state may try to assert for itself greater freedom of action, however, by avoiding any use of refugee terminology. Asylum-seekers can thus find themselves classified as 'displaced persons', 'illegal immigrants', 'quasi-refugees','aliens', 'depart-ees', 'boat-people', or 'stowaways'. The intention may be to allow those arriving to be dealt with at discretion, but the clear implication is that, for states at large, refugees are a class known to general international law and, as a matter of law, entitled to a somewhat better and higher standard of treatment.

Chapter II

# DETERMINATION OF REFUGEE STATUS: ANALYSIS AND APPLICATION

The legal consequences which flow from the formal definition of refugee status are necessarily predicated upon determination by some or other authority that the individual or group in question satisfies the relevant legal criteria. In principle, a person becomes a refugee at the moment when he or she satisfies the definition, so that formal determination of status is declaratory, rather than constitutive; problems arise, however, where states decline to determine refugee status, or where different determinations are reached by states and by UNHCR.[1]

## 1. Respective competence of UNHCR and of states parties to the Convention and Protocol

The UNHCR Statute and the 1951 Convention contain very similar definitions of the term 'refugee'. It is for UNHCR to determine status under the Statute and any relevant General Assembly resolutions, and for states parties to the Convention and the Protocol to determine status under those instruments.[2] Given the differences in definition, an individual may be recognized as both a mandate,[3] and a Convention[4] refugee; or as a mandate

---

[1] See generally, Grahl-Madsen, *The Status of Refugees in International Law* (1966) i.173-216; Weis, 'The Concept of the Refugee in International Law' *Journal du droit international* (1960) 1; Schnyder, 'Les aspects juridiques actuels du problème des réfugiés' Hague *Recueil* (1965-I) 339; Sadruddin Aga Khan, 'Legal Problems relating to Refugees and Displaced Persons' Hague *Recueil* (1976-I) 287.

[2] The situation of refugees acknowledged under earlier arrangements and formally included in both Statute and Convention is not examined further; cf. Statute, para. 6(a)(1) and 1951 Convention art. 1A(1): below, annexes III and IV; Grahl-Madsen, *Status of Refugees*, i.108-41.

[3] The term 'mandate refugee' will signify a refugee within the competence of UNHCR according to its Statute, according to specific General Assembly resolutions, or according to general resolutions on displaced persons.

[4] The term 'Convention refugee' will signify a refugee within the meaning of the 1951 Convention and/or 1967 Protocol.

refugee but not as a Convention refugee.[5] The latter can arise, for example, where the individual is in a non-contracting state or a state which adheres to the temporal or geographical limitations permitted under the Convention.[6] Divergence between mandate and Convention status can also result from differences of opinion between states and UNHCR, although a number of factors reduce that possibility. UNHCR, for example, has the statutory function of supervising the application of international conventions for the protection of refugees,[7] and states parties to the Convention and Protocol formally undertake to facilitate this duty.[8] Moreover, many states accept direct or indirect participation by UNHCR in procedures for the determination of refugee status, so that the potential for harmonization of decisions is increased.

## 2. Determination of refugee status by UNHCR

The basic elements of the refugee definition are common to states and to UNHCR and are examined more fully in Section 3. UNHCR itself will be concerned to determine status (1) as a condition precedent to providing international protection (e.g. intervention with a government to prevent expulsion); or (2) as a prerequisite to providing assistance to a government which requests it in respect of certain groups within its territory. Except in individual cases, formal determination of refugee status may not be necessary. Intervention to secure temporary refuge, for example, can be based on prima-facie elements in the particular case—the fact of flight across an international frontier, evidence of valid reasons for flight from the country of origin, and the material needs of the group in question. Where assistance is expressly requested by a receiving country, that invitation alone would justify UNHCR's involvement in the absence of hard evidence that those to be helped were not refugees or displaced persons, or of any coherent, persuasive opposition by the country of origin or other members of the international community.[9]

---

[5] Recognition as a Convention, but not as a mandate refugee would import no consequences of significance.

[6] These optional limitations are not discussed further; see Grahl-Madsen, *Status of Refugees*, i.164-72.

[7] Para. 8(a).

[8] Art. 35 of the Convention; art. II of the Protocol.

[9] Cf. objections raised by Ethiopia and Afghanistan, cited above, ch. I, s. 3(2).

Formal determination of mandate status, however, is often necessary in individual cases. Only comparatively few states have instituted procedures for assessing refugee claims, so that intervention by UNHCR on the basis of a positive determination of refugee status may be required to protect the individual. Some countries also make access to their refugee resettlement programmes conditional upon certification by the UNHCR office in the country of first admission that the individuals in question fall within the mandate of the High Commissioner.[10]

## 3. Determination of refugee status by states

The 1951 Convention defines refugees and provides for certain standards of treatment to be accorded to refugees. It says nothing about procedures for determining refugee status, and leaves to states the choice of means as to implementation at the national level.[11] Given the nature of the definition, the assessment of claims to refugee status thus involves a complex of subjective and objective factors, while the context of such assessment—interpretation of an international instrument with fundamentally humanitarian objectives—implies certain ground rules.[12]

Clearly, the onus is on the applicant to establish his or her case, but practical considerations and the trauma which can face a person in flight, impose a corresponding duty upon whomever must ascertain and evaluate the relevant facts and the credibility of the applicant. Given 'protection' of refugees as one of the Convention's objectives, a liberal interpretation of the criteria is called for. A decision on the well-foundedness or not of a fear of persecution is essentially an essay in hypothesis, an attempt to prophesy what might happen to the applicant in the future, if returned to his or her country of origin. Particular care needs to be exercised, therefore, in applying the correct standard of proof.

In civil and criminal cases, two 'standards of proof' are commonly advanced: 'proof on a balance of probability' for the former, and 'proof beyond a reasonable doubt' for the latter. In practice, there can be no absolute standard in either case, and it

[10] Australia, which previously relied on UNHCR's mandate determinations, announced on 16 Mar. 1982 that henceforth its officials overseas would determine refugee status on a case-by-case basis, using the Convention criteria: Ministerial Statement on Refugee Policy *Parliamentary Debates* 16 Mar. 1982, 989-94 (House of Representatives).

[11] See further below, ch. VI, s. 2(2).

[12] Cf. art. 31(1), Vienna Convention on the Law of Treaties.

will vary with the subject-matter. In the United Kingdom, for example, in habeas corpus proceedings, the applicant must cast some doubt on the validity of his or her detention. But in matters of fact, it is enough that the applicant presents such evidence as raises the possibility of a favourable inference. It then falls to the respondent, the detaining authority, to rebut that inference.[13] It might be argued that, in a refugee status case, the 'likelihood of persecution' must be established on a balance of probabilities. In civil cases, the typical issue is whether a close, legally relevant relation exists between *past* causes and *past* effects.[14] The applicant for refugee status, however, is adducing a future speculative risk as the basis for a claim to protection. Analogous issues were considered by the House of Lords in 1971 in an extradition case, *Fernandez* v. *Government of Singapore*.[15] Here, Lord Diplock noted that the phrase 'balance of probability' was 'inappropriate when applied not to ascertaining what has happened, but to prophesying what, if it happens at all, can only happen in the future'.[16] He went on to note that the relevant provision of the Fugitive Offenders Act:

... calls upon the court to prophesy what will happen to the fugitive in the future if he is returned ... The degree of confidence that the events specified will occur which the court should have to justify refusal to return the fugitive ... should, as a matter of common sense and common humanity, depend upon the gravity of the consequences contemplated on the one hand of permitting and on the other hand of refusing, the return of the fugitive if the court's expectation should be wrong. The general policy of the Act, viz. that persons against whom a prima facie case is established that they have committed a crime ... should be returned to stand their trial ..., is departed from if the return of a person who will not be detained or restricted for any of the reasons specified in paragraph (c) is refused. But it is departed from only in one case. On the other hand, detention or restriction in his personal liberty, *the consequence which the relevant words are intended to avert*, is grave indeed to the individual fugitive concerned.

[13] *R.* v. *Governor of Brixton Prison, ex parte Ahsan* [1969] 2 QB 222 per GODDARD LCJ at 233.

[14] For example, did war service cause or contribute to cancer of the gullet leading to death? Cf. *Miller* v. *Minister of Pensions* [1947] 2 All ER 372.

[15] [1971] 1 WLR 987. The Court considered and applied section 4(1)(c) of the Fugitive Offenders Act 1967 which provides: 'A person shall not be returned under this Act ... if it appears ... that he might, if returned, be prejudiced at his trial or punished, detained or restricted in his personal liberty by reason of his race, religion, nationality or political opinion.'

[16] [1971] 1 WLR 987, at 993-4. Cf. the quantification of future losses, both pecuniary and non-pecuniary, which courts undertake in personal injury claims; see for example, *Davies* v. *Taylor* [1972] All ER 836, *Jefford* v. *Gee* [1970] 2 QB 130.

One significant difference between the principle of non-extradition and that of protection of refugees lies in the risk to society if return is refused when, in fact, persecution would not have occurred. On the one hand, a suspected or actual criminal is allowed to remain, while on the other hand, someone who is innocent and against whom no allegations are made is allowed to remain. The attitude to the asylum-seeker should be at least as benevolent as that accorded to the fugitive from justice. Lord Diplock took account of the relative gravity of the consequences of the court's expectations proving wrong either one way or the other, and concluded that the appellant need not show that it was more likely than not that he or she would be detained or restricted if returned. A lesser degree of likelihood sufficed such as 'a reasonable chance', 'substantial grounds for thinking', or 'a serious possibility'.[17]

Considered in isolation, these terms lack precision. In practice, however, they are appropriate, beyond the context of municipal law, for the unique task of assessing a claim to refugee status. The examiner must make a reasoned guess as to the future, while also taking account of the element of relativity between the degree of persecution feared (whether death, torture, imprisonment, discrimination, or prejudice, for example), and the degree of likelihood of its eventuating.

## 4. Analysis of the definition

### (1) GENERAL MATTERS

A claimant to refugee status must be 'outside' his or her country of origin, and the fact of having fled, of having crossed an international frontier, is an intrinsic part of the quality of refugee, understood in its ordinary sense. Certain states may provide for those who would be considered as refugees once they took flight,[18] but this in no way alters the basic international rule.[19]

---

[17] Art. 2, Draft Convention on Territorial Asylum proposed a 'definite possibility' of persecution as the criterion for the grant of asylum.

[18] See United States Refugee Act 1980 s. 201. UK immigration rules on asylum have been held not to apply to a refugee in a third country (*Secretary of State* v. *Two citizens of Chile* [1977] ImmAR 36) or to a would-be refugee in his or her country of origin (*Secretary of State* v. *X. (a Chilean citizen)* [1978] ImmAR 73).

[19] On the question of *non-refoulement* and the rejection of refugees at the frontier, see further below, ch. IV, s. 2(1).

The Convention neither requires that the putative refugee shall have fled by reason of fear of persecution, nor that persecution should have actually occurred. The fear may derive from conditions arising during an ordinary absence abroad (for example, as a diplomat or holiday-maker), while the element of well-foundedness looks more to the future, than to the past. This latter element is itself a combination of subjective and objective factors. Fear, and the degree to which it is felt by a particular individual, are incapable of precise quantification.[20] It may be exaggerated or understated, but still be reasonable. If the applicant's statements in regard to that fear are consistent and credible, then little more can be required in the way of formal proof. The next question is whether that subjective fear is well-founded; whether there are sufficient facts to permit the finding that the applicant would face a serious possibility of persecution.[21]

Problems of assessment cannot be pursued very far in the abstract. All the circumstances of the case have to be considered, including the relation between the nature of the persecution feared and the degree of likelihood of its happening. At each stage, hard evidence is likely to be absent, so that finally the asylum-seeker's own statements, their force, coherence, and credibility must be relied on, in the light of what is known generally, from a variety of sources,[22] regarding conditions in the country of origin.

Article 1A(2) of the Convention makes separate provision for refugees with a nationality and for those who are stateless. For the former, the relevant criterion is that they should be unable or unwilling to avail themselves of the protection of their state of nationality, while the latter should be unable or unwilling to return to their state of former residence.[23] In cases of dual or

---

[20] Assessment of this element may be particularly difficult in cases involving minority or mental disturbance.

[21] The *Ad Hoc* Committee referred to a refugee as a person who 'has either actually been a victim of persecution or can show good reasons why he fears persecution': UN doc. E/1618, 39.

[22] In practical terms, reports by Amnesty International, the Minority Rights Group, the International Commission of Jurists, and various United Nations bodies, such as the Commission on Human Rights, can be of great assistance.

[23] See report of the *Ad Hoc* Committee: UN doc. E/1618, 39: 'The Committee agreed that for the purposes [of this provision], and therefore the draft Convention as a whole, "unable" refers primarily to stateless refugees but includes also refugees possessing a nationality who are refused passports or other protection by their own government. "Unwilling" refers to refugees who refuse to accept the protection of the government of their nationality.'

multiple nationality, refugee status will only arise where the individual in question is unable or unwilling, on the basis of well-founded fear, to secure the protection of any of the states of nationality. In this context, whether the link of nationality is effective in the sense of general international law will be a relevant consideration.[24]

Statelessness and refugee status are by no means identical phenomena.[25] On occasion, those fleeing may be deprived of their nationality, but it is quite common also for the formal link to remain. Following the Russian revolution in 1917, large numbers of citizens were stripped of their status and even today Soviet Jews leaving the country permanently are required to renounce their citizenship. Refugee status in such cases might appear determinable in the light of the situation prevailing in the Soviet Union as the 'country of former habitual residence'. However, in addition to internal repressive measures applied to those seeking to leave that country,[26] account must be taken of the denationalization, itself testimony of denial of protection. Whether it severs the effective link for all purposes of international law, including the responsibility of states, is less clear, but the expulsion of an unwanted minority could not justifiably be predicated upon the municipal act of deprivation of citizenship.[27]

## (2) REASONS FOR PERSECUTION

The Convention identifies five relevant grounds of persecution, all of which, in varying degrees, have been correspondingly

---

[24] Cf. Goodwin-Gill, *International Law and the Movement of Persons between States* (1978) 46-9.

[25] A stateless person has been defined as 'a person who is not considered as a national by any State under the operation of its law' in art. 1, 1954 Convention relating to the Status of Stateless Persons: 360 UNTS 117. By 16 votes to 1 with 4 abstentions the Conference preceding the Convention adopted a recommendation that each contracting state 'when it recognises as valid the reasons for which a person has renounced the protection of the State of which he is a national' should consider sympathetically extending the Convention to such persons. See also the 1961 Convention on the Reduction of Statelessness: UN doc. A/CONF.9/15, Final Act, where the Conference recommended that 'persons who are stateless *de facto* should as far as possible be treated as stateless *de jure* to enable them to acquire an effective nationality'. Cf. Weis, who has long criticized the terminology of *de facto* and *de jure* statelessness, for example, in 72 *AJIL* 680-1 (1978), reviewing Mutharika, *The Regulation of Statelessness under International and National Law: Texts and Documents* (1977); see also Weis's articles in 30 *BYIL* 480 (1953); 10 *ICLQ* 255 (1961); 11 *ICLQ* 1073 (1962).

[26] Cf. *Religious Minorities in the Soviet Union* (Minority Rights Group, report no. 1, rev. ed. 1977) 18-20.

[27] See Fischer Williams, 'Denationalization' 8 *BYIL* 45 (1927).

developed in the field of non-discrimination.[28] With regard to *race* for example, account should be taken of Article I of the 1965 Convention on the Elimination of All Forms of Racial Discrimination which defines that practice to include distinctions based on 'race, colour, descent, or national or ethnic origin'. Given legal developments affecting this topic over the last thirty years, the broad meaning can be considered valid also for the purposes of the 1951 Convention. Persecution on account of race has frequently figured as the background to refugee movements. For example, Ugandan citizens of Asian origin were persecuted and expelled in 1972;[29] the same year, large numbers of Burundi citizens of the Hutu tribe were massacred, while many others fled into neighbouring countries;[30] in the years after 1975 thousands of Vietnamese citizens of Chinese ethnic origin, felt compelled, along with many others, to seek protection in the countries of South-East Asia;[31] and the development and application of the policies of apartheid by the Government of South Africa, has caused many of its citizens to flee institutionalized discrimination.[32] The international community has expressed particular abhorrence at discrimination on racial grounds, as evidenced by repeated resolutions of the General Assembly, but it is less clear whether such practices themselves amount to persecution.[33]

*Religion* has long been the basis upon which governments and peoples have singled out others for persecution. In 1685, thousands of Huguenots fled from France to England and Prussia after revocation of the Edict of Nantes opened the way to massacre and oppression. The late nineteenth century witnessed pogroms of Jews in Russia and of Armenian Christians in Ottoman Turkey. The present century has likewise seen large-scale persecution of Jews under the hegemony of Nazi and Axis powers up to 1945, while more recent targets have included Jehovah's

[28] Vierdag, *The Concept of Discrimination in International Law* (1973); McKean, 'The Meaning of Discrimination in International and Municipal Law' 44 *BYIL* 177 (1970); Bossuyt, *L'interdiction de la discrimination dans le droit international des droits de l'homme* (1976); Goodwin-Gill *Movement of Persons*, 75-87.

[29] Goodwin-Gill, *Movement of Persons,* 212-16.

[30] See *Selective Genocide in Burundi* (Minority Rights Group, report no. 20, 1974).

[31] See above, ch. I, n. 27, and sources cited.

[32] 'Human Rights, War and Mass Exodus', *Transnational Perspectives* (1982), 11, 14.

[33] See further below, s. 5(2). The European Commission on Human Rights has expressed the view that discrimination on racial grounds could, in certain circumstances, constitute degrading treatment within the meaning of art. 3 of the European Convention on Human Rights: Decision on Admissibility, *Patel* (application 4403/70) *et al.* v. *United Kingdom* Oct. 1970, p. 30. Cf. *Ali* v. *Secretary of State* [1978] ImmAR 126 (discrimination likely to be faced by Kenyan citizen of Asian origin did not amount to persecution).

Witnesses in Africa,[34] Moslems in Burma, Baha'is in Iran[35] and believers of all persuasions in totalitarian and self-proclaimed atheist states.

Article 18 of the 1966 Covenant on Civil and Political Rights, elaborating Article 18 of the Universal Declaration of Human Rights, prescribes that everyone shall have the right to freedom of thought, conscience, and religion, which shall include the freedom to have or adopt a religion or belief of choice and the freedom to manifest such religion or belief.[36] Moreover, no one is to be subject to coercion which would impair the freedom to have or adopt a religion or belief of choice. In 1962, the General Assembly requested the Commission on Human Rights to draw up a draft declaration and a draft convention on the elimination of all forms of intolerance based on religion or belief,[37] and in 1967 it took note of the Preamble and Article 1 of a proposed convention,[38] in which the Third Committee had suggested that the expression 'religion or belief' should include 'theistic, non-theistic and atheistic beliefs'.[39] The content of the right to freedom of thought, conscience, and religion has also been examined in various forums,[40] and the Declaration on the Elimination of All Forms of Intolerance and of Discrimination Based on Religion or Belief, adopted in 1981, indicates the interests to be protected, the infringement of which may signal persecution.[41]

---

[34] *Jehovah's Witnesses in Central Africa* (Minority Rights Group, report no. 29, 1976).

[35] In Sept. 1980 the United Nations Subcommission on the Prevention of Discrimination and Protection of Minorities requested the Secretary-General to transmit its concern to the Government of Iran and to invite that Government to express its commitment to the guarantees provided in the 1966 Covenant on Civil and Political Rights by granting full protection to the Baha'i religious community in Iran: *Press Release* HR/2003, 15 Sept. 1980.

[36] See to similar effect art. 9, European Convention on Human Rights, which also expressly recognizes the freedom to change religion or belief.

[37] GA Res. 1781(XVII), 7 Dec. 1962.

[38] GA Res. 2295(XXII), 11 Dec. 1967.

[39] Article reproduced in *Elimination of All Forms of Religious Intolerance, Note by the Secretary-General*: UN doc. A/8330, 8. This article, which includes definitions of discrimination on religious grounds and of religious intolerance, was adopted by 91 votes in favour, 2 against, with 6 abstentions. See report of the Commission on Human Rights Working Group, cited in UN doc. E/1980/13, at 115, 118.

[40] See UN doc. A/8330 annexe i, 3, art. VI (proposed by the Subcommission on the Prevention of Discrimination and Protection of Minorities); ibid. annexe ii, 3, art. VI (proposed by the working group set up by the Commission on Human Rights); ibid. annexe iii, 2-3, art. III (draft convention article adopted by the Commission on Human Rights); UN doc. E/1980/13, at 117 (text of art. VI proposed by the United States representative).

[41] Declaration adopted without vote by GA Res. 36/55 of 25 Nov. 1981; see further below, s. 5(1).

The reference to persecution for reasons of *nationality* is somewhat odd, given the absurdity of a state persecuting its own nationals on account of their membership of the body politic. Furthermore, those who possess the nationality of another state will, in normal circumstances, be entitled to its protection and so fall outside the refugee definition. Conceivably, the nationals of state B resident in state A could find themselves persecuted on account of their nationality, driven out to a neighbouring country and yet still denied the protection of state B, particularly that aspect which includes the right of nationals to enter their own state.[42] However, nationality in Article 1B of the 1951 Convention is usually interpreted broadly, to include origins and the membership of particular ethnic, religious, cultural, and linguistic communities.[43] It is not necessary that those persecuted should constitute a minority in their own country, for oligarchies traditionally tend to resort to oppression.[44] Nationality, interpreted broadly, illustrates the points of distinction which can serve as the basis for the policy and practice of persecution. There may be some overlap between the various grounds and, likewise, factors derived from two or more of the criteria may contribute cumulatively to a well-founded fear of persecution.

Further potential overlap lies in the criterion, *membership of a particular social group*. The 1951 Convention is not alone in recognizing 'social' factors as a potential irrelevant distinction giving

---

[42] Such denial of protection could easily arise through the haphazard workings of citizenship and immigration laws; cf. the situation of citizens of the United Kingdom and Colonies resident in East Africa, discussed in Goodwin-Gill, *Movement of Persons*, 101-3, 164-7; also, Whitaker, ed., *The Fourth World: Victims of Group Oppression* (1973) 37-71.

[43] Cf. *London Borough of Ealing* v. *Race Relations Board* [1972] AC 342, in which the court *excluded* nationality from the generic term 'national origins'. Note art. 27 of the 1966 Covenant on Civil and Political Rights: 'In those States in which ethnic, religious or linguistic minorities exist, persons belonging to such minorities shall not be denied the right, in community with the other members of their group, to enjoy their own culture, to profess and practise their own religion, or to use their own language.' Related work in the Commission on Human Rights has also included 'national minorities', but considerable controversy has surrounded the meaning of this term. It has also been argued that inclusion of national minorities in the Commission's work was inappropriate in view of the wording of art. 27. See UN doc. E/1980/13, 126-34; Res. 37(XXXVI), 12 Mar. 1980: ibid. 198; also Capotorti, *Study on the Rights of Persons belonging to Ethnic, Religious and Linguistic Minorities* (1978): UN doc. E/CN.4/Sub.2/384/Rev.1, 5-15, 95-6; cf. Martinez Cobo, *Study of the Problem of Discrimination against indigenous Populations* (1979): UN doc. E/CN.4/Sub.2/L.707; Elles, *International Provisions protecting the Human Rights of Non-Citizens* (1980): UN doc. E/CN.4/Sub.2/392/Rev. 1, 25 f.

[44] *Selective Genocide in Burundi*, above, n. 30; see also the interesting analysis in *The two Irelands—the double Minority* (Minority Rights Group, report. no. 2, rev. ed., 1979).

rise to arbitrary or repressive treatment. Article 2 of the 1948 Universal Declaration of Human Rights includes 'national or social origin, property, birth or other status' as prohibited grounds of distinction and this form of words is repeated in Article 2 of the 1966 Covenants on Economic, Social, and Cultural Rights and Civil and Political Rights; it also appears in Article 26 of the latter Covenant, which calls for equality before and equal protection of the law.

Jurisprudence on the interpretation of the term 'social group' is sparse.[45] A superficial linguistic analysis suggests people in a certain relation or having a certain degree of similarity, or a coming together of those of like class or kindred interests. A fully comprehensive definition is impracticable, if not impossible, but the essential element in any description would be the factor of shared interests, values, or background—a combination of matters of choice with other matters over which members of the group have no control. In determining whether a particular group of people constitutes a 'social group' within the meaning of the Convention, attention should therefore be given to the presence of uniting factors such as ethnic, cultural, and linguistic origin; education; family background; economic activity; shared values, outlook, and aspirations. Also relevant are the attitude to the putative social group of other groups in the same society and, in particular, the treatment accorded to it by state authorities. The importance, and therefore the identity, of a social group may well be in direct proportion to the notice taken of it by others, particularly the authorities of the state. The notion of social group thus possesses an element of open-endedness which states, in their discretion, could expand in favour of a variety of different classes susceptible to persecution. Whether they would be prepared to do so is another matter, but in arguing for expansion appropriate reference could be made to the unifying factors of the group in

---

[45] Cf. cases cited by Grahl-Madsen, *Status of Refugees*, i. 219-20. Tajfel, in *The Social Psychology of Minorities* (Minority Rights Group, report no. 38, 1978) cites at p. 3 Simpson and Yinger (*Racial and Cultural Minorities* (1965) 17) for the following set of definitional criteria appropriate for the identification of social minorities: '(1) Minorities are subordinate segments of complex state societies; (2) minorities have special physical or cultural traits which are held in low esteem by the dominant segments of the society; (3) minorities are self-conscious units bound together by the special traits which their members share and by the special disabilities which these bring; (4) membership in a minority is transmitted by a rule of descent which is capable of affiliating succeeding generations even in the absence of readily apparent special cultural or physical traits; (5) minority peoples, by choice or necessity, tend to marry within the group.' On 'social group' see Tajfel, ibid. 4.

question and to the elements of distinction which make it the object of persecution.[46]

Finally, the Convention adduces fear of persecution for reasons of *political opinion*. Article 19 of the Universal Declaration of Human Rights states that: 'Everyone has the right to freedom of opinion and expression; the right includes freedom to hold opinions without interference and to seek, receive and impart information and ideas through any media and regardless of frontiers.' The basic principle is restated in Article 19 of the Covenant on Civil and Political Rights, but the right to freedom of expression is qualified there by reference to 'special duties and responsibilities'. Certain types of opinion may therefore be judged unacceptable.[47]

In the 1951 Convention, 'political opinion' should be understood in the broad sense, to incorporate, within substantive limitations now developing generally in the field of human rights, any opinion on any matter in which the machinery of state, government, and policy may be engaged. The typical 'political refugee' is one pursued by the government of a state on account of his or her opinions, which are an actual or perceived threat to that government or its institutions. Political opinions may or may not be expressed, and they may be rightly or wrongly attributed to the applicant for refugee status. If they have been expressed, and if the applicant (or others similarly placed) has suffered or been threatened with repressive measures, then a well-founded fear may be made out. Problems arise, however, in assessing the value of the 'political act', particularly if the act itself stands more or less alone, unaccompanied by evident or overt expressions of opinion.

The issue of *Republikflucht* illustrates the case. Many totalitarian states severely restrict travel abroad by their nationals. Passports are difficult to obtain, while illegal border-crossing and absence abroad beyond the validity of an exit permit can attract heavy penalties.[48] The question is, whether fear of prosecution and

---

[46] Again there may be a relation of degree between the nature of the particular group and the type of persecution alleged. Thus, it *may* be the case that the discrimination suffered by women in many countries on account of their sex alone, though severe, is not yet sufficient to justify the conclusion that they, as a group, have a fear of persecution within the meaning of the Convention.

[47] Cf. art. 4, Convention on the Elimination of All Forms of Racial Discrimination; art. 10, European Convention on Human Rights.

[48] See, for example, Bulgaria, Penal Code of 1968, arts. 101, 279-81 (defection, illegal border crossing, refusal to return); Czechoslovakia, Penal Code as published by Law

punishment under such laws can be equated with a well-founded fear of persecution on grounds of political opinion, especially where the claim to refugee status is based on nothing more than the anticipation of such prosecution and punishment. It may be argued that the individual in question, if returned, would be subject merely to prosecution for breach of a law of general application; he or she would not be 'singled out' for treatment amounting to persecution. Alternatively, more weight might be accorded to the object and purpose of such laws. In one case in the Federal Republic of Germany in 1971, the Court observed:

[Die Bestrafung wegen Republikflucht] diente dem Zweck, die politische Herrschaft des Kommunismus zu sichern. Sie ist nicht vergleicher mit Strafen, durch die auch in Rechtsstaaten dem unerlaubten Grenzubertritt gewehrt wird.[49]

Here, the fact of leaving or staying abroad is seen as a political act. It may reflect an actual political opinion of the individual, in which case the necessary subjective element is present; or dissident political opinion may be attributed to the individual by the authorities of the state of origin.[50]

Some states have been wary of recognizing refugee status in such cases, for fear of attracting asylum-seekers motivated by purely economic considerations. Other states adopt more liberal policies, for example, Austria. Here, a ministerial directive expressly provides for recognition of refugee status where penal sanctions apply to overstayers, where the asylum-seeker has overstayed, and where he or she declares an unwillingness to return to the country of origin for political reasons considered in the widest sense.[51] A decision of the *Bundesverwaltungsgericht* of the Federal

---

no. 113/1973, para. 109 (abandonment of the republic); Romania, Penal Code of 1968 (amended 1973), paras. 245, 253 (fraudulent border crossing, refusal to return); USSR, Law on Criminal Offences against the State 1958, para. 20; Criminal Code of the RSFSR 1960, arts. 64a, 83-4. Amnesty International has taken up the cases of numbers of those punished under such laws; see *1979 Report*, 123, 133; *1980 Report*, 255, 269 f., 277 f., 291, 303; *1982 Report*, 270 f., 286 f.

[49] '[Punishment for the crime of flight from the Republic] serves the goal of securing the political sovereign authority of communism. It is not comparable with the penalties with which, even in "constitutional states", unauthorized border crossing is punished.' *BVerwGE*, Bd.39, S.27, 28-9. The nature of such penalties was to be distinguished by reference to their purpose, which should not be to hinder or prevent journeys abroad.

[50] Note, however, the class of 'self-exiled persons' who may qualify for admission under Canada's 1976 Immigration Act; see above, ch. I, n. 68.

[51] Directive of the Minister of the Interior: 22.501/4-II/0/75, part ii.

Republic of Germany in 1977 has also stressed that the reasons motivating the prosecuting state are of greater importance than any opinion actually held by the asylum-seeker.[52]

Similar issues are raised by asylum-seekers who base their claim upon the fear of prosecution and punishment for conscientious objection to military service. Objectors may be motivated by reasons of conscience or convictions of a religious, ethical, moral, humanitarian, philosophical, or other nature.[53] Again, it may be argued that they are punished not on account of their beliefs, but because of their failure to obey a law of universal application; moreover, it does not necessarily follow that such punishment amounts to persecution. In one case in 1976, the United Kingdom's Immigration Appeal Tribunal found that, on the basis of the law and practice then applying in Greece,[54] punishment of conscientious objectors amounted to persecution. However, the Tribunal doubted that this was persecution for reasons of religion or political opinion. It observed:

The immediate cause of the persecution is a refusal to obey the law of the land, and the fact that such refusal may be due to religious beliefs or political opinion is ... only the secondary cause. If the Jehovah's Witnesses in Greece were being persecuted for reasons of religion one would expect that their teachings and meetings would be proscribed. This is evidently not the case ... We do not consider that the relevant law is discriminatory, because it appears to us that other religious beliefs with

---

[52] File no. IC33.71. Account should be taken not only of the laws and prescribed penalties, but also of their application in practice.

[53] See Council of Europe Res. 337(1967) calling for recognition of the right to be excused from military service in such cases; cf. the view of the delegate of Cyprus expressed in the Commission on Human Rights: UN doc. E/1980/13, 134. It is not always appropriate to view the (objective) political act as equivalent to the (subjective) notion of political opinion. The asylum-seeker's actual motivation can make such an approximation pure fiction; the same applies in the case of the individual who is likely to be persecuted for political opinions *wrongly* attributed to him or her. The humanitarian aspects of such cases are better accommodated in a liberal asylum practice, than in a forced interpretation of refugee status criteria.

[54] Art. 13 of the Constitution of the Republic of Greece, which deals with freedom of conscience, provides in para 4 that 'No person shall, by reason of his religious convictions, be exempt from discharging his obligations to the State, or refuse to comply with the laws'. Art. 4(6) obliges every Greek able to bear arms to assist in the defence of the nation. Various penalties were provided under Law no. 2803 of 21 Feb. 1941 (the Greek Military Code, art. 43(c)) and Legislative Decree 720/1970 on conscription. Prior to recent legislative reforms, the practice tended to be for conscientious objectors to be sentenced to repeated terms of four and one-half years imprisonment throughout the period of military age. See Amnesty International, *1981 Report*, 300; *1982 Report*, 272 f.

similar views ... and indeed persons with no religious beliefs at all ...,
would all be treated in the same way.[55]

Military service and objection thereto, seen from the point of
view of the state, are issues which go to the heart of the body politic. Refusal to bear arms, however motivated, reflects an essentially political opinion regarding the permissible limits of state
authority; it is a political act. The 'law of universal application'
can thus be seen as singling out or discriminating against those
holding certain political views. While the state has a justifiable
interest in the maintenance of its own defence,[56] the measures
taken to that end should at least be 'reasonably necessary in a
democratic society';[57] specifically, there ought to exist a reasonable relationship of proportionality between the end and the
means.[58] The element of proportionality is especially important
in this context, where the right in question is not generally accepted
by states as falling within the corpus of fundamental human
rights.[59]

To argue that breach of the law, rather than the belief in question, is the relevant causative factor does no more than beg the
question—the law itself being frequently the instrument of repression. Whether prosecution and punishment amount to persecution in the sense of the Convention depends on the following

[55] *Dounetas* v. *Secretary of State*, approved and applied in *Atibo* v. *Immigration Officer,
London (Heathrow) Airport* [1978] ImmAR 93.

[56] Clearly a value judgment has to be made at this point; introducing Res. 38 (XXXVI)
before the Commission on Human Rights on 12 Mar. 1980, the representative of the
Netherlands noted that of some 90 countries with compulsory military service, 37 made
legislative or administrative provision for conscientious objectors, while 'broad public
support ... appeared to be growing': UN doc. E/1980/13, 106-7, 198-9.

[57] Cf. *Akar* v. *Attorney-General of Sierra Leone* [1970] AC 853, in which the Privy Council
declined to accept that a law dealing with citizenship was by that fact alone 'reasonably
necessary in a democratic society' so as to avoid constitutional limitations, including
provisions on discrimination. The law in question purported to limit citizenship to
persons of 'Negro African descent'.

[58] In the United Kingdom, throughout the Second World War, conscientious objectors were permitted the alternative of civilian service. Exemption from that was also
permitted if reasons of religion or conscience demanded, while the criterion for exemption
was the honesty or sincerity, rather than the 'validity' of the views held.

[59] In a case in the Federal Republic of Germany in 1976 (*Verwaltungsgericht, Ansbach Nr.*
AN3220-II(IV)/73, cited with approval by the same court in 1977: *VG Ansbach Nr.*
AN8341-IV/76), the court expressly conceded the widest discretion to other states in
the regulation of military service, which it considered to fall within the reserved domain
of domestic jurisdiction (*innerstaatliche Rechtsordnung*). The court declined to apply the
standard of exemption recognized by art. 4 of the 1949 Constitution of the Federal
Republic; moreover, its reasoning would not appear wholly consistent with that adopted
in cases of *Republikflucht*.

factors: the object and purpose of the law, the precise motivation of the individual who breaches such law, the 'interest' which such individual asserts and the nature and extent of the punishment.

Similar considerations apply to the related question of non-extradition of political offenders. The IRO Constitution excluded 'ordinary criminals who are extraditable by treaty' as well as 'war criminals, quislings, and traitors' and a variety of other 'undeserving' groups; the UNHCR Statute and the 1951 Convention contain equivalent provisions.[60] The exception in favour of political offenders developed in the nineteenth century in the context of bilateral extradition arrangements, and is not the consequence of any rule of general international law. No duty obliges states to surrender fugitive criminals and extradition itself may be but a gloss upon the rule which permits the grant of territorial asylum.[61] In practice, characterization of an offence as 'political' is left to the authorities of the state from which extradition is requested, and the function of characterization itself is evidently one in which political considerations will be involved, including the self-interest of the requested state as reflected by its military and other alliances.[62] Not surprisingly, divergent attitudes are revealed in municipal law. For example, the political offence exception does not appear in the extradition arrangements existing between Eastern European states,[63] although their constitutions commonly recognize the institution of asylum.[64] In contrast, certain Western European states have developed a comprehensive approach to purely political offences, complex political offences, and related political offences, all of which may justify non-extradition.[65] Nevertheless, the weight to be accorded to the motives of the offender varies from jurisdiction to juris-

---

[60] Para. 7(d) and art. 1F, respectively. See further below, ch. III, s. 4.

[61] O'Connell, *International Law* (2nd ed. 1970) 720; *Asylum* case, ICJ Rep. 1950, 266, at 274; cf. Lauterpacht, 'The Law of Nations and the Punishment of War Crimes' 21 *BYIL* (1944).

[62] Goodwin-Gill, *Movement of Persons*, 143 ff, 226-8.

[63] See Shearer, *Extradition in International Law* (1971) 65-6; Epps, 'The Validity of the Political Offence Exception in Extradition Treaties in Anglo-American Jurisprudence' 20 *Harv. ILJ* (1979) 61, 86; Gold, 'Non-extradition for political offences: the Communist perspective' 11 *Harv. ILJ* (1970) 191.

[64] See the provisions listed in *A Select Bibliography on Territorial Asylum* (1977): UN doc. ST/GENEVA/LIB.SER.B/Ref.9, 68-74.

[65] See, in particular, the Swiss cases: *Pavan*, Ann. Dig., 1927-8, 347 (in which the theory of predominance is advanced); *Ficorilli* 18 ILR 345 (1951); *Kavic* 19 ILR 371 (1952); also, Whiteman, *Digest of International Law* vi. 799 ff.

diction,[66] as does the practice on substantive limitations to the political offence exception. Some states have long excluded assassination of the head of state, while others have explicitly excluded acts of barbarism or offences the suppression of which is required under international obligations.[67] Moreover, appreciation of the political character of offences is clearly likely to vary according to the particular perspective of the requested state.[68]

In debates preceding the enactment of extradition powers in the United Kingdom, John Stuart Mill suggested including within the political offence exception not only acts committed in an insurrection, but also acts committed with a view to, or as a first step towards, an insurrection.[69] The 1870 Extradition Act itself provides for non-extradition either in respect of offences 'of a political character', or where the request for surrender is made with a view to try or punish the fugitive in respect of such an offence. Successive decisions of the United Kingdom courts have limited this provision to offences committed in the context of parties in opposition and conflict.[70] The word 'political', it was suggested in one case, 'indicate[s] ... that the requesting State is

---

[66] In *Giovanni Gatti* Ann. Dig. 1947 case no. 70; Kiss, *Répertoire de la pratique française en matière de droit international public* (1966) ii. 213-14, the Court of Appeal of Grenoble took the view that motive alone does not give a common crime the character of a political offence; such offence springs from the nature of the rights of the State which are injured. Cf. *Public Prosecutor* v. *Zind* 40 ILR 214 (Ct. of Cassation, Italy, 1961); here a German national had been convicted of making anti-Jewish comments in Germany. The court noted that in Italian law, the expression 'political offence' included an ordinary offence committed wholly or in part for political motives. Motives were especially important, 'whatever may be the legal right or interest offended against'.

[67] Kiss, *Répertoire de la pratique française*, ii. 210, 212, 216-17; cf. art. 3, 1957 European Convention on Extradition.

[68] See *VerwRspr*, Bd.20, S.332 (OVG Münster, 1968). A Belgian was sentenced to 12 years imprisonment for having served in the *Wehrmacht* during the Second World War. Released on parole, he was subsequently sentenced to serve the remainder of his sentence. He fled to the Federal Republic of Germany where the court upheld his appeal against expulsion and noted that he would in any event be immune from extradition by reason of the political character of his offence. Cf. *In re Pohle* 46 *BVerfGE*, 214, noted 73 *AJIL* 305-6 (1979), where the Federal Constitutional Court, in an appeal by a convicted member of the Baader-Meinhof group subsequently extradited from Greece, maintained the traditional rule that extradition treaties confer no rights on individuals, save if expressly mentioned. It construed the treaty with Greece as neither conferring rights on political offenders nor as barring a request for surrender of an offender who might be covered by an exception clause. It further held that membership in a 'criminal organization', even if politically motivated, did not constitute a political offence from the perspective of the German legal system. See also the 'collaboration cases' cited in Goodwin-Gill, *Movement of Persons*, 143, n. 2.

[69] 6 *BDIL* 661 ff.

[70] *Re Castioni* [1891] 1 QB 149; *Re Meunier* [1894] 2 QB 415; *R.* v. *Governor of Brixton Prison, ex parte Schtraks* [1964] AC 556.

after [the fugitive] for reasons other than the enforcement of the criminal law in its ordinary, ... common or international aspect'.[71] To categorize as political all offences committed for a political object, with a political motive or for the furtherance of some political cause would be to ignore the fundamental requirement of political disturbance and opposition.[72] In a later United Kingdom case, Lord Diplock said that an offence could not be considered political 'unless the only purpose sought to be achieved by the offender ... were to change the government of the state in which it was committed, or to enable ... escape from the jurisdiction of a government of whose political policies the offender disapproved but despaired of altering ...'.[73]

Lord Diplock explained that the political offence exception had the dual purpose of avoiding the United Kingdom's involvement in the internal political conflicts of foreign states; and preventing, on humanitarian grounds, the surrender of an offender to a jurisdiction in which trial and punishment might be unfairly prejudiced by political considerations.[74] As regards the latter, international legal principles relating to the protection of refugees are immediately involved. Not only must the offence in respect of which extradition is requested be examined, but also the broader context, with due consideration given to humanitarian issues and the fundamental rights of the individual.[75] The good faith and motives of the requesting state may require investigation. Some courts are wary of this highly political arena,[76] but others have been prepared to apply 'persecution criteria' more generously.[77] State practice suggests, at the least, that these factors should be taken into account at some level, either judicial or executive.[78]

---

[71] LORD RADCLIFFE in *Schtraks*, loc. cit. 591; see also LORD EVERSHED, ibid. 598; Amerasinghe, 'The *Schtraks* Case' 28 MLR 27 (1965).

[72] But cf. LORD REID, [1964] AC 556, 583.

[73] *Cheng.* v. *Governor of Pentonville Prison* [1973] 2 All ER 204, per LORD DIPLOCK at 209. Cf. *R.*v. *Governor of Brixton Prison, ex parte Kolczynksi* [1955] 2 WLR 116.

[74] Cf. United Kingdom Fugitive Offenders Act 1967, s. 4.

[75] See Austria, Extradition Law 1979, s. 14: 1979 *BGBl* 2551 ff.; Austria-Poland Extradition Treaty 1980, arts. 4, 5: *BGBl* 1104 ff.; Austria-Hungary Extradition Treaty 1976, art. 3: *BGBl* 1262 ff.

[76] See, for example, *Re Arton* [1896] 1 QB 108, 110, 115; *R.* v. *Governor of Brixton Prison, ex parte Kotronis* [1971] AC 250; *Zacharia* v. *Cyrpus* [1962] 2 A11 ER 438; *R.* v. *Governor of Brixton Prison, ex parte Keane* [1971] 2 WLR 1243; similarly in the United States of America, see *Re Lincoln* 228 F. 70 (1915); *Re Gonzalez* 217 F. Supp. 717 (1963).

[77] NB developments in the Federal Republic of Germany cited in Goodwin-Gill, *Movement of Persons*, 144-6.

[78] Moore, *Digest* iv. s. 604; 6 *BDIL* 665-8 (USA-UK discussions 1870-6); cf. art. 3, 1957 European Convention on Extradition.

The international community does not exist for the purpose of preserving established governments, and the political offence exception may be considered valuable for its dynamic quality. International law, however, provides no guidance on the substance of the concept, other than its outermost limits; states retain the broadest discretion, almost a 'unilateral right of qualification'. Nevertheless, exclusive attention to the concept should not lead to total disregard of the broader humanitarian issues which underlie it. It is arguable (though few might care to do so), that the mere commission of a political offence is not sufficient to qualify a person for refugee status, which arises only where the anticipated punishment shades into persecution. Alternatively, it may be that certain offences are inherently political, that their commission reflects the failure of a state to protect a greater and more valued interest, so that any punishment would be equivalent to persecution.

## 5. Persecution and Lack of Protection

'Persecution' is not defined in the 1951 Convention or in any other international instrument. Articles 31 and 33 of the Convention refer to those whose 'life or freedom may be threatened', but otherwise a wide margin of appreciation is left to states in interpreting this fundamental term, and state practice reveals no coherent or consistent jurisprudence. Specific decisions by national authorities are some evidence of the content of the concept, as understood by states, but comprehensive analysis requires the general notion to be related to developments within the broad field of human rights.

Fear of persecution and lack of protection are themselves interrelated elements. The persecuted clearly do not enjoy the protection of their country of origin, while evidence of the lack of protection on either the internal or external level may create a presumption as to the likelihood of persecution and to the wellfoundedness of any fear. The core meaning of persecution readily includes the threat of deprivation of life or physical freedom.[79] In its broader sense, however, it remains very much a question of degree and proportion; less overt measures may suffice, such as the imposition of serious economic disadvantage, denial of access to employment, to the professions, or to education, or other restrictions on the freedoms traditionally guaranteed in a demo-

[79] See Grahl-Madsen, ibid. 193, quoting Zink's 'restrictive' interpretation.

cratic society, such as speech, assembly, worship, or freedom of movement.[80] Whether such restrictions amount to persecution within the 1951 Convention will again turn on an assessment of a complex of factors, including (a) the nature of the freedom threatened, (b) the nature of the restriction, and (c) the likelihood of the restriction eventuating in the individual case.

## (1) PROTECTED INTERESTS

The references to 'race, religion, nationality, membership of a particular social group, or political opinion' illustrate briefly the characteristics of individuals and groups which are considered worthy of special protection. These same factors have figured in the development of the fundamental principle of non-discrimination in general international law,[81] and have contributed to the formulation of other fundamental human rights. In a judgment in 1970, the International Court of Justice referred to the outlawing of genocide, slavery, and racial discrimination as falling within the emergent notion of obligations *erga omnes*.[82] The resulting rights, in so far as they are embodied in international conventions, figure generally among those from which no derogation is permitted, even in exceptional circumstances.[83] These basic rights include: the right to life, in so far as the individual is protected against 'arbitrary' deprivation;[84] the right to be protected against torture, or cruel or inhuman treatment or punishment;[85] the right not to be subjected to slavery or servitude;[86] the right not to be subjected to retroactive criminal penalties;[87] the right to recognition as a person before the law;[88] and the right to freedom of thought, conscience, and religion.[89] Although not included within the same fundamental class, the following rights are also relevant in view of the frequent close connection between persecution and personal freedom: the right to liberty and security of the person, including freedom from arbitrary arrest and detention;[90]

---

[80] Ibid., citing the liberal interpretations of Weis ('other measures in disregard of human dignity') and Vernant ('severe measures and sanctions of an arbitrary nature, incompatible with the principles set forth in the Universal Declaration of Human Rights').

[81] Cf. Goodwin-Gill, *Movement of Persons,* 66-87.

[82] *Barcelona Traction* case, ICJ Rep. (1970) 3, at 32.

[83] Cf. art. 15(2), European Convention on Human Rights; art. 4, Covenant on Civil and Political Rights; art. 27, American Convention of Human Rights.

[84] Art. 6, Covenant on Civil and Political Rights.

[85] Ibid. art. 7.      [86] Ibid. art. 8.

[87] Ibid. art. 15.     [88] Ibid. art. 16.

[89] Ibid. art. 18.     [90] Ibid. art. 9.

and the right to freedom from arbitrary interference in private, home, and family life.[91]

Recognition of these rights is essential to the maintenance of the integrity and inherent human dignity of the individual. Persecution within the Convention thus comprehends measures, taken on the basis of one or more of the stated grounds, which threaten: deprivation of life or liberty; torture or cruel, inhuman, or degrading treatment; subjection to slavery or servitude; non-recognition as a person (particularly where the consequences of such non-recognition impinge directly on an individual's life, liberty, livelihood, security, or integrity); and oppression, discrimination, or harassment of a person in his or her private, home, or family life.

## (2) THE WAYS AND MEANS OF PERSECUTION

There being no limits to the perverse side of human imagination, little purpose is served by attempting to list all known measures of persecution. Assessments must be made from case to case by taking account, on the one hand, of the notion of individual integrity and human dignity and, on the other hand, of the manner and degree to which they stand to be injured. A straightforward threat to life or liberty is widely accepted.[92] United States law, for example, formerly employed the notion of 'physical persecution' as the basis for withholding deportation,[93] until 'persecution on account of race, religion or political opinion' was substituted in 1965.[94] Further statutory amendments have been

---

[91] Ibid. art. 17.

[92] See, for example, statements on United Kingdom policy: 529 HC Deb. cols. 1507-16 (1 July 1954); 595 HC Deb. col. 1343 (20 Nov. 1958); 649 HC Deb. col. 431 (15 Nov. 1961).

[93] Initially introduced by the Internal Security Act 1950: 64 Stat. 987, s. 23, this provision was substantially re-enacted in the Immigration and Nationality Act 1952: 66 Stat. 163, s. 243 (h). See further below, ch. VIII, s. 2(7).

[94] 79 Stat. 911, s. 11(f); 8 USC s. 1253(h). This was interpreted in *Kovac* v. *INS* 407 F.2d 102, 106 (1969) as effecting 'a significant, broadening change' and the applicant was no longer required to show the likelihood of actual bodily harm. In *INS* v. *Stanisic* 395 US 62 (1969), the Supreme Court remanded a persecution claim decided according to the earlier criteria for reconsideration in the light of the 1965 amendment. United States courts, however, have generally been wary of reviewing the merits of persecution claims, and have limited themselves to ensuring procedural due process. See *Muskardin* v. *INS* 415 F.2d 865 (Ct. of Appeals 1969); *Kam* v. *Esperdy* 274 F. Supp. 485 (D. Ct. 1967); *Blazina* v. *Bouchard* 286 F.2d 510 (Ct. of Appeals 1961); *Lena* v. *INS* 379 F.2d 536 (Ct. of Appeals 1967); *Fleurinor* v. *INS* 585 F.2d 129 (Ct. of Appeals 1978); cf. the influence of the 'political question' doctrine: *Mathews* v. *Diaz* 426 US 67, 81 (Supreme Court 1976).

introduced by the 1980 Refugee Act,[95] but the earlier jurisprudence may still be relevant generally and in understanding the concept of persecution in United States law. In 1961, for example, the Court of Appeals interpreted 'physical persecution' to mean confinement, torture, or death inflicted on account of race, religion, or political viewpoint,[96] and subsequently expanded the notion to include economic restrictions so severe as to deprive a person of all means of earning a livelihood.[97] Likelihood of punishment for defection or desertion,[98] and liability to compulsory military service[99] have been rejected, unless the individual was likely to face long imprisonment.[100] On the other hand, in 1964, a court noted that it was 'a matter of common knowledge', of which it would take judicial notice, that the regime in Haiti might well represent a danger of physical persecution to members of an opposition family.[101] In 1969, the Court of Appeals interpreted persecution to mean 'the infliction of suffering or harm upon those who differ in race, religion or political opinion in a way regarded as offensive'.[102] Moreover, persecution might exist where there was a probability of deliberate imposition of 'substantial economic disadvantage' for any of the stated reasons.[103] Persecution, it may be argued, also includes punishment or repeated punishment for breach of the law which is out of proportion to the offence.[104]

Certain measures, such as the forcible expulsion of an ethnic minority or of an individual, will clearly show the severance of the normal relationship between citizen and state, but the relation of

---

[95] In addition, substantial limitations were imposed on opportunities for judicial review; see below, ch. VIII, s. 2(7).

[96] *Blazina* v. *Bouchard* 286 F.2d 510 (1961). In *Lena* v. *INS* 379 F.2d 536 (1967), the Court of Appeals ruled that a refusal to stay deportation was not arbitrary where the immigration judge had found that Greeks in Turkey do, and are permitted to, practice their religion. Such discrimination as does exist, said the Court, was directed against the Greek Orthodox Church, rather than against individuals.

[97] *Dunat* v. *Hurney* 297 F.2d 744 (Ct. of Appeals 1961); *Kasravi* v. *INS* 400 F.2d 675 (Ct. of Appeals 1968).

[98] *Blazina* v. *Bouchard* 286 F.2d 510 (Ct. of Appeals 1961).

[99] *Glavic* v. *Beechie* 225 F. Supp. 24 (D. Ct. 1963).

[100] *Sovich* v. *Esperdy* 206 F. Supp. 558; 319 F.2d 21 (Ct. of Appeals 1963).

[101] *Mercer* v. *Esperdy* 234 F. Supp. 611 (D. Ct. 1964); see also, in particular, *Haitian Refugee Center* v. *Civiletti* 503 F. Supp. 422, 474-510 (D. Ct. 1980), for comment on conditions in Haiti and the limits of the political question doctrine.

[102] *Kovac* v. *INS* 407 F.2d 102 (1969); reasoning approved and reaffirmed in *Moghanian* v. *Board of Immigration Appeals* 577 F.2d 141 (Ct. of Appeals 1978).

[103] Cf. *Berdo* v. *INS* 432 F.2d 824 (1970).

[104] See above, s. 4(2).

cause and effect may be less clear in other cases. For example, expulsion may be encouraged indirectly, either by threats[105] or by the implementation of apparently unconnected policies. Thus, in Vietnam after 1978, state policies aimed at the restructuring of society and the abolition of the bourgeoisie[106] began to be implemented, giving rise among those affected to serious concern for their future life and security. Those in any way associated with the previous government of South Vietnam were already liable not only to 're-education',[107] but thereafter also to surveillance, to denial of access to employment and the ration system, or to relocation in a 'new economic zone'.[108] The situation of ethnic Chinese was exacerbated by the deterioration in relations and subsequent armed conflict with the People's Republic of China.[109] The net result was a massive exodus of asylum-seekers by boat and land to countries in the region.

Cause and effect are yet more indirect where the government of the country of origin cannot be immediately implicated. Refugees, for example, have fled mob violence[110] or the activities of so-called 'death squads'.[111] Governments may be unable to suppress such activities, they may be unwilling or reluctant to do so, or they may even be colluding with those responsible. In such cases, where protection is in fact unavailable, persecution within the Convention can result, for it does not follow that the concept is limited to the actions of governments or their agents.[112] There is also no reason in principle why the fear of persecution should relate to the whole of the asylum-seeker's country of origin; for various reasons, it may be unreasonable to expect the asylum-seeker to move internally, rather than to cross an international frontier.[113]

Persecution under the Convention is thus a complex of reasons,

---

[105] As was done by President Amin in the case of the Uganda expulsions in 1972.

[106] Foreign Language Press, Hanoi, *The Hoa in Vietnam* (1978) 12.

[107] Cf. Amnesty International *1980 Report* 241-6, *1982 Report* 249-52.

[108] Grahl-Madsen includes 'removal to a remote or designated place within the home country' in a list of measures which may amount to persecution: *Status of Refugees*, i.201.

[109] Osborne, 'Indo-China's refugees: causes and effects' *International Affairs* (1980) 37, 38-44.

[110] Cf. *The Biharis in Bangladesh* (Minority Rights Group, report no. 11, 1977).

[111] 'Death squads' have been particularly active in Latin American countries in recent years; see, for example, Amnesty International, *Guatemala: A government program of political murder* (1981). See also the work of the UN Commission on Human Rights Working Group on Enforced or Involuntary Disappearances: UN doc. E/1980/13, 74-6; Res. 20 (XXXVI), ibid. 180 f.

[112] Persecution for reasons of race or religion will often spring from hostile sections of the populace, while that for reasons of political opinion will more commonly derive from direct, official action.     [113] Cf. OAU Convention, art. I(2).

interests, and measures. The measures affect or are directed against groups or individuals for reasons of race, religion, nationality, membership of a particular social group, or political opinion. These reasons in turn show that the groups or individuals are identified by reference to a classification which ought to be irrelevant to the enjoyment of fundamental, protected interests. Persecution results where the measures in question harm those interests and the integrity and inherent dignity of the human being to a degree considered unacceptable under prevailing international standards or under higher standards prevailing in the state faced with determining a claim to asylum or refugee status.[114] An element of relativity exists, moreover, between the value to be attributed to the protected interest (for example, life and freedom of conscience) and the nature of the measure threatened (for example, death and some lesser interference).

Although persecution itself is undefined by any international instrument, an approach in terms of reasons, interests, and measures receives support by analogy in the International Convention on the Suppression and Punishment of the Crime of Apartheid.[115] The term 'the crime of apartheid', declares Article II, shall apply to the following:

inhuman acts committed for the purpose of establishing and maintaining domination by one racial group of persons over any other racial group of persons and systematically oppressing them:

---

[114] The following historical examples provide illustrations of measures which may amount to persecution; the treatment accorded to those returned to the USSR after the Second World War: Bethell, *The Last Secret* (1974); Tolstoy, *Victims of Yalta* (rev. ed. 1979); relocation of national minorities in the USSR: *The Crimean Tatars, Volga Germans and Meskhetians* (Minority Rights Group, report no. 6, rev. ed. 1980); mob and institutionalized attacks on members of the Baha'i faith in Iran: *The Baha' is in Iran* (Baha'i International Community, New York, June 1981, updated Nov. 1981); measures taken against ethnic minorities: *Selective Genocide in Burundi* (Minority Rights Group, report no. 20, 1974); *What future for the Amerindians of South America?* (Minority Rights Group, report no. 15, rev. ed. 1977); institutional and individual measures of repression against religious groups: *Religious Minorities in the Soviet Union*, (Minority Rights Group, report no. 1, rev. ed. 1977); *Jehovah's Witnesses in Central Africa* (Minority Rights Group, report no. 29, 1976); economic measures affecting Asians in East and Central Africa: *The Asian Minorities of East and Central Africa* (Minority Rights Group, report no. 4, 1971); *Problems of a Displaced Minority: the new position of East Africa's Asians* (Minority Rights Group, report no. 16, rev. ed. 1978); the complex of measures aimed or calculated to deny self-determination: *The Kurds* (Minority Rights Group, report no. 23, rev. ed. 1981); *The Namibians of South West Africa* (Minority Rights Group, report no. 19, rev. ed. 1978); *The Palestinians* (Minority Rights Group, report no. 24, rev. ed. 1979).

[115] Adopted by the UN General Assembly on 30 Nov. 1973: Res. 3068(XXVIII). The Convention entered into force on 18 July 1976; as of 1 July 1982, 67 states were parties to the Convention.

(a) Denial to a member or members of a racial group or groups of the right to life and liberty of person:

(i) By murder of members of a racial group or groups;

(ii) By the infliction upon the members of a racial group or groups of serious bodily or mental harm by the infringement of their freedom or dignity, or by subjecting them to torture or to cruel, inhuman or degrading treatment or punishment;

(iii) By arbitrary arrest and illegal imprisonment of the members of a racial group or groups;

(b) Deliberate imposition on a racial group or groups of living conditions calculated to cause its or their physical destruction in whole or in part;

(c) Any legislative measures and other measures calculated to prevent a racial group or groups from participating in the political, social, economic and cultural life of the country and the deliberate creation of conditions preventing the full development of such a group or groups, in particular by denying to members of a racial group or groups basic human rights and freedoms, including the right to work, the right to form recognised trade unions, the right to education, the right to a nationality, the right to freedom of movement and residence, the right to freedom of opinion and expression, and the right to freedom of peaceful assembly and association;

(d) Any measures, including legislative measures, designed to divide the population along racial lines by the creation of separate reserves and ghettos for the members of a racial group or groups, the prohibition of mixed marriages among members of various racial groups, the expropriation of landed property belonging to a racial group or groups or to members thereof;

(e) Exploitation of the labour of the members of a racial group or groups, in particular by submitting them to forced labour;

(d) Persecution of organisations and persons, by depriving them of fundamental rights and freedoms, because they oppose *apartheid.*[116]

This provision also invites consideration of the question whether each member of a group subject to a repressive policy of general application, can, by reason of such membership alone, be considered to have a well-founded fear of persecution; or does persecution necessarily imply a further act of specific discrimination, a singling out of the individual?[117] Where large groups are seriously affected by a government's political, economic, and social policies

[116] Art. III.
[117] *Lena.* v. *INS*, loc. cit. above, n. 96.

or by the outbreak of uncontrolled communal violence, it would appear wrong in principle to limit the concept of persecution to measures immediately identifiable as direct and individual.[118] General measures, often aimed at 'restructuring' society,[119] will frequently be directed at groups identifiable by reference to the Convention reasons for persecution, and carried through with the object, express or implied, of excluding them from or forcing them into the mainstream of the new society. Where individual or collective measures of enforcement are employed, such as coercion by denial of employment or education, restrictions on language and culture, denial of access to food supplies, expropriation of property without compensation, and forcible or involuntary relocation, then fear of persecution in the above sense may exist; mere membership of the affected group can be sufficient. Likewise, where punishment under a law of general application may result, any necessary condition of singling out would be met by the decision to prosecute in a given case. Whether a well-founded fear of persecution exists will depend upon an examination of the class of persons in fact affected, of the interests in respect of which they stand to be punished, of the likelihood of punishment, and the nature and extent of the penalties.

## (3) LACK OF PROTECTION

The criteria for refugee status posited by Article I of the 1951 Convention have the individual asylum-seeker very much in mind. In the case of large numbers of asylum-seekers, establishing a well-founded fear of persecution on a case-by-case basis can be impossible and impracticable. A prima-facie or group determination, based on evidence of lack of protection, may therefore be the answer.[120] This solution is implied by the second leg of the refugee

---

[118] Grahl-Madsen, *Status of Refugees*, i.213.

[119] Economic reasons or motivation alone will not entitle a person to refugee status; but a government's 'economic measures' may well be the cloak for action calculated to destroy the economic livelihood of specific groups. In such cases, a fear of persecution can be well founded. Cf. Palley, *Constitutional Law and Minorities* (Minority Rights Group, report no. 36, 1978) on the subject of laws and administrative action designed to remedy economic imbalances, at 10: 'If the emphasis is on remedying disadvantage and lack of opportunity (such as special educational programmes, special technical assistance programmes, special loan programmes in setting up co-operatives) or is protective (protection of native land against sale to capitalist entrepreneurs) it can be more readily tolerated by non-recipients. If it becomes an instrument of economic attack on other communities by denial of the right to engage in their traditional occupations, then it is proper to describe the technique as one of domination.'

[120] Cf. Sadruddin Aga Khan, Hague *Receuil* (1965-I) at 341.

definition adopted in the 1969 OAU Convention, which extends to 'every person who, owing to external aggression, occupation, foreign domination, or events seriously disturbing public order in either part or the whole of his country of origin or nationality', is compelled to seek refuge in another country.[121] Establishing that civil war has broken out, that law and order have broken down, or that aggression is under way is relatively simple. The notion of lack of protection, however, is potentially wider and invites attention to the general issue of a state's duty to protect and promote human rights. Clearly, not every failure by the state to promote and protect, for example, the various rights recognized by the 1966 Covenants, will justify flight across an international frontier and a claim to refugee status. Not all the rights are fundamental, some are subject to progressive implementation only, while others may in turn be the subject of permissible derogations.

The list of fundamental protected interests proposed above can be expanded in the future, as recognition grows of the value of certain economic and social rights.[122] It is doubtful, however, whether states at present are prepared to support any formal extension of the refugee definition.[123] Nevertheless, one legal implication of developments in favour of refugees is that there are limits to the legitimate or permissible extent of state power. If individuals, social groups, and classes are at the absolute disposal of the state, then repression, re-education, relocation or even expulsion aimed at the restructuring of society can be considered comprehensible, even acceptable. But where there are limits to state power, and individuals and groups have rights against the state or interests entitled to recognition and protection, then such measures may amount to persecution.

[121] Art. 1(2); see also above, ch. I, s. 3(2).

[122] Cf. Bossuyt, *L'interdiction de la discrimination*, at 169-217. He analyses the distinction between civil and political rights, on the one hand, and economic, social, and cultural rights, on the other hand. He concludes that there is an intrinsic difference in the nature of the two groups of rights, which reflects that between negative and positive obligations of the state.

[123] In this respect, the provisions of Swiss law quoted above, ch. I, s. 6 with its concept of 'serious prejudice' are ahead of the views of most states.

Chapter III

# LOSS AND DENIAL OF REFUGEE STATUS AND ITS BENEFITS

Most recent international instruments not only define refugees, but also provide for the circumstances in which refugee status shall terminate or in which the benefits of status shall be denied or withdrawn.[1] For example, the IRO Constitution excluded refugees who were 'ordinary criminals ... extraditable by treaty', and Article 14 of the Universal Declaration of Human Rights prohibits invocation of the right of asylum 'in the case of prosecutions genuinely arising from non-political crimes or from acts contrary to the purposes and principles of the United Nations'. These categories have been expanded in other instruments and in state practice so that, broadly, there are four sets of circumstances in which refugee status may be lost or denied: (1) by reason of voluntary acts of the individual; (2) by reason of change of circumstances; (3) by reason of protection accorded by other states or international agencies; and (4) in the case of criminals or other undeserving cases.

## 1. Voluntary acts of the individual

Both the UNHCR Statute and the 1951 Convention provide for loss of refugee status where the individual, by his or her own actions, indicates that a well-founded fear of persecution no longer exists or that international protection is no longer required.[2] The circumstances include voluntary reavailment of the protection of the country of origin, voluntary reacquisition of nationality, acquisition of a new nationality and the protection which derives therefrom, and voluntary re-establishment in the country of origin.

---

[1] See generally, Grahl-Madsen, *The Status of Refugees in International Law* (1966) i.367-412; Weis, 'The Concept of the Refugee in International Law' *Journal du dr. inter.* (1960) 1, at 25-30.

[2] Statute, para. 6(a)-(d); Convention, art. 1 C (1)-(4).

For the purposes of *reavailment of protection*, the refugee must not only act voluntarily, but must also intend to and actually obtain protection. Protection comprises all such actions by the refugee as indicate the establishment of normal relations with the authorities of the country of origin—for example, registration at consulates or application for and renewal of passports or certificates of nationality. Sometimes, however, a refugee may be unwillingly obliged to seek a measure of protection from those authorities, as where a passport or travel document is essential to obtain the issue of a residence permit in the country of asylum.[3] Being involuntary, the protection obtained should not bring refugee status to an end.

In other cases of application for and obtaining a national passport or the renewal of a passport, it may be presumed, in the absence of evidence to the contrary, that reavailment of protection is intended. The presumption may be strengthened where the refugee in fact makes use of the passport for travel, or for return to the country of origin, or in order to obtain some advantage in the country of asylum. Possession of a national passport and a visit to the country of origin would seem conclusive as to cessation of refugee status. Grahl-Madsen, however, suggests that 'physical presence in the territory of the home country does not *per se* constitute reavailment of protection ... it is the conscious subjection under the government of that country ... the normalization of the relationship between State and individual which matters.'[4] Indeed, on leaving the country of origin for the second time, the individual in question may well be able to show that he or she, still or once again, has a well-founded fear of persecution within the Convention.[5]

All the circumstances of the contact between the individual and the authorities of the country of origin must be taken into account.

[3] See, for example, *Jurisprudence de la Commission de Recours des Réfugiés* (1961), hereafter *JCRR*, case no. 174, 10 (*Molina Toledo*)—reference to consular authorities at request of French authorities not reavailment of protection; case no. 1209-10, 81 f. (*Chimeno*)—nationality certificate obtained in similar circumstances not reavailment; case no. 185, 11 (*Grunberg*)—passport for journey to third country obtained from consular authorities at invitation of *Préfecture de Police* not reavailment. See also, ibid. case no. 407, 31 (*Romerales Millera*); case no. 682, 27 f. (*Gheorghiu*); case no. 949, 66 (*Estop Caranto*); case no. 1558, 94 f. (*Andujar Alonso*).

[4] *Status of Refugees*, i.384 f. See also *JCRR*, case no. 593, 39 (*Dominquez del Rey*)—brief, clandestine return journeys to the country of origin not considered reavailment of protection; cf. ibid. case no. 60, 5 (*Sasiain Arrue*).

[5] Note that art. 1 C (4) of the Convention, which provides for cessation of refugee status on 'voluntary re-establishment' in the country of origin, clearly implies something more than mere presence.

It is therefore relevant to consider the age of the refugee,[6] the object to be attained by the contact,[7] whether the contact was successful,[8] whether it was repeated,[9] and what advantages were actually obtained.[10] In cases involving passports, it will be relevant if the refugee's country of residence is a party to the 1951 Convention and/or the 1967 Protocol, and so bound under Article 28 to issue travel documents to refugees lawfully staying in its territory.[11] If not a party, that state may yet issue aliens passports or certificates of identity which enable the refugee to avoid recourse to his or her national authorities. In addition, it will be necessary to determine whether the national passport which the refugee obtains in fact reflects the full measure of national protection, for example, by enabling him or her to return freely to the country of issue.

These various issues were illustrated in the late 1970s when many Chilean refugees were found to be obtaining and renewing

[6] See *JCRR*, case no. 4145, 111 (*Ibanez bel Ramon*); cf. case no. 2049, 99 (*Lopez Perez*); the fact that the contact has been made on behalf of the refugee by a third party is not generally sufficient to rebut a finding of reavailment of protection; see *JCRR*, case no. 135, 9 (*Morales Fernandez*); case no. 1263, 84 f. (*Broseta Marti*).

[7] See *JCRR*, case no. 3355, 105 (*Borensztajn David*)—passport renewed in order to obtain foreign visas for urgent journeys for professional purposes not reavailment; case no. 1486, 93 f. (*Mendez Perez*), passport obtained and renewed by seaman for whom such document essential to pursue his profession not reavailment, particularly as document not valid for return to home country.

[8] See *JCRR*, case no. 1727, 97 (*Bata Lojos*)—unsuccessful approach to consular authorities with view to repatriation not reavailment; cf. case no. 3975, 108 (*Szlabowicz*)—visa for return to country of origin stamped in French travel document nevertheless amounted to reavailment of protection; case no. 534, 35 (*Kjosev*)—repatriation requested and passport permitting return obtained amounted to reavailment in absence any proof that refugee acted in moment of severe depression. In *Gasinskaya* in 1981 the Australian DORS Committee decided to keep under review the case of a refugee who had approached the authorities of her country of origin with a view to possible return and reacquisition of citizenship.

[9] See *JCRR*, case no. 288, p. 17 f. (*Llesta Escanilla*)—nationality certificate obtained, apparently to facilitate reunion with minor daughter, but twice renewed and considered reavailment of protection; case no. 55, 4 (*Rebay Lazlo*)—unsuccessful application for passport but stated intention to apply again indicative of absence of fear, thus justifying refusal of recognition of refugee status; case no. 133, 8 f. (*Caballero Martin*)—obtaining and renewing passport amounted to reavailment of protection.

[10] See *JCRR*, case no. 271, 17 (*Roldan, Antonia*)—nationality certificate obtained to complete sale of property in country of origin, but not renewed or used to obtain any other advantage, not considered reavailment; case no. 332, 25 (*Martin Cotorruelo*)—similarly. Cf. case no. 291, 18 (*Rodriguez Martin*)—nationality certificate obtained and used to renew residence permit amounted to reavailment; case no. 257, 14 f. (*Nogueira*) and case no. 562, 37 f. (*Callado Sierra*)—similarly; case no. 941, 65 f. (*Codina Bea*)—initial reference to consular authorities with agreement of *Office français de protection des réfugiés et apatrides* followed by second reference with object of benefitting from advantages granted to those of applicant's nationality considered reavailment of protection.

[11] See further below, ch. VII, s. 1(2)(a).

national passports, apparently without difficulty. In 1976 the Chilean government had decided that passports might be issued or renewed for Chilean nationals abroad, even if they had refugee status and asylum in their country of residence. However, under a 1973 legislative decree,[12] persons who had left Chile to seek asylum, who had left illegally or been expelled or forced to leave, were prohibited from returning without express authorization by the Minister of the Interior. Moreover, those returning without such permission were liable to prosecution.[13] Holding a Chilean passport could thus still be compatible with refugee status, although the holder might reasonably be required to explain why alternative documentation had not been obtained.[14]

Voluntary action is also explicitly required in respect of *re-acquisition of nationality*.[15] Such an act is more immediately verifiable than the notion of reavailment of protection, yet perhaps constitutes the supreme manifestation of the latter. There is less scope for explanation or extenuating circumstances: the intention of the individual and the effectiveness of the act will suffice in most cases.[16]

In the case of *acquisition of a new nationality*,[17] however, the individual must also enjoy protection in virtue of that status. The new nationality must be effective, in that at least the fundamental incidents of nationality should be recognized, including the right of return and residence in the state.[18] In a number of decisions in the 1950s, the French *Commission de Recours* considered the refugee status of Jews who had travelled to and resided in Israel. The general view adopted was that acquisition of Israeli nationality

---

[12] Art. 3 of Decree Law no. 81 of 11 Oct. 1973: *Diario Oficial,* no. 28694, 6 Nov. 1973.

[13] Cf. Amnesty International *1978 Report,* 111; *1980 Report,* 118; *1981 Report,* pp. 122-3.

[14] See *JCRR,* case no. 637, 42 (*Petrow*), where the *Commission de Recours* took the view that use of a 'passport of convenience' issued by a third state had no effect on the holder's true nationality such as to remove the basis for her claim to refugee status; see also case no. 577, 39 f. (*Berline*); case no. 313, 12 f. (*Ekmekdjian*); case no. 1165, 77 f. (*Pitharoulis*). In a series of cases in 1980, the Australian DORS Committee considered the weight to be accorded to Taiwanese passports held by Indo-Chinese seeking refugee status in Australia. The Committee noted that the Taiwanese authorities issued two types of passport, only one of which (the so-called 'MFA' passport) enabled the holder to return to and reside in Taiwan. Other passports, issued freely to 'overseas Chinese', amounted to no more than a travel facility and could not be equated with the full protection normally accorded to passport holders by the state of issue. See generally, Goodwin-Gill, *Movement of Persons,* 24-50.

[15] Statute, para. 6(b); Convention, art. 1 C (2).

[16] Cf. *JCRR,* case no. 772, 41 (*Gorbatcheff*).

[17] Statute, para. 6(c); Convention, art. 1 C (3).

[18] Cf. Goodwin-Gill, *Movement of Persons* 45-9.

under the provisions of the Law of Return brought the individuals within the scope of Article 1C(3), particularly where Israeli passports were later used.[19] In one case, the *Commission* held that the *'très graves difficultés d'existence'* which had motivated the individual to leave Israel were not attributable to the political or administrative authorities and could not be equated with persecution or lack of protection.[20]

Finally, refugee status may be lost by *voluntary re-establishment in the country of origin.*[21] Something more than a visit or mere presence is required; the individual must have settlement on a permanent basis in view, with no evident intention of leaving.[22] Should the individual leave again and claim refugee status, the case will need to be considered in the light of events subsequent to re-establishment.

## 2. Change of circumstances

The 'change of circumstances' anticipated is clearly intended to comprehend fundamental changes in the country which remove the basis of any fear of persecution.[23] The replacement of a tyrannical by a democratic regime is an obvious example,[24] but the process of change may be more subtle and reflected over a number of years by legal reforms and gradual improvements in human rights. Amnesties are important and may also indicate that the grounds for refugee status have disappeared. For example, following the overthrow of the government of President Masie Ngnuema in Equatorial Guinea in 1979, the new government enacted a general amnesty for all who had fled abroad for political reasons during the previous eleven years.[25] The efficacy of such amnesties, of course, is critical but on that occasion the text of the law was required to be transmitted to interested governments, the

---

[19] See *JCRR*, case no. 208, 13 (*Breitholz*); case no. 237, 15 (*Schapira*)—no steps taken to avoid the acquisition of nationality; case no. 432, 21 (*Mincu, Benjamin*)—similarly, and no evidence that the individual applied for or was refused a Convention Travel Document; see also case no. 3973, 107 f. (*Rosenthal, E.*).

[20] See *JCRR*, case no. 1093, 75 f. (*Yarhi*).

[21] Statute, para. 6(d); Convention, art. 1 C (4). Cf. IRO Constitution, part I D, below, annexe I.

[22] See *JCRR*, case no. 59, 2 (*Maqueda, Jean*)—two years' residence amounted to voluntary re-establishment; cf. case no. 593, 39 (*Dominquez del Rey*), above, n. 4.

[23] Statute, para. 6(e), (f); Convention, art. 1 C (5), (6). The difference in the wording of the two paragraphs reflects that between refugees with and refugees without a nationality.

[24] Cf. IRO Constitution, annexe I below, part I C 2.

[25] Ministerial decree 45/1979 of 10 Oct. 1979.

United Nations Secretary-General, the OAU Secretary-General, and UNHCR.[26] Involvement by UNHCR in repatriation operations may well confirm the fundamental nature of any change of circumstances.[27]

The UNHCR Statute and the 1951 Convention deal somewhat differently with those who, having fled, may still be considered as having valid reasons for continuing to enjoy the status of refugee, any change in their country of origin notwithstanding. The Convention expressly acknowledges the weight to be accorded to 'compelling reasons arising out of previous persecution',[28] yet perversely limits the right to invoke such reasons to refugees recognized under earlier agreements. The Statute refers to 'grounds other than those of personal convenience' as justifying a refusal to have recourse to the protection of the country of origin, but without limiting their availability.[29] The object of the exception to the effects of a change of circumstances is clearly the continuation of protection for those who have suffered most seriously in their country of origin. One commentator has suggested that the provision is 'mainly intended to cover the case of victims of racial persecution where, unlike political persecution, the population as well as the government often took an active part'.[30] However, the continuing nature of the injuries often suffered by the persecuted is a reason for the exception to be liberally applied.[31]

## 3. Protection or assistance by other states or United Nations agencies

### (1) THE COUNTRY OF FIRST ASYLUM PRINCIPLE

States have so far not accepted an obligation to grant asylum to refugees,[32] and have likewise failed to agree upon principles

---

[26] Cf. Amnesty International *1979 Report,* 46-7; *1980 Report,* 43-4; for UNHCR's involvement in repatriation to Equatorial Guinea, see UN doc. A/AC.96/575, para. 381 (Aug. 1980).

[27] Cf. UNHCR's involvement in repatriation of refugees from Angola and Zaire: UN docs. A/AC.96/564, paras. 4-5, 255-6, 262, 275-80 (1979); A/AC.96/577, paras. 6-8, 20-2, 304, 315, 321-5 (1980); and in repatriation of Zimbabweans following independence: ibid. paras. 368-75.

[28] Cf. IRO Constitution, annexe I below, part I C (a) (iii).

[29] The precise relationship between the various parts of para. 6 is far from clear.

[30] Pompe, 'The Convention of 28 July 1951 and the international protection of refugees' HCR/INF/42 (May 1958) 10, n. 3; originally published in Dutch in *Rechtsgeleerd Magazyn Themis* (1956) 425-91.

[31] See *JCRR,* case no. 1786, 74 f. (*Pilarsky*); case no. 2909, 106 (*Tillmann*); cf. case no. 584, 38 (*Grynszpan*).

[32] In the general sense of protection and residence; see further below, ch. V, ss. 1, 5.

which would establish the appropriate state to consider applications in any given case. Article 31 of the 1951 Convention requires refugees guilty of illegal entry not to be penalized, but is limited to those 'coming directly from a territory where their life or freedom was threatened'. With the background of this somewhat ambiguous reference, a practice has developed in certain states of excluding from consideration the cases of those who have found or are deemed to have found asylum or protection elsewhere, or who are considered to have spent too long in transit.[33]

This practice is sometimes backed by legal provisions. For example, in the Federal Republic of Germany, the law declares that those entitled to asylum shall include, *inter alia*, refugees under the 1951 Convention 'so far as they have not already been recognised as refugees in another state ... or otherwise found protection from persecution'.[34] An applicant for refugee status may also be barred from submitting or pursuing a claim if it is not made within a determined period after departure from the country of origin, or after the occurrence of events there which give rise to the fear of persecution, or after entry to the potential asylum country.[35]

In resettlement countries, too, eligibility for special entry programmes may be conditional upon the refugee not otherwise having found a durable solution. Thus, under United States law, a refugee has long been liable to refusal of admission if already established in another state. The requirement that the refugee be 'not firmly resettled' in the first state of refuge, absent from the original legislation, was already apparent in administrative practice,[36] and has been approved in a number of court decisions. In 1968 the United States District Court of California held that aliens who had left China in 1950 and 1955 and who entered the United States after extended residence in the Dominican Republic were outside the scope of the Act. They had stopped fleeing, and

---

[33] This and related problems, as well as the disharmony of practice and standards which produce them, are analysed in detail in Melander, *Refugees in Orbit* (1978); see also, Grahl-Madsen, *Territorial Asylum* (1980) 95-101.

[34] *AsylVfG* 1982, art. 2. Cf. Kimminich, *Der internationale Rechtsstatus des Flüchtlings*, (1962) 406-7; in respect of Canadian practice, see Wydryzynski, 'Refugees and the Immigration Act' 25 *McGill LJ* 154 (1979) at 170-3.

[35] See examples cited by Melander, *Refugees in Orbit*, 14-24.

[36] Evans, 'Political Refugees "not firmly resettled" as in section 203(A) (7) of the Immigration Act 1952 as amended' 66 *AJIL* (1972) 101; id. 'Political Refugees and the United States Immigration Laws: Further Developments' ibid. 571. There are parallels in earlier United Kingdom practice; see 469 HC Deb. col. 811 (1949).

'a non-resettled status is a *sine qua non* for qualification'.[37] The Supreme Court has also held that presence in the United States must be a consequence of the flight in search of refuge, 'reasonably proximate to the flight and not following a flight remote in point of time or intervening residence in a third country reasonably constituting a termination of the original flight in search of refuge'.[38] A temporary refuge in another state may not prejudice status, but what is temporary will clearly depend on all the circumstances, including whether the individual has established any business, whether any official position inconsistent with status has been occupied and the duration of stay.[39] This limitation is now maintained in the United States 1980 Refugee Act,[40] and it is also embodied as an essential criterion for qualification in Canada's designated classes.[41]

In many states, the criteria for recognition of refugee status also serve as the criteria for the grant of asylum in the sense of residence and protection.[42] It may thus be reasonable for states to

[37] *Min Chin Wu* v. *Fullilove* 282 F. Supp. 63 (D. Ct. 1968). See also *Alidede* v. *Hurney* 301 F. Supp. 1031 (1969), in which the District Court considered that the fact that the applicant had obtained Turkish citizenship and had run his own restaurant in Turkey for eight years subsequent to fleeing a Communist country, meant that he was no longer a refugee.

[38] *Rosenberg* v. *Yee Chien Woo* 402 US 49 (1971): 65 *AJIL* 828 (1971); see also *Chinese American Civic Council* v. *Attorney General* 566 F.2d 321 (Ct. of Appeals 1978); 72 *AJIL* 672 (1978).

[39] For example, in 1979, the Australian DORS Committee dealt with a number of applications by Indo-Chinese who had spent some time in camps in Malaysia and Thailand before travelling on by boat to Australia. The Committee decided that it was entitled to disregard that element, in that the 'transit' states could not be considered as potential countries of asylum. See, to similar effect, *JCRR* case no. 2629, 91 f. (*Protic*).

[40] S. 201 introducing new s. 207(c) into the Immigration and Nationality Act 1952. 8 CFR 207.1(b) (Interim Regulations, 2 June 1980) provided that a 'refugee is considered to be firmly resettled if he has been offered resident status, citizenship, or some other type of permanent resettlement by another nation and has travelled to and entered that nation as a consequence of his flight from persecution, unless the refugee establishes, to the satisfaction of the United States Government officer reviewing the case, that the conditions of his residence in that nation have been so substantially and consciously restricted by the authorities of that country that he has not in fact been resettled. In making this determination, the officer shall consider, in light of the conditions under which other residents of the country live, the type of housing, whether permanent or temporary, made available to the refugee, the types and extent of employment available to the refugee, and the extent to which the refugee has received permission to hold property and to enjoy other rights and privileges (such as travel documentation, education, public relief, or naturalization) available to other residents in the country.' The wording was revised in 1983.

[41] The Indo-Chinese and Self-Exiled Designated Classes regulations (SOR/78-931 and 933, continued and amended by SOR/80-334, 908 and 910) refer to persons who 'have not become permanently resettled'. See Wydryzynski, 25 *McGill LJ* 165-6.

[42] See further below, ch. VIII, s. 5(3).

limit their response in this field to refugees in need. Consequently, a refugee formally recognized by one state, or who holds an identity certificate or travel document issued under the 1951 Convention,[43] generally has no claim to transfer residence to another state, otherwise than in accordance with normal immigration policies. Like principles may apply to a refugee who, though not formally recognized, has found protection in any state. 'Protection' in this context should mean, as a minimum, the right of residence and re-entry, the right to work, and some form of guarantee against return to a country of persecution.[44] Given evidence of recognition, asylum and protection elsewhere, the only issue which might otherwise be raised in the refugee's favour is that those measures are not in fact effective; this would amount to a new claim, directed in part at least against the country of first asylum.

Serious problems arise, however, where the candidate for refugee status has not been formally recognized, has no asylum or protection elsewhere, but is nevertheless considered by the state in which application is made to be some other state's responsibility. Individuals can end up in limbo, unable to return to the alleged country of asylum or to pursue an application and regularize status in the country in which they now find themselves. The absence of agreement between states on responsibility in such cases, the variety of procedural limitations governing applications for refugee status and asylum, as well as the tendency of states to interpret their own and other states' duties in the light of sovereign self-interest, all contribute to a negative situation potentially capable of leading to breach of the fundamental principle of *non-refoulement*.

The problem was recognized and some steps taken to avoid it at the abortive 1977 United Nations Conference on Territorial Asylum. There a measure of agreement was reached on the following paragraph:

Asylum should not be refused by a Contracting State solely on the ground that it could be sought from another State. However, where it

---

[43] Under art. 27 and 28; see further below, ch. VII, s. 1(2)(a).

[44] For example, the right to raise the issue of refugee status or fear of persecution on appeal against deportation. In a case in New Zealand in 1980, the Inter-Departmental Committee on Refugees declined to consider further the case of an Iranian Baha'i who held a permit valid for residence in the Federal Republic of Germany, where he had lived for several years. See also *JCRR*, case no. 1242, 83 f. (*Marcus*) and cf. arts. 1 C (3) and 1 E of the Convention.

appears that a person before requesting asylum from a Contracting State already has a connexion or close links with another State, the Contracting State may, if it appears fair and reasonable, require him first to request asylum from that State.[45]

At its 1979 session the Executive Committee also stressed the need for agreement on criteria which would allow identification of the responsible state in a positive manner, and recommended that account be taken of the duration and nature of any stay in another country, as well as of the asylum-seeker's intentions.[46]

It is difficult to predict whether states will go beyond present *ad hoc* arrangements, and agree on appropriate criteria.[47] The paramountcy of the principle of *non-refoulement*, however, ought to be maintained and was indeed stressed in a decision of the Australian Determination of Refugee Status (DORS) Committee in 1981 involving applications for refugee status by two seamen. The Committee considered that in view of their service on a Greek ship, their connexion with Greece and Article 11 of the 1951 Convention, their claims for refugee status ought to be presented to that country. Nevertheless, if for any reason it looked as though the individuals might be returned to their country of origin,[48] then Article 33 of the Convention required that their claims to refugee status be examined by the Committee.

## (2) REFUGEES RECEIVING UNITED NATIONS PROTECTION AND ASSISTANCE

Palestinians are the only group in effect excluded by the words of the Statute and the Convention.[49] The competence of the High Commissioner in the political issues surrounding the Palestinian question was once thought incompatible with the proclaimed non-political character of UNHCR's work.[50] Solutions to the Palestinian problem by way of repatriation or indemnification were

---

[45] See below, annexe VII.

[46] UN doc. A/AC.96/572, para. 72(2). In a case decided on 10 Apr. 1979, the Judicial Division of the Council of State of the Netherlands held that an Eritrean should not be prejudiced by reason of his failure to apply for asylum in Italy, where he had spent some months. The geographical reservation to the 1951 Convention and the 1967 Protocol maintained by that country would have prevented his being granted refugee status.

[47] Cf. the draft convention proposed by Melander, *Refugees in Orbit*, 113-15.

[48] For example, if having been ordered to be deported, the ship's master refused to re-employ the men and the ship's agents decided to repatriate them rather than find them work on another vessel.

[49] Para. 7(c) and art. 1 D, respectively.

[50] UN doc. E/AC.7/SR.172.

under consideration at the time,[51] but have not eventuated;[52] Palestinians continue to be the responsibility of, and to receive assistance from, the United Nations Relief and Works Agency (UNRWA), established as a subsidiary organ by the General Assembly in 1949.[53] UNRWA's competence extends to those who left Palestine as a result of the 1948 conflict, and it operates in Jordan, Syria, Lebanon, and the Gaza Strip.[54] If UNRWA assistance is terminated without the situation of those affected having been resolved, then the Convention provides that they shall *ipso facto* be entitled to its benefits.[55] In addition, if Palestinians leave UNRWA's area of operation, they may well qualify independently as refugees within the Statute and the Convention.

### (3) OTHER REFUGEES NOT CONSIDERED TO REQUIRE INTERNATIONAL PROTECTION

Finally, the Statute and the Convention exclude from any entitlement to protection those who, in their country of residence, are considered by the competent authorities 'as having the rights and obligations which are attached to the possession of the nationality of that country'.[56] The reference is clearly intended to take account of an effective nationality, such as that enjoyed by the so-called *Volksdeutsche*, or ethnic Germans, under Article 116 of the Constitution of the Federal Republic of Germany.[57] The constitution of the IRO excluded Germans by name,[58] but the general scope of the later provision is capable of extending to many other groups. The British Nationality Act 1948, for example, declared the citizens of independent Commonwealth countries to be British subjects or Commonwealth citizens, the expressions having the same meaning.[59] The assimilation of Commonwealth citizens

---

[51] See, for example, GA Resolutions 194(III), 11 Dec. 1948, and 393(V), 2 Dec. 1950.

[52] A useful analysis of aspects of this problem is provided in Radley, 'The Palestinian Refugees: The Right to return in international law' 72 *AJIL* 586 (1978); see also Dimitrijevic, 'Legal Position of Palestinian Refugees' 19 *Rev. of Int. Affs.* 18 (1965).

[53] GA Res. 302(IV), 8 Dec. 1949.

[54] By Res. 2252(ES-V), 4 July 1967, the mandate for assistance was extended to other persons in the area in serious need as a result of the June 1967 war; operations were extended to Egypt on behalf of those displaced from the Gaza Strip.

[55] UNRWA faced serious financial difficulties in 1980-1; see report of the Working Group on the Financing of UNRWA: UN doc. A/36/615; GA Res. 36/146E, 16 Dec. 1981.

[56] Statute, para. 7(b); Convention, art. 1 E.

[57] See further, Goodwin-Gill, *Movement of Persons*, 16-20.

[58] Annexe I, part II, s. 4; see below, Annexe I. See also de Zayas, *Die Anglo-Amerikaner und die Vertreibung der Deutschen*, (1977); published in English as *Nemesis at Potsdam: the Anglo-Americans and the Expulsion of the Germans* (1977).

[59] S. 1(2).

to United Kingdom nationals strictly so-called was most fully realized in the years up to 1962, when all British subjects (Commonwealth citizens) had the unrestricted right of entry into the United Kingdom, whatever their country of origin. They were free to settle, they enjoyed the right to work and the right to vote, and they were not subject to removal; they also enjoyed the right after 12 months of residence to register as citizens of the United Kingdom. However, the most important of these indices of nationality have now been specifically removed, namely, the right to enter freely and the right not to be expelled. The distinction between non-patrial Commonwealth citizens and patrial citizens of the United Kingdom and Colonies is stated clearly in the Immigration Act 1971 which limits the 'right of abode' to the latter.[60] Simply describing non-patrial Commonwealth citizens as 'British subjects' did not constitute them nationals of the United Kingdom for the purposes of international law generally or Article 1E of the 1951 Convention in particular. The term was a matter of internal law, from which the United Kingdom derived none of the rights (such as that of protection) or obligations (such as the duty of admission) that are the normal attributes of nationality in international law.[61] The 1981 British Nationality Act establishes a new 'British citizenship', which itself will now become the sole criterion for the right of entry and residence in the United Kingdom.[62]

Article 1E of the Convention and the corresponding statutory provision do not require that the individuals in question should enjoy the full range of rights incidental to citizenship. Given the fundamental objective of protection, however, the right of entry to the state and freedom from removal are to be considered essential.

## 4. Undeserving cases

A different drafting approach is used in the Statute and the Convention to describe those not deserving the benefits of refugee status,[63] but without great differences of substance.

---

[60] S. 1(1), (2). Non-patrials are also liable to deportation; ibid. s. 3(5). Exemptions from deportation provided by s. 7 are limited to those ordinarily resident in the United Kingdom on 1 Jan. 1973.

[61] See Goodwin-Gill, *Movement of Persons*, 174-5.

[62] The 1981 Act abandons use of the term 'British subject' as a common description of all Commonwealth citizens, with certain savings.

[63] Statute, para. 7(d); Convention, art. 1F.

## (1) CRIMES AGAINST PEACE, WAR CRIMES, AND CRIMES AGAINST HUMANITY

Excluded first are those 'with respect to whom there are serious reasons for considering' that they have committed any of the above crimes, as defined in the relevant international instruments.[64] 'Crimes against peace' are defined by the Charter of the International Military Tribunal to include 'planning, preparation, initiation or waging of a war of aggression or a war in violation of international treaties, agreements, or assurances or participation in a common plan or conspiracy for any of the foregoing'.[65]

'War crimes' are defined as violations of the laws or customs of war, including 'murder, ill-treatment or deportation to slave labour or for any other purpose of civilian population of or in occupied territory, murder or ill-treatment of prisoners of war or persons on the seas, killing of hostages, plunder of public or private property, wanton destruction of cities, towns or villages, or devastation not justified by military necessity'.[66] Also included in the concept are the 'grave breaches' set out in the 1949 Geneva Conventions for the protection of war victims,[67] which comprise wilful killing, torture, inhuman treatment, including biological experiments, and wilfully causing great suffering or serious injury to body or health.[68]

Finally, 'crimes against humanity' are defined as: 'Murder, extermination, enslavement, deportation, and other inhumane acts committed against any civilian population, before or during the war, or persecutions on political, racial or religious grounds in execution of or in connexion with any crime within the jurisdiction of the Tribunal, whether or not in violation of the domestic law of the country where perpetrated'.[69] The notion of crimes against humanity inspired directly the 1948 Genocide Convention, Article II of which defines the 'crime under international

---

[64] Cf. the comparable provisions in the IRO Constitution, annexe i, part II, ss. 1, 2. The sufficiency of 'serious reasons' indicates that previous prosecution, conviction, and sentence are not required.

[65] Art. 6(a): 82 UNTS 279; Charter confirmed by GA Res. 3(I), 13 Feb. 1946, and 94(I), 11 Dec. 1946.

[66] Art. 6(b).

[67] See generally Draper, *The Red Cross Conventions* (1958). Note also art. 1 of the Convention on the Non-Applicability of Statutory Limitations to War Crimes and Crimes against Humanity, adopted by GA Res. 2391(XXIII), 26 Nov. 1968.

[68] Note also related developments in the field of arms control; see the 1971 Convention on Biological Weapons, adopted by GA Res. 2826(XXVI), 16 Dec. 1971, in force 26 Mar. 1975.

[69] Art. 6(c).

law', and Article VII of which prescribes that it shall not be a political crime for the purpose of the principle of non-extradition.[70] More recently, in 1973, the General Assembly, recalling its conviction that apartheid constitutes both a total negation of the purposes and principles of the United Nations and a crime against humanity, adopted the International Convention on the Suppression and Punishment of the Crime of Apartheid.[71] Further to Article I, states parties declare apartheid to be a crime against humanity, undertake to adopt appropriate legislative and administrative measures to prosecute and punish those responsible, and agree that the acts constituting the crime shall not be considered political crimes.[72]

## (2) SERIOUS NON-POLITICAL CRIMES

While the IRO Constitution and the Statute refer to extradition crimes,[73] the Convention uses the deceptively simple phrase 'serious non-political crime' as the basis for exclusion from the benefits of refugee status, and limits such crimes to those committed 'outside the country of refuge prior to ... admission ... as a refugee'.[74] The potential state of refuge thus has some discretion in determining whether the criminal character of the applicant for refugee status in fact outweighs his or her character as bona fide refugee, and so constitutes a threat to its internal order.[75]

The problem of determining whether a crime is political has already been considered.[76] The nature and purpose of the offence require examination, including whether it was committed out of genuine political motives or merely for personal reasons or gain,

[70] 78 UNTS 277.

[71] GA Res. 3068(XXVIII), 30 Nov. 1973, adopted by 91 votes in favour, 4 against, with 26 abstentions.

[72] On the relation between war crimes, crimes against humanity, genocide, and apartheid, see generally Ruhashyankiko, *Study of the Question of the Prevention and Punishment of the Crime of Genocide*: UN doc. E/CN.4/Sub.2/416 (1978) paras. 377-408.

[73] The IRO's *Eligibility Manual* included the following extradition crimes: murder, poisoning, rape, arson, forgery, issuing counterfeit money, perjury, theft, bankruptcy, receiving stolen goods, embezzlement, bigamy, assault, grave injury, and malicious destruction. Cf. Shearer, *Extradition in International Law* (1971) ch. 5.

[74] Cf. art. 32 regarding the circumstances in which lawfully resident refugees may be expelled, below, ch. IV, s. 2(4), and ch. VII, s. 1(2)(c). Art. 14(2) of the Universal Declaration of Human Rights excludes invocation of the right of asylum 'in the case of prosecutions genuinely arising from non-political crimes'.

[75] At the Conference of Plenipotentiaries reference was made to striking a balance 'between the offences committed ... and the extent to which [the] fear of persecution was well-founded': UN doc. A/CONF.2/SR.29, 23; cf. Weis, *Journal du dr. inter.* (1960) 30.

[76] See ch. II, s. 4(2).

whether it was directed towards a modification of the political organization or the very structure of the state, and whether there is a close and direct causal link between the crime committed and its alleged political purpose and object. <u>The political element should in principle outweigh the common law character of the offence, which may not be the case if the acts committed are grossly disproportionate to the objective, or are of an atrocious or barbarous nature.</u>[77] The recent tendency to 'depoliticize' certain offences, such as hijacking, hostage-taking, offences against diplomats, and terrorism, is a potential source of difficulties[78] which are not entirely resolved by inclusion in certain of the conventions of the principle, *aut dedire aut punire*. This may still leave open the option of *refoulement* to persecution and is considered further below.[79]

The political aspect apart, the phrase 'serious non-political crime' is not easy to define given the different connotations of the term 'crime' in different legal systems.[80] The standard finally to be applied is an international standard, in that a provision of a multilateral treaty is involved, but standards relating to criminal prosecution and treatment of offenders current in the potential country of asylum are also relevant. Each case will require examination on its merits, with regard paid to both mitigating and aggravating factors.

Article 1F excludes 'persons', rather than 'refugees' from the benefits of the Convention, suggesting that the issue of a well-founded fear of persecution is irrelevant and need not be examined at all if there are 'serious reasons for considering' that an individual comes within its terms. In practice, the claim to be a refugee can rarely be ignored, for a balance must also be struck between the nature of the offence presumed to have been committed and

---

[77] Cf. the case of *Rodriguez Martinez Manuel* (1941) cited by Kiss, *Répertoire de la pratique français en matière de droit international public* (1966) ii.216; and of *Morelli*, ibid. 217.

[78] See, for example, art. 16, 1963 Tokyo Convention on Offences and Certain other Acts committed on board Aircraft; art 7, 1970 Hague Convention for the Suppression of Unlawful Seizure of Aircraft; art. 7, 1971 Montreal Convention for the Suppression of Unlawful Acts against the Safety of Civil Aviation; art. 7, 1973 Convention on the Prevention and Punishment of Crimes against Internationally Protected Persons, including Diplomatic Agents; art. 3, 1957 European Convention on Extradition; art. 5, 1977 European Convention on the Suppression of Terrorism; art. 9, 1979 United Nations Convention on the Taking of Hostages; art. 9, 1971 OAS Convention to prevent and punish Acts of Terrorism taking the form of Crimes against Persons and related Extortion that are of International Significance; art. 3, 1981 OAS Inter-American Convention on Extradition.

[79] See further below, ch. IV, s. 2(2).

[80] Cf. Grahl-Madsen, *Status of Refugees*, i, at 289-99.

the degree of persecution feared. A person with a well-founded fear of very severe persecution, such as would endanger life or freedom, should only be excluded for the most serious reasons. If the persecution feared is less, then the nature of the crime or crimes in question must be assessed to see whether criminal character in fact outweighs the applicant's character as a bona fide refugee.

In 1980, following the arrival of some 125,000 Cuban asylum-seekers in the United States, UNHCR was requested by the authorities *inter alia*, to advise on asylum applications which were likely to be refused on account of the applicants' criminal background.[81] The size of the influx made individual case-by-case assessment difficult, and it was later decided to accord the majority an interim status in anticipation of their situation being regularized by special legislation.[82] Suspected criminal cases, however, were examined in a joint UNHCR/State Department exercise, in which the author was closely involved during June and July 1980.

With a view to promoting consistent decisions, UNHCR proposed that, in the absence of any political factors, a presumption of serious crime might be considered as raised by evidence of commission of any of the following offences: homicide, rape, child molesting, wounding, arson, drugs traffic, and armed robbery.[83] However, that presumption should be capable of rebuttal by evidence of mitigating factors, some of which are set out below. The following offences might also be considered to constitute serious crimes, provided other factors were present: breaking and entering (burglary); stealing (theft and simple robbery); receiving stolen property; embezzlement; drugs possession and use; and assault. Factors to support a finding of seriousness included: use of weapons, injury to persons; value of property involved; type of drugs involved;[84] evidence of habitual criminal conduct. With

---

[81] The text of the United States request for assistance is in 19 *Int. Leg. Mat.* 1296. The 1980 Refugee Act incorporates the substance of art. 1 F (b) of the Convention as an exception to the prohibition on the deportation or return of an alien to a country in which his or her life or freedom may be threatened: s. 203(e), amending s. 243(h) of the Immigration and Nationality Act 1952. ·

[82] See 'Cuban-Haitian Arrivals in US' *Current Policy no. 193*, June 20 1980, statement by Victor H. Palmieri, US Co-ordinator for Refugee Affairs. Legislation introduced into Congress in Oct. 1981 had not been enacted at the time of writing.

[83] The evidence in question was provided by the asylum-seekers themselves, in interviews with United States officials.

[84] Mere possession of marijuana for personal use was not considered to amount to a serious non-political crime.

respect to all cases, the following elements were suggested as tending to rebut a presumption or finding of serious crime: minority of the offender; parole; elapse of five years since conviction or completion of sentence; general good character (for example, one offence only); offender was merely accomplice; other circumstances surrounding commission of the offence (for example, provocation and self-defence).[85]

These criteria may be of general value in the interpretation of the Convention and the Statute, bearing in mind that the objective of such provisions is to obtain a humanitarian balance between a potential threat to the community of refuge and the interests of the individual who has a well-founded fear of persecution.

### (3) ACTS CONTRARY TO THE PURPOSES AND PRINCIPLES OF THE UNITED NATIONS

The purposes and principles of the United Nations are proclaimed in Articles 1 and 2 of the Charter, but they offer little clarification of the type of acts which would deprive a person of the benefits of refugee status.[86] The principal interests are the maintenance of international peace and security, respect for the equal rights and self-determination of peoples, international co-operation in economic, social, cultural, and humanitarian matters, and the promotion of human rights for all without distinction. The present exception from refugee status potentially accords a very wide discretion to states, although the nature of the relevant acts may become clearer in time, as the United Nations indicates its interests more concretely.

The general principle of respect for human rights has been developed specifically through the Universal Declaration and the 1966 Covenants, so that an individual who has denied or

---

[85] There was ample evidence in statements by convicts from different jails that an incentive to leave Cuba had been the threat by officials of a further term of imprisonment. Others, particularly former convicts, were threatened with up to four years' jail under Cuba's *Ley de Peligrosidad*, while some were issued with passports on simple production of their release certificates at local police stations. During a period of some seven weeks, 1021 cases were examined. The greater part of the case-load provided few problems, in that the commission of serious crimes was clearly indicated. A number of cases, however, were discussed at length, resulting in final agreement on the serious or non-serious nature of the crime, or in deferral for further inquiries and reinterview regarding either the circumstances of the offence or political and refugee elements.

[86] The Convention, art. 1 F (c), refers simply to being 'guilty' of the acts in question, whereas the Statute and its point of reference (art. 14(2) of the Universal Declaration of Human Rights) add a specifically criminal element by citing '*prosecutions* genuinely arising from ...' such acts.

restricted the human rights of others may thus be argued to fall within the exception. Those who had persecuted others were expressly excluded from the IRO's mandate, and a similar provision is included in United States legislation.[87] Also relevant are the notions of an individual's duties to the community and of the limitations inherent in human rights.[88] Article 17 of the European Convention on Human Rights, for example, provides:[89] 'Nothing in this Convention may be interpreted as implying for any State, group or person any right to engage in any activity or perform any act aimed at the destruction of any of the rights and freedoms set forth herein or at their limitation to a greater extent than is provided for in the Convention.' Such a principle is sometimes incorporated or reflected in municipal law,[90] and can then indicate the factors to be taken into account in the exercise of discretion.

In 1982 the DORS Committee was faced with an application for refugee status by one who admitted to have been present for some of the time at the occupation of the United States Embassy in Tehran, when diplomatic and consular staff were held hostage. Conflicting views were expressed in the Committee on the preliminary question, whether the application should even be examined. In its judgment in 1980, the International Court of Justice characterized the detention of the hostages as 'manifestly incompatible' with the purposes and principles of the United Nations.[91] Relying upon this, some argued that the mere fact of presence or involvement was sufficient to bring the applicant within Article 1F(c) of the Convention and that, given his admission in this regard, no further examination of the case was required. Others, however, took the view that the Court had been principally concerned in its judgment with issues of state responsibility;[92] its views on the initially independent actions of individuals[93] should not be taken as excluding an applicant for all time and all purposes from the benefits of refugee status. The nature and extent of

---

[87] Refugee Act 1980, s. 203(e), amending INA s. 243(h). See also *JCRR*, case no. 304, 19 f. (*Milosek*).

[88] Art. 29, Universal Declaration of Human Rights; see generally Daes, *Study of the Individual's Duties to the Community and the Limitations of Human Rights and Freedoms under Article 29 of the Universal Declaration of Human Rights*: UN doc. E/CN.4/Sub.2/432/Rev.1 (1980).

[89] Cf. also art. 18.

[90] See art. 18, 1949 Constitution of the Federal Republic of Germany.

[91] *United States Diplomatic and Consular Staff in Tehran* (*USA* v. *Iran*) ICJ Rep. 1980, 3, at 42 (para. 91).

[92] Ibid. at 35 (para. 74).

[93] Ibid. at 29-30 (paras 58-9).

the individual's role in the occupation should be examined, as well as his motives and intentions and current situation *vis-à-vis* his country of origin. After lengthy debate it was agreed that the applicant should be interviewed on the subject of his involvement and the results then considered by the Committee; the conflicting views regarding the implications of such involvement nevertheless remained.[94]

Article 1F(c) of the Convention is potentially very wide. Besides promoting action to combat hostage-taking, hijacking, and apartheid and to promote human rights, the United Nations has also recognized the international standing of liberation movements. This may imply that those responsible for the maintenance of colonial and colonial-style regimes should not subsequently be entitled to recognition of refugee status, but such issues remain moot. The exception is not often invoked, and broad agreement on its interpretation and development is probably unlikely, given the disparate interests of the sovereign states members of the United Nations.[95]

[94] In December 1982 the committee recommended that the applicant be excluded under art. 1 F (c) on the ground of the degree of his involvement in the hostages incident. That he would also be exposed to very serious danger if returned to his country of origin seemed likely, and final resolution of the case was still pending at the year's end.

[95] Cf. statements in respect of the United Kingdom's earlier unwillingness to ratify the Genocide Convention: 663 HC Deb. cols. 442-4; 1202-12 (1962).

# PART TWO

## ASYLUM

# Chapter IV

# NON-REFOULEMENT

The principle of *non-refoulement* states, broadly, that no refugee should be returned to any country where he or she is likely to face persecution or danger to life or freedom. The present chapter examines its origins, its meaning, scope, and standing in general international law, with reference to particularly difficult issues, including rejection at the frontier, extradition, and exceptions to the principle.[1]

## 1. Evolution of the principle

The term *non-refoulement* derives from the French *refouler*, which means to drive back or to repel, as of an enemy who fails to breach one's defences. In the context of immigration control in continental Europe, *refoulement* is a term of art covering, in particular, summary reconduction to the frontier of those discovered to have entered illegally and summary refusal of admission of those without valid papers.[2] *Refoulement* is thus to be distinguished from expulsion or deportation, the more formal process whereby a lawfully resident alien may be required to leave a state, or be forcibly ejected therefrom.

The idea that a state ought not to return persons to other states in certain circumstances is of comparatively recent origin. Common in the past were formal agreements between sovereigns for the reciprocal surrender of subversives, dissidents, and traitors.[3] Only in the early- to mid-nineteenth century do the concept of

---

[1] Some of the ideas developed below first appeared in Goodwin-Gill, 'Entry and Exclusion of Refugees: The Obligations of States and the Protection Function of the United Nations High Commissioner for Refugees' (1982) *Michigan Yearbook of International Legal Studies*, 291.

[2] A number of agreements have institutionalized the practice on a bilateral basis; see the *'conventions de prise en charge à la frontière'* discussed in Batiffol and Lagarde, *Droit international privé* (5th. ed., 1970) i.198; and *'Übernahme-'* or *'Schubabkommen'* discussed in Schiedermair, *Handbuch des Ausländerrechts der Bundesrepublik Deutschland*, 178, 227-30 (1968).

[3] See examples cited in Goodwin-Gill, *International Law and the Movement of Persons between States* (1978) 143, n. 2.

asylum and the principle of non-extradition of political offenders begin to concretize, in the sense of that protection which the territorial sovereign can, and perhaps should, accord. At that time, the principle of non-extradition reflected popular sentiment that those fleeing their own country for political reasons were worthy of protection.[4] It was a period of political turmoil in Europe and South America, as well as of mass movements of populations occasioned by pogroms against Jewish and Christian minorities in Russia and the Ottoman Empire.

A sense of the need to protect the latter can be gathered from the United Kingdom's 1905 Aliens Act, where an exception to refusal of entry for want of means was prescribed in respect of those 'seeking to avoid prosecution or punishment on religious or political grounds or for an offence of a political character, or persecution involving danger of imprisonment or danger to life or limb on account of religious belief'.[5] Not until after the First World War, however, did international practice begin to display some recognition of an emerging principle of non-return of refugees.

Initial efforts to resolve refugee problems concentrated on repatriation and resettlement, so that the first agreement between League of Nations members in 1922 was concerned with the issue of *identity* certificates to Russian refugees for the purpose of onward travel.[6] Only in 1933 is the first reference found in an international agreement to the principle that refugees should not be returned to their country of origin.[7] In Article 3 of the Convention relating to the International Status of Refugees, the contracting parties undertook not to remove resident refugees or keep them from their territory, 'by application of police measures, such as expulsions or non-admittance at the frontier (*refoulement*)', unless dictated by national security or public order.[8] Moreover, in the second paragraph, each state undertook 'in any case not to refuse entry to refugees at the frontiers of their countries

---

[4] See, for example, the views cited in 6 *British Digest of International Law*, 53-4, 64-5.

[5] S. 1.

[6] This and other related arrangements are cited above, ch. I, s. 2.

[7] Under a 1928 arrangement (89 LNTS no. 2005), states had adopted a recommendation (no. 7), 'that measures for expelling foreigners or for taking such other action against them be avoided or suspended in regard to Russian and Armenian refugees in cases where the person concerned is not in a position to enter a neighbouring country in a regular manner'. The recommendation was not to apply to a refugee who had entered a state in intentional violation of national law.

[8] 159 LNTS no. 3663; official text in French.

of origin'. Only eight states ratified this Convention; three of them, by reservations and declarations, emphasized their retention of sovereign competence in the matter of expulsion, while the United Kingdom expressly objected to the principle of non-rejection at the frontier.

Agreements regarding refugees from Germany in 1936 and 1938 also contained some limitation on expulsion or return.[9] The instruments varied slightly: broadly, refugees required to leave a contracting state were to be allowed a suitable period to make arrangements; lawfully resident refugees were not to be expelled or sent back across the frontier[10] save 'for reasons of national security or public order'; and even in such cases, governments undertook not to return refugees to the German Reich,[11] 'unless they have been warned and have refused to make the necessary arrangements to proceed to another country or to take advantage of the arrangements made for them with that object'.

The inter-war period was characterized by principally administrative arrangements aimed at facilitating resettlement and relieving the burden on countries of first asylum. The need for protective principles for refugees began to be recognized, but limited ratifications of instruments containing equivocal and much qualified provisions effectively prevented the emergence of a formal principle of *non-refoulement*. Nevertheless, the period was also remarkable for the very large numbers of refugees not in fact sent back to their countries of origin, whether they fled Russia after the revolution, Spain, Germany, or the Ottoman Empire.[12] In February 1946, the United Nations expressly accepted that 'refugees or displaced persons' who have expressed 'valid objections' to returning to their country of origin should not be compelled to do so.[13] The International Refugee Organization,

---

[9] Art. 4, provisional arrangement concerning the status of refugees coming from Germany, 1936: 171 LNTS no. 3952; official text in English and French. The arrangement was definitively signed by seven states; the United Kingdom excluded refugees subject to extradition proceedings from the ambit of art. 4, and likewise, for most purposes, refugees admitted for a temporary visit or purpose. Art. 5, Convention concerning the Status of Refugees coming from Germany, 1938: 192 LNTS no. 4461; official texts in English and French. The Convention was ratified by only three states; the United Kingdom repeated its 1936 reservations.

[10] The 1938 Convention substituted 'measures of expulsion or reconduction ...'

[11] The 1936 arrangement read: 'refugees shall not be sent back across the frontier of the Reich'; the 1938 Convention provided that states parties 'undertake not to reconduct refugees to German territory'.

[12] Kiss notes, for example, that in 1939 France admitted 400,000 refugees from Spain in just ten days: *Répertoire de la pratique française en droit international public* (1966) iv.433-5.

[13] GA Res. 8(1), 12 Feb. 1946, para. (c)(ii).

established the same year, facilitated the resettlement and integration of some 1,620,000 refugees, while many others fleeing political developments in Eastern Europe were readily admitted to Western countries. State practice of the immediate post-war period, however, is regrettably inconclusive. Writing in 1954, Weis found that *refoulement* was rare, save 'in the case of some Russians and Ukrainians covered by certain wartime agreements'.[14] The release of relevant documents to public scrutiny thirty years later showed the full extent of a forcible repatriation policy which meant death or horrific treatment for well over two million, by no means all of them covered by those wartime agreements.[15]

States in this period also resisted inclusion of a right to be granted asylum, both in the 1948 Universal Declaration of Human Rights and in the 1951 Convention. The *Ad Hoc* Committee responsible for the draft text of the latter had prepared the following provision: 'No contracting State shall expel or return ("refouler") a refugee in any manner whatsoever to the frontiers of territories where his life or freedom would be threatened on account of his race, religion, nationality, membership of a particular social group or political opinion.' It was considered so fundamental that no exceptions were proposed,[16] but the Conference of Plenipotentiaries demurred and added the following paragraph to what was to become Article 33:

The benefit of the present provision may not, however, be claimed by a refugee whom there are reasonable grounds for regarding as a danger to the security of the country in which he is, or who, having been convicted by a final judgment of a particularly serious crime, constitutes a danger to the community of that country.[17]

As expressed in Article 33, the principle of *non-refoulement* raises questions of its scope of application *ratione personae*, and its relation to the issues of admission and non-rejection at the frontier. It is a rule clearly designed to benefit the refugee, the person who, in the

[14] Weis, 'The International Protection of Refugees' 48 *AJIL* 193-221, at 196 (1954).

[15] The story is thoroughly recounted and documented in Tolstoy, *Victims of Yalta* (1977, rev. ed. 1979); see also Bethell, *The Last Secret* (1974).

[16] UN doc. E/1850, para. 35; Robinson, *Convention relating to the Status of Refugees: A Commentary* (1953) 160-6; Pompe, 'The Convention of 28 July 1951 and the International Protection of Refugees' UN doc. HCR/INF/42, May 1958, 20-1 (first published in Dutch in *Rechtsgeleerd Magazyn Themis* (1956) 425-91).

[17] The change in the international situation between the meeting of the *Ad Hoc* Committee in Aug. 1950 and the Conference in July 1951 is usually cited as responsible for the introduction of exceptions; see UN doc. A/CONF.2/SR.16, 8 (views of the United Kingdom).

sense of Article 1 of the Convention, has a well-founded fear of being persecuted on grounds of race, religion, nationality, membership of a particular social group, or political opinion. In principle, its benefit ought not to be predicated upon formal recognition of refugee status which, indeed, may be impractical in the absence of effective procedures or in the case of a mass influx.[18] Likewise, it would scarcely be consonant with considerations of good faith for a state to seek to avoid the principle of *non-refoulement* by declining to make a determination of status.

From the point of general, as opposed to conventional, international law, the issue is rendered more problematic by developments in the refugee definition, as well as by doubts which may be raised as to the scope and standing of *non-refoulement* outside the relevant international instruments. Recent extensions of UNHCR's mandate might be considered purely functional in that they authorize the channelling of material assistance but do not justify the exercise of protection. States may in turn argue that, in regard to the expanded class, their obligations are humanitarian rather than legal. Early General Assembly resolutions certainly did limit UNHCR operations to the assistance field, but latterly the protection requirements of the broad class of refugees and displaced persons have been repeatedly stressed.[19] State practice in cases of mass influx also offers some support for the view that *non-refoulement* applies both to the individual refugee with a well-founded fear of persecution, and to the frequently large groups of persons who do not in fact enjoy the protection of the government of their country of origin. The principle, in both its conventional and general international law aspects, must be interpreted in the context of overall developments in the refugee concept.

[18] In 1977, the Executive Committee of the High Commissioner's Programme reaffirmed the principle of *non-refoulement*, irrespective of formal recognition of refugee status: UN doc. A/AC.96/549, para. 53.4(c). In 1979, the Arusha Conference on the Situation of Refugees in Africa observed, *inter alia*, that procedures for determination of refugee status might be impractical in the case of large-scale movements of asylum-seekers in Africa, and that special arrangements might be necessary. As a minimum, however, the conference recommended that provision be made for appeal or review in the case of refusal of refugee status and that the protection of individuals by virtue of the principle of *non-refoulement* be ensured. Report published in summary form in UN doc. A/AC.96/INF.158; see p. 9.

[19] See above, ch. I, s. 3(2).

## 2. Relation of the principle of *non-refoulement* to particular issues

### (1) ADMISSION AND NON-REJECTION AT THE FRONTIER

At the 1951 Conference, no formal objection appears to have been raised to the Swiss interpretation of *non-refoulement*, limiting its application to those who have already entered state territory.[20] This narrow view, premissed on the notion that a state was not obliged to allow large groups of asylum-seekers to cross its frontiers, did not fully square with the practice of *refoulement* in European immigration law or with the letter of Article 3 of the 1933 Convention. The words 'expel or return' in the English version of Article 33 have no precise meaning in general international law. The former may describe any measure, judicial, administrative, or police, which secures the departure of an alien, although Article 32 possibly implies that measures of expulsion are reserved for lawfully resident aliens. The word 'return' is even more vague; to the Danish representative it suggested such action as a state might take in response to a request for extradition.[21] Probably the most accurate assessment of states' views in 1951 is that there was no unanimity, perhaps deliberately so. At the same time, however, the fact remains that states were not prepared to include in the Convention any article on admission of refugees; *non-refoulement* in the sense of even a limited obligation to allow entry may well have been seen as coming too close to the unwished-for duty to grant asylum.

The views of commentators have varied. Robinson, in 1953, declared that Article 33 'concerns refugees who have gained entry into the territory of a contracting State, legally or illegally, but not to refugees who seek entrance into this territory'.[22] Weis, in the same year, suggested that Article 33 'simply codifies ... what is the practice of civilized States'. The principle of *non-refoulement* is a usage, rather than a customary rule, but one which 'leads the way to the adoption of the principle that a State shall not refuse admission to a refugee, i.e. it shall grant him at least temporary asylum ... if non-admission is tantamount to surrender to the

---

[20] UN doc. A/CONF.2/SR.16, 6; see also the views of the Dutch representative, cited by Weis in 'Legal Aspects of the Convention of 28 July 1951 relating to the Status of Refugees' 30 *BYIL* 478, at 482 (1953); Robinson, *Commentary*, 161-2.

[21] UN doc. A/CONF.2/SR.16, 10.

[22] Robinson, *Commentary*, 163; Pompe, UN doc. HCR/INF/42, 20-2, is more equivocal, but favours a liberal interpretation.

country of persecution'.[23] In 1966, the same writer argued for extension of the principle to non-rejection at the frontier, otherwise protection becomes dependent on 'the fortuitous circumstance' that the refugee has successfully entered state territory.[24] The previous year, the then High Commissioner for Refugees had written that the principles of non-rejection and temporary asylum were becoming more and more recognized;[25] yet eleven years later, his successor concluded that states do not accept the rule of non-rejection.[26] Grahl-Madsen has likewise consistently argued that Article 33 is limited to those present, lawfully or unlawfully, in the territory of contracting states, that protection depends upon having 'set foot' in that territory.[27]

Little is to be gained today by any further analysis of the motives of states or the meaning of words in 1951. Likewise, it is fruitless to pay too much attention to moments of entry or presence, legal or physical. As a matter of *fact*, anyone presenting themselves at a frontier post, port, or airport will already be within state territory and jurisdiction; it is for this reason, and the better to retain sovereign control, that states have devised fictions to keep even the physically present alien technically, legally, unadmitted.[28] Similarly, no consequence of significance can be derived from repeated reliance on the proposition that states have no duty to admit refugees, or indeed, any other aliens. 'No duty to admit' begs many questions; in particular, whether states are obliged to protect refugees to the extent of not adopting measures which will result in their persecution or exposure to danger. State practice attributes little weight to the precise issue of admission, but far

---

[23] Weis, 30 *BYIL* (1953) at 482-3.

[24] Weis, 'Territorial Asylum' 6 *Indian Journal of International Law* (1966) 173, at 183.

[25] Schnyder, 'Les aspects juridiques actuels du problème des réfugiés' Hague *Recueil* (1965-I) 339-450, at 381.

[26] Sadruddin Aga Khan, 'Legal problems relating to refugees and displaced persons' Hague *Recueil* (1976-I) 287-352, at 318-22.

[27] Grahl-Madsen, *The Status of Refugees in International Law* (1966) ii.94-9; id. *Territorial Asylum* (1980) 40 ff.; he also argues that *non-refoulement* does not prevent 'extradition under a mandatory treaty provision'; again, views were divided in 1951 and such a sweeping generalization otherwise finds scant support; see further below, ch. IV, s. 2(2).

[28] See, for example, the elaborations of LORD DENNING in *R.* v. *Governor of Brixton Prison, ex parte Soblen* [1963] 2 QB 243; also the United States decisions cited by Pugash, 'The Dilemma of the Sea Refugee: Rescue without Refuge' 18 *Harv. ILJ* (1977) 577, at 592 ff. *A Study on Statelessness* (UN doc. E/1112 and Add. 1, 1949, at 60) defines *reconduction* as 'the mere physical act of ejecting from the national territory a person who has gained entry or is residing therein irregularly' and *expulsion* as 'the juridical decision taken by the judicial or administrative authorities whereby an individual is ordered to leave the territory of the country'. The study observes that terminology varies, but for its purposes the term *refoulement* (reconduction) was not used to signify the act of preventing a foreigner present at the frontier from entering the national territory.

more to the necessity for *non-refoulement* through time, pending the obtaining of durable solutions.

Let it be assumed that, in 1951, the principle of *non-refoulement* was binding solely on the conventional level, and that it did not encompass non-rejection at the frontier. Analysis of its scope today requires full account to be taken of state practice since that date,[29] as well as that of international organizations. Over the last thirty years, the broader interpretation of *non-refoulement* has established itself. States have allowed large numbers of asylum-seekers not only to cross their frontiers, for example, in Africa from the early 1960s and more recently, in South East Asia, but also to remain pending a solution.[30] State practice, as manifested within international organizations, has contributed to further progressive development of the law. Thus, the 1967 Declaration on Territorial Asylum, adopted unanimously by the General Assembly, provides that no one entitled to seek asylum 'shall be subjected to measures such as rejection at the frontier or, if he has already entered the territory in which he seeks asylum, expulsion or compulsory return to any State where he may be subjected to persecution'.[31]

A resolution adopted by the Committee of Ministers of the Council of Europe the same year similarly acknowledged that member states should 'ensure that no one shall be subjected to refusal of admission at the frontier, rejection, expulsion or any other measure which would have the result of compelling him to return to, or remain in, a territory where he would be in danger of persecution ...'[32] Two years later, states in Africa formulated a principle in like terms for inclusion in the OAU Convention.[33]

Resolutions of the General Assembly, such as that on territorial

---

[29] Note Vienna Convention on the Law of Treaties, art. 31: '(1) A treaty shall be interpreted in good faith in accordance with the ordinary meaning to be given to the terms of the treaty in their context and in the light of its object and purpose ... (2) There shall be taken into account, together with the context ... (b) any subsequent practice in the application of the treaty which establishes the agreement of the parties regarding its application ...'

[30] See also the statement by the French Minister of the Interior in 1953, advising the Parliament that asylum-seekers from Spain were still arriving. He gave assurances that none was refused admission; all were allowed to remain pending determination of refugee status, when those not recognized as refugees were invited to return to their country: Kiss, *Répertoire de la pratique française*, vol. iv, 434-5; In 1956, following the Hungarian crisis, some 180,000 were granted immediate first asylum in Austria, and a further 20,000 in Yugoslavia: UNHCR, *A Mandate to Protect and Assist Refugees* (1971) 67-77.

[31] Art. 3(1); GA Res. 2312(XXII) of 14 Dec. 1967.

[32] Res. (67) 14 on Asylum to Persons in danger of Persecution, adopted 29 June 1967.

[33] Art. II; see below, annexe VIII.

asylum, even if adopted unanimously, have no direct, legally binding force. They may create some expectation of observance in good faith,[34] but it is what states actually do that remains of critical importance. Exceptions to the principles of *non-refoulement* and non-rejection at the frontier have occurred in recent years, but have generally been vigorously protested by other states and by UNHCR. In October 1979, for example, Thailand announced the reversal of a policy which had earlier led to the forcible return of some 40,000 Kampucheans; henceforth, all asylum-seekers were to be allowed to enter.[35] Staggering numbers have since been allowed entry and refuge, with admitting states frequently justifying their actions on the basis of established principles favouring refugees.

The broad interpretation of *non-refoulement*, however, was far from conclusively supported at the 1977 United Nations Conference on Territorial Asylum. Contrary to the Carnegie Draft,[36] the UN Group of Experts had proposed only that a state should 'use its best endeavours' to ensure non-rejection of asylum-seekers at the frontier.[37] One group of states moved that 'endeavour' be substituted for 'best endeavours',[38] while another state favoured deletion of any reference to non-rejection.[39] In the event, neither of those amendments was put to the vote;[40] the text reflecting the broader view was adopted, but the voting (45 in favour, 25 against, 18 abstentions) was scarcely conclusive.[41]

Since 1977, the General Assembly has nevertheless repeatedly urged governments scrupulously to observe humanitarian principles, including *non-refoulement* and the grant of asylum to those seeking refuge.[42] By and large, states in their practice and in their recorded views, have recognized that the former applies to the moment at which asylum-seekers present themselves for entry. Certain factual elements may be necessary (such as human rights

---

[34] Weis, 'The United Nations Declaration on Territorial Asylum' 7 *Can. Y'book of Int'l Law* (1969) 92, 147-9; Tunkin, *Theory of International Law* (1974) 66, 165-76.

[35] See report of the Secretary-General: UN doc. A/34/627, para. 48; annexe 1, para. 8.

[36] Art. 2; text in Grahl-Madsen, *Territorial Asylum* (1980) annexe KK.

[37] Art. 3(1); UN doc. A/10177; text in Grahl-Madsen, *Territorial Asylum*, annexe RR.

[38] Indonesia, Malaysia, and the Philippines; see UN doc. A/CONF.78/C.1/L.60/Rev/1.

[39] USSR; see UN doc. A/CONF.78/C.1/L/69.

[40] UN doc. A/CONF.78/12, para. 63.

[41] Ibid. para. 62; for text see below, annexe VII.

[42] See, for example, GA Resolutions 32/67, 8 Dec. 1977; 33/26, 29 Nov. 1978; 34/60, 29 Nov. 1979; 35/41, 25 Nov. 1980; 36/125, 14 Dec. 1981; 37/195, 18 Dec. 1982.

violations in the country of origin) before the principle of *non-refoulement* is triggered, but the concept now encompasses both non-return and non-rejection. A realistic appraisal of the normative aspect of *non-refoulement* in turn requires that the rule be examined not in isolation, but in its dynamic sense and in relation to the concept of asylum and the pursuit of durable solutions.

## (2) NON-REFOULEMENT AND EXTRADITION

The 1951 Convention says nothing about the extradition of refugees. In principle, *non-refoulement* should also apply in this context, for other provisions of the Convention already recognize the interests of the state of refuge in not committing itself to the reception of serious criminals. In 1951, however, a number of representatives formally expressed the view that Article 33 did not prejudice extradition.[43] One suspected of a serious non-political crime would in any event be excluded from the benefits of refugee status;[44] but one suspected or guilty of a non-serious non-political crime would remain liable to extradition, even to the state in which he or she had a well-founded fear of persecution. Any conflict of treaty obligations might be further dependent upon which obligation was contracted first.

This issue today again requires analysis of state practice since 1951, in the light of the object and purpose of the Convention and of the principle of *non-refoulement*. The political offender is considered worthy of protection, and it has become increasingly recognized that the non-serious, non-political offender, if a refugee, should also be entitled to the benefit of *non-refoulement*. The 1957 European Convention on Extradition, for example, prohibits extradition, 'if the requested Party has substantial grounds for believing that a request for extradition for an ordinary criminal offence has been made for the purpose of prosecuting or punishing a person on account of his race, religion, nationality or political opinion, *or that that person's position may be prejudiced for any of those reasons.*'[45] The Committee of Experts of the Council of Europe expanded this article expressly to include the basic elements of the refugee definition, although declining to write in 'membership of a particular social group' on the ground that it might be interpreted too freely. That apart, every indication is that the Committee intended to close the gap between the political

---

[43] See UN doc. A/CONF.2/SR.24, 10 (United Kingdom); ibid. SR.35, 21 (France).
[44] See above, ch. III, s. 4(2).
[45] Art. 3(2); ETS no. 24 (emphasis supplied); see below, annexe XII.

offender and the refugee. It further proposed that the transit of those extradited be excluded through any territory where the life or freedom of the person claimed could be threatened for any of the stated reasons, and this was included in Article 21.[46]

Article 3 of the European Convention now serves as a model for bilateral treaties and municipal laws.[47] It clearly influenced the Scheme for the Rendition of Fugitive Offenders adopted in 1966 by the Meeting of Commonwealth Law Ministers,[48] where somewhat different wording was chosen for the reference to 'prejudice'. In the form adopted in section 4(1)(c) of the United Kingdom's Fugitive Offenders Act 1967, non-return is called for where the person requested 'may be prejudiced at his trial or punished, detained or restricted in his personal liberty by reason of his race, religion, nationality or political opinions'.[49]

The substance of Article 3 is repeated in Article 5 of the 1977 European Convention on the Suppression of Terrorism, save that non-extradition is optional ('Nothing in this Convention shall be interpreted as imposing an obligation to extradite if ...').[50] On the other hand, Article 9 of the 1979 International Convention against the Taking of Hostages,[51] reverts to the 'extradition shall not be

[46] See generally *Supplementary Report of the Committee of Experts on Extradition to the Committee of Ministers*, Council of Europe doc. CM(57)52.

[47] See, for example, art. 19, 1979 Austrian Extradition Law (*Auslieferungs- und Rechtshilfegesetz: BGBl Nr.* 529/1979), which provides, *inter alia*, for non-extradition where the proceedings in the requesting state are likely to offend arts. 3 and 6 of the European Convention on Human Rights; where the likely punishment is likely to offend art. 3 of that Convention; or where the requested person may face persecution or other serious consequences on grounds akin to those in art. 1 of the 1951 Convention. Art. 3 of the 1976 Austria-Hungary Extradition Treaty (*BGBl Nr.* 340/1976) likewise provides for non-extradition (1) in respect of political offences; (2) when the person sought enjoys asylum in the requested state; and (3) when it is not in accord with other international obligations of the requested state. Art. 4 of the 1980 Austria-Poland Extradition Treaty (*BGBl Nr.* 146/1980) is to similar effect.

[48] Cmnd. 3008. The United Kingdom has not ratified the European Convention on Extradition, but did contribute two experts to the discussions cited above, n. 46.

[49] The words are more detailed than those of art. 3 (in the sense that they attempt in part to give meaning to the word 'prejudice') and yet potentially capable of narrower application, in the sense that prejudice at large is confined to that arising at trial or otherwise specifically defined in terms of punishment, detention, or restriction 'in personal liberty' for any of the stated reasons.

[50] The United Kingdom's implementing legislation, the Suppression of Terrorism Act 1978, s. 2, nevertheless maintains a *right* not to be extradited if the person requested makes out a case within the exception.

[51] Adopted by GA Res. 34/146, 17 Dec. 1979, by consensus. Art. 9 was adopted in the Sixth Committee by 103 votes to 10, with 4 abstentions. Contrary votes were cast by the Soviet Union, Eastern European countries (less Romania), Cuba, and Mongolia. The objections of these countries were based in particular on the inclusion of 'political opinion' in the list of relevant grounds; and on para. 2 of the article modifying 'all extradition

granted' formula. It also includes ethnic origin within the list of relevant grounds while adding one further likely cause of prejudice, 'the reason that communication with [the person requested] by the appropriate authorities of the State entitled to exercise rights of protection cannot be effected'. Where extradition is not granted, then according to Article 8, the state in which the alleged offender is found 'shall ... be obliged, without exception whatsoever and whether or not the offence was committed in its territory' to submit the case for prosecution.

The inclusion of the principle *aut dedere aut punire* in instruments aimed at suppressing certain crimes with an international dimension[52] is further acknowledgement that even the serious criminal may deserve protection against persecution or prejudice, while not escaping trial or punishment. Where non-extradition in such cases is stated as an *obligation*, the discretion of the state is significantly confined. *Non-refoulement* becomes obligatory[53] in respect of a class of alleged serious offenders, and no less should be required for the non-serious criminal who would otherwise fall within the exception.

While the tendency to extend the principle of *non-refoulement* to include non-extradition is clear, the position of certain states on this and on the more general issues of protection remains ambivalent. The practice of East European and Communist states is difficult to assess; the fact that United Nations resolutions on asylum and UNHCR are generally adopted unanimously or by consensus only adds to the sense of equivocation. The constitutions of the states in question frequently acknowledge the principle of asylum, thus indicating both awareness of the institution

treaties ... applicable between States Parties ... to the extent that they are incompatible with (the) Convention'. In the view of the objecting states, such a provision infringed their sovereign rights. See UN doc. A/C.6/34/SR.62, 12, cited by Verwey, 'The International Hostages Convention and National Liberation Movements' 75 *AJIL* 69, at 91 (1981) and generally.

[52] Art. 16, 1963 Tokyo Convention on Offences and certain Other Acts Committed on board Aircraft: art. 7, 1970 Hague Convention for the Suppression of Unlawful Seizure of Aircraft: art. 7, 1971 Montreal Convention for the Suppression of Unlawful Acts against the Safety of Civil Aircraft: art. 7, 1973 Convention on the Prevention and Punishment of Crimes against Internationally Protected Persons, including Diplomatic Agents.

[53] Given that the 'obligation' only arises where the state 'has substantial grounds' (i.e. it has a discretion), it must be considered imperfect. That *non-refoulement* is obligatory does not entail either a duty to grant asylum or a duty not to expel; see further below, and ch. V.

and recognition of a class of persons worthy of protection.[54] Yet the political offence exception, so closely related to principles of protection of refugees, finds no place in the extradition arrangements existing between such states.[55] At the 1977 United Nations Conference on Territorial Asylum, one article proposed would have protected refugees against extradition to a country in which they might face persecution.[56] The German Democratic Republic and the USSR, however, both prepared amendments reiterating the paramountcy of states' extradition obligations.[57] With the failure of the conference, these conflicting approaches were not resolved.

The extradition of refugees was also examined in 1980 by the Executive Committee, which reaffirmed the fundamental character of the principle of *non-refoulement*.[58] Although the views of states are not unanimous, the greater body of opinion, representing those most active in the protection of refugees and the development of refugee law, regards the principle of *non-refoulement* as likewise protecting the refugee from extradition.[59]

---

[54] See the provisions listed in *A Select Bibliography on Territorial Asylum*, UN doc. ST/GENEVA/LIB.SER.B/Ref.9, 68-74 (1977).

[55] Shearer, *Extradition in International Law*, (1971), 65-6. One commentator has noted that, constitutional provisions notwithstanding, asylum in communist countries may be refused to one who, though anti-capitalist, refuses to espouse communism: Epps, 'The Validity of the Political Offence Exception in Extradition Treaties in Anglo-American Jurisprudence' 20 *Harv. ILJ* 61, 86 (1979).

[56] See, for example, the proposal by the Federal Republic of Germany and Senegal: UN docs. A/CONF.78/C.1/L/105 and A/CONF.78/12, annexe 1, at 66 (1977). See also discussion of the issue by the Group of Experts: UN doc. A/10177, paras. 78-81 (1975).

[57] UN doc. A/CONF.78/12, annexe 1 at 43-6; the text finally referred to the drafting committee omitted any mention of extradition, ibid. 50-1, but the Committee of the Whole agreed that the issue should be considered later: ibid. at 47.

[58] They were based on the report of the Subcommittee of the Whole on International Protection: UN doc. A/AC.96/586. See also UN doc. A/AC.96/588, para. 48(2); the Subcommittee's recommendations regarding the refugee, recognized in one state, whose extradition is then sought from another state which he or she is temporarily visiting (UN doc. A/AC.96/586, para. 16, conclusions 8 and 9) were not adopted by the Executive Committee. On the extraterritorial effect of refugee status determinations, see further below, ch. IX, s. 1(2).

[59] See also art. 13, 1981 OAS Inter-American Convention on Extradition: 'No provision of this Convention shall be interpreted as a limitation on the right of asylum when applicable'. Also recommendation no. R(80)9 of the Committee of Ministers of the Council of Europe concerning extradition to states not parties to the European Convention on Human Rights; governments are recommended not to allow extradition in such cases, where there are substantial grounds to believe that art. 3(2) of the European Convention on Extradition would otherwise be applicable.

## (3) *NON-REFOULEMENT* AND EXPULSION[60]

While states may be bound by the principle of *non-refoulement*, they as yet retain discretion as regards both the grant of 'durable asylum' and the conditions under which it may be enjoyed or terminated. States parties to the Convention and Protocol, however, have acknowledged that the expulsion of refugees raises special problems and under Article 32 they undertake not to 'expel a refugee lawfully in their territory save on grounds of national security or public order'. Decisions to expel are further required to be in accordance with due process of law and 'except where compelling reasons of national security otherwise require' refugees shall be accorded the right of appeal.[61] Moreover, refugees under order of expulsion are to be allowed a reasonable period within which to seek legal admission into another country, though states retain discretion in this period to apply 'such internal measures as they may deem necessary'.

The restricted grounds of expulsion have been adopted in the laws of many states,[62] and have been taken into account in a number of judicial decisions.[63] The benefit is limited to refugees who enjoy what might loosely be called 'resident status' in the state in question, and one admitted temporarily remains liable to removal in the same way as any other alien.[64] The permitted power of expulsion, however, does not include the power to return the individual to the country in which his or her life or freedom would be threatened, unless the further exacting provisions which regulate exceptions to the principle of *non-refoulement* are also met.[65] Article 32 may yet have both advantages and dis-

---

[60] Generally on states' powers of expulsion, see Goodwin-Gill, *Movement of Persons*, 201-310; and on expulsion to a particular state, 218-28.

[61] See also art. 13, 1966 Covenant on Civil and Political Rights.

[62] See, for example, art. 11(2) of the Aliens Law 1965 (*Ausländergesetz*) of the Federal Republic of Germany: '*Ausländer, die als politisch Verfolgte Asylrecht geniessen, heimatlose Ausländer und ausländische Flüchtlinge können, wenn sie rechtmässig im Geltungsbereich dieses Gesetzes aufhalten, nur aus schwerwiegenden Gründen der öffentlichen Sicherheit und Ordnung ausgewiesen werden.*' Art. 43, Asylum Law 1979 (*loi sur l'asile*) of Switzerland: '(1) *Un réfugié auquel la Suisse a accordé l'asile ne peut être expulsé que s'il compromet la sûreté intérieure ou extérieure de la Suisse ou s'il a porté gravement atteinte à l'ordre public.* (2) *L'asile prend fin par l'exécution de l'expulsion administrative ou judiciaire.*'

[63] See, for example, *Yugoslav Refugee (Germany)* case 26 ILR 496; *Homeless Alien (Germany)* case 26 ILR 503; *Refugee (Germany)* case 28 ILR 297; *Expulsion of an Alien (Austria)* case 28 ILR 310.

[64] Robinson, *Commentary*, 157; Pompe, UN doc. HCR/INF/42, 19.

[65] In the *Refugee (Germany)* case (above, n. 63) the Federal Administrative Court held that a refugee unlawfully in the country could be expelled, provided he or she was not

advantages for the refugee. Thus, one expelled for the serious reasons stated in Article 32(1) is likely to face major difficulties in securing admission into any other country. Return to the country of origin being ruled out, the refugee may be exposed to prosecution and detention for failure to depart. As only the state of nationality is obliged to admit the refugee,[66] the expelling country may find itself frustrated in its attempts at removal. For these reasons, in 1977, the Executive Committee recommended that expulsion should be employed only in very exceptional cases. Where execution of the order was impracticable, it further recommended that states consider giving refugee delinquents the same treatment as national delinquents, and that the refugee be detained only if absolutely necessary for reasons of national security or public order.[67]

## (4) ILLEGAL ENTRY

In view of the normative aspects of *non-refoulement* in international law, the precise legal status of refugees under the immigration or aliens law of the state of refuge is irrelevant, although a state seeking to avoid liability will often classify them as prohibited or illegal immigrants. Refugees who flee frequently have no time for immigration formalities, and allowance for this is contained in Article 31 of the Convention, which of all articles comes closest to dealing with the controversial question of admission of refugees. Admission is not formally required. Instead, it is provided that penalties on account of illegal entry or presence shall not be imposed on refugees 'coming directly from a territory where their life or freedom was threatened ... provided they present themselves without delay ... and show good cause for their illegal entry or presence'. Refugees are not required to have come directly

---

returned to a country in which life or freedom would be threatened. An almost identical conclusion was reached in a 1974 United States decision, *Chim Ming* v. *Marks* 505 F.2d 1170 (2nd. Cir.). In the *Expulsion of an Alien (Austria)* case (above, n. 63), the Austrian Supreme Court observed when upholding an expulsion order that it merely required a person to leave the state, but did not render him or her liable to be returned to a specific foreign country.

[66] See Goodwin-Gill, *Movement of Persons*, 20-1, 44-6, 136-7.

[67] Report of the 28th Session, UN doc. A/AC.96/549, para. 53.5. In France, under art. 28 of the ordonnance no. 45-2658 of 2 Nov. 1946, *'assignation à résidence'* may be the consequence for the alien who finds it impossible to leave. See also art. 3(3) of the 1933 Convention (above, n. 8).

from their country of origin, but other countries or territories passed through should also have constituted actual or potential threats to life or freedom. What remains unclear is whether the refugee is entitled to invoke Article 31 when continued flight has been dictated more by the refusal of other countries to grant asylum.[68] Whether this is a 'good cause' for illegal entry rests very much with the state authorities.

At the 1951 Conference, several representatives considered that the undertaking not to impose penalties did not exclude the possibility of resort to expulsion.[69] Article 31 does not require that refugees be permitted to remain, and paragraph 2 emphasizes this point indirectly, by providing:

> The Contracting States shall not apply to the movements of such refugees restrictions other than those which are necessary and ... [they] shall only be applied *until their status in the country is regularized or they obtain admission into another country.* The Contracting States shall allow such refugees a reasonable period and all the necessary facilities to obtain admission into another country.

Given that the principle of *non-refoulement* remains applicable, the freedom of the state finally to refuse regularization of status can well be circumscribed in practice. As a matter of law, however, it would seem that the state may continue to keep the unresettled refugee under a regime of restricted movement, either in prison or a refugee camp.[70]

## (5) MEASURES NOT AMOUNTING TO *REFOULEMENT*

The core of meaning of *non-refoulement* requires states not to return refugees in any manner whatsoever to territories in which they face the possibility of persecution. But states may deny admission to bona fide asylum-seekers in ways not obviously amounting to breach of the principle. For example, stowaways and refugees rescued at sea may be refused entry; refugee boats may be towed back out to sea and advised to sail on; or military operations may render border crossing too dangerous to contemplate.

---

[68] See above, ch. III, s. 3(1).

[69] UN doc. A/CONF.2/SR.13, 12-14 (Canada, United Kingdom). Cf. art. 5, 1954 Caracas Convention on Territorial Asylum; see below, annexe IX.

[70] See further below, ch. V, ss. 4, 5, on the implications of *non-refoulement* through time.

## (a) *Stowaways*

Without breaching the principle of *non-refoulement*, the state where a stowaway asylum-seeker arrives may require the ship's master to keep the stowaway on board and travel on to the next port of call; or it may call upon the flag state to assume responsibility where the next port of call is unacceptable; or it may allow temporary disembarkation pending resettlement elsewhere. In the absence of rules regulating the appropriate state to consider the asylum claim, the situation is comparable to that of refugees in orbit,[71] while practical solutions are made more difficult to obtain by the tendency of states' immigration laws to deal summarily with stowaways.[72]

In October 1979, a Greek owned and registered bulk grain carrier, the *M.V. Dimitris*, under contract to a Soviet company, arrived in Australia with nine stowaways aboard; it had travelled directly from Vietnam, having spent some eight and a half hours bunkering in Singapore. The Australian authorities initially invoked the element of flag-state responsibility by analogy with the practice governing rescue of asylum-seekers at sea which had developed in the South East Asia region in the preceding years. A guarantee of resettlement was requested as a pre-condition to disembarkation. UNHCR argued that the asylum-seekers' status as stowaways under local law ought not to prejudice their entitlement to apply for recognition of refugee status, although for those with relatives in other countries, resettlement elsewhere might be the appropriate durable solution. The practice of requesting and obtaining resettlement guarantees from the flag states of rescuing ships had been developed to promote rescue at sea in the special circumstances pertaining in South East Asia, where disembarkation in first-port-of-call countries was seriously hampered by the lack of possibilities for local settlement. No rule of general or conventional international law governs responsibility for stowaway asylum-seekers,[73] and they should be treated as any other direct arrivals.

---

[71] See above, ch. III, s. 3(3).

[72] See, for example, the United States Immigration and Nationality Act 1952, 8 USC s. 1182(a) (18).

[73] None of the states involved in the case had ratified the 1957 Brussels Convention on Stowaways, which still awaits entry into force. Art. 5(2) provides that in considering application of the Convention, 'the Master and the appropriate authorities of the port of disembarkation will take into account the reasons which may be put forward by the stowaway for not being disembarked at or returned to' various ports or states. Art. 5(3) declares that 'The provisions of [the] Convention shall not in any way affect the power or

In the event, no resettlement guarantee was forthcoming. In view of Article 33 and the fact that the ship's next port of call was in the Soviet Union, which was not a party to the 1951 Convention or the 1967 Protocol, the Australian Government decided to allow disembarkation on humanitarian grounds. It reiterated its view, however, that in determining the appropriate country to respond to an asylum request, all the various factors should be weighed, including the flag state of the ship carrying the stowaways, their physical presence within the territory of the state of port of call, as well as the intentions of the asylum-seekers and any connection which they might have with third states. Eight of the nine stowaways were allowed to submit claims to the Australian Determination of Refugee Status Committee where they were recommended for recognition of refugee status and subsequently granted residence; the ninth was resettled with close relatives in a third country.[74]

The issue of stowaway asylum-seekers was briefly examined by a working group which met in Geneva in July 1982 to consider problems related to rescue at sea. While there was agreement on the importance of maintaining the principle of *non-refoulement*, there were otherwise widely diverging views on how problems should be solved; the general recommendations made by the working group on the questions of stowaways were not adopted by the Executive Committee at its October 1982 session.[75]

The discretion of the coastal state may be limited, however, by the particular facts of the case. If the flag state refuses to accept any responsibility for resettlement and if the ship's next

obligation [*sic*] of a Contracting State to grant political asylum.' Art. 3 provides, *inter alia*, that where a stowaway is otherwise unreturnable to any other state, he may be returned to 'the Contracting State whose flag was flown by the ship in which he was found' unless subject to 'a previous individual order of deportation or prohibition from entry'. The text of the Convention is printed in *Conférence diplomatique de droit maritime, 10ème session, Bruxelles,* 491-503 (1958). Both the United Kingdom and the Netherlands opposed these aspects of the Convention on the ground that they made too many inroads on national immigration control: ibid. 200, 436-7, 441-3, and 632-3.

[74] A similar solution was reached in Dec. 1980/Jan. 1981 following the arrival of an Italian owned and registered vessel, the M.V. *Simonetta*, with three stowaways on board; two were recognized as refugees and allowed to remain in Australia and the third was resettled with relatives in another state. In a case in 1982, involving a Danish vessel, the M.V. *Pacific Skou*, the flag state (which had ratified the Stowaways Convention) appears at least to have given serious consideration to Australia's request for a resettlement guarantee. Two stowaways were disembarked without a firm offer, but subject to UNHCR's undertaking to use its best endeavours to effect resettlement. One stowaway was resettled in a third state, while the other was eventually allowed to stay in Australia.

[75] Report of the Working Group on problems related to the rescue of asylum-seekers in distress at sea: UN doc. EC/SCP/21, paras. 22ff.

port of call is in a country in which the stowaway asylum-seekers' life or freedom may be threatened, then the practical effect of refusal of entry is *refoulement*. The nominal authority of the flag state to require diversion to a safe port, which would anyway be controversial where a charter party was involved, can hardly be considered a practical alternative, or 'last opportunity', to avoid *refoulement*. The paramount consideration remains the refugee status of those on board; a refusal to take account of their claims, either on the specious basis that they have not 'entered' state territory or on the (disputed) ground that they are the responsibility of the flag or any other state, would not suffice to avoid liability for breach of the principle of *non-refoulement*.

## (b) Rescue at sea

Asylum-seekers have been escaping by sea for years, only the most recent examples being Cubans, Haitians, and Indo-Chinese. As with stowaways, several options are open to the state where those rescued arrive; it may refuse disembarkation absolutely and require ships' masters to remove them from the jurisdiction, or it may make disembarkation conditional upon satisfactory guarantees as to resettlement, care and maintenance, to be provided by flag or other states, or by international organizations. Once again, a categorical refusal of disembarkation cannot be equated with breach of the principle of *non-refoulement*, even though it may result in serious consequences for asylum-seekers.

The duty to rescue those in distress at sea is firmly established in both general[76] and conventional[77] international law. Little provision has been made, however, in respect of the rescue of those who do not in fact enjoy the protection of their country of origin.[78] In recent years, given the expense and delay which often

[76] This view was expressed by the International Law Commission with regard to its proposed draft of art. 12 of the 1958 Convention on the High Seas; see UN doc. A/3179 (1956).

[77] See, for example, art. 11, 1910 Brussels International Convention with respect to Assistance and Salvage at Sea: 1 *Bevans* 780 (1968); art. 45 (1), 1929 International Convention on the Safety of Life at Sea: 136 LNTS 82; ch. V, Reg. 10a, 1960 International Convention on the Safety of Life at Sea; art. 12, 1958 Convention on the High Seas; art. 98, 1982 Convention on the Law of the Sea.

[78] See generally, Grant, *The Boat People* (1980), 68-72. Pugash, 'The Dilemma of the Sea Refugee: Rescue without Refuge' 18 *Harv. ILJ* 577-604 (1977). Art. 11 of the 1951 Convention requires contracting states to give 'sympathetic consideration' to the establishment within their territory of 'refugees regularly serving as crew members' on ships flying their flag. At the 1951 conference, it was stated that this provision was intended to benefit genuine seamen, not those escaping by sea; see Grahl-Madsen, *Status of Refugees*, ii.271-2 and sources there cited. Likewise, the 1957 agreement relating to refugee seamen

resulted from attempting to disembark those rescued at sea, many in distress were ignored by ships' masters and left to their fate. The problem was recognized as early as 1975[79] and the following year the Executive Committee stressed the obligations of ships' masters and states under the 1910 Brussels and 1958 Geneva Conventions, and appealed for the grant of first asylum.[80] The situation continued to worsen; on 3 October 1977, UNHCR appealed jointly with the Inter-governmental Maritime Consultative Organization (IMCO) to the shipping community directly, through the London-based International Chamber of Shipping, requesting owners to instruct ships' masters of the need for scrupulous observance of obligations relating to rescue at sea.[81]

The fears of first-port-of-call countries had also to be allayed by developing the practice of resettlement guarantees. In October 1978, the Executive Committee called for at least temporary admission to be granted, and appealed to the international community to support efforts to obtain the resettlement assurances that would facilitate disembarkation.[82] The general situation regarding Indo-Chinese refugees in South East Asia deteriorated rapidly in the first half of 1979, with the escalation in numbers leading to forcible measures against asylum-seekers. A United Nations Meeting convened in Geneva in July resulted in substantially increased resettlement offers, financial aid, and a number of practical proposals regarding rescue at sea.[83] A follow-

---

(updated by the 1973 protocol thereto) offers little solace to the asylum-seeker at sea. Art. 1 defines a 'refugee seaman' as a refugee within the meaning of the Convention and Protocol, who 'is serving as a seafarer in any capacity on a mercantile ship, or habitually earns his living as a seafarer on such ship'. The objective of the agreement is to determine the links which a refugee seaman may have with contracting states, with a view to establishing entitlement to residence and/or the issue of travel documents. The qualifying links are such as generally to exclude the seafaring asylum-seeker; for example, 600 days service under the flag of a contracting state; previous lawful residence in a contracting state; or travel documents previously issued by a contracting state: arts. 2, 3. 'Sympathetic consideration' is to be given to extending the agreement's benefits to those not otherwise qualifying: art. 5.

[79] Report of the 26th Session of the Executive Committee: UN doc. A/AC.96/516/Add.I, para. 92.

[80] Report of the 27th Session of the Executive Committee: UN doc. A/AC.96/534, para. 87(f), (g), (h).

[81] Cf. report of the 28th Session of the Executive Committee: UN doc. A/AC.86/549, paras. 21, 36.B(d), (e); also UN doc. E/1978/75, para. 9. The appeal was renewed 11 Dec. 1978. At the 29th Session of the Executive Committee it was recommended that UNHCR advise IMCO of the names of ships which ignored distress signals, with a view to their being reported to countries of ownership or registration: UN doc. A/AC.96/559, para. 38.E.

[82] Report of the 29th Session of the Executive Committee: UN doc. A/AC.96/559, para. 38.E.          [83] See UN doc. A/34/627, paras. 31-6; annexe I.

up meeting of experts[84] in August took note of the principle of flag-state responsibility and also proposed for consideration a further principle of responsibility for nationally owned vessels sailing under a flag of convenience. A pool of joint resettlement offers was suggested for difficult cases, to be available to UNHCR in its efforts to secure disembarkation where the flag state was unable to provide a guarantee or where it was unreasonable to expect that state to offer resettlement.[85]

In 1979, after rescue by 128 ships, 8,624 individuals known to UNHCR were disembarked, mostly in Hong Kong, the Philippines, Singapore, Thailand, and Japan, most of them against flag-state guarantees. In 1980, the numbers rose to 15,563 from 217 ships, and in 1981 to 14,589 from 213 ships, but already the principle of flag-state responsibility was being questioned. Doubt as to its general applicability had already emerged with the rescue in November 1979 of some 150 Vietnamese by the British registered vessel *Entalina* which was then heading for Darwin. The Australian Government requested a resettlement guarantee as a pre-condition to disembarkation, but the British Government appears initially to have considered that that practice was geographically limited to South East Asia, where all possibility of local settlement was ruled out; in other cases in other regions the principle of first-port-of-call responsibility should apply. In the event, the British Government did accept for ultimate settlement in the United Kingdom any refugees not resettled in other countries. The Australian Government in turn announced that it would consider accepting any who met Australian requirements, and who had relatives in the country or other special reasons to support their applications.[86]

At the 1980 Executive Committee Meeting, the United Kingdom representative called for a special approach to the problem of rescue cases.[87] He was supported by the Netherlands represen-

---

[84] The meeting was attended by representatives of Australia, Canada, France, Federal Republic of Germany, Italy, Japan, the Netherlands, the United Kingdom and the United States of America.

[85] This became known as the DISERO (Disembarkation Resettlement Offers) Scheme; it operated principally in Singapore.

[86] Department of Immigration and Ethnic Affairs, press releases 173/79(a), 30 Nov. 1979, 176/79, 4 Dec. 1979, 177/79, 5 Dec. 1979, and 180/79, 6 Dec. 1979. In June 1980 Australia announced that it accepted responsibility for some 70 refugees rescued by one of its naval vessels, referring to 'accepted international practice': press release 64/80, 17 June 1980. The following month the British Government gave a further guarantee in respect of 51 Vietnamese rescued by the bulk carrier *Glenpark:* press release 78/80, 3 July 1980.        [87] UN doc. A/AC.96/SR.317, para. 47.

tative who pointed out that, while numerous guarantees had been given by his country, the growth in numbers was becoming more difficult to handle. With the overall decline in refugee arrivals, he hoped that first-port-of-call states would reconsider their policy of requiring time-limited guarantees from flag states.[88] The representative for Greece was more direct. In his view, the rescue of refugees at sea should not impose flag-state responsibility; that responsibility rested with all signatories of the Convention and Protocol and the problem should be thoroughly re-examined with a view to an equitable sharing of the burden.[89]

A working group on problems related to rescue at sea was duly set up, composed of the representatives of the maritime and coastal states most concerned, of the potential resettlement countries and competent international bodies. The working group met in July 1982 and its report was considered at the thirty-third session of the Executive Committee in October.[90] The fundamental character of the duty to rescue was reiterated and it was generally acknowledged that the rescue of refugees at sea entailed a division of responsibilities between flag states, coastal states and resettlement states. The problem was to delimit more precisely their scope and content.

✓ The Netherlands representative proposed that coastal states no longer demand resettlement guarantees, which themselves led to an unacceptable disparity in the resettlement opportunities available, on the one hand, for those rescued at sea; and, on the other hand, for those who succeeded in arriving directly in countries of first refuge.[91] The Australian representative thought impractical any attempt to formulate detailed, legally binding principles on state responsibility, and that the key to solutions lay in international solidarity.[92] It was generally agreed that, as a

[88] UN doc. A/AC.96/SR.319, para. 27; see also the views of the Netherlands and others expressed at the July 1982 working group of government representatives on rescue at sea: UN doc. EC/SCP/21 paras. 11, 12, 16.

[89] UN doc. A/AC.96/SR.319, para. 4; the representative cited Colombos, *The International Law of the Sea* (6th ed., 1967) 285, and Simonet, *La Convention sur la haute mer* (1966) 78, in support of the argument against obligation. In 1979/80, British, Dutch, and Greek ships rescued a total of 6,223 persons, or 27.5% of the total. Representatives of maritime nations reiterated their concern at the 1981 Executive Committee meeting; see UN doc. A/AC.96/SR.332, para. 3; UN doc. A/AC.96/601, para. 52.

[90] See Report of the Working Group on problems related to the rescue of asylum-seekers in distress at sea: UN docs. EC/SCP/21 and EC/SCP/24; Report of the Meeting of the Sub-Committee of the Whole on International Protection: UN doc. A/AC.96/613, paras. 3-12; Report on the 33rd Session of the Executive Committee: UN doc. A/AC. 96/614, paras. 61, 70(2).

[91] UN doc. EC/SCP/21, para. 6.          [92] Ibid., para. 7.

matter of law, the responsibilities of flag states *after* disembarkation were uncertain. Some saw legal responsibility as limited to
the point of rescue, with any resettlement obligations thereafter
deriving from flag states' membership of the international community. The issue of disembarkation was also unclear. It might
be called for in application of the principle that those in search of
asylum should always receive temporary admission. Alternatively,
there may be an *imputed* obligation to allow disembarkation,
binding at least the states parties to the various conventions
dealing with rescue at sea and without which effective implementation of the rescue duty may be hindered.[93] The IMO representative, however, observed that there existed no 'formal, multilateral agreement' embodying a principle of disembarkation at
the next scheduled port of call. Coastal states were prepared to
continue to allow disembarkation, but only where resettlement
guarantees were given and those disembarked were rapidly
moved out. The Executive Committee in 1982 acknowledged the
divergence of views and recommended that solutions be sought
not only through legal norms but also through practical arrangements.[94]

In the light of the above, the principle of flag-state responsibility
can hardly be said to have established itself as 'international
custom, as evidence of a general practice accepted as law'. The
special circumstances which affected the finding of solutions to
the South East Asia refugee problem dictated the emergence of a
particular usage. In other situations it may be appropriate to
emphasize the responsibility of the first port of call, given the
inescapable but internationally relevant fact of the refugees' presence within the territory of the state.[95] As with stowaways,
effective solutions ought in principle to be attainable through a
weighing of competing interests, taking account not only of the
prospects, if any, of local integration, but also of notions of

---

[93] The author is indebted to Professor Luke T. Lee for calling his attention to this
aspect of the problem during a course on refugee law at the International Institute of
Humanitarian Law, San Remo, November 1982.

[94] Report on the 33rd Session of the Executive Committee: UN doc. A/AC.96/614,
paras. 61, 70(2). The Working Group suggested further contributions to DISERO, which
was generally favoured, as was the idea of expanding the scheme to include a funding
element to meet costs related to rescue, disembarkation and temporary admission: UN
doc. EC/SCP/21, para. 18.

[95] Although municipal law concepts of presence are not irrelevant (cf. Pugash, 18
*Harvard ILJ* 594 ff.), they can hardly be considered controlling for the purposes of interpreting treaty obligations.

international solidarity and burden-sharing,[96] as well as the extent to which refusal of disembarkation may lead in fact to *refoulement*, or to other serious harm for the asylum-seekers.

### (c)  *Arrival of asylum-seekers by boat*

The arrival of asylum-seekers by boat puts at issue not only the interpretation of *non-refoulement*, but also the extent of freedom of navigation and of coastal states' right of police and control. In South East Asia in 1979 and again in 1982, states employed measures to prevent boats landing, and towed back to the high seas many which had penetrated the territorial sea and internal waters. In 1981, President Reagan announced a policy of 'interdiction' of boats on the high seas which were believed to be bringing illegal aliens to the United States.

It is trite knowledge that the high seas[97] are not subject to the exercise of sovereignty by any state, and that ships are liable to the exclusive jurisdiction of the flag state, save in exceptional cases provided for by treaty or under general international law. The freedom of the high seas, however, is generally expressed as a freedom common to states,[98] while the boats of asylum-seekers, like their passengers, will most usually be denied flag-state protection. Similarly, the right of innocent passage for the purpose of traversing the territorial sea or entering internal waters is framed with normal circumstances in mind. A coastal state may argue, first, that boats of asylum-seekers are to be assimilated to ships without nationality[99] and are subject to boarding and other measures on the high seas. Additionally, it may argue that existing exceptions to the principle of freedom of navigation, applying within the territorial sea and the contiguous zone,[100] justify such preventive measures as the coastal state deems necessary to avoid landings on its shores.

Under general international law, ships on the high seas may be

---

[96] At the 1981 Executive Committee meeting, one speaker suggested that arrangements relating to rescue and resettlement 'already reflected the principle of burden-sharing between maritime and coastal States and should therefore be maintained': UN doc. A/AC.96/601, para. 52. Similar views were reiterated at the 1982 working group, see above, n. 88.

[97] Art. 1, 1958 Geneva Convention on the High Seas.

[98] Ibid.

[99] Ibid. art. 6(2).

[100] See arts. 14-20, 24, 1958 Geneva Convention on the Territorial Sea and the Contiguous Zone.

boarded only in very limited circumstances, namely, suspicion of piracy or slave trading, where the ship has no nationality or has the same nationality as the warship purporting to exercise authority, and where the ship is engaged in unauthorized broadcasting.[101] The third exception is most relevant to the situation of asylum-seekers, but even if their boats are without the effective protection of the country of origin, it is doubtful whether they can be assimilated to ships without nationality. Colombos points out, in a related context, that in certain circumstances a ship may take on the 'national character' of its owners.[102] Moreover, there is some authority for the view that a ship's owners can themselves sue in respect of illegal interference on the high seas.[103] In any event, no boat is ever entirely without the protection of the law. Obligations with regard to the rescue of those in distress at sea will circumscribe a state's freedom of action in certain cases.[104] In others, elementary considerations of humanity[105] require that account be taken of the right to life, liberty, and security of the person, and to freedom from torture, cruel, inhuman, and degrading treatment, as proclaimed and reaffirmed in the Universal Declaration and the 1966 Covenant on Civil and Political Rights. As the latter instrument notes, no derogation from the provisions protecting these interests is permitted, even 'in time of public emergency which threatens the life of the nation'.[106]

In the absence of an armed attack, the use of force against asylum-seekers cannot be justified on the ground of self-defence.[107] Notions of necessity[108] or self-preservation,[109] as well as exceptions relating to the 'peace, good order or security' of the coastal

---

[101] Art. 22, 1958 Geneva Convention on the High Seas; Art. 110, 1982 Convention on the Law of the Sea.

[102] Colombos, *The International Law of the Sea* (6th ed., 1967) 501.

[103] *The Paquete Habana* 175 US 677 (1900).

[104] See above, s. 2(5)(b).

[105] *Corfu Channel* case, ICJ Rep. 1949, 4, at 22; Brownlie, *Principles of Public International Law*, (3rd ed. 1979) 243.

[106] Art. 4.

[107] Brownlie, *International Law and the Use of Force by States* (1963) 264 ff., 278-9. Schwarzenberger and Brown, *A Manual of International Law* (6th ed.) 150. On the distinction between self-defence and self-help, see Bowett, *Self-Defence in International Law* (1958) 11-12.

[108] Brownlie, *Principles of Public International Law* (3rd ed., 1979) 464-6.

[109] Cf. Johnson, 'Refugees, Departees and Illegal Migrants' 9 *Sydney LR* 11, at 30-1; Bowett, *Self-Defence*, 22.

state[110] would in any event be subject to the limitations just set out. While a state necessarily enjoys a margin of appreciation in determining whether an influx of asylum-seekers constitutes a threat, the lawfulness of measures taken to meet it will depend on there being some relationship of proportionality between the means and the end. International procedures for assistance and for finding solutions to refugee problems exist and it is doubtful whether the use of such force as is reasonably likely to result in injury or death can ever be justified.[111]

Somewhat different considerations arise where, under a bilateral agreement, a flag state agrees to permit the authorities of another state to intercept its vessels. Precedents have existed for many years in regard to smuggling, slaving, and fisheries conservation, and in late 1981 the United States initiated a policy of 'interdiction' on the high seas, following an exchange of letters with the Government of Haiti and a Presidential proclamation.[112] The US Coast Guard was instructed to stop and board specified vessels, including those of US nationality, or no nationality, or possessing the nationality of a state which had agreed to such measures. Those on board were to be examined and returned to their country of origin 'when there is reason to believe that an offense is being committed against the United States immigration laws, or appropriate laws of a foreign country [with which an agreement exists]; provided, however, that no person who is a refugee will be returned without his consent'.[113]

---

[110] See Arts. 14, 19, and 24, 1958 Geneva Convention on the Territorial Sea and the Contiguous Zone; as Brownlie points out, *Principles*, 215, coastal states' powers are essentially powers of police and control.

[111] Cf. Johnson, 9 *Sydney LR* at 32, who concludes that 'Such force, and only such force, may be used as will prevent the attempted incursion of illegal immigrants from becoming a danger to the preservation of the State'.

[112] See also the Emergency Interdiction Act and the Immigration Emergency Act, part of the Omnibus Immigration Control Act (HR 4832/51765) introduced into Congress at the request of the Administration in 1981: *Interpreter Releases*, vol. 58, no. 42, 30 Oct. 1981, 557-60. A less comprehensive package was eventually proposed; see below ch. VIII, s. 2(7).

[113] Executive Order no. 12324 of 29 Sept. 1981, *Interdiction of Illegal Aliens*, sec. 2(c) (3). S. 3 in turn requires the Attorney General to take whatever steps are necessary to ensure the fair enforcement of the immigration law and 'the strict observance of ... international obligations concerning those who genuinely flee persecution in their homeland'. The United States Ambassador's letter to the Government of Haiti also noted that it was 'understood' that the US did not intend to return to Haiti any whom it determined to qualify for refugee status. Text of Executive Order and Presidential Proclamation 4865 in *Interpreter Releases* vol. 58, no. 40, 17 Oct. 1981, 529-31.

This express recognition of the substance of the principle of *non-refoulement* acknowledges the potential liability of the United States for the actions of its officials in actually returning refugees to a country where they may be endangered, even though such actions take place in an area wholly outside its territorial jurisdiction.[114] Notwithstanding this, the asylum-seekers themselves will be denied the procedural guarantees accruing to the physically present,[115] and the effective protection of bona fide refugees is rendered impracticable, if not impossible. In the case of measures designed to prevent landings and which fall short of returning refugees to a country in which they may be endangered, *non-refoulement* remains inapplicable. It does not follow that states enjoy complete freedom of action over arriving boats, even if they come in substantial numbers and without nationality. The range of permissible measures is limited by obligations relating to rescue at sea and arising from elementary considerations of humanity, while action which would directly effect return is enjoined by the principle of *non-refoulement*. Whether on the high seas or in waters subject to the jurisdiction of any state, refugees may be protected by UNHCR in the exercise of its functional protection role.[116]

## 3. Exceptions to the principle of *non-refoulement*

*Non-refoulement* is not an absolute principle, and 'national security' and 'public order' have long been recognized as potential justifications for derogation.[117] Nevertheless, as the principle has become more entrenched, so too has the exceptional privilege of derogation become somewhat more closely circumscribed. Article 33(2) expressly provides that the benefit of *non-refoulement* may not be claimed by a refugee, 'whom there are reasonable grounds for regarding as a danger to the security of the country ... or who, having been convicted by a final judgment of a particularly serious crime, constitutes a danger to the community of that country'. The exceptions to *non-refoulement* are thus framed in terms of the individual, but whether he or she may be considered

---

[114] US Coast Guard vessels took up position in the Windward Passage, close to the coast of Haiti.

[115] See below, ch. VIII, s. 2(7).      [116] Ibid.

[117] See, for example, art. 3, 1933 Convention relating to the International Status of Refugees: 159 LNTS 199; art. 5(2), 1938 Convention concerning the Status of Refugees coming from Germany: 192 LNTS 59.

a security risk appears to be left very much to the judgment of the state authorities.[118] This, at least, was the intention of the British representative at the 1951 Conference, who proposed the inclusion of Article 33(2), and such an approach to security cases is supported both by Article 32(2) of the Convention and by immigration law and practice generally.[119]

It is unclear to what extent, if at all, one convicted of a particularly serious crime must also be shown to constitute a danger to the community. The jurisprudence is sparse, and the notion of 'particularly serious crime' is not a term of art,[120] but principles of natural justice and due process of law require something more than mere mechanical application of the exception. An approach in terms of the penalty imposed alone will always be somewhat arbitrary, and the application of Article 33(2) ought always to involve the question of proportionality, with account taken of the nature of the consequences likely to befall the refugee on return. The offence in question and the perceived threat to the community would need to be extremely grave if danger to the life of the refugee were to be disregarded, although a less serious offence and a lesser threat might justify the return of an individual likely to face only some harassment or discrimination.

In contrast to the 1951 Convention, the 1969 OAU Convention declares the principle of *non-refoulement* strongly and without exception. No formal concession is made to overriding considerations of national security, although in cases of difficulty 'in continuing to grant asylum' appeal may be made directly to other member states and through the OAU. Provision is then made for temporary residence pending resettlement, although its grant is not mandatory.[121] The absence of any formal exception to the principle is the more remarkable in view of the dimensions of the refugee problems which have faced individual African states. Indeed, Article 3 of the Declaration on Territorial Asylum, adop--

---

[118] The reference to 'reasonable grounds' was interpreted by one representative at the 1951 Conference as allowing states to determine whether there were sufficient grounds for regarding the refugee as a danger and whether the danger likely to be encountered by the refugee on *refoulement* was outweighed by the threat to the community: UN doc. A/CONF. 2/SR.16, 8.

[119] See Goodwin-Gill, *Movement of Persons*, 241-2, 247-50.

[120] Analysing art. 1F(b), Grahl-Madsen proposes as a yardstick for interpretation of serious non-political crime, 'any offence for which the maximum penalty in the majority of countries of western Europe and North America [*sic*] is imprisonment for more than five years or death'. He rejects the narrower interpretation advanced by those who would limit the term to offences against life or limb: *Status of Refugees,* i.284.    [121] Art. II.

ted by the General Assembly only two years before the OAU
Convention, not only acknowledges the national security exception, but also appears to authorize further exceptions 'in order to
safeguard the population, as in the case of a mass influx of persons'.
Though strongly criticized for its vagueness,[122] this provision
remains of concern, particularly in the light of recent refugee
crises. The exception reappeared, however, at the 1977 Conference on Territorial Asylum. Turkey proposed an amendment
whereby *non-refoulement* might not be claimed 'in exceptional
cases, by a great number of persons whose massive influx may
constitute a serious problem to the security of a Contracting
State'.[123] Although each case will differ, a mass influx ought not
to be considered in itself sufficient to justify *refoulement*; the likelihood of an international response, including financial and material
assistance with voluntary repatriation, local integration or resettlement in other states, is an important factor to be set against
any potential threat to national security. *Non-refoulement*, moreover, implies refuge through time, with due regard to the attainment of appropriate solutions.[124]

## 4. The status of the principle of *non-refoulement* in general international law

The evidence relating to the meaning and scope of *non-refoulement*
in its conventional sense also amply supports the conclusion that
today the principle forms part of general international law. There
is substantial, if not conclusive, authority that the principle is
binding in all states, independently of specific assent. State
practice before 1951 is, at the least, equivocal as to whether, in
that year, Article 33 of the Convention reflected or crystallized a
rule of customary international law.[125] State practice since then,

---

[122] Weis, 'The United Nations Declaration on Territorial Asylum' 7 *Can. YIL* 92, 113,
142-3 (1969). Weis nevertheless applauds rejection of the 'public order' exception, which
he sees as too wide and susceptible of different connotations in civil and common law
countries. For an examination of the *ordre public* concept in the context of entry and expulsion generally, see Goodwin-Gill, *Movement of Persons,* 168-9, 229-37, 298-9.

[123] UN doc. A/CONF.78/C.1/L.28/Rev.1 adopted in the Committee of the Whole by
24 votes to 20, with 40 abstentions. The paragraph of exceptions as a whole was adopted
by 68 votes to 5, with 8 abstentions: UN doc. A/CONF.78/12, para. 62.

[124] See below, ch. V, ss. 4, 5.

[125] This conclusion represents a modification of views set out in Goodwin-Gill,
*Movement of Persons,* 141.

however, is persuasive evidence of the concretization of a customary rule, even in the absence of any formal judicial pronouncement.[126] In this context, special regard should also be paid to the practice of international organizations, such as the United Nations General Assembly and the United Nations High Commissioner for Refugees. Latterly, General Assembly resolutions dealing with the report of the High Commissioner and consistently endorsing the principle of *non-refoulement* have tended to be adopted by consensus. While consensus decision-making denotes the absence of formal dissent,[127] it still allows states the opportunity to express opposing views in debate and in summary records.[128] No formal or informal opposition to the principle of *non-refoulement* is to be found, and where objection has been made on occasion to the protection and assistance activities of UNHCR, it has been founded on a challenge to the status as refugees of the individuals involved.

Article 33 of the 1951 Convention is of a 'fundamentally norm-creating character' in the sense in which that phrase was used by the International Court of Justice in the *North Sea Continental Shelf* cases.[129] That *refoulement* may be permitted in exceptional circumstances does not deny this premiss; instead, it indicates the boundaries of discretion.

The practice examined hitherto has necessarily been selective

---

[126] See *United States Diplomatic and Consular Staff in Tehran* ICJ Rep. 1980, 3, at 41 (para. 88), in which the Court hints at the 'legal difficulties, in internal or international law' which might have resulted from the United States acceding to Iran's request for the extradition of the former Shah.

[127] The Special Committee on the Rationalization of the Procedures and Organization of the General Assembly concluded that 'the adoption of decisions and resolutions by consensus is desirable when it contributes to the effective and lasting settlement of differences, thus strengthening the authority of the United Nations'. The Committee emphasized, however, 'that the right of every Member State to set forth its views in full must not be prejudiced by this procedure': report of the Special Committee, *GAOR*, 26th Session, Supplement no. 26 (A/8426), 1971, paras. 28-9; Rules of Procedure of the General Assembly, A/520/Rev.12 (1974), annexe V, para. 104. See D'Amato, 'On Consensus' 8 *Can. YIL* 104-22 (1970); Buzan, 'Negotiating by Consensus: Developments in Technique at the United Nations Conference on the Law of the Sea' 75 *AJIL* 324-48 (1981).

[128] On 16 Dec. 1981, the General Assembly adopted without a vote Res. 36/148 on International Co-operation to Avert New Flows of Refugees, on the recommendation of the Special Political Committee (report: UN doc. A/36/790). In the course of debate in the Committee, a number of delegates made statements in explanation which included substantial reservations regarding the draft resolution; other delegates expressly stated that they would have abstained, had the draft been put to the vote: UN doc. A/SPC/36/SR.45, paras. 49 ff.

[129] ICJ Rep. 1969, 3 at 42. No reservations may be made to art. 33; see art. 42.

and far from embracing the views of all states. The position of certain countries remains ambivalent, even though no state today claims any general right to return refugees or bona fide asylum-seekers to a territory in which they may face persecution or danger to life or limb. Where states do claim not to be bound by any obligation, their arguments either dispute the status of the individuals in question, or invoke exceptions to the principle of *non-refoulement*, particularly on the basis of threats to national security. Nevertheless, one further possible objection to including *non-refoulement* within the corpus of general international law lies in the so-called 'right of unilateral qualification'. Article 1(3) of the 1967 Declaration on Territorial Asylum declares that, 'It shall rest with the State granting asylum to evaluate the grounds for the grant of asylum'.[130] This provision, which Poland introduced during discussions in the Third Committee, is of uncertain scope. In so far as the grant of *asylum* remains discretionary and a manifestation of sovereignty by the territorial state, it is redundant. Some commentators fear, however, that, rather than facilitate liberal policies, such a provision might be invoked to justify decisions to *refoule* refugees.[131] The disparate interpretations of 'political offence' in extradition, and its tendency to become dominated by political considerations, emphasize how, in the absence of directly applicable international standards, states' discretion can remain paramount.

If each state remains absolutely free to determine the status of asylum-seekers and either to abide by or ignore the principle of *non-refoulement*, then the refugee's status in international law is denied and the standing, authority, and effectiveness of the principles and institutions of protection are seriously undermined. The weight of the evidence, though, is in favour of the limits to discretion which flow, first, from an international legal definition

---

[130] The 1975 Group of Experts' text (UN doc. A/10177) proposed the following article for inclusion in a convention on territorial asylum: 'Qualification of the grounds for granting asylum *or applying the provisions of this Convention* appertains to the Contracting State whose territory the person concerned has entered or seeks to enter and seeks asylum' (art. 9; emphasis supplied). Various amendments were proposed, including deletion of the article, but none was considered by the Committee of the Whole: UN doc. A/CONF.78/12, 63.

[131] Grahl-Madsen, *Territorial Asylum* (1980) 46, 88. See also Epps, 20 *Harvard ILJ* 61, 86, and the various provisions on the right of qualification in Latin American treaties, for example, art. 23, 1889 Montevideo Treaty on International Penal Law: OAS TS no. 34, 1; art. 3, 1933 Montevideo Convention on Political Asylum: OAS TS no. 34, 27; arts. 20, 23; 1940 Montevideo Treaty on International Penal Law: OAS TS no. 34, 71; art. 4, 1954 Caracas Convention on Diplomatic Asylum: OAS TS no. 34, 82; below annexe X.

of the refugee; and secondly, from general recognition of the principle of *non-refoulement*. That certain grey areas exist in the formulation of *non-refoulement* hardly confirms its lack of status in general international law. As Brierly noted some fifty-six years ago, 'the principles of international law are not susceptible of precise formulation ... [the] rules are ... constantly changing and modelling themselves on the ever-changing needs of international life.'[132]

[132] 'The Shortcomings of International Law' in Brierly, *The Basis of Obligation in International Law* (1958, ed. Lauterpacht and Waldock) 68, 74.

# Chapter V

# THE CONCEPT OF ASYLUM

## 1. Introduction

The meaning of the word 'asylum' tends to be assumed by those who use it, but its content is rarely explained. The Universal Declaration of Human Rights refers to 'asylum from persecution', the UN General Assembly urges the grant of asylum and observance of the principle of asylum, and states' constitutions and laws offer the promise of asylum, yet nowhere is this act of states' defined. The word itself and the phrase 'right of asylum' have lost much of their pristine simplicity.[1] With the growth of nation states and the corresponding development of notions of territorial jurisdiction and supremacy, the institution of asylum underwent a radical change. It came to imply not only a place of refuge, but also the right to give protection, not so much to the ordinary criminal, as to the one class previously excluded, namely, exiles and refugees.[2] The anomalous position of exiles had already been noted by the jurist Wolff who, writing in 1764, observed that 'exiles do not cease to be men ... [By] nature the right belongs to them to dwell in any place in the world which is subject to some other nation.'[3] But this was a 'right' which even Wolff tempered with recognition of the fact of sovereignty. Compassion ought to be shown to those in flight, but admission might be refused for good reasons.[4] The interest of the state in admission or non-admission continued to predominate.[5] Moore, in 1908, noted that

---

[1] See generally Reale, 'Le droit d'asile' Hague *Recueil* (1938-I) 473-601; Koziebrodski, *Le droit d'asile* (1962); Reville, *'L'abjuratio regni*: histoire d'une institution anglaise' *Revue historique* (1892) 1; Trenholme, *The Right of Sanctuary in England* (1903); Kimminich, *Der internationale Rechtsstatus des Flüchtlings* (1962) 65-98; Sinha, *Asylum and International Law* (1971) 5-15 and *passim*; Grahl-Madsen, *The Status of Refugees in International Law*, vol. 2 (1972); Garcia-Mora, *International Law and Asylum as a Human Right* (1956).

[2] Reale, Hague *Recueil* (1938-I) 499-500, 544-54, locates the beginning of this development in the mid-eighteenth century, with its hardening into an institution after the events of 1848-9.

[3] *Jus Gentium Methodo Scientifica Pertractatum* (1764) s. 147.

[4] Ibid. s. 148; see also Vattel, ed. Chitty (1834) I.19. 229-30; Grotius, *De Jure Belli et Pacis* (1646) iii. 20. xli.

[5] Generally on states' powers over entry and exclusion, see Goodwin-Gill, *International Law and the Movement of Persons between States* (1978).

the right to grant asylum 'is to be exercised by the government in the light of its own interests, and of its obligations as a representative of social order'.[6] Hackworth, similarly observed the freedom of each sovereign state to deal with refugees 'as its domestic policy or its international obligations may seem to dictate'.[7] In 1949, Morgenstern settled the competence of states to grant asylum upon 'the undisputed rule of international law' that every state has exclusive control over the individuals in its territory, including all matters relating to exclusion, admission, expulsion, and protection against the exercise of jurisdiction by other states.[8]

This element, protection granted to a foreign national against the exercise of jurisdiction by another state, lies at the heart of the institution of asylum.[9] It remains important, however, to distinguish between the international law and municipal law aspects. In international law, protection is founded either in an exercise of territorial jurisdiction or on the basis of treaty or some regional or local custom. The latter bases are particularly relevant to the institution of 'diplomatic asylum', understood in the sense of protection against *local* jurisdiction granted in embassies and consulates and on warships.[10] The notion of extraterritoriality has been adduced in support of the practice, but regional treaty and custom appear to be its surer foundations.[11] In the *Asylum* case in 1950 the

---

[6] Moore, *Digest* ii.757.

[7] Hackworth, *Digest* ii.622.

[8] 'The Right of Asylum' 26 *BYIL* (1949) 327. See also Koziebrodski, *Droit d'asile*, 24, 79-81; Simpson, *The Refugee Problem* (1939) 230: 'Asylum is a privilege conferred by the State. It is not a condition inherent in the individual.'

[9] Cf. the definition adopted by the Institute of International Law at its 1950 Bath Session: 'Asylum is the protection which a State grants on its territory or in some other place under the control of its organs to a person who comes to seek it.' 1 *Annuaire* (1950) 167, art. 1.

[10] Note also the recognition given after the 1973 coup in Chile to UNHCR 'safe havens'; see UN doc. A/AC.96/508, 5.

[11] Many states do not accept the institution of diplomatic asylum, or do so only in very limited cases; see debate in the International Law Commission in 1949: *Yearbook of the ILC*, paras. 49, 87-8; debate on the draft Declaration on the Right of Asylum in 1966: UN doc. A/6570, para. 11; Moore, *Digest* ii.755 ff.; Hackworth, *Digest* ii.623 ff.; Whiteman, *Digest* vi.445 ff.; McNair, 'Extradition and Exterritorial Asylum' 28 *BYIL* (1951) 172; 7 *British Digest of International Law* 905-23. In 1974, on an Australian initiative, the General Assembly requested the Secretary-General to prepare and circulate a report on the practice of diplomatic asylum and invited member states to make known their views: GA Res. 3321(XXIX), 14 Dec. 1974. The report (UN doc. A/10139) confirmed the regional nature of the practice; of 25 states which made known their views, only seven favoured drawing up an international convention on the matter. Further consideration of the subject was postponed indefinitely: GA Res. 3497(XXX), 15 Dec. 1975.

International Court of Justice described the practice as involving,

a derogation from the sovereignty of [the local] State. It withdraws the offender from the jurisdiction of the territorial State and constitutes an intervention in matters which are exclusively within the competence of that State ... In the case of extradition, the refugee is within the territory of the State of refuge. A decision with regard to extradition implies only the normal exercise of territorial sovereignty. The refugee is outside the territory of the State where the offence was committed, and a decision to grant him asylum in no way derogates from the sovereignty of that State.[12]

The generality of these last dicta can be misleading unless the normative effect of extradition treaties is taken into account, as well as more recent developments which limit or qualify the 'normal exercise' of sovereignty.[13] From the point of view of international law, therefore, the grant of protection in its territory derives from the state's sovereign competence, a statement of the obvious. The content of that grant of protection—whether it embraces permanent or temporary residence, freedom of movement and integration or confinement in camps, freedom to work and attain self-sufficiency or dependence on national and international charity—is less easy to determine. What cannot be ignored, however, is the close relationship existing between the issue of refugee status and the principle of *non-refoulement*, on the one hand, and the concept of asylum, on the other hand. These three elements are, as it were, all links in the chain between the refugee's flight and his or her attainment of a durable solution.

Certain legal consequences flow from the existence of a class of refugees known to and defined by general international law and, in particular, from the principle of *non-refoulement*. In regard to asylum, however, it will be seen that the argument for obligation fails, both on account of the vagueness of the institution and of the

---

[12] ICJ Rep. 1955, 266, at 274. In this and the *Haya de la Torre* case, ICJ Rep. 1951, 71, the Court was concerned *inter alia* with interpretation of the 1928 Havana Convention on Asylum, in force between the parties to the dispute, Colombia and Peru, which embodied the right to grant asylum in embassies to political offenders in urgent cases. Colombia's claim that it was entitled to qualify the offence in question as political and also to determine the urgency of the case was rejected by the Court, as was its further claim that the territorial state was bound to allow the asylee to leave. Nevertheless, the Court agreed that the offence was political, but disagreed on the issue of urgency. The resulting stalemate, in which Colombia was not bound to hand over the fugitive, notwithstanding the improper grant of asylum, and Peru was not bound to allow safe passage, was not covered by the Convention or by any regional custom; the parties were urged to reach a friendly settlement.

[13] On which, see above ch. III, s. 4(1).

continuing reluctance of states formally to accept such obligation and to accord a right of asylum enforceable at the instance of the individual.

## 2. Asylum in international conventions, other instruments and acts, 1945-70

The refusal of states to accept an obligation to grant asylum, in the sense of residence and lasting protection against the jurisdiction of another state, is amply evidenced by the history of international conventions and other instruments. Measures taken between the two world wars related, initially, to arrangements for the issue of travel documents which would facilitate the resettlement of refugees, but no obligations to resettle were assumed. The 1933 Convention, which proposed non-rejection of refugees at the frontier, was ratified by only a few states, while it, too, made no provision in respect of permanent asylum. Likewise, those states which subscribed to the constitution of the IRO, though urged to co-operate in its function of resettling refugees, accepted no obligations to that end. Little progress was achieved by the statement in Article 14(1) of the Universal Declaration of Human Rights that 'everyone has the right to seek and to enjoy ... asylum'. Lauterpacht rightly noted that there was no intention among states to assume even a moral obligation in the matter.[14] The proposal to substitute 'to be granted' for 'to enjoy'[15] was vigorously opposed,[16] as was the suggestion that the United Nations itself should be empowered to secure asylum.[17] Contemporary opinion held that to grant asylum to refugees within its territory was the sovereign right of every state, while the corresponding duty was that of respect for that asylum by all other states.

This approach was substantially reiterated in the UN General Assembly resolution establishing UNHCR, which merely urged states to co-operate with the High Commissioner, *inter alia*, by admitting refugees.[18] Draft conventions submitted by France and

---

[14] *International Law and Human Rights* (1950) 421. As Kimminich succinctly states: '*Das Recht, Asyl zu suchen, bedeutet nichts anderes als das Recht, sich auf die Flucht zu begeben.*' (*Internationale Rechtsstatus des Flüchtlings*, 81.)

[15] UN doc. A/C.3/285/Rev. 1.

[16] For example, by the United Kingdom: UN doc. A/C.3/SR.121, 4-6.

[17] UN doc. A/C.3/244 (France).

[18] GA Res. 428(V), 14 Dec. 1950; see also GA Res. 430(V) of the same date, urgently appealing to states to assist the IRO in its resettlement efforts.

the UN Secretariat in the course of debate on the 1951 Convention both contained an article on admission of refugees,[19] but the Conference of Plenipotentiaries preferred to leave asylum and admission to be covered by exhortatory statements in the Final Act. Nevertheless, efforts continued in other forums. In 1957, France proposed a declaration on the right of asylum to the Economic and Social Council,[20] and in 1959, the General Assembly called on the International Law Commission to take up codification of the right of asylum.[21] The subject was included in the Commission's future work programme in 1962,[22] but in the absence of progress generally it fell to the Commission on Human Rights and to the Third and Sixth Committees to take up the cause, culminating in the 1967 Declaration on Territorial Asylum, adopted unanimously by the General Assembly.[23]

The Declaration recommends that states should base their asylum practice upon the principles declared, but it stresses throughout the sovereign competence aspect of territorial asylum and reaffirms the position of each state as sole judge of the grounds upon which it will extend such protection.[24] Article 2, however, acknowledges that the plight of refugees remains of concern to the international community, and that where a state finds difficulty in granting or continuing to grant asylum, other states 'shall consider', in a spirit of international solidarity, measures to lighten the burden. Article 3 declares the principle of *non-refoulement* and states contemplating derogation, once again, 'shall consider' the possibility of according those affected the opportunity, 'by way of provisional asylum or otherwise', of going to another state.

The 1967 Protocol relating to the Status of Refugees is limited to updating the refugee definition and no other instruments of a universal character have specifically contributed to strengthening

---

[19] UN doc. E/AC.32/2, 22, cited by Weis, 'Legal Aspects of the Convention of 28 July 1951 relating to the Status of Refugees' 30 *BYIL* 478-89 at 481 (1953).

[20] ECOSOC OR 22nd Session, Supplement, paras. 109-12. Other states objected by reference to issues of sovereignty and domestic jurisdiction; see UN doc. E/CN.4/781, 3 (Czechoslovakia); ibid. 10-11 (United Kingdom).

[21] GA Res. 1400(XIV) of 21 Sept. 1959. The ILC had been tentatively involved with the issue some ten years previously, in debate on an article proposed for inclusion in a draft declaration on the rights and duties of states: *Yearbook of the ILC* (1949) 125, paras. 49 ff.

[22] UN doc. A/CN.4/245.

[23] GA Res. 2312(XXII), 14 Dec. 1967. For text, see below, annexe VI. For a detailed account of the background and steps leading to the Declaration see Weis, 'The United Nations Declaration on Territorial Asylum' 7 Can. *YIL* (1969) 92-149.

[24] Art. 1(1), (2).

the institution of asylum. On a regional level, however, some slight progress can be discerned. Thus, the European Convention on Human Rights has facilitated an overall improvement in the situation of individuals at large, whether citizens, aliens or refugees. The 1957 European Convention on Extradition formulates the principle of non-extradition for political offences in the form of an obligation ('extradition shall not be granted') and applies the same principle where the request is made for the purpose of prosecuting or punishing a person on account of race, religion, nationality, or political opinion, or where a person's position may be prejudiced for any of these reasons.[25] In a resolution of 1967, the Committee of Ministers of the Council of Europe recommended that member governments 'should act in a particularly liberal and humanitarian spirit in relation to persons who seek asylum in their territory', but also recognized 'the necessity of safeguarding national security and of protecting the community from serious danger'.[26] Observance of the principle of *non-refoulement* was called for and, where exceptions were contemplated, the individual should 'as far as possible and under such conditions as [were considered] appropriate' be accorded the opportunity of going to another state.

Within Latin America, the 1954 Caracas Convention on Territorial Asylum reaffirmed the territorial state's sovereign right to grant asylum, the duty of other states to respect such asylum, and the exemption from any obligation to surrender or expel persons 'sought for political offences' or 'persecuted for political reasons or offences'.[27] As regards diplomatic asylum,[28] another Caracas Convention of the same year stressed that while 'every State has the right to grant asylum … it is not obligated to do so or state its reasons for refusing it'; and that it rested with 'the State granting asylum to determine the nature of the offence or the motives for the persecution'.[29] The Convention provides further that 'the

---

[25] ETS no. 24, art. 3(2).

[26] Res. (67) 14 of 29 June 1967 on Asylum to Persons in Danger of Persecution, Preamble and para. 1. See also the precursors to this Resolution: Recommendation 293 of 26 Sept. 1961 of the Consultative Assembly of the Council of Europe, proposing that the Committee of Experts be instructed to include an article on asylum in a protocol to the European Convention on Human Rights; this was rejected by the Committee of Experts, which favoured either a separate convention or a resolution. The principles of the 1967 resolution were reaffirmed in the Declaration on Territorial Asylum adopted by the Committee of Ministers on 18 Nov. 1977.

[27] Arts. 1-4, see below, annexe IX.

[28] i.e. asylum granted 'in legations, war vessels, and military camps or aircraft, to persons being sought for political offences': art. 1; see below, annexe X.

[29] Ibid., art. 2, 4.

State granting asylum is not bound to settle him in its territory, but it may not return him to his country of origin, unless this is the express wish of the asylee'.[30]

The 1969 OAU Convention, besides broadening the refugee definition, also strengthens the institution of asylum. Member states of the OAU, proclaims Article II, 'shall use their best endeavours ... to receive refugees and to secure the settlement' of those unable or unwilling to be repatriated. The principle of *non-refoulement* is stated without exception, although once again a call is made to lighten the burden borne by countries of first refuge.[31] A further provision, dealing with the case of a refugee who has not received the right to reside in any country, merely acknowledges that he or she 'may' be granted temporary residence pending resettlement. On asylum at large, the Convention affirms that its grant is a peaceful and humanitarian act, and thus not to be regarded as unfriendly. It also emphasizes the duty of refugees to abide by the laws of the country in which they find themselves and to refrain from subversive activities against any member state.

Despite the encouraging tone of the OAU Convention, neither this instrument nor any other permits the conclusion that states have accepted an international obligation to grant asylum to refugees, in the sense of lasting protection against persecution and/or the exercise of jurisdiction by another state. The period under review, however, is replete with examples of asylum given; the humanitarian practice exists, but the sense of obligation is missing. The practice of international organizations tends to support this view; at the same time, pragmatically, it illustrates an awareness of the need for a flexible response to refugee problems. In the years after the Second World War, for example, many thousands of refugees had the benefit, at least, of asylum in the refugee camps of Europe.[32] Their principal need was for resettlement, and the General Assembly repeatedly called upon immigration countries to allow refugees access to their programmes.[33] On other occasions, the General Assembly reiterated that permanent solutions should be sought in voluntary repatriation and assimilation within

[30] Ibid., art. 17.

[31] Art. II(4); see below, annexe VIII.

[32] See generally, Vernant, *The Refugee in the Post-War World* (1953); Holborn, *The International Refugee Organization* (1956).

[33] See, for example, GA Res. 430(V), 14 Dec. 1950, urgently appealing to all states to assist the IRO with resettlement; GA Res. 538(VI) of 2 Feb. 1952, appealing specially to states interested in migration.

new national communities, either locally in countries of first refuge or in countries of immigration.[34] The initial burden may fall in fact upon the receiving country,[35] but solutions are the responsibility of the international community at large.[36]

General Assembly resolutions are not the most consistent of sources from which to extract the views of states. Those adopted in the period under review are significant for the extent to which the notion of asylum is left unexplained and unexplored. There is, as it were, implicit recognition of the plight of the refugee as a state of exception, in which no assumptions can be made as to the appropriateness of any particular solution. Thus, in the case of refugees in European camps in the 1950s, the international community acknowledged that resettlement or aid with local integration were the most suitable courses.[37] In the case of refugees from Algeria in Morocco and Tunisia fleeing the struggle for independence, the temporary nature of the problem was recognized; living conditions required improvement until the refugees were able to return home.[38] A similar anticipation was expressed in regard to Angolan refugees in the Congo,[39] and generally in regard to refugees in Africa.[40] Although no *a priori* assumptions may be possible as to the appropriateness of particular solutions, it is nevertheless evident that in the hierarchy of voluntary repatriation, local integration, and resettlement in third countries, the first mentioned is seen as the most desirable. Voluntary repatriation puts an end to the situation of exception; asylum is a link in

[34] See GA Res. 1166(XII), 26 Nov. 1957, para. 2, reaffirming the basic approach set out in para. 1 of the UNHCR Statute; also GA Res. 1285(XIII) of 5 Dec. 1958, on special efforts to be made in the context of World Refugee Year.

[35] See GA Res. 832(IX) of 21 Oct. 1954, '*Considering* that, while the ultimate responsibility for ... refugees ... falls in fact upon the countries of residence, certain of these countries have to face particularly heavy burdens as a result of their geographical situation, and some complementary aid has been shown to be necessary ...'

[36] See GA Res. 1167(XII) of 26 Nov. 1957, recognizing the heavy burden placed on the government of Hong Kong by the massive influx of Chinese refugees, but noting that the problem is such 'as to be of concern to the international community'.

[37] See GA Res. 538(VI), of 2 Feb. 1952, 638(VII), 20 Dec. 1952; 639(VII) of the same date, 832(IX), 21 Oct. 1954, 1166(XII), 26 Nov. 1957, 1284(XIII), of 5 Dec. 1958, 1388(XIV), 20 Nov. 1959. Note also GA Res. 1039(XI) of 23 Jan. 1957, 1129(XI), 21 Nov. 1956, and 1006(ES-II), 9 Nov. 1956 on the situation of Hungarian refugees 'obliged ... to seek asylum in neighbouring countries'.

[38] See GA Res. 1500(XV), 5 Dec. 1960, and 1672(XVI), 18 Dec. 1961.

[39] See GA Res. 1671(XVI) of 18 Dec. 1961, noting efforts to provide immediate assistance and to help the refugees become self-supporting until they can return home; also recognizing that the needs of the refugees may not be separable from those of the local population.

[40] See GA Res. 2040(XX), 7 Dec. 1965.

the chain between the refugees' flight and re-establishment in their old communities.

## 3. The decade of drafts, 1971-80, and after

The 1970s were characterized by wide ranging activity. Some progress could be noted on the level of individual protection and certain major refugee problems were resolved through repatriation and resettlement, but hopes and expectations centring on asylum were dashed by the failure of the 1977 United Nations conference. Efforts to promote a convention and states' responses to refugee crises show, on the one hand, continuing reluctance to do more than recognize the humanitarian aspects of refugees in need; and, on the other hand, increasing recognition of the normative quality of the principle of *non-refoulement* and of the responsibility of the international community to find solutions. Contemporaneous with these developments, some states began to enquire into the root causes of refugee problems, particularly those producing a massive exodus of refugees.[41]

Discussions in the UN Sixth Committee shortly before adoption of the 1967 Declaration on Territorial Asylum revealed a degree of expectation that that instrument would be the precursor to a universal convention.[42] The first draft was in fact proposed, not by the International Law Commission (as General Assembly resolutions might have anticipated) but by a group of experts meeting in 1971 and 1972 under the auspices of the Carnegie Endowment for International Peace, in consultation with UNHCR. Article I of their text proposed that contracting states 'acting in an international and humanitarian spirit, *shall use [their] best endeavours to grant asylum* in [their] territory, which ... includes permission to remain in that territory'.[43] The draft was discussed in the Third Committee later in 1972, where it was decided that the High Commissioner should consult Governments, with a view to the eventual convening of an international conference.[44] The

---

[41] See further below, ch. IX, s. 4.

[42] See UN doc. A/C.6/SR. 983-9, *passim*; doc. A/6912, report of the Sixth Committee, paras. 64-5; also the Preamble to the 1967 Declaration, adopted by GA Res. 2312(XXII), 14 Dec. 1967.

[43] UN doc. A/8712, appx., annexe 1. This and other drafts are collected in Grahl-Madsen, *Territorial Asylum* (1980) annexes KK *et seq.*

[44] UN doc. A/C.3/SR.1956 and 1957, paras. 25, 32.

opinions of Governments were canvassed[45] and the General Assembly decided that the text should be reviewed.[46] The UN Group of Experts' revision indicated continuing adherence to the discretionary aspect of asylum practice.[47] Article I proposed that 'Each Contracting State, *acting in the exercise of its sovereign rights, shall use its best endeavours* in a humanitarian spirit to grant asylum in its territory ...'.[48] The same 'best endeavours' formula was again introduced in Article 3 where, following a statement of the principle of *non-refoulement* on behalf of those 'in the territory of a contracting State', it operated to reduce the level of obligation in relation to rejection at the frontier from that previously adopted in both the 1967 Declaration and the 1969 OAU Convention.[49] Acting on the Group of Experts' report, the General Assembly requested the Secretary-General, in consultation with the High Commissioner, to convene a conference on territorial asylum in early 1977.[50]

Dissatisfaction with much of the proposed texts inspired a working group of non-governmental organizations to suggest an alternative version,[51] the asylum provisions of which were largely supported by consensus at a Nansen Symposium held in 1976.[52] In both cases, the proposals favoured an obligation to grant asylum, subject to certain exceptions; inclusion of the notion of non-rejection at the frontier within the principle of *non-refoulement*; and general recognition of the principle of provisional admission as a minimum requirement.

[45] UN doc. A(9612/Add.3, annexe (1974). Of 91 states which made known their views, 76 favoured elaboration of a convention on territorial asylum. See also doc. A/C.3/SR. 2098-2101 and 2103, paras. 44-60 (1974).

[46] GA Res. 3272(XXIX), 9 Jan. 1975.

[47] UN doc. A/10177 and Corr. 1 (1975); Grahl-Madsen, *Territorial Asylum,* annexe RR. See also doc. A/C.3/SR.2161-4.

[48] Cf. the draft prepared by the International Law Association at its 55th Conference in 1972, under which states would 'undertake to grant refuge in their territories to all those who are seeking asylum ...', save where danger to the security of the country or to the safety and welfare of the community was apprehended (art. 1(b)). Art. 3 of this draft, however, proposed that 'A grant of asylum does not imply any right of permanent immigration'. ILA, report of 55th Session, (1972); text also in Grahl-Madsen, *Territorial Asylum,* annexe LL.

[49] Art. 4 did provide for provisional admission pending consideration of a request for asylum, but meeting the qualifications still gave no entitlement to the grant of asylum.

[50] GA Res. 3456(XXX), 9 Dec. 1975.

[51] Text in Grahl-Madsen, *Territorial Asylum,* annexe TT.

[52] *Towards an Asylum Convention,* report of the Nansen Symposium (1977); text of draft convention proposed by Grahl-Madsen and Melander also in Grahl-Madsen, *Territorial Asylum,* annexe UU.

The 1977 United Nations Conference on Territorial Asylum was an abject failure, with close voting on major issues indicative of the divisions between states.[53] One article only, that on asylum, was considered by the drafting committee, which reduced the 'best endeavours' formula of the Group of Experts draft to that of 'shall endeavour ... to grant asylum'.[54] On the other hand, non-rejection at the frontier was proposed for inclusion overall within the principle of *non-refoulement*, though the principle was subject generally to qualifications reflecting states' preoccupation with numbers and security. Recognizing that little of substance had been achieved, the Conference at its final session recommended that the General Assembly consider is reconvening at a suitable time.[55] Later that year, however, the Third Committee declined to submit any formal proposal to that effect, and it was thought more appropriate that the High Commissioner continue consultations with governments.[56] At the time of writing, no further progress towards reconvening the Conference had been noted.

The overall experience must be assessed not only on its own terms, but in the light also of the events and responses of the period. The years since 1970 have been remarkable for the magnitude and frequency of refugee crises and for the increasing attention paid to them within international organizations. With the events leading to the partition of Pakistan in 1971-2, India underwent a massive influx of refugees, principally from East Bengal. By December 1971, their number was estimated at some 10 million, and the only possible solution was voluntary repatriation. The Indian Government insisted on a maximum stay of six months, the General Assembly endorsed repatriation,[57] and by February 1972 over ninety per cent of the refugees had returned to the newly independent state of Bangladesh. That political development and the acceptance by all parties concerned of the principle of voluntary repatriation, were clearly the controlling conditions for the ultimate solution.

Similar factors were present in refugee problems resulting from the struggle for liberation from colonial rule, particularly in Africa.

---

[53] See generally, Grahl-Madsen, *Territorial Asylum*; Weis, 'The Draft Convention on Territorial Asylum' 50 *BYIL* 176 (1979).

[54] For full text of the articles considered by the Committee of the Whole and by the Drafting Committee, see below, annexe VII.

[55] See report of the conference: UN doc. A/CONF.78/12, para. 25; also report of the UNHCR to ECOSOC: doc. E/5987, paras. 10-16 (June 1977).

[56] UN doc. A/C.3/32/SR.49, paras. 16-19 (Nov. 1977).

[57] GA Res. 2790(XXVI), 6 Dec. 1971.

The provisional nature of such refugee problems was acknowledged in anticipation of repatriation on independence, with, where appropriate, international assistance in rehabilitation being given to those returning.[58] Where such solutions are more remote in time, attention has focused on the need for the international community to relieve the pressure borne by countries of first refuge. Thus, in 1976, the General Assembly formally recognized the heavy burden placed in Botswana, Lesotho, and Swaziland by the influx after Soweto of large numbers of South African student refugees.[59] In succeeding years, it has urged other governments to assist by providing opportunities for settlement, education, and vocational training.[60] Where the attainment of the political conditions essential to voluntary repatriation is uncertain, interim and long-term self-sufficiency programmes may be called for. African states generally have been prepared in these situations to allow refugees to remain, and internationally funded schemes have contributed to a degree of local integration.[61] Where repatriation is altogether excluded, the local integration process is often completed by naturalization.

In Latin America, in the period under review, solutions to refugee problems were more problematic. Following the *coup d'état* in Chile in 1973, large numbers of Chileans and foreign refugees previously resident there fled to neighbouring countries. Some states, for example, Peru, indicated that they were only prepared to allow refugees a transit facility. In Argentina, a certain proportion was allowed to remain, but resettlement was demanded of others and the personal security of many was so severely threatened by the activities of so-called paramilitary groups that a solution beyond the region was urgently called for. As a result of numerous appeals by UNHCR, some 14,000 refugees were resettled by other countries in the period 1973-80.[62]

In Asia, apart from limited exceptions, opportunities for voluntary repatriation or local integration in countries of first refuge

---

[58] See GA Res. 3271(XXIX), 10 Dec. 1974.

[59] See GA Res. 31/126, 16 Dec. 1976.

[60] See GA Res. 32/70, 8 Dec. 1977, 32/119, 16 Dec. 1977, 33/164, 20 Dec. 1978; 34/174, 17 Dec. 1979; 35/184, 15 Dec. 1980; 36/170, 16 Dec. 1981.

[61] Details of various programmes may be found in UNHCR reports on assistance activities, submitted each year to the Executive Committee of the High Commissioner's Programme.

[62] See 'Human Rights, War and Mass Exodus', *Transnational Perspectives* (1982) 8-9.

have been minimal.[63] Even temporary admission pending other solutions was difficult to obtain and in May 1975 Singapore refused to admit some 8,000 Vietnamese who arrived in sixty ships.[64] Subsequently, even the disembarkation of refugees rescued at sea became problematic notwithstanding resettlement guarantees by flag or other states. In the years after 1975, the Indo-Chinese refugee problem developed into one of the largest and most intractable. Over one million people fled Kampuchea, Laos, and Vietnam, and almost without exception the countries of first refuge declined to allow refugees to settle locally.[65] Their repeated calls for more assistance were interspersed with threatened and actual forcible action against asylum-seekers.[66] The international community finally responded with increased financial aid and more resettlement offers, while calling upon receiving countries to respect the principles of asylum and *non-refoulement*.[67] Following a major international conference in July 1979, the resettlement rate rose dramatically. Vietnam announced efforts to curb illegal departures and declared that it would co-operate with UNHCR in expanding and implementing a programme for 'orderly depar-

---

[63] The principal exception as regards voluntary repatriation was the successful return of Burmese Moslem refugees from Bangladesh in 1978-9; UN doc. A/AC.96/564, paras. 392 ff. In 1981, there were also small scale returns of Laotian refugees from Thailand: UN doc. A/AC.96/594, para. 552, while in 1980, some 7,000 Khmers repatriated to Kampuchea, also from Thailand. The Kampuchean authorities, their Vietnamese allies, and a number of independent observers considered that most of those returning were active Khmer Rouge forces, which made further repatriation operations difficult. Discussions between UNHCR, Thailand, Kampuchea, and Vietnam continued in 1981 and 1982. As regards local integration, the principal exception was the settlement of some 267,000 refugees who entered the People's Republic of China from Vietnam in 1979: UN doc. A/AC.96/594, paras. 505 ff. Malaysia also admitted some 90,000 refugees from the southern Philippines during 1979/80: ibid., paras. 582 ff.

[64] The asylum-seekers eventually made their way to the US territory of Guam.

[65] Indonesia, Malaysia, the Philippines, Singapore, and Thailand each adduced various objections to local integration, including racial, religious, cultural, financial, and security grounds. The exceptions were Australia, which was prepared to grant asylum to those arriving directly who were recognized as refugees by the Determination of Refugee Status Committee (the small number of direct arrivals—just over 2,000 from 1975-81—was clearly an important factor in this policy); Hong Kong, which granted residence to some 14,500 Vietnamese, though calling on the international community to resettle many thousands of others; and the People's Republic of China (above, n. 63).

[66] Thus, Malaysia in Jan. and Mar. 1979 announced it would permit no more landings; Thailand in May 1979 ordered an (ineffective) blockade of its coast and later forcibly repatriated some 40,000 Kampucheans. In June of that year Indonesia announced it could support no more and Malaysia threatened to tow boats out to sea and to shoot asylum-seekers on sight. The threat to shoot was subsequently withdrawn, but numerous boats were turned away or towed out to sea, with resulting loss of life. See generally, Grant, *The Boat People* (1980); Wain, *The Refused: The Agony of the Indochina Refugee* (1982).

[67] GA Res. 33/26, 29 Nov. 1978.

tures';[68] and the first steps were taken towards establishing refugee processing centres in Indonesia and the Philippines.[69] First refuge countries modified their threats of forcible measures against asylum-seekers. Thereafter, with a few exceptions, states in the region continued to allow admission on a temporary basis pending a solution elsewhere, but their practice must be seen in the context of other states preparedness to shoulder financial and resettlement costs.

By contrast, Pakistan in this period was much more ready to admit refugees, and by 31 August 1982 had accepted over 2½ million from Afghanistan. Resettlement was recognized as inappropriate, while the weight of numbers likewise militated against long-term local integration, despite common aspects of language and culture. The expectation was that voluntary repatriation would be the eventual solution, but a realistic appreciation of political realities required that provision be made for accommodation and for measures to assist the refugees to attain a degree of self-sufficiency.[70]

## 4. *Non-refoulement* and asylum in cases of mass influx

Recent large-scale population movements have been the source of many of the most intractable problems affecting refugees. In some cases, ethnic similarities encouraged reception and hospitality, but where the flow was cross-cultural, serious political problems arose, in addition to the usual logistical and economic ones. Assistance to refugees can also be the source of difficulty, as where the local, often displaced, population perceives refugees receiving benefits which have hitherto been denied to them.

---

[68] Report of the Secretary-General on the Meeting on Refugees and Displaced Persons in South East Asia, Geneva, 20-1 July 1979, and subsequent developments: UN doc. A/34/627. In Jan. 1979, Vietnam announced that it would permit the emigration of those who wished to leave, subject to certain exceptions. UNHCR missions to Vietnam in Mar. and May of that year resulted in a Memorandum of Understanding whereby the legal emigration of family reunion and 'other humanitarian cases' was to be facilitated.

[69] See UN docs. A/AC.96/577, paras. 541, 628-31; A/AC.96/594; paras. 548-9, 632. In proposing such centres in Dec. 1978, the ASEAN states had insisted on guarantees that they would face 'no residual problem'. In Bangkok in Feb. 1979, ASEAN foreign Ministers announced the terms for the centres: refugees would be admitted only on the basis of firm commitments from third countries that they would be resettled within a reasonable time; the country providing the site would be entitled to limit numbers, would retain sovereignty, administrative control and responsibility for security, and should not bear the cost.

[70] See UN doc. A/AC.96/594, paras. 595 ff.

The 1951 Convention was drawn up very much with the individual asylum-seeker in mind, and yet it contains no provision on admission. Article 31 gives some protection to refugees entering illegally, but at the same time acknowledges that no refugee can expect, as a matter of right, to regularize his or her stay in the state of first refuge. The refugee unable to secure entry to another state, denied local settlement and yet benefitting from *non-refoulement* thus falls into limbo. This indeed was the condition of many refugees in European camps in the 1950s and of others in South East Asia and Africa in the 1970s and the 1980s. The principle of *non-refoulement* has developed to include non-rejection at the frontier, thus promoting admission, but there has been no corresponding development with regard to the concept of asylum, understood in the sense of a duty upon states to accord a lasting solution. *Non-refoulement* has to that extent become divorced from the notion of asylum, and this has been the price demanded by states in otherwise accepting the obligation to admit to their territories large numbers of refugees.

Traditional notions of asylum are still relevant to an understanding of the past and to the future promotion of the rights of the individual in the municipal laws of states, but it is doubtful whether these notions are consistent or appropriate enough for application to the political and humanitarian problems of today. This was especially apparent in the discussion in the Executive Committee of the notion of temporary refuge in 1980 and 1981. Temporary refuge, it was claimed, would erode present practices on asylum and undermine the principle of *non-refoulement*; it was a 'new concept', and states had no need of it. In fact, the practice of temporary refuge, of admission and protection (i.e. asylum) on a temporary basis has a long history, even if the attempt at conceptualization is relatively recent.

It is important, first, to appreciate the extent to which finding durable solutions to refugee problems has long been acknowledged as the responsibility of the international community. Thus, in the Preamble to the 1951 Convention the parties noted expressly 'that the grant of asylum may place unduly heavy burdens on certain countries', and that satisfactory solutions to problems international in scope depend upon international co-operation. These sentiments were repeated in Recommendation D of the Final Act, calling upon governments to continue to receive refugees and to act in concert that such refugees 'may find asylum and the possibility of resettlement'. In this context, 'asylum' is used broadly, to mean the protection given by the state of first refuge, which may be continued or which may be taken over by another state in the spirit of international co-operation. Such an approach well describes the situation in Europe in the 1950s. The thousands who fled Hungary in 1956, for example, were granted what turned out to be relatively temporary 'asylum' in Austria and Yugoslavia, prior to onward movement (some 170,000 being resettled within eighteen months). It was evident that generous admission policies were dependent on, if not conditioned by, generous resettlement policies maintained by other countries. That situation prevails to this day, with Australia, Canada, and the United States running resettlement programmes for East European asylum-seekers admitted to West European countries, while the precise legal status of refugees prior to resettlement varies from country to country.

The idea of 'temporary' or 'provisional' asylum or admission, or residence pending movement of another country has also figured in a number of international instruments, as an alternative to *refoulement*.[71] Some provisions encompass the individual who is considered a security or equally serious threat to the state of refuge; others cover groups of persons who, by reason of their numbers, are thereby considered a danger to the community of the state. There is nevertheless not only a quantitative, but also a qualitative difference between the two types of case. In that of the individual, recognition of refugee status may properly give rise to a presumption that asylum in the sense of a local, lasting solution will be forthcoming. As a matter of principle, that presumption should only be rebutted by evidence clearly indicating the personal unacceptability of the refugee. In the case of the mass influx, however, formal determination of status may be impracticable in view of the numbers or the absence of appropriate machinery; or impossible in strict terms owing to the mixed motives of those fleeing, for example, from a combination of civil disorder, hostilities, and famine. In addition, any presumption that a local solution will be forthcoming may be fully rebutted by evidence of cross-cultural, ethnic, or religious conflict.

---

[71] Cf. the various formulations in art. III(4), principles concerning treatment of refugees, adopted by the Asian-African Legal Consultative Committee, 8th Session, Bangkok, 1966, cited in Jahn, in 27 *Zeitschrift für ausländisches öffentliches Recht und Völkerrecht*, 122 (1967); art. 3(3), 1967 Declaration on Territorial Asylum; art. 11(5), 1969 OAU Convention; para. 3, Council of Europe Res. 14(1967) on Asylum to Persons in Danger of Persecution; art. 3(3), adopted by the Committee of the Whole of the 1977 United Nations Conference on Territorial Asylum.

In searching for solutions, it will be important to distinguish between refugees in the strict sense who have a well-founded fear of persecution, and refugees in the broader sense, who may be motivated by a combination of factors. Causes cannot be ignored; they condition the protection which is required in the short and medium term and bear on the solutions which are possible. The immediate need, however, is for admission to a state of refuge. In December 1978, summing up the results of a consultative meeting on refugees and displaced persons in South East Asia, the High Commissioner acknowledged that there could be no solutions unless Governments granted at least temporary asylum. The consultations had noted, as a corollary, that facilities in receiving countries were already overloaded, 'and that for such countries temporary asylum depended on commitments for resettlement in third countries and the avoidance of residual problems in the area'.[72]

At its 1979 Session, the Executive Committee stressed the humanitarian obligation of coastal states 'to allow vessels in distress to seek haven in their waters and to grant asylum, or at least temporary refuge' to those on board seeking it.[73] Similarly, it noted that in 'cases of large-scale influx, persons seeking asylum should always receive at least temporary refuge' and that states 'faced with a large-scale influx, should as necessary and at the request of the State concerned receive immediate assistance from other States in accordance with the principle of equitable burden-sharing'.[74] General discussion of the notion of temporary refuge at that session revealed divergent views, with some states apprehensive lest it upset established principles.[75] In 1980, as the result of an Australian initiative, the Executive Committee requested the High Commissioner to convene a group of experts 'to examine

[72] UN doc. A/AC.96/549, para. 53.3(b) (28th Session, 1977); recalling this conclusion at its 29th Session, the Executive Committee noted that refugees 'still encountered difficulties in obtaining permanent or even temporary *asylum*': UN doc. A/AC.96/559, para. 68.1(d) (emphasis supplied). The equation of those seeking asylum or refuge with those in fact entitled to protection begs many questions; it seems not to have been intended.

[73] UN doc. A/AC.96/572, para. 72(2) (c).

[74] Ibid., para. 72(2) (f). The Committee also urgently appealed to Governments 'to grant at least temporary *asylum* to those seeking refuge pending alternative solutions being found for them': ibid., para. 43C(c) (emphasis supplied).

[75] UN doc. A/AC.96/SR.309, paras. 22-3, 26, 33, 43-4, 59, 60. The Australian representative had earlier expressed the view that solidarity and assistance would enable states of first asylum or refuge to meet fundamental humanitarian obligations; he also described *non-refoulement* as having a normative character independent of international instruments: ibid., paras. 18-19.

temporary refuge in all its aspects within the framework of the problems raised by large-scale influx.'[76] Once again, fears were expressed that 'codification' of the temporary refuge practice might endanger basic principles of protection,[77] but others, while maintaining the peremptory character of *non-refoulement*, considered there were positive aspects to temporary refuge. Columbia, for example, noted that while durable refuge was obviously the better solution, strengthening the principles governing temporary refuge would also strengthen the principle of *non-refoulement*.[78]

The Group of Experts on Temporary Refuge in Situations of Large-Scale Influx met in Geneva in April 1981. The Australian expert, who had contributed a working paper, referred to many refugee situations which clearly illustrated that receiving states were often not in a position to offer permanent settlement at the time of admission. It was essential, however, to establish basic minimum standards for the protection of refugees, and also principles for the attainment of satisfactory durable solutions. The debate and conclusions were inconclusive and remarkable chiefly for the imprecise and inconsistent use of terminology, as well as for the adherence of many participants to a methodology appropriate to the individual asylum-seeker but not necessarily to the situation of mass influx. 'Asylum' itself, though often invoked, was never defined in the report; it was recognized that there might be asylum on a permanent basis and asylum on a temporary basis, but the consequences of that distinction were not pursued. It was said that asylum was not necessarily linked to the grant of a durable solution; that the grant of asylum was the prerogative of states, but that where life was in danger, states 'should give at least temporary asylum'.[79]

The report of the Group of Experts does contain general but helpful conclusions on international solidarity, burden-sharing and minimum standards of treatment; these were endorsed by the Executive Committee at its 32nd Session in October 1981 in its conclusions on protection in situations of large-scale influx. On

[76] UN doc. A/AC.96/588, para. 48(4) (e).
[77] UN doc. A/AC.96/SR.322, paras. 24, 34, 46, and 48.
[78] Ibid., para. 41.
[79] One expert even claimed, though without adducing evidence in support, that it was 'generally recognized that the country of asylum [*sic*] should be obliged to regularise the situation of an asylum-seeker if, after a certain period, a durable solution was not forthcoming': UN doc. EC/SCP/16, para. 21. While this sentiment may well be appropriate to the case of the individual asylum-seeker, recent examples show it is hardly a candidate for the status of general principle.

the whole, the Committee preferred the language of admission to that of asylum as used by the Group of Experts:

1. In situations of large-scale influx, asylum-seekers should be admitted to the State in which they first seek refuge and if that State is unable to admit them on a durable basis, it should always admit them at least on a temporary basis and provide them with protection according to the principles set out below. They should be admitted without any discrimination as to race, religion, political opinion, nationality, country of origin or physical incapacity.

2. In all cases the fundamental principle of *non-refoulement*—including non-rejection at the frontier—must be scrupulously observed.[80]

The references to 'asylum-seekers' in this context must be interpreted as presupposing refugee status (in the broad sense) as the necessary condition of entitlement, if the relevant principles and concepts are not to lose all meaning. Admission on a temporary basis, especially in situations of large-scale influx, remains an inescapable fact of life, and is practised by states throughout the world. Conceptualization of the practice may none the less offer significant practical advantages in securing the entry of large groups, in improving their protection, and in working towards durable solutions.

The political and legal reality is that states generally have not undertaken, and foreseeably will not undertake, an obligation to grant asylum in the sense of a lasting solution. The peremptory norm of *non-refoulement* secures admission and, in the individual case, may further raise the presumption that a local durable solution will be forthcoming. In the case of large-scale movements, however, no such presumption is raised. In attaining its present universal and peremptory character, *non-refoulement* has cut itself off from asylum in the sense of a lasting solution. *Non-refoulement* through time is none the less the core element both promoting admission and simultaneously emphasizing the responsibility of the international community at large in finding the solutions to large-scale problems.[81] As recent experience shows, these will vary in complexity, duration, and solvability. In the case of Indo-China, cultural and political factors ruled out repatriation and local integration; *non-refoulement* through time allowed eventual resettlement. In the case of Afghan refugees, resettlement was

---

[80] UN doc. A/AC.96/601, para. 57(2)II,A.

[81] Thus in admitting large numbers of persons of concern to the international community and in scrupulously observing *non-refoulement*, the state of first admission can be seen as acting on behalf of the international community.

considered inappropriate and repatriation hoped for, but remote; *non-refoulement* through time has facilitated international aid and assistance and the establishment of a degree of interim self-sufficiency. In neither case could the condition of temporary refuge be considered a satisfactory durable solution in itself; that was an objective which remained to be pursued.

The concept of temporary refuge as the practical consequence of *non-refoulement* through time provides, first, the necessary theoretical nexus between the admission of refugees and the attainment of a lasting solution. It establishes, *a priori,* no hierarchy in the field of solutions, but allows a pragmatic yet principled approach to the idiosyncracies of each situation. So, for example, it does not rule out the eventual local integration of all or a proportion of a mass influx in the state of first refuge, acting in concert with others and pursuant to principles of international solidarity and equitable burden-sharing.[82] Secondly, the concept provides a platform upon which to build principles of protection for refugees pending a durable solution, whereby minimum rights and standards of treatment may be secured.

The practice of temporary refuge is not new, though the terminology may be. Far from undermining established principles, the use of the word 'refuge' offers substantial advantages over any comparable use of the word 'asylum' in situations of mass influx. The latter is undefined; it can be used broadly to signify protection of refugees, or it can be used in the narrow sense of a durable or permanent solution, involving residence and lasting protection against the exercise of jurisdiction by the state of origin. A receiving state called upon to grant 'asylum' to large numbers may well demur; admission is more likely to be facilitated by reference to the peremptory norm of *non-refoulement* and to its manifestation in the dynamic sense, through time, pending arrangements for whatever solution is appropriate to the particular problem. The peremptory character of *non-refoulement* makes it independent of principles of solidarity and burden-sharing, but these cannot be ignored in a society of inter-dependent states. In situations of large-scale influx, protection cannot cease with the fact of admission; on the contrary, it must proceed in full knowledge of the political and practical consequences which result from a state abiding by *non-refoulement*.

---

[82] These principles may find expression not just in offers of resettlement, but also in the provision of financial and material assistance, and moral and political support.

The concept of temporary refuge, in the context of large-scale influx, thus stands paradoxically as both the link and the line between the peremptory, normative aspects of *non-refoulement* and the continuing discretionary aspect of a state's right in the matter of asylum as a permanent or lasting solution.

## 5. Conclusions

The plight of the refugee in search of asylum remained a dominant theme in the late 1970s and early 1980s, as is evident from repeated appeals of the Executive Committee, the General Assembly, inter-governmental organizations and other concerned bodies.[83] State practice, however, permits only one conclusion: the individual still has no right to be granted asylum. The right appertains to states and the correlative duty, if any, is that which obliges other states to respect the grant of asylum, as any other exercise of territorial jurisdiction. The right itself is in the form of a discretionary power. The state has discretion whether to exercise its right, as to whom it will favour, as to the form and content of the asylum to be granted. Save in so far as treaty or other rules confine its discretion, for example, by requiring the extradition of war criminals, the state remains free to grant asylum to refugees as defined by international law or to any other person or group it deems fit. It is likewise free to prescribe the conditions under which asylum is to be enjoyed. It may thus accord the refugee the right to permanent or temporary residence, it may permit or decline the right to work, or confine refugees to camps, dependent on international assistance pending some future solution, such as repatriation or re-settlement.

To pursue an ideal of asylum in the sense of an obligation imposed on states to accord lasting solutions, with or without a correlative right of the individual, is currently a vain task. Asylum remains an institution which operates between subjects of international law. In an era of mass exodus, of actual or perceived threats to national security, states are not prepared to accept an obligation without determinable content or dimension. Recent

---

[83] See, for example, report of the 30th Session (1979), UN doc. A/AC.96/522, paras. 43C(c), 72(1) (c), 72(2); report of the 31st Session (1980), UN doc. A/AC.96/588, para. 48(4); GA Res. 34/60, 29 Nov. 1979, 35/41, 25 Nov. 1980, 36/125, 14 Dec. 1981; Manila Declaration adopted by the Round Table of Asian Experts on International Protection of Refugees and Displaced Persons, 14-18 Apr. 1980: UN doc. A/AC. 96/INF.162.

experience shows that efforts to secure agreement on such a divisive issue are more likely to produce equivocation, qualification, and exception, that can tend only to dilute the rules and principles already established in state practice.[84] But asylum in the sense of a lasting solution, though the preferred sense, represents one aspect only. State practice is not solely concerned with permanent protection, and the concept of asylum in its broad sense cannot be analysed adequately apart from the normative principle of *non-refoulement*. In so far as states *are* obliged to protect refugees, they are obliged to abide by *non-refoulement* through time. That time is not and cannot be determined by any principle of international law, but likewise the duty to accord *non-refoulement* through time cannot be separated in practice from that other complex duty which recognizes the responsibility of states at large in finding durable solutions.[85]

The duty not to return refugees to persecution or to a situation of danger to life or limb is owed to the international community of states, as represented by UNHCR. The international community is likewise entitled to require of individual states, not only that they accord to refugees the benefit of *non-refoulement* through time, but also the opportunity of finding a lasting solution to their plight. The degree of protection required is that commensurate with the occasion, and given the present level of development of international law, certain exceptions in favour of the state remain. The area continues to be governed by discretion, rather than duty, but analysis reveals that discretion to be not only confined by principle, but also structured in the light of other legally relevant considerations, including national security, international solidarity, burden-sharing, and the right of functional protection enjoyed by UNHCR.

Freedom to grant or to refuse permanent asylum remains, but save in exceptional circumstances, states do not enjoy the right to return refugees to persecution or any situation of personal danger. Protection against the immediate eventuality is the responsibility of the country of first refuge. In so far as a state is required to grant that protection, the minimum content of which is *non-*

---

[84] This is not to say that promotion of an individual's right to asylum may not have some future; merely that progress is more likely to be achieved through the development of regional instruments and the promotion of effective municipal laws, particularly with a view to maintaining and protecting the integrity of the principle of *non-refoulement*.

[85] International solidarity and equitable burden-sharing are admittedly still principles lacking precision.

*refoulement* through time, it is required also to treat the refugee in accordance with such standards as will permit an appropriate solution, whether voluntary repatriation, local integration, or resettlement in another country. There was some support in the past for the overall primary responsibility in fact falling on the first country of refuge,[86] but the experience of South East Asia, where so many states declined to allow refugees to remain within their borders, has served to emphasize the international dimension to burden-sharing.

[86] Cf. GA Res. 832(IX), 21 Oct. 1954, and 1166(XII), 26 Nov. 1957.

# PART THREE

PROTECTION

## Chapter VI

# INTERNATIONAL PROTECTION

The lack or denial of protection is a principal feature of refugee character, and it is for international law, in turn, to substitute its own protection for that which the country of origin cannot or will not provide. *Non-refoulement* is the foundation-stone of international protection, and in this and the following chapter the content of that protection is examined in more detail, with attention specifically to international institutions, treaties, and the incorporation of international standards in municipal law.

## 1. International institutions

The first intergovernmental arrangements on behalf of refugees were contemporaneous with the establishment of various institutions charged with their implementation.[1] Thus, in June 1921 the Council of the League of Nations decided to appoint a High Commissioner for Russian Refugees, naming Dr Fridtjof Nansen to the post some two months later.[2] The tasks of the High Commissioner included defining the legal status of refugees; organizing their repatriation or allocation to potential resettlement countries and finding employment; and undertaking relief work, with the aid of philanthropic societies.[3] In 1924, the mandate of the High Commissioner was extended to Armenian refugees, and in 1929 to 'other categories of refugees', including Assyrians, Assyro-Chaldeans, Syrians, and Kurdish and Turkish refugees. Under a 1928 arrangement,[4] it was recommended that the services normally rendered to nationals abroad by consular authorities should be discharged on behalf of refugees by representatives of the High

---

[1] For further information and detail on the inter-war years, see Simpson, *The Refugee Problem* (1939); Reale, 'Le problème des passeports' 50 Hague *Recueil* (1934-IV) 89; *A Study of Statelessness* (1949): UN doc. E/1112 and Add. 1, 34-8.

[2] See generally Reynolds, *Nansen* (1932, rev. ed. 1949).

[3] Annexe 224, minutes of the 13th Session of the Council of the League of Nations, Geneva, 17-28 June 1921; cited by Weis, 'The International Protection of Refugees' 48 *AJIL* 193-221, 207-8 (1954).

[4] Arrangement relating to the legal status of Russian and Armenian refugees, 30 June 1928: 89 LNTS no. 2005. It came into force between 10 states.

Commissioner. Unless within the exclusive competence of national authorities, such services were to include: certifying the identity and position of refugees; certifying their family position and civil status, in so far as that was based on documents issued or action taken in the refugees' country of origin; testifying to the regularity, validity, and conformity with the previous law of their country of origin of documents issued in that country; certifying the signature of refugees and copies and translations of documents drawn up in their own language; testifying before the authorities of the country to the good character and conduct of individual refugees, their previous record, professional qualifications, and university or academic standing; and recommending individual refugees to the competent authorities with a view to obtaining visas, residence permits, admission to schools, libraries, etc.[5] In order to give legal effect to these recommendations two states, France and Belgium, concluded an agreement authorizing the High Commissioner's representatives to issue the documents in question.[6]

In the period 1923-9, certain 'technical services' principally relating to assistance, were entrusted to the International Labour Organization, leaving the High Commissioner responsible for the political and legal protection of refugees. With Nansen's death in 1930, the Assembly of the League of Nations established the Nansen Office to undertake humanitarian activities on behalf of refugees, and entrusted protection to the Secretary-General. A succession of other bodies followed: first, the High Commissioner's Office for Refugees Coming from Germany was established in 1933;[7] then, in 1938, came the High Commissioner's office for all refugees, charged with providing political and legal protection, superintending the entry into force of the relevant conventions, co-ordinating humanitarian assistance, and assisting governments and private organizations in their efforts to promote emigration and permanent settlement.[8] Finally, in this period, as a result of

[5] Ibid. Res. (1). Other resolutions made recommendations, *inter alia*, in respect of choice of law in matters of marriage and divorce; that refugees not be denied certain rights and privileges on the basis of lack of reciprocity; that they be exempt from the *cautio judicatum solvi*; that they be accorded national treatment in matters of taxation.

[6] Agreement concerning the functions of the representatives of the League of Nations High Commissioner for Refugees: 93 LNTS no. 2126. In France, this function was taken over by the IRO (agreement cited by Weis, 'Legal Aspects of the Convention of 28 July 1951 relating to the Status of Refugees' 30 *BYIL* 478-89, 484 (1953), and subsequently by the *Office français de protection des réfugiés et apatrides* (*OFPRA*): *loi no.* 52-893 of 25 July 1952, art. 4; *décret no.* 53-377 of 2 May 1953, art. 5.

[7] Originally, this office was set up outside the League, owing to German Government opposition.

[8] League of Nations *OJ* Special Supplement no. 189, (1938) 86.

the thirty-two nation Evian Conference which met in July 1938 on the initiative of the United States of America, the Intergovernmental Committee on Refugees was established.[9]

During the Second World War, the United Nations Relief and Rehabilitation Administration (UNRRA) was set up to assist and eventually repatriate those displaced by the conflict, but it had no competence specifically with regard to refugees. In 1946, however, the United Nations recognized the fundamental principle that no refugees with valid objections to returning to their countries of origin should be compelled to do so,[10] and later that year it created the International Refugee Organization (IRO) and its preparatory commission (PCIRO).[11] The IRO operated until 28 February 1952,[12] its functions being defined in its constitution to include: repatriation; identification; registration and classification; care and assistance; legal and political protection; and transport, re-settlement, and re-establishment of persons of concern to the Organization.[13] The IRO existed to deal with the aftermath of the Second World War and the immediate consequences of political change. Even during its lifetime, the United Nations General Assembly acknowledged the need for a successor organization, deciding in 1949 to establish a High Commissioner's Office for Refugees.[14]

## (1) THE OFFICE OF THE UNITED NATIONS HIGH COMMISSIONER FOR REFUGEES (UNHCR)

At its 1950 session, the General Assembly formally adopted the Statute of UNHCR as an annexe to Resolution 428(V),[15] in which it also called upon governments to co-operate with the Office. The functions of UNHCR encompass 'providing international protection' and 'seeking permanent solutions' to the

---

[9] The functions of the Committee were defined in a resolution adopted 14 July 1938; text in *A Study of Statelessness* (above, n.1) 116-18.

[10] GA Res. 8(I), 12 Feb. 1946.

[11] GA Res. 62(I), 15 Dec. 1946. The Preparatory Commission was set up in order to ensure continuity between the work of UNRRA and the IGCR (both of which were wound up on 30 June 1947) and that of the IRO, pending sufficient ratifications to bring the latter's constitution into force. This became effective 20 Aug. 1948.

[12] See generally Holborn, *The International Refugee Organization* (1956).

[13] Art. 2, constitution of the IRO.

[14] GA Res. 319(IV), 3 Dec. 1949. For completeness sake, mention should also be made of the United Nations Relief and Works Agency for Palestine Refugees in the Near East (UNRWA), established by GA Res. 302(iv), 8 Dec. 1949; the agency's duties relate principally to assistance; and the United Nations Korean Reconstruction Agency established by GA Res. 401A and B(v), 1 Dec. 1950; this agency was principally concerned with relief and economic reconstruction, and concluded its activities in 1958.

[15] See full text of resolution and Statute below, annexe III.

problems of refugees by way of voluntary repatriation or assimilation in new national communities.[16] The Statute expressly provides that 'the work of the High Commissioner shall be of an entirely non-political character; it shall be humanitarian and social and shall relate, as a rule, to groups and categories of refugees.'[17] Of the two functions, the provision of international protection is of primary importance, for without protection, such as intervention by the Office to secure admission of refugees, there can be no possibility of finding lasting solutions. Besides defining refugees the UNHCR Statute prescribes the relationship of the High Commissioner with the General Assembly and the Economic and Social Council (ECOSOC), makes provision for organization and finance, and identifies ways in which the High Commissioner is to provide for protection.[18] These develop the functions engaged in by predecessor organizations and include: (i) promoting the conclusion of international conventions for the protection of refugees, supervising their application and proposing amendments thereto; (ii) promoting through special agreements with governments the execution of any measures calculated to improve the situation of refugees and to reduce the number requiring protection; and (iii) promoting the admission of refugees.[19]

Notwithstanding the statutory injunction that the work of the Office shall relate, as a rule, to groups and categories of refugees, a major part of UNHCR's protection work is concerned with individual cases, as was that of its predecessor organizations. No state has objected to UNHCR taking up individual cases as such,[20] although states may, and do, question whether an individual is indeed a refugee.[21] Nevertheless, the individual dimension to the protection function is a natural corollary to the declared task of supervising the application of international conventions.

---

[16] Statute, para. 1.

[17] Ibid. para. 2. Para. 3, however, obliges the High Commissioner to follow policy directives of the General Assembly and the Economic and Social Council.

[18] Statute, para. 8.

[19] In addition to the declared functions, UNHCR's indirect or promotional activities encompass the enforcement of national laws and regulations benefitting refugees, the development and adoption of appropriate national laws, regulations, and procedures, promotion of accession to international instruments, and the development of new legal instruments. Latterly, the Executive Committee has also included with approval the dissemination of refugee law in the list of activities; see, for example, UN doc. A/AC.96/588, para. 48(1) (k) (report of the 31st Session of the Executive Committee, 1980).

[20] Sadruddin Aga Khan, 'Legal problems relating to refugees and displaced persons' Hague *Recueil* (1976-I) 331-2; Schnyder, 'Les aspects juridiques actuels du problème des réfugiés' Hague *Recueil* (1965-I) 319, 416; Weis, 30 *BYIL*, at 214.

[21] See above, ch. I, s. 3(2).

Such instruments define refugees in essentially individualistic terms and provide rights on behalf of refugees which can only be understood in the sense of the particular. The acquiescence of states in the individual protection function of UNHCR, however, significantly delineates both the competence of the Office and the status of the individual refugee in international law.

## (2) RELATION OF UNHCR TO THE GENERAL ASSEMBLY AND ITS STANDING IN GENERAL INTERNATIONAL LAW

UNHCR was established by the General Assembly as a subsidiary organ under Article 22 of the UN Charter,[22] and the parent body has continued to play an active role in expanding the mandate of the Office. The relationship of the two organizations is clarified in the Statute, which declares that UNHCR acts 'under the authority of the General Assembly',[23] that it shall 'follow policy directives given by [that body] or the Economic and Social Council',[24] and that it 'shall engage in such additional activities, including repatriation and resettlement, as the General Assembly may determine'.[25] The High Commissioner is further required to report annually to the General Assembly, through the Economic and Social Council, and the report is to be considered as a separate item on the agenda of the former.[26] Finally, the Statute calls upon the High Commissioner, particularly where difficulties arise, to request the opinion of the advisory committee on refugees, if it is created.[27] Such a committee was first established in 1951,[28] and replaced four years later by the UN Refugee Fund Executive Committee,[29] whose functions included supervision of material assistance progammes financed by the fund. The General Assembly

---

[22] Art. 22 provides: 'The General Assembly may establish such subsidiary organs as it deems necessary for the performance of its functions.' UNHCR was originally constituted for three years and its mandate is now subject to renewal every five years.

[23] Statute, para. 3. The High Commissioner is elected by the General Asembly, on the nomination of the Secretary-General: ibid. para. 13.

[24] Ibid. para. 4.

[25] Ibid. para. 9.

[26] Ibid. para. 11. As a corollary, the same paragraph entitles the High Commissioner to present his or her views before the General Assembly and ECOSOC and their subsidiary bodies. Since 1969, the practice has been to transmit the report without debate to the General Assembly, unless one or more members of ECOSOC or the High Commissioner request otherwise: Decision on Item 9, ECOSOC *OR* Resumed 47th Session, (E/4735/Add.1).

[27] Statute, para. 1. By para. 4 ECOSOC was empowered to establish such a committee.

[28] ECOSOC Res. 393B(XIII), 10 Sept. 1951.

[29] ECOSOC Res. 565(XIX), 31 Mar. 1955, further to GA Res. 832(IX), 21 Oct. 1954.

called for its replacement in turn by the Executive Committee of the High Commissioner's Programme, which was set up by the Economic and Social Council in 1958.[30] Originally made up of twenty-four states, it has been progressively enlarged to its present membership of forty-one.[31] The Committee's terms of reference include advising the High Commissioner, on request, in the exercise of the Office's statutory functions; and advising on the appropriateness of providing international assistance through the Office in order to solve any specific refugee problems. In 1975, the Executive Committee decided to set up a Subcommittee of the Whole on International Protection,[32] which makes a continuing contribution to the development and strengthening of refugee law.

Each of the above elements involves the participation of states, at varying levels, in the international institutions protecting refugees. The practice of such organizations is relevant in assessing the standing both of UNHCR and of the rules benefitting refugees in general international law. An international organization such as UNHCR is not only a forum in which the views of states may be represented; it is also, as a subject of international law, an actor in the relevant field whose actions count in the process of law formation. Specific authority to involve itself in the protection of refugees has been accorded to the Office by states parties to the 1951 Convention and/or the 1967 Protocol relating to the Status of Refugees. Article 35 of the Convention, for example, provides: 'The contracting States undertake to co-operate with the Office of the United Nations High Commissioner for Refugees ... in the exercise of its functions, and shall in particular facilitate its duty of supervising the application of the provisions of this Convention.'[33] The 1969 OAU Convention requires member states to co-operate similarly, while declaring itself to be the 'effective regional complement in Africa' of the 1951 Convention.[34] UNHCR, however, is not itself a party to those instruments, and its standing must be located in more general principles.

---

[30] GA Res. 1166(XII), 26 Nov. 1957, and ECOSOC Res. 672(XXV), 30 Apr. 1958.

[31] See below, annexe XIV.

[32] Report of the Executive Committee, 26th Session, 1975, UN doc. A/AC.96/521, para. 69(h).

[33] Art. II of the 1967 Protocol is to similar effect.

[34] Art. VIII.

Clearly, by derivation and intention, UNHCR does enjoy international personality. As a subsidiary organ of the General Assembly, its 'personality' (its capacity to possess international rights and duties) can be traced to the United Nations at large.[35] Moreover, its Statute shows that the Office was intended by the General Assembly to act on the international plane.[36] Its standing in regard to protection has been further reinforced by successive General Assembly resolutions urging all states to support the High Commissioner's activities, for example, by granting asylum, observing the principle of *non-refoulement* and acceding to the relevant international treaties. While it is trite knowledge that General Assembly resolutions are not legally binding, 'it is another thing', as Judge Lauterpacht noted in the *Voting Procedure* case, 'to give currency to the view that they have no force at all, whether legal or other, and that therefore they cannot be regarded as forming in any sense part of a legal system of supervision'.[37] On this occasion, the 'legal system of supervision' was the mandate in respect of South West Africa. In his separate opinion, Judge Lauterpacht noted that, while the mandatory had the right not to accept a recommendation of the supervising body, it was nevertheless bound to give it due consideration in good faith, which in turn entailed giving reasons for non-acceptance.

Admittedly, General Assembly resolutions with regard to refugees and to UNHCR do not have the same degree of particularity as a recommendation relating to the administration of a mandate. Nevertheless, against the background of the UN Charter and general international law, UNHCR, with its principal function of providing 'international protection' to refugees, can be seen to occupy the central role in an analogous legal system of supervision. Indeed, though discretions continue to favour states in certain of their dealings with refugees, the peremptory character of the principle of *non-refoulement* clearly puts it in a higher class than the 'intangible and almost nominal' obligation to consider in

---

[35] See generally, *Reparations* case, ICJ Rep. 1949, 174 at 178-9.

[36] For example, the Statute refers to the High Commissioner supervising the application of international conventions, promoting certain measures through special agreements with governments, and consulting governments on the need to appoint local representatives: paras. 8(a), (b), 16.

[37] See generally, *South West Africa, Voting Procedure,* advisory opinion, ICJ Rep 1955, 67, at 120-2 (separate opinion of JUDGE LAUTERPACHT). JUDGE LAUTERPACHT noted at 122 that General Assembly resolutions are 'one of the principal instrumentalities of the formation of the collective will and judgment of the community of nations represented by the United Nations'. See also Brownlie, *Principles of Public International Law* (3rd ed., 1979), 14, 696.

good faith a recommendation of a supervisory body, such as Judge Lauterpacht discerned in the *Voting Procedure* case.[38] The entitlement of UNHCR to exercise protection on the basis of a universal jurisdiction receives additional support from the decision of the International Court of Justice in the *Reparations* case. There, the Court read into the rights and duties of the United Nations Organization, as a 'necessary intendment', the capacity to exercise a measure of functional protection on behalf of its agents.[39] UNHCR, moreover, is *expressly* ascribed the function of providing international protection to refugees; state practice reflects 'recognition or acquiescence in the assumption of such jurisdiction'[40] universally, and without regard to any requirement of treaty ratification. The 'effective discharge'[41] of this function evidently requires capacity to assert claims on behalf of individuals falling within the competence of the Office.

Given states obligations with regard to refugees, the question must yet be considered, to whom are they owed? The individual is still not considered to be a subject of international law, capable of enforcing his or her rights on the international plane,[42] while the problems faced by refugees are not such as would prompt the exercise of the right of diplomatic protection on the part of the state of nationality. In the case of states parties to the 1951 Convention and the 1967 Protocol, the existence of obligations *inter se* is established. Both instruments expressly provide for the settlement of disputes relating to their interpretation or application, and for reference to the International Court of Justice at the request of any of the parties to the dispute, should other means of

---

[38] *Voting Procedure* case ICJ Rep. 1955, 67, at 119. See also JUDGE LAUTERPACHT'S remarks generally in regard to good faith in the exercise of discretion: ibid. 120.

[39] *Reparations* case ICJ Rep. 1949, 174, at 184.

[40] Schwarzenberger and Brown, *A Manual of International Law* (6th ed., 1976) 115, commenting on the movement of an implied consensual right to exercise functional protection from its basis in consent to its acquisition of 'an increasingly absolute validity'. Cf. below, n. 42.

[41] *Reparations* case ICJ Rep. 1949, 174, at 180.

[42] In Schwarzenberger and Brown, *Manual,* the traditional view is stated thus: 'Whether [the individual] is entitled to benefit from customary or consensual rules of international law depends on his own link—primarily through nationality—with a subject of international law which, on the international level, is alone competent to assert his rights against another subject of international law.' (At 64.) Later in the same work it is noted that 'By means of conventions, attempts have been made to alleviate the position of refugees and stateless persons. Otherwise, they are objects of international law for whom no subject of international law is internationally responsible—a notable twentieth-century contribution to the category of *res nullius.*' (At 114-5.) *Sed quaere.*

settlement fail.[43] No litigation has resulted, and, in the absence of injury to an individual related to a claimant state by the link of nationality, the results of any such litigation are likely to be without practical consequence.[44] There are precedents, however, by which states may yet have legal interests in matters other than those which affect directly their material interests.[45]

Under Article 24 of the European Convention on Human Rights, for example, any contracting state may refer to the European Commission an alleged breach of the Convention by another party. The instrument itself thus provides for a 'European public order', a regime in which all states parties have a sufficient interest in the observance of the European Convention's provisions to allow for the assertion of claims. While there are similarities in the objectives of the European Convention and the refugee conventions—both call for certain standards of treatment to be accorded to certain groups of persons—the refugee conventions lack effective investigation, adjudication, and enforcement procedures; they can hardly be considered to offer the same opportunity for judicial or quasi-judicial solutions. None the less, in view of the importance of the rights involved, it may be argued that all states have an interest in their protection;[46] and that UNHCR, by express agreement of some states and by the acquiescence of others, is the qualified representative of the 'international public order' in such matters. A cogent theory of responsibility remains to be developed to cover this situation, and the legal consequences that may flow from a breach of the international obligations in question are as yet unclear. International claims can take the form of protest, a call for an inquiry, negotiation, or a request for submission to arbitration or to the International Court of Justice. Both the nature of breaches of obligation affecting refugees and the nature of the protecting organization rule out certain types of claims, such as arbitration, while strictly legal considerations exclude, for example, recourse to the International Court of

[43] 1951 Convention, art. 38; 1967 Protocol, art. IV. Under the Protocol, but not under the Convention, states are entitled to make reservations to the article on settlement of disputes.

[44] See *Northern Cameroons case, Preliminary Objections,* ICJ Rep. 1963, 15, at 34-5. Cf. below, n. 47.

[45] See *South West Africa* cases, preliminary objections, ICJ Rep. 1962, 319, at 424-33 (separate opinion of JUDGE JESSUP). But cf. *South West Africa* cases, second phase, ICJ Rep. 1966, 6 at 32-3, 47 (holding that individual states do not have a legal right to require the performance of South Africa's mandate over South West Africa).

[46] *Barcelona Traction* case ICJ Rep. 1970, 3 at 32. See also 1967 Declaration on Territorial Asylum, art. 2(1).

Justice.[47] Currently, the simple existence of obligations owed at large may provide sufficient justification, not just for 'expressions of international concern',[48] but also for formal protest on the part of UNHCR.[49] The significance of this development for the individual's standing in general international law should not be underestimated.

## 2. Protection of refugees: standards of treatment deriving from general international law and treaty

Day-to-day protection activities are necessarily dictated by the needs of refugees, but a summary reading of both the Statute of the Office and the 1951 Convention gives a general picture. There are, first, both direct and indirect aspects to the protection function with the latter comprising the promotion activities of the Office already mentioned. Direct protection activities, including intervention on behalf of individuals or groups, involve protection of the refugee's basic human rights, for example, non-discrimination, liberty, and security of the person. UNHCR is also concerned specifically with the following: (1) the prevention of the return of refugees to a country or territory in which their life or liberty may be endangered; (2) the determination of refugee status; (3) the grant of asylum; (4) the prevention of expulsion; (5) the issue of identity and travel documents; (6) the facilitation of voluntary repatriation; (7) the facilitation of family reunion; (8) the assurance of access to educational institutions; (9) the

---

[47] The possibility of interim measures ordered by the International Court of Justice, however, should not be ignored entirely. In *United States Diplomatic and Consular Staff in Tehran* (request for the indication of provisional measures), ICJ Rep. 1979, 7, the Court noted (p. 19, para. 36) that its power to indicate such measures has as its object to preserve the respective rights of the parties pending the decision of the Court and presupposes that irreparable prejudice should not be caused to rights which are the subject of dispute in judicial proceedings. The rights of the United States to which the Court referred included the rights of its nationals to life, liberty, protection, and security (para. 37). It held (para. 42) that continuation of the situation exposed those individuals to privation, hardship, anguish, and even danger to health and life and thus to a serious possibility of irreparable harm. The Government of the Islamic Republic of Iran was ordered, among others, to ensure the immediate release of those held. In its judgment, ICJ Rep. 1980, 3 at 42 (para. 91), the Court noted that 'Wrongfully to deprive human beings of their freedom and to subject them to physical constraint in conditions of hardship is in itself manifestly incompatible with the principles of the Charter of the United Nations, as well as with the fundamental principles enunciated in the Universal Declaration of Human Rights'.

[48] See Goodwin-Gill, *International Law and the Movement of Persons between States* (1978) 23.

[49] Where *refoulement* has taken place or is believed to be imminent, UNHCR will intervene either with the authorities locally, through its representative on the spot, and/or through the country's Permanent Mission to the United Nations in Geneva or New York.

assurance of the right to work and the benefit of other economic and social rights; (10) the facilitation of naturalization. Of these, the first four, together with the general function, are clearly of prime importance, with the principle of *non-refoulement* standing as the *sine qua non* of the search for permanent solutions.[50]

The precise standard of treatment to be accorded to refugees will vary, depending on whether the state in which they find themselves has ratified the Convention and Protocol or any other relevant treaty. It may further depend on whether the refugee falls within the narrow or broad sense of the term, is lawfully or unlawfully in the territory of the state, or has been formally recognized as a refugee.

## (1) GENERAL INTERNATIONAL LAW

With regard to basic standards, however, the lawfulness or otherwise of presence is as irrelevant as the distinction between national and alien.[51] Certain provisions of the 1966 Covenants on human rights are indicative of standards going beyond the purely conventional regime. Article 2(1) of the Covenant on Civil and Political Rights, for example, obliges states to respect and to ensure the rights declared to 'all individuals within its territory and subject to its jurisdiction'. The same article elaborates a principle of non-discrimination in broad terms, including national or social origin, birth or other status, within the list of prohibited grounds of distinction. Article 4(1), it is true, permits derogation in certain

---

[50] The protection of refugees may also be promoted, directly and indirectly, by regional and non-governmental organizations, including, for example, the Organization of African Unity, the Organization of American States, and the Council of Europe. These have generated, among others, instruments such as the 1969 OAU Convention on the Specific Aspects of Refugee Problems in Africa, the American Convention on Human Rights, the European Convention on Human Rights, the European Agreement on the Abolition of Visas for Refugees, the European Agreement on Social Security and its Supplementary Agreement, the European Agreement on Consular Functions, together with the Protocol concerning the Protection of Refugees, and the European Agreement on Transfer of Responsibility for Refugees. In the non-governmental field, account should be taken of the work of the International Committee of the Red Cross, of National Red Cross and Red Crescent Societies, and of Amnesty International. There is a clear complementarity between protection of refugees and Amnesty International's statutory concern with 'prisoners of conscience', that is, men and women 'imprisoned, detained or otherwise physically restricted by reason of their political, religious or other conscientiously held beliefs or by reason of their ethnic origin, sex, colour or language, provided that they have not used or advocated violence' (art. 1(a), Statute of Amnesty International, as amended by the 12th International Council, Louvain, Belgium 6-9 Sept. 1979: *1980 Report*, appx. 1, 383.

[51] Applicable standards, with particular regard to immigration, are analysed in more detail in Goodwin-Gill, *Movement of Persons*, chs. iv and v.

circumstances,[52] and contains a narrower statement of the principle of non-discrimination, which would allow states to distinguish between nationals and aliens. Nevertheless, any measures in derogation must be consistent with states' other obligations under international law,[53] and no derogation is allowed from those provisions which guarantee the right to life, or which forbid torture or inhuman treatment, slavery, servitude, or conviction or punishment under retroactive laws. The right to recognition as a person before the law and the right to freedom of conscience, thought, and religion are also declared in absolute terms.[54]

The Covenant is in force, but still lacks universal acceptance. Certain rights and standards, however, enjoy a more positive foundation in general international law. In one dictum the International Court of Justice observed that 'the principles and rules concerning the basic human rights of the human person, including protection from slavery and racial discrimination'[55] figured within the class of obligations owed by states *erga omnes*. The rights in question frequently appear in conventions among those from which no derogation is permitted even in exceptional circumstances. Other rights of a similar fundamental character ought likewise to benefit everyone, and they would include the right to life; the right to be protected against torture or cruel or inhuman treatment or punishment; the right not to be subject to retroactive criminal penalties and the right to recognition as a person before the law.[56] Such rights clearly allow for no distinction between national and alien, whether the latter be a migrant, visitor, refugee, or asylum-seeker, and whether lawfully or unlawfully in the state.[57] The obligations of respect and protection are incumbent

[52] Derogation is permitted in 'time of public emergency which threatens the life of the nation and the existence of which is officially proclaimed'.

[53] Thus, in view of the peremptory character of the rule of non-discrimination on the ground of race, measures taken against a particular class of foreign nationals determinable solely by reference to race or colour would not appear to be justified.

[54] Art. 4(2). Cf. annexe III, Elles, *International Provisions protecting the Human Rights of Non-Citizens*: UN doc. E/CN.4/Sub.2/392/Rev.1 (1980) 57.

[55] *Barcelona Traction* case, ICJ Rep. 1970, 3, at 32.

[56] See Goodwin-Gill, *Movement of Persons*, 72-3, 85-7.

[57] Cf. ILO Migrant Workers (Supplementary Provisions) Convention 1975 (no. 143). Art. 1 affirms that 'Each Member for which this Convention is in force undertakes to respect the basic human rights of all migrant workers'. The ILO Committee of Experts proposed for inclusion within this category of rights, the right to life, to protection against torture, cruel, inhuman or degrading treatment or punishment, liberty and security of the person, protection against arbitrary arrest and detention, and the right to a fair trial: *Migrant Workers,* report of the Committee of Experts, International Labour Conference, 66th Session, 1980, 68-9. Art. 9(1) of this same convention requires further that illegal migrant workers, whose position cannot be regularized, should receive 'equal treatment'

on states, irrespective of ratification of treaties, and refugees ought in principle to benefit, whether admitted on a temporary, indefinite, or a permanent basis. In practice, however, this objective may remain elusive, particularly where the state of refuge is unable or unwilling to take the necessary measures. Refugees have thus fallen victim to external, armed aggression;[58] to attacks by pirates resulting in murder, rape, abduction, and robbery;[59] to abandonment when in distress at sea;[60] to actual and potential threats to life and security by para-military 'death squads';[61] and to arbitrary detention and torture.[62] The exercise of protection on such occasions is a difficult and delicate task, whether attempted by UNHCR or by concerned states, and the problem is further exacerbated where the injury takes place in an area formally beyond the jurisdiction of any state. While international solidarity may manifest itself in calls for action,[63] practical results can be far harder to obtain.[64]

Once refugees have secured admission, however, the desirability of attaining a lasting solution to their plight would seem to entail certain further standards of treatment geared to that objective. The Group of Experts, which considered the implications of the concept of temporary refuge in 1981, proposed a list of some sixteen 'basic human standards' which, in its view, should govern the treatment of those temporarily admitted, and they were duly endorsed by the Executive Committee later that year.[65] The objective was rather the promotion of certain practically attainable standards, than the formulation of rules. The Executive Committee thus reiterated the need to observe fundamental rights,

for themselves and their families in respect of rights arising out of past employment in matters of pay, social security, etc. See also Hevener and Mosher, 'General Principles of Law and the United Nations Covenant on Civil and Political Rights' 27 *ICLQ* 596-613 (1978).

[58] UN doc. A/AC.96/527, Note on International Protection (1976), paras. 14, 15; UN docs. E/1980/79, para. 30 and E/1981/45, para. 30 (reports of the High Commissioner to the General Assembly).

[59] UN docs. A/AC.96/579, Note on International Protection (1980), para 11; E/1980/79, para. 29; E/1981/45, paras. 27-9.

[60] UN doc. E/1980/79, paras. 21-2.

[61] UN doc. E/1981/45, para. 31.

[62] UN docs. E/1980/79, paras. 31-2; E/1981/45, paras. 32-3.

[63] GA Res. 33/26 of 29 Nov. 1978.

[64] In June 1982, following a number of *ad hoc* measures which had included donation to the Thai Government of $2 million by the USA and an unarmed patrol boat by UNHCR, a further $3.6 million was contributed by twelve donor countries to strengthen anti-piracy measures.

[65] UN doc. A/AC.96/101, para. 57(2) II B.

including the principle of non-discrimination. It also recommended that asylum-seekers be located by reference to their safety and well-being, as well as the security of the state of refuge; that they be provided with the basic necessities of life; that the principle of family unity be respected and that assistance with tracing of relatives be given; that minors and unaccompanied children be adequately protected; that the sending and receiving of mail, and receipt of material assistance from friends be allowed; that, where possible, appropriate arrangements be made for the registration of births, deaths, and marriages; that they be permitted to transfer to the country in which a lasting solution is found, any assets brought into the country of temporary refuge; and that all necessary facilities be granted to enable the attainment of a satisfactory durable solution, including voluntary repatriation. The recommendations, although clearly oriented towards solutions, are not of a normative character. The Executive Committee was somewhat more peremptory, however, in its statement on co-operation with UNHCR: 'Asylum-seekers *shall* be entitled to contact the Office of UNHCR. UNHCR *shall* be given access to asylum-seekers. UNHCR *shall* also be given the possibility of exercising its function of international protection *and shall be allowed to supervise the well-being of persons entering reception or other refugee centres.*'[66]

## (2) STATE RESPONSIBILITY, TREATIES AND MUNICIPAL LAW

Basic human rights derive their force from customary international law, and indicate the content of the *general* obligations which control and structure the treatment by states of nationals and aliens. For states which have ratified treaties specifically benefitting refugees, the particular standards required ought to be easier to determine. This, however, raises the problem of the obligation, if any, incumbent on ratifying states to incorporate or otherwise implement the provisions of the treaties in question in their municipal law. The 1951 Convention contains no provision requiring legislative incorporation or any other formal implementing step; indeed, Article 36, which obliges states to provide information on national legislation, refers only to such laws and regulations as states 'may' adopt to ensure application of the Convention. Similarly, nothing is said with regard to the establishment of procedures for the determination of refugee status, or otherwise for ascertaining and identifying those who are to benefit from the substantive provisions of the Convention.

---

[66] Ibid. para. 57(2) III, (emphasis supplied).

Although it offers little assistance in the solution of specific problems, the *general* duty of a party to a treaty to ensure that its domestic law is in conformity with its international obligations is beyond contradiction.[67] The governing principles, however, do not include an obligation, *per se*, to incorporate the provisions of treaties into domestic law.[68] The fundamental distinction is between an obligation of conduct or means, and an obligation of result.[69] This is often easier to declare than to apply, but it remains crucial in any assessment of a state's performance in the light of its participation in international treaties. Obligations of conduct tend on the whole to be less frequent than obligations of result, and are commonly encountered where action is required at the level of direct relations between states. Obligations of result, on the other hand, incorporating acknowledgement of the principle of choice of means, are most usually found where states are required to bring about a certain situation within their system of internal law.[70]

So, for example, Article 22(1) of the 1961 Vienna Convention on Diplomatic Relations declares a clear obligation of conduct: 'The premises of the mission shall be inviolable. The agents of the receiving State may not enter them, except with the consent of the head of the mission.'[71] In this case, the internationally required conduct is that of omission by the organs of the receiving state; in other cases, positive action may be required. Thus, states parties to the 1965 Convention on the Elimination of All Forms of Racial Discrimination agree, *inter alia*, 'to amend, rescind or nullify any laws or regulations which have the effect of creating or perpetuating racial discrimination wherever it exists'.[72] Similarly, the specific *enactment* of legislation may be required, as by Article 20 of the 1966 Covenant on Civil and Political Rights. ('Any propaganda for war shall be prohibited by law.')[73] In all such cases,

---

[67] McNair *The Law of Treaties* (1961) 78-9; see also Brownlie, *Principles of Public International Law* (3rd. ed. 1979) 36-8; *Treatment of Polish Nationals in Danzig* PCIJ ser. A/B no. 44 at 24; *Greco-Bulgarian Communities* PCIJ, ser. B, no. 17, 32; *Free Zones* PCIJ ser. A, no. 24, 12; ser. A/B, no. 46, 167; art. 27, 1969 Vienna Convention on the Law of Treaties.

[68] The International Court has stressed that failure to enact legislation necessary to ensure fulfilment of international obligations will not relieve a state of responsibility; see *Exchange of Greek and Turkish Populations* PCIJ ser. B, no. 10, 20.

[69] See generally *Yearbook of the ILC* (1977) ii.11-50.

[70] Ibid. 13.

[71] 500 UNTS 95; Brownlie, *Basic Documents in International Law* (2nd. ed. 1972) 233.

[72] Art. 2(1) (c): 660 UNTS 195.

[73] Text annexed to GA Res. 2200(XXI), 16 Dec. 1966. A number of states have entered reservations to this article, on the basis of its inconsistency with the freedom of expression recognized in art. 19. See UN doc. ST/LEG/SER.D/13 (*Multilateral Treaties*

the international obligation requires a specifically determined course of conduct; ascertaining if the obligation has been fulfilled simply turns on whether the state's act or omission is or is not in fact in conformity with the internationally required conduct, the sufficient injury being the breach of legal duty.[74]

International obligations requiring the achievement of a specified result often concede the state's full freedom in its choice of means for implementation. Article 22(2) of the 1961 Vienna Convention on Diplomatic Relations declares the receiving state's 'special duty to take all appropriate steps to protect the premises of the mission', but defines those steps no further. Article 10 of the ILO Migrant Workers (Supplementary Provisions) Convention 1975 (no. 143) obliges 'Each Member for which the Convention is in force ... to declare and pursue a national policy designed to promote and to guarantee, *by methods appropriate to national conditions and practice*, equality of opportunity and treatment ...'.[75] The obligation of result is especially common in standard-setting treaties (for example, treaties of establishment guaranteeing most-favoured-nation treatment) and in human rights instruments. On occasion, full freedom of choice may be implied from the terms of the treaty itself, while in other cases a preference for the adoption of legislative measures may be indi-

---

*in respect of which the Secretary-General performs Depositary functions; List of Signatures, Ratifications, Accessions, etc. as at 31 Dec. 1979*), 111-20, recording reservations by Denmark, Finland, Iceland, Netherlands, New Zealand, Norway, Sweden, and the United Kingdom.

[74] *United States Diplomatic and Consular Staff in Tehran (USA v. Iran)*, ICJ Rep. 1980, 3 at 30-1. The International Law Commission's draft articles on state responsibility include: 'Article 16. There is a breach of an international obligation by a State when an act of the State is not in conformity with what is required of it by that obligation. ... Article 20. There is a breach by a State of an international obligation requiring it to adopt a particular course of conduct when the conduct of that State is not in conformity with that required of it by that obligation': *Yearbook of the ILC* (1977) ii.10-11. In commenting on the irrelevance whether harmful consequences actually result, the ILC suggests as one example that art. 10(3) of the 1966 Covenant on Economic, Social, and Cultural Rights ('...States Parties ... recognize that [child employment in certain circumstances] should be prohibited and punishable by law') is breached by simple failure to enact legislation. This conclusion seems erroneous; art. 2(1) of the Covenant refers expressly to 'achieving progressively the full realization of the rights recognized', while art. 10 alone in that instrument employs the ambivalent 'should', rather than the peremptory 'shall'. The provision in question is rather an obligation of result, than of conduct. On the terminological issue, cf. 1979 International Convention on Maritime Search and Rescue (IMCO, 1979) annexe I, art. 1.1: ' "Shall" is used ... to indicate a provision, the uniform application of which by all Parties is required in the interest of safety of life at sea.'

[75] See also art. 24, ILO Constitution, whereby every member state 'binds itself effectively to observe within its jurisdiction any Convention to which it is a party'.

cated. Nevertheless, though legislation may be considered appropriate, even essential, it is evidently only one way in which the internationally required result can be obtained. It is not so much the law which counts, as that compliance with international obligations be assured. As the International Law Commission noted in 1977 '... so long as the State has not failed to achieve *in concreto* the result required by an international obligation, the fact that it has not taken a certain measure which would have seemed especially suitable for that purpose—in particular, that it has not enacted a law—cannot be held against it as a breach of that obligation'.[76] In two recent treaties, states are called upon to enact 'such legislative or other measures as may be necessary'[77] to give effect to rights; and to 'prohibit and bring to an end' certain conduct, 'by all appropriate means, including legislation as required by circumstances'.[78] Words such as 'necessary' and 'appropriate' indicate that the state enjoys discretion in its choice of implementing measures, but the standard of compliance remains an international one. The question is one of effective or efficient implementation of the treaty provisions, *in fact*, and in the light of the principle of effectiveness of obligations.[79] Just as taking the theoretically most appropriate measures of implementation is not conclusive as to the fulfilment of an international obligation, so failing to take such measures is not conclusive as to breach.[80] The same holds good with regard to a state's adoption of a potentially obstructive measure, so long as such measure does not itself create a specific situation incompatible with the required result; what counts is what in fact results, not enactment and promulgation, but application and enforcement.[81]

[76] The ILC invoked particularly clear statements of the principle submitted by Poland and Switzerland to the Preparatory Committee of the 1930 Hague Conference for the Codification of International Law; cited in *Yearbook of the ILC* (1977) ii. 23.

[77] Art. 2(1), 1966 Covenant on Civil and Political Rights.

[78] Art. 2(1) (d), 1965 International Covenant on the Elimination of All Forms of Racial Discrimination.

[79] See generally Lauterpacht, *The Development of International Law by the International Court* (1958) 257, 282 ff; art. 31(1), 1969 Vienna Convention on the Law of Treaties; McNair, *Treaties* 540-1.

[80] See *Tolls on the Panama Canal* (1911-12): Hackworth, *Digest* vi.59 (views of the United States); *German Interests in Polish Upper Silesia* (merits) PCIJ (1926) ser. A, no. 7, 19. The Permanent Court's reference in the *German Settlers in Poland* case to the necessity for '... equality in fact ... as well as ostensible legal equality in the sense of absence of discrimination in the words of the law' (PCIJ (1923) ser. B, no. 6, 24) is founded on an equivalent principle. See further *Yearbook of the ILC* (1977) ii.23-7.

[81] Judgment of the Court *Ireland* v. *United Kingdom* (application 5301/71) paras. 236 ff. 17 ILM 680 (1978). Art. 1 of the European Convention provides: 'The High Contracting Parties shall secure to everyone within their jurisdiction the rights and freedoms defined ...'

In theory at least, the test of implementation of an international obligation of result might appear as straightforward as that for an obligation of conduct: compare the result in fact achieved with that which the state ought to have achieved.[82] In practice, however, major problems of interpretation and appreciation arise in view of, amongst others, the relative imprecision of the terminology employed in standard-setting conventions; the variety of legal systems and practices of states: the role of discretion, first, in the state's initial choice of means, and secondly, in its privilege on occasion to require resort to such remedial measures as it may provide; and finally the possibility that the state may be entitled to avoid responsibility by providing an 'equivalent alternative',[83] to the required result, such as compensation for arbitrary detention. The question whether a state has fulfilled an obligation of result must be examined in the light of the initial means chosen for implementation, the remedies available in the event that an initially incompatible situation ensues, and the option, if permitted by the obligation, of substituting an equivalent alternative result in the event that the principal required result is rendered unattainable. In the context of standard setting, local remedies are especially important;[84] their availability and effectiveness will often determine the question of fulfilment or breach of obligation, the 'generation' of international responsibility and the implementation of this responsibility.[85] Nevertheless, it is also clear that a

[82] Cf. ILC draft art. 21: '(1) There is a breach by a State of an international obligation requiring it to achieve, by means of its own choice, a specified result if, by the conduct adopted, the State does not achieve the result required of it by that obligation. (2) When the conduct of the State has created a situation not in conformity with the result required of it by an international obligation, but the obligation allows that this or an equivalent result may nevertheless be achieved by subsequent conduct of the State, there is a breach of the obligation only if the State also fails by its subsequent conduct to achieve the result required of it by that obligation.' *Yearbook of the ILC* (1977) ii.18 f.

[83] Ibid. 22, 28.

[84] The local remedies rule is firmly based in general international law, but also figures increasingly in human rights instruments; see, for example, art. 26, European Convention on Human Rights; art. 11(3), 14(7) (a), International Convention on the Elimination of All Forms of Racial Discrimination; art. 41(1) (c), Covenant on Civil and Political Rights, art. 5 (2) (b), Optional Protocol thereto.

[85] *Yearbook of the ILC* ii.36. Cf. ILC draft art. 22: 'When the conduct of a State has created a situation not in conformity with the result required of it by an international obligation concerning the treatment to be accorded to aliens, whether natural or juridical persons, but the obligation allows that this or an equivalent result may nevertheless be achieved by subsequent conduct of the State, there is a breach of the obligation only if the aliens concerned have exhausted the effective local remedies available to them without obtaining the treatment called for by the obligation or, where that is not possible, an equivalent treatment'. The United States has expressed some reservations as to the 'possibility that in the further drafting of Article 22 a "substantive" approach to the

conventional standard of treatment may be expressed as an obligation of *conduct*, in which case no requirement of exhaustion of local remedies would arise.[86] In the present context, the principle of *non-refoulement* of refugees, including non-rejection at the frontier falls within this category of obligation.

The difficulties attaching to the general issue of incorporation are illustrated by two occasions on which the United Kingdom's performance in the light of its international obligations was called in question. In 1979, that country was examined by the Human Rights Committee with regard to its report on the implementation of the Covenant on Civil and Political Rights. One expert noted that the United Kingdom had no written constitution and that the Covenant was not part of its internal legal order; if there were no laws, he wondered how the Committee could determine the degree of compliance with the Covenant.[87] Another expert believed that Article 2(2) required the adoption of specific measures and that it was not sufficient to state that existing laws were consonant with the Covenant.[88] The United Kingdom's representative disagreed with the view that states were obliged to adopt positive measures; what mattered was the treatment that people received and the way in which the law worked in practice.[89]

The following month, incorporation and effective implementation of the 1951 Convention relating to the Status of Refugees

calculation of damages as of the exhaustion of local remedies might result in the accrual of interest not from time of injury, but at the time of exhaustion'. 1977 *Digest of United States Practice in International Law* 762.

[86] *Yearbook of the ILC* ii.30-50 at 48.
[87] Mr Movchan, expert from the Soviet Union: UN doc. CCPR/C/SR.147, paras. 8, 9. (For a more lively account, see United Nations press releases HR/1792-4, 25-6 Apr. 1979.) It may be noted in passing that the Soviet Union figures among those states which, despite the apparently express requirement of art. V of the Genocide Convention, have not found it necessary to enact specific legislation: UN doc. E/CN.4/Sub.2/416, para. 501 (Ruhashyankiko, *Study of the Question of the Prevention and Punishment of the Crime of Genocide* (1978)).
[88] Mr Sadi, expert from Jordan: UN doc. CCPR/C/SR.147, para. 13; Mr Movchan agreed: ibid., para. 31. Schachter, 73 *AJIL* 464 F. (1979) 464 f., doubts whether proposed United States reservations designed, in the view of the State Department, to harmonize the treaties with existing provision of domestic law, but in fact aiming to avoid any need to modify the said law, can be regarded as compatible with the object and purpose of the Covenant, especially in the light of the obligations of conduct which he finds expressed in art. 2. He considers that the object of art. 2 was to require all parties to adopt measures wherever necessary to give effect to the Covenant; reservations intended to deprive art. 2 of all effect themselves challenge the general principle reflected in art. 27 of the Vienna Convention on the Law of Treaties.
[89] Mr Richard (United Kingdom): UN doc. CCPR/C/SR.147, para. 18 and SR.149, para. 18; also Mr Cairncross (United Kingdom): ibid. SR.147, para. 32.

were discussed in the House of Commons.[90] The debate, which continued that of the previous year in the House of Lords,[91] arose out of a note submitted to the British Government by UNHCR, in which certain suggestions for reform were made. The two principal proposals were that 'all those provisions of the 1951 Convention and the 1967 Protocol which are not provided for in the existing law', should be specifically incorporated; and that there should be established 'a formal procedure for the determination of refugee status by an independent body' in accordance with recommendations made by the Executive Committee of the High Commissioner's Programme.[92] The Minister for State, in reply, noted that nothing in the Convention required incorporation. He explained that the normal procedure, before ratification, was to consider whether the existing provisions of the law covered any new obligations to be assumed in the treaty. If they did not, the law was amended and ratification followed; if they did, then no further steps were considered necessary. In the case of the Convention, he observed that the government of the day (the United Kingdom ratified in 1954) had been satisfied that 'legislative coverage was adequate' and no implementing laws were required.[93] The Convention imposed no obligation and offered no guidance in the matter of procedures for the determination of refugee status. While accepting that the Executive Committee's 1977 recommendations[94] might comprehend 'the basic requirements for the effective implementation of the Convention', he nevertheless felt that the United Kingdom's existing procedure was sufficient. Moreover, he noted that it was accepted by UNHCR that no Convention refugee had been expelled from the United Kingdom in recent years.[95]

The arguments regarding legislative implementation and establishment of a procedure, while formally correct in the light of

[90] 967 HC Deb. cols. 1363-81 (25 May 1979).

[91] 392 HL Deb. cols. 799-819 (22 May 1978).

[92] Ibid. cols. 815-6 (Lord Wells-Pestell).

[93] 967 HC Deb. col. 1376 (Mr Raison). A similar argument was stated the previous year in the Executive Committee by the United Kingdom's representative, Mr Gould, who noted that 'the States Parties to the 1951 Convention and the 1967 Protocol were under a duty to comply with those instruments and it was entirely for them to decide whether the provisions of those texts should for that purpose be incorporated in their national law'. UN doc. A/AC.96/SR.302, para. 17, commenting on UN doc. A/C.96/555, para. 6; also UN doc. A/AC.96/553, paras. 517-18.

[94] UN doc. A/AC.96/549, para. 53.6 (report of the Executive Committee, 28th Session, 1977).

[95] 967 HC Deb. cols. 1378-9.

obligations actually assumed, fail to go to the heart of the matter, which is effectiveness of implementation. That existing laws were adequate in 1954 might be conceded, but law and practice have undergone significant changes since then, particularly as regards entry and expulsion, the one area in which refugees face major problems.[96] That incompatibilities with the Convention had developed was impliedly admitted in the Minister's announcement of certain changes in practice.[97] While it is correct that no direct conflict or incompatibility exists between the provisions of the Convention and the Protocol and provisions of United Kingdom law, closer examination reveals that the law, like that of many countries, is of general application, making no special provision for refugees. It must therefore be supplemented by a judicious use of administrative discretion, both to avoid the application of the general law and to secure appropriate benefits. Under Article 28 of the Convention for example, refugees lawfully staying in the territory of contracting states are entitled to be issued with travel documents. If 'refugee status' is not recognized at law, and if no procedure exists whereby claims to refugee status can be determined, it may be difficult, if not impossible, for the contracting state effectively to implement its international obligations.[98]

In addition to assuming obligations with regard to the status and treatment of refugees, states ratifying the 1951 Convention and the 1967 Protocol necessarily undertake to implement those instruments effectively and in good faith. The choice of means in implementing most of the provisions is left to the states themselves; they may select legislative incorporation, administrative regulation, informal and *ad hoc* procedures, or a combination thereof. In no case will mere formal compliance itself suffice to discharge a state's responsibility; the test is whether, in the light of domestic law and practice, including the exercise of administrative

[96] The development of relevant legislation is summarized in Goodwin-Gill, *Movement of Persons*, 97 ff.

[97] 967 HC Deb. cols. 1379-80. The changes included provision for the recognition of refugees from Commonwealth countries, who even if granted asylum had not been accepted as Convention refugees because of their status as 'British subjects' (see above, ch. III, s. 3(3)); the issue of a refugee identity paper; and changes in the 'last resort' character of the immigration rules on asylum, which appeared to apply only to those who did not otherwise qualify for entry, for example, as a student or business person. See now revised immigration rules: 1980 HC no. 394, replacing 1973 HC nos. 79-82).

[98] See also art. 24(3), under which states agree to extend to refugees the benefits of treaties covering the maintenance of acquired rights and rights in the process of acquisition in regard to social security. Again, effective implementation would appear to be contingent on effective procedures for the determination of status. Cf. EEC Regulation 1408/71, art. 2(1), (2).

discretion, the state has attained the international standard of reasonable efficacy and efficient implementation of the treaty provisions concerned.

The following further conclusions are relevant to the broad question of effective implementation. First, states parties have undertaken particularly important obligations governing (a) the legal definition of the term 'refugee'; (b) the application of the Convention to refugees without discrimination; (c) the issue of travel documents to refugees; (d) the treatment of refugees entering illegally; (e) the expulsion of refugees; and (f) the *non-refoulement* of refugees. These topics all fall, somewhat loosely, within the field of immigration or aliens law; such law itself is most usually of general application, so that if special measures are not taken to single out the refugee, he or she is likely to be denied the rights and benefits due under the Convention and Protocol. Secondly, the Convention defines a status to which it attaches consequences, but says nothing about procedures for identifying those who are to benefit. While the choice of means may be left to states, some such procedure would seem essential for the effective implementation and fulfilment of convention obligations. It should be available to deal with claims to refugee status, whether made in the context of applications for asylum, for a travel document, or for a social security benefit, or in an appeal against expulsion.[99]

Specific *legislative* action in the areas cited above may well operate sufficiently to remove the refugee from the ambit of the general law; it might therefore be considered a necessary condition for effective implementation. The establishment of a procedure for the determination of refugee status, given the object and purpose of the instruments in question, may likewise be considered a further necessary condition. Whether in any given case such measures, either together or alone, are sufficient conditions for effective implementation remains to be judged in the light of the actual workings of the municipal system as a whole.[100]

---

[99] The state again benefits from choice of means, but the standard of effective implementation itself will be affected by the practice of other states and the recommendations of bodies such as the Executive Committee. Cf. art. 6, 1954 Caracas Convention on Territorial Asylum (below, annexe IX) which declares that states are under no obligation to make any distinction in the laws, regulations, or administrative acts applicable to aliens, solely because they are political asylees or refugees.

[100] The laws and procedure of the United Kingdom are examined more fully below; see ch. VIII, s. 2(6).

Chapter VII

# TREATY STANDARDS

The main treaties governing the status and treatment of refugees
have not yet achieved universal acceptance, and they do not in
fact either comprehend every refugee known to the world, or, in
many cases, offer any but the most basic guarantees. Nevertheless,
both the 1951 Convention and the 1967 Protocol are increasingly
and widely accepted, while the benefits which they call for are
commonly improved upon in actual practice, and supplemented
substantially by the provisions of regional and related instruments.
The Convention and the Protocol represent a point of departure
in considering the appropriate standard of treatment of refugees,
often exceeded, but still at base proclaiming the fundamental
principles of protection, without which no refugee can hope to
attain a satisfactory and lasting solution to his or her plight. The
present chapter briefly examines the provisions of these and
related agreements, with a view to determining the appropriate
conventional standards of treatment applicable to refugees and
asylum-seekers, whether lawfully or unlawfully in the territory of
contracting states.[1]

## 1. The 1951 Convention and the 1967 Protocol relating to the Status of Refugees

The importance of the 1951 Convention as a statement of the
minimum rights of refugees has been stressed repeatedly in the
preceding chapters. Time has shown its provisions to be inad-
equate to deal with certain aspects of today's refugee problems,
but its principal objective was always the regulation of issues of
legal status and treatment, rather than the grand design of universally acceptable solutions. It should not be forgotten that the Convention has its origin in the cold war climate of the late 1940s and
early 1950s, when concern centred on refugees in Europe. Similarly, the very European flavour of many of the provisions can be

[1] As of 31 Dec. 1982, 93 states had ratified the 1951 Convention and/or the 1967
Protocol. For full texts see annexes IV and V, and for parties, annexe XIV.

readily understood when it is realized that of the twenty-six states which participated in drafting and adopting the Convention, seventeen were from Europe and four more of a Western European/North American disposition. What is remarkable is that the 1951 Convention still attracts both ratifications and the continuing loyalty of state parties.

By Resolution 429(V) of 14 December 1950, the United Nations General Assembly decided to convene a Conference of Plenipotentiaries to draft and sign a convention on refugees and stateless persons; it duly convened in July 1951, but was able only to complete its work with regard to the former.[2] The Conference took as its basis for discussion a draft prepared by the *Ad hoc* Committee on Refugees and Stateless Persons, adopted at its second session in Geneva in August 1950,[3] save that the Preamble was that adopted by the Economic and Social Council,[4] while Article 1 was as recommended by the General Assembly and annexed to Resolution 429(V). The Conference also unanimously adopted five recommendations covering travel documents, family unity, non-governmental organizations, asylum, and application of the Convention beyond its contractual scope.

As noted in Chapter I, Article 1 limited the definition of refugees by reference not only to a well-founded fear of persecution, but also to a dateline (those resulting from 'events occurring before 1 January 1951'), and offered states the option of further restricting their obligations to refugees resulting from events occurring *in Europe* before the critical date. It was the object of the 1967 Protocol to remove that stipulative date, but the geographical option remains.[5] For convenience's sake, the 1967 Protocol has been referred to as 'amending' the 1951 Convention; in fact, it does no such thing. The Protocol is an independent instrument, not a revision within the meaning of Article 45 of the Convention.[6]

---

[2] The proposed Protocol formed the basis of the 1954 Convention relating to the Status of Stateless Persons: 360 UNTS 117, finalized after a further conference.

[3] UN doc. E/1850. This draft, and that adopted by the *Ad Hoc* Committee at its first session (UN doc. E/1618), are reprinted in Robinson, *Convention relating to the Status of Refugees: A Commentary* (1953), appendices ii and iii, 190-214. See also the draft prepared by the UN Secretariat (UN doc E/AC.32/2): ibid. 181-9.

[4] ECOSOC Res. 319 B II (XI), 11 Aug. 1950.

[5] As of 31 Dec. 1980, nine states maintained the geographical limitation: Argentina, Brazil, Italy, Madagascar, Malta, Monaco, Paraguay, Peru, and Turkey: *Multilateral Treaties in respect of which the Secretary-General performs depositary Functions* (1981) 123-51: UN doc. ST/LEG/SER.D/13.

[6] See generally Weis, 'The 1967 Protocol relating to the Status of Refugees and some questions of the law of treaties' 42 *BYIL* 39-70 (1967).

States parties to the Protocol, which can be ratified or acceded to by a state without becoming a party to the Convention,[7] simply agree to apply Articles 2 to 34 of the Convention to refugees defined in Article 1 thereof as if the dateline were omitted.[8] While reservations are generally permitted under both instruments, the integrity of certain articles is absolutely protected, including in particular, Articles 1 (definition); 3 (non-discrimination), 4 (religion), 16(1) (access to courts), and 33 (*non-refoulement*).[9]

(1) REQUIRED STANDARDS OF TREATMENT

As was the case with some of the inter-war arrangements,[10] the objective of the 1951 Convention and the 1967 Protocol is both to establish certain fundamental rights, such as *non-refoulement*, and to prescribe certain standards of treatment. The refugee may be stateless and therefore, as a matter of law, unable to secure the benefits accorded to nationals of his or her country of origin. Alternatively, even if nationality is retained, the refugee's unprotected status can make obtaining such benefits a practical impossibility. The Convention consequently proposes, as a minimum standard, that refugees should receive at least that treatment which is accorded to aliens generally.[11] Most-favoured-nation treatment[12] is called for in respect of the right of association and the right to engage in wage-earning employment (Articles 15 and 17(1)). The latter is of major importance to the refugee in search of an effective solution, but it is also the provision which has attracted most reservations.[13] Many states have thus emphasized that the reference to most-favoured-nation shall not be interpreted as entitling refugees to the benefit of special or regional customs, or economic or political agreements.[14] Other states have expressly

---

[7] Swaziland and the United States of America have acceded only to the Protocol.

[8] Art. I of the Protocol. Note also art. I(3), on the geographical limitation.

[9] Under the Convention, reservations are further prohibited with respect to Arts. 36-46, which include a provision entitling any party to a dispute to refer the matter to the International Court of Justice (art. 38). The corresponding provision of the Protocol (art. IV) may be the subject of reservation, and such has been made by Botswana, the Congo, Ghana, Jamaica, Rwanda, and Tanzania. It is also not clear from art. VII of the Protocol whether reservations may be made to art. II (co-operation with the United Nations); they are clearly permissible under the corresponding Convention provision (art. 35) although none has been made.

[10] Art. 37 lists the agreements replaced, as between the parties, by the Convention.

[11] Art. 7(1). Note also arts. 5, 6, 13, 18, 19, 21, 22(2); see further below on art. 26.

[12] Goodwin-Gill, *International Law and the Movement of Persons between States* (1978) 186 and note, and sources cited.

[13] For location of reservations cited, see above, n. 5.

[14] See reservations by Belgium, Denmark, Finland, Iran, Luxembourg, Madagascar, Netherlands, Norway, Peru, Spain, Sweden, and Uganda. See also Kiss, 'La convention européenne et la clause de la nation la plus favorisée' *Ann. Fr.* 478-89 (1957).

rejected most-favoured-nation treatment, limiting their obligation to accord only that standard applicable to aliens generally,[15] while some view Article 17 merely as a recommendation,[16] or agree to apply it 'so far as the law allows'.[17]

National treatment, finally, is to be granted in respect of a wide variety of matters, including the freedom to practice religion and as regards the religious education of children (Article 4); the protection of artistic rights and industrial property (Article 14); access to courts, legal assistance, and exemption from the *cautio judicatum solvi* (Article 16(2)); rationing (Article 20); elementary education (Article 22(1)),[18] public relief (Article 23);[19] labour legislation and social security (Article 24(1));[20] and fiscal charges (Article 29).

## (2) STANDARDS APPLICABLE TO REFUGEES QUA REFUGEES

Although the stipulative provisions of Article 1 are excluded from reservation, three states have made declarations which may affect claims to refugee status. The Netherlands, for example, declared on ratification that Ambionese transported to that country after 17 December 1949 (the date of Indonesia's accession to independence) were not considered eligible for refugee status. Turkey, on the other hand, stated on signature that it considered the Convention should apply also to 'Bulgarian refugees of Turkish extraction ... who, being unable to enter Turkey, might seek refuge on the territory of another Contracting State'.[21] Somalia, somewhat portentously, declared that its accession to the Convention was not to be construed so as to prejudice or adversely affect 'the national status or political aspiration of displaced people from Somali territories under alien domination'. Such evidently political statements, not amounting to reservations, appear to have had little if any susbtantive effect on the application of the Con-

---

[15] Ireland, Liechtenstein, Switzerland, and Zambia.

[16] Italy and Ethiopia.

[17] Jamaica; see also reservations by Malta, Sweden, the United Kingdom, and Zambia.

[18] Ethiopia, Monaco, and Zambia consider this provision a recommendation only.

[19] Iran and Monaco consider this a recommendation only, while it is not accepted by Malta; for Canada's reservation, see further below, n. 62.

[20] Reservations have been made to this article by Canada, Finland, Iran, Jamaica, Liechtenstein, Monaco, New Zealand, Sweden, Switzerland, the United Kingdom, and the United States of America. Turkey has declared that refugees shall not enjoy greater rights than Turkish citizens in Turkey.

[21] On ratification, Turkey also expressed its understanding that the terms 'reavailment' and 'reacquisition' in art. 1C implied not only a request by the individual concerned, but also the consent of the state in question.

vention generally or on the interpretation of the basic refugee definition.

Of greater importance is the varying degree to which states have been prepared to accept and to apply benefits and standards of treatment established by the Convention on behalf of refugees *qua* refugees. Article 8, for example, makes a half-hearted attempt to exempt refugees from the application of exceptional measures which might otherwise affect them by reason only of their nationality. Several states have made reservations, of which some exclude entirely any obligation, some regard the article as a recommendation only, while others expressly retain the right to take measures based on nationality in the interests of national security.[22] Article 9, indeed, expressly preserves the right of states to take 'provisional measures' on the grounds of national security against a particular person, 'pending a determination by the Contracting State that that person is in fact a refugee and that the continuance of such measures is necessary ... in the interests of national security'. Nevertheless, this has not prevented certain states from seeking further to entrench their powers by way of reservation.[23] Similar concern is evident in states' responses to Article 26, which prescribes such freedom of movement for refugees as is accorded to aliens generally in the same circumstances. Eight states have made reservations, six of which expressly retain the right to designate places of residence, either generally, or on grounds of national security, public order (*ordre public*) or the public interest.[24] Burundi, reflecting concerns shared by many African countries and reiterated in the 1969 OAU Convention,[25] declares that it accepts Article 26 provided refugees (a) do not choose their place of residence in a region bordering on their country of origin; and (b) refrain in any event, when exercising their right to move freely,

---

[22] Reservations by Ethiopia, Fiji, Finland, Israel, Jamaica, Madagascar, Malta, Spain, Sweden, Uganda, and the United Kingdom.

[23] Reservations by Ethiopia, Fiji, Finland, Jamaica, Madagascar, Malta, Uganda, and the United Kingdom.

[24] Reservations by Burundi, Greece, Netherlands, Rwanda, Spain, and Zambia; Botswana has made an 'open' reservation, while Iran considers art. 26 to be a recommendation only. At the 1951 Conference, the view was expressed that art. 26 was not infringed where, under a labour contract or group-settlement scheme, refugees who were admitted were required to remain in a particular job for a particular time: UN doc. E/AC.32/SR.11, 6. Robinson further considers that art. 26 would not be breached in the case of 'special situations where refugees have to be accommodated in special camps or in special areas even if this does not apply to aliens generally': *Commentary*, 133, n. 207. See further below, s. 1(2)(b).

[25] Arts. II(6) and III.

from any activity or incursion of a subversive nature with respect to the country of which they are nationals.

The principal articles still to be considered fall loosely into two groups: first, those under which states parties agree to provide certain facilities to refugees; and secondly, those by which states have undertaken to recognize and protect certain 'rights' on behalf of refugees. The first group includes the provision of administrative assistance (Article 25);[26] the issue of identity papers (Article 27); the issue of travel documents (Article 28);[27] the grant of permission to transfer assets (Article 30); and the facilitation of naturalization (Article 34). Within the second group are included the following specific 'rights'[28]: recognition of the law of personal status (Article 12);[29] exemption from penalties in respect of illegal entry or presence (Article 31); limitations on the liability to expulsion (Article 32); and the benefit of *non-refoulement* (Article 33).

## (a) *The Convention Travel Document: Article 28*

Article 28 of the 1951 Convention maintains the practice of issuing travel documents to refugees, initiated under the League of Nations, and provides in paragraph 2 for documents issued under earlier arrangements to continue to be recognized.[30] The operative part of Article 28 is succinct: 'The Contracting States shall issue to refugees lawfully staying in their territory travel documents for the purpose of travel outside their territory unless compelling reasons of national security or public order otherwise require ...'. The criterion of entitlement, 'lawfully staying', is examined more fully below, but it is evident that the words of this provision may well place the refugee in a better position with regard to the issue

---

[26] Some 'common law' countries, where affidavits and statutory declarations may take the place of official documents, have made reservations; see, for example, those of Fiji, Ireland, Jamaica, Uganda, and the United Kingdom. Finland and Sweden have also limited their obligations.

[27] Finland does not accept an obligation to issue travel documents, but agrees to recognize those issued by other contracting states. Israel agrees to issue CTDs subject to the limitations provided for in its passport law, while Zambia does not consider itself bound to issue a travel document with a return clause, where another state has accepted a refugee from Zambia.

[28] Art. 10, which protects certain types of residence otherwise affected by the events of the Second World War, is not considered further. Art. 11, in respect of refugee seamen, is examined above, ch. IV, s. 2(5)(b).

[29] The general rule is that personal status shall be governed by the law of a refugee's country of domicile or residence. Finland and Sweden maintain that status is governed by the law of nationality; Botswana and Israel do not accept art. 12, while Spain reserves its position with regard to para. 1.

[30] See also Recommendation A of the Final Act.

of travel documentation than the citizen of the state in which he or she resides.[31] A Schedule to the Convention prescribes the form of the travel document and makes provision, *inter alia,* for renewal, recognition, and return to the state of issue. Article 28(1) also empowers states, in their discretion, to issue travel documents to refugees not linked to them by the nexus of lawful stay, who may be present temporarily or even illegally.[32]

Where the applicant for a travel document is indeed a refugee within the Convention and/or the Protocol, and meets the requirement of lawful stay, Article 28 permits few exceptions to the obligation to issue. The reference to 'compelling' reasons of national security and public order as justifying an exception clearly indicates that restrictive interpretation is called for. It was thus emphasized at the 1951 Conference that the refugee is not required to justify his or her proposed travel;[33] on the other hand, paragraph 14 of the Schedule to the Convention (which declares that the Schedule's provisions in no way affect laws and regulations governing admission, transit, residence, establishment, and departure), might be interpreted as permitting a somewhat broader range of restrictions. In this context, 'public order' (*ordre public*) still remains a relatively fluid concept, and certain states have not excluded the possibility of applying to the issue of Convention travel documents the same restrictions as they would apply with regard to national passports.[34]

A more serious obstacle in practice to the issue of Convention travel documents can result from the absence within a state's administration of any procedure for consideration and deter-

[31] Generally on passports and the right to travel, see Goodwin-Gill, *Movement of Persons*, ch. II. Robinson notes that at the 1951 Conference, the representative of Venezuela, despite the wording of art. 28(1), held to the view that the issue of travel documents to refugees would not be considered mandatory in the absence of a similar obligation benefitting nationals: *Commentary*, 135, n. 212. Cf. Turkey's 'general' declaration that 'no provisions of [the] Convention may be interpreted as granting to refugees greater rights than those accorded to Turkish citizens in Turkey': Weis, 42 *BYIL* 39-70.

[32] Amended regulations governing the issue of CTDs in the United States, adopted in 1974, emphasized that issue was discretionary rather than mandatory in the case of a refugee so briefly in the country (for example, as a crewmember or in transit) that his or her presence did not imply residence even of a temporary nature: 8 CFR, 223a.3; cited in 1974 *Digest of United States Practice in International Law* 107.

[33] UN docs. E/AC.32/SR.16, 13-15; SR.42, 5-7; A/CONF.2/SR.12, 4-13; SR.17, 4-11.

[34] See the reservation by Israel; also the comment by an unidentified state representative in the Executive Committee's Sub-Committee of the Whole on International Protection in 1978: UN doc. A/AC.96/558, para. 34, who noted that issue would be precluded, *inter alia*, to a refugee who was not fulfilling family maintenance obligations.

mination of applications for refugee status. Even where such procedures do exist, they may be limited to consideration of refugee status in the context of asylum, i.e. at the point at which questions of admission, residence, and expulsion arise. The refugee admitted under a resettlement programme, or allowed to remain otherwise than by reference to his or her refugee status (for example, as a student or business person, or by reason of marriage to a local citizen) may be unable, quite simply, to invoke such status and thereby to secure treatment in accordance with the Convention. The standard of reasonably efficient and efficacious implementation suggests that some sort of procedure is required, if states are to meet their obligations under provisions such as Article 28.

The Schedule referred to above prescribes the format of the Convention travel document,[35] and further regulates its issue and renewal, extension, recognition by other states, and guarantee of the holder's returnability to the country of issue.[36] Geographical validity for the largest possible number of countries is called for, and the document is to be valid for one or two years, at the discretion of the issuing state.[37] Renewal shall be by the state of issue, so long as the holder has not established lawful residence in another country,[38] and diplomatic and consular offices abroad are to be empowered to effect limited extensions of validity.[39] Contracting states undertake to recognize Convention travel documents issued by other parties (even, it may be supposed, if they do not accept that the holder is a refugee)[40] and to accept them for visa purposes.[41] Paragraph 13(1) of the Schedule makes clear the obligation of the issuing state to readmit the holder of one of its travel documents 'at any time during the period of its validity'.[42]

[35] See also UN doc. EC/SCP/10 (1978), *passim.*

[36] On 'returnability' as an essential incident to travel documentation, see Goodwin-Gill, *Movement of Persons*, 44-6.

[37] Schedule, paras. 4, 5.

[38] Ibid., paras. 6(1), 11, 12.

[39] Schedule, para. 6(2); see also para. 6(3).

[40] On the 'extraterritorial' effect of determinations of refugee status, see further below, ch. IX, s. 1(2).

[41] Schedule, paras. 7, 8, 9. The obligation to recognize CTDs, of course, does not oblige states to admit their holders.

[42] The return clause only gradually became an integral part of the refugee travel document; see Goodwin-Gill, 42-4. Some states, on a bilateral basis, have agreed to re-admission even after expiration of validity; see, for example, art. 2 and 4, 1974 Austria-France Agreement on the Residence of Refugees (collected with other related instruments in Council of Europe doc. EXP/AT.Re(77) 3, 21-3). A similar provision is included in art. 4, 1980 European Agreement on Transfer of Responsibility for Refugees: ETS no. 107.

Paragraph 13(3) nevertheless empowers states 'in exceptional cases, or in cases where the refugee's stay is authorized for a specific period ...' to limit the return clause to not less than three months. Article 28 already acknowledges states' discretionary competence to issue travel documents to refugees not otherwise 'lawfully staying' in their territory. The Schedule confirms that discretion, by allowing states to avoid any long-term responsibility towards refugees whom they wish simply to assist with resettlement in a third state.[43] In practice, however, it is clear that excessive limitation of the return clause can result in serious problems for refugees, who may find themselves unable to return to the country of issue of their travel document and yet without any entitlement to residence elsewhere.[44]

With the aim of resolving some at least of those problems a number of states have concluded agreements regulating 'transfer of responsibility' for refugees who change their lawful residence from one country to another. Paragraph 6 of the Schedule predicates responsibility for renewal and extension of CTDs on the fact that 'the holder has not established lawful residence in another territory and resides lawfully in the territory' of the renewing authority. Paragraph 11, in turn, predicates transfer of responsibility for the issue of a CTD on the fact that the refugee 'has lawfully taken up residence in the territory of another Contracting State'. Given the divergence in national immigration laws and concepts, these terms are clearly capable of many different interpretations. Inter-state agreements have therefore attempted to provide objective criteria for ascertaining the moment of transfer. Article 2 of the 1980 European Agreement, for example, declares: '1. Responsibility shall be considered to be transferred on the expiry of a period of two years of actual and continuous stay in the second State with the agreement of its authorities or earlier if the second State has permitted the refugee to remain in its territory either on a permanent basis or for a period exceeding the validity of the travel document.'[45] The same article provides a method of

---

[43] Robinson, *Commentary*, 145; see also the general discussion in UN doc. A/AC.96/558, paras. 35-7.

[44] See UN docs. EC/SCP/12, paras. 19-23 (1979); A/AC.96/572, (report of the Executive Committee, 30th Session, 1979), paras. 60, 72(2) (m), (n). In 1978, the Observer for Botswana, in urging other countries to offer resettlement opportunities, noted that it was unfair that Botswana should be asked to readmit those who had gone abroad for education, solely because it had been the country of first refuge: UN doc. A/AC.96/SR.302, para. 14.

[45] See also the earlier bilateral agreements, loc. cit. above, n. 42.

calculation of the relevant period, and permits disregard of stay allowed solely for study, training, or medical care, and of periods of imprisonment.[46]

Finally, paragraph 15 of the Schedule to the Convention declares that neither the issue of a CTD nor entries on it shall affect the status of the holder, particularly as to nationality, and paragraph 16 affirms that the CTD holder is not entitled to diplomatic protection by the issuing state, and that that state acquires no right to exercise such protection. In practice, however, diplomatic assistance falling short of full protection is often accorded by issuing states, while the fact of possession of a CTD would constitute prima-facie evidence at least of the holder's entitlement to protection by UNHCR.

### (b)  *Treatment of refugees entering illegally: Article 31*

Article 31 has already been analysed in the context of *non-refoulement* and asylum.[47] Although not comprehensive, this provision serves as a point of departure in determining the minimum standard of treatment to be accorded to those whose situation remains unregularized in the country of first refuge. First, they are not to be subjected to 'penalties', a term which appears to comprehend prosecution, fine, and imprisonment, but not administrative detention. Article 31(2) makes it clear that states may impose 'necessary' restrictions on movement, which would include those prompted by security considerations or special circumstances like a large influx.[48] Such measures also come within Article 9, and are an exception to the freedom of movement called for by Article 26. Article 31(2) nevertheless calls for restrictions to be applied only until status in the country of refuge is regularized,[49] or admission obtained into another country; moreover, contracting states are to allow refugees a reasonable period and all necessary facilities to obtain such admission. Those facilities clearly include access to the representatives of other states and of UNHCR.

---

[46] Art. 2(2). Temporary absences not exceeding three months on any one occasion or six months in all are not deemed to interrupt stay.

[47] See above, ch. IV, s. 2(4). See also art. 5, 1954 Caracas Convention on Territorial Asylum; below, annexe IX.

[48] Robinson, *Commentary,* 154.

[49] Cf. art. 9: 'pending a determination ... that [the] person is in fact a refugee ...'. Under amendments introduced in Hong Kong in 1982, Vietnamese arriving after 2 July of that year who were detained were to be given 'all reasonable facilities' to obtain authorization to enter another state, or to leave Hong Kong, with or without such authorization: Immigration Amendment Ordinance 1982 (no. 42/82) s. 7 (adding new s. 13D).

Secondly, account should be taken of Article 31's categorical references to 'refugees'. It might be argued that the benefit of this provision is only to be accorded to refugees formally recognized as such. In practice, however, recognition procedures, if they exist, may well be overburdened and inoperative on the occasion of a mass influx, or the state of refuge may be unwilling, for political and other reasons, to make any formal determination of status. Article 31(2), however, does contemplate regularization of status, which would include determination of the refugee issue, and Article 9 has a similarly forward-looking aspect. In these circumstances it is believed that the benefit of Article 31 is due to the broad class of bona fide asylum-seekers defined above,[50] pending formal determination, if any, of refugee status.

### (c) *Expulsion of refugees: Article 32*

Article 32, which limits the circumstances in which refugees 'lawfully in their territory' may be expelled by contracting states, has also been analysed above in the context of *non-refoulement*.[51] The meaning of 'lawfully' in Article 32 is examined further below, and for the present it suffices to recall that this provision limits expulsion to grounds of national security or public order; that it requires a decision to be reached in accordance with due process of law; that some form of appeal should be generally permitted; and that the refugee should be allowed a reasonable period in which to seek admission into another country. As with most Convention provisions, the state clearly enjoys choice of means with regard to its implementation of Article 32. Thus, it may be sufficient to adopt internal, *ad hoc* administrative procedures regulating the exercise of the discretion to set removal machinery in motion, so that formal incorporation of the limitations on explusion is not necessary. Moreover, some uncertainty surrounds the precise implications of the reference to decisions in accordance with due process of law. The French version of the text ('*une décision rendue conformément à la procédure prévue par la loi*') suggests that formal compliance with the law is all that is required.[52] Alternatively, the concept of

---

[50] See above, ch. I, s. 7; ch. IV, s. 4.

[51] See above, ch. IV, s, 2(3).

[52] This appears to be Ireland's interpretation, as stated on ratification: loc. cit. above, n. 5. Cf. Uganda's reservation to art. 32: 'Without recourse to legal process the Government ... shall, in the public interest, have the unfettered right to expel any refugee ... and may at any time apply such internal measures as the Government may deem necessary in the circumstances; so however that any action taken by the Government ... in this regard shall not operate to the prejudice of the provisions of art. 33 ...' (Ibid.).

due process today can be considered to include, as minimum requirements, (a) knowledge of the case against one, (b) an opportunity to submit evidence to rebut that case, and (c) the right to appeal against an adverse decision before an impartial tribunal independent of the initial decision-making body. It is a moot point to what extent these higher standards of procedural due process are now required by the precepts of general international law.[53]

### (d)  Non-refoulement: *Article 33*

The scope of the principle of *non-refoulement*, both as a conventional rule and as a rule of general international law, has been fully analysed in Chapter IV.

## (3)  THE CRITERIA OF ENTITLEMENT TO TREATMENT IN ACCORDANCE WITH THE CONVENTION

Some provisions of the Convention are limited to refugees 'lawfully staying' in contracting states, some apply to those 'lawfully in' such states, while others apply to refugees *tout court,* whether lawfully or unlawfully present. Regrettably, there is little consistency in the language of the Convention, be it English or French, but three general categories may be distinguished: simple presence, lawful presence, and lawful residence.

### (a)  *Simple presence*

Some benefits extend to refugees, by virtue of their status alone as refugees, without in any way being dependent upon their legal situation. Article 33, for example, refers simply to refugees, as does Article 3.[54] Articles 2, 4, and 27 are predicated on the fact of presence ('the country in which he finds himself'; 'refugees within their territories'; 'any refugee in their territory'/'*du pays où il se trouve*'; '*réfugiés sur leur territoire*'; '*tout réfugié se trouvant sur leur territoire*'), while Article 31 is specifically applicable to cases of illegal entry or presence ('in their territory without authorization'/'*se trouve sur leur territoire sans autorisation*').

### (b)  *Lawful presence*

Lawful presence is to be distinguished from lawful residence; it implies admission in accordance with the applicable immigration law, for a temporary purpose, for example, as a student, visitor, or recipient of medical attention. Owing to the different ap-

---

[53] Cf. Goodwin-Gill, *Movement of Persons* 227-8, 238-40, 308-9.
[54] See also art. 16(1).

proaches adopted within national systems, the distinction is often difficult to maintain in practice. For the purposes of the Convention, Articles 18, 26, and 32 apply to refugees whose presence is lawful (lawfully in/*qui se trouvent régulièrement*).[55]

The extension of Article 32 benefits to refugees who are merely lawfully present in contracting states, even if only on a temporary basis, may be disputed in the light of state practice. Thus, Article 43 of the 1979 Swiss law on asylum affords the benefit of restricted grounds of expulsion to the refugee '*auquel la Suisse a accordé l'asile*'.[56] A similar approach is found in other jurisdictions,[57] and in principle there appears to be no reason why the temporarily present refugee should not be subject to the same regime of deportation as applies to aliens generally. It may be assumed that he or she will still enjoy the right of return to the state which issued a travel document and the benefit of Article 33 will apply in any event. It may be argued that the grounds of public order/*ordre public* include breach of any aspect of a country's immigration or aliens law,[58] in which case little substantive protection is offered to distinguish the refugee lawfully present from the refugee lawfully resident. On balance, Article 32 should be interpreted as a substantial limitation upon the state's power of expulsion, but with its benefits confined to lawfully resident refugees, i.e. those in the state on a more or less indefinite basis.

### (c) *Lawful residence*

Finally, there are many articles only applicable to refugees lawfully resident in the contracting state, i.e. those who are, as it were, enjoying asylum in the sense of residence and lasting protection.

---

[55] Cf. art. 11, which refers to refugees 'regularly serving as crew members /*réguilièrement employés comme membres de l'équipage*'.

[56] FF 1979 II 977. A similar limitation on the scope of art. 32 has also been expressed to the author by senior government officials in a number of countries.

[57] See, for example, *AuslG*, 1965, art. 11 as amended , *AsylVFG*, 1982, art. 39, Federal Republic of Germany. In *Kan Kim Lin* v. *Rinaldi* 361 F. Supp. 177 (1973), the US District Court, referring to the *travaux préparatoires* on art. 32, observed that the term 'lawfully in their territory' would 'exclude a refugee who, while lawfully admitted, has overstayed the period for which he was admitted or was authorized to stay or who has violated any other condition attached to his admission or stay' (at 186; judgment affirmed 493 F.2d (1974) Ct. of Appeals). In *Chim Ming* v. *Marks* 505 F.2d 1170 (1974), the Court of Appeals considered that the 'only rational interpretation' of the phrase was 'one consistent with the definition of unlawfulness in Article 31 as involving the status of being in a nation "without authorization". Since a nation's immigration laws provide authorization, one unlawfully in the country is in violation of those laws.'

[58] See cases cited in Goodwin-Gill, *Movement of Persons* 298, n. 1, and generally, 295-9.

Again the terminology varies. Article 25 refers to states 'in whose territory (the refugee) is residing/*sur le territoire duquel il réside*'. Articles 14 and 16(2) invoke the country of the refugee's 'habitual residence/*résidence habituelle*', while Articles, 15, 17(1), 19, 21, 23, 24, and 28 employ, in English, the somewhat imprecise term 'lawfully staying'.[59] The corresponding phrase in the French text is '*résident régulièrement*' (or some variation thereof); it is evident from the *travaux préparatoires* concerning Article 28, for example, that the English phrase was selected for its approximation to the French term, particularly as the concept of residence in common law systems is often replete with contradiction. The terminology adopted in the Convention, however, is not free from difficulty. It was noted at the 1951 Conference that a resident in France may be a privileged, ordinary, or temporary resident.[60] The cases of those present only for a short period of time might cause problems, but in the view of the French representative, '... an examination of the various articles in which the words 'résident régulièrement' appeared would show that they all implied a settling down and consequently a certain length of residence'.[61] In order to obtain the benefit of the articles cited above, the refugee must show something more than mere lawful presence.[62] Generalizations are difficult in the face of different systems of immigration control, but evidence of permanent or other residence status, recognition as a refugee, issue of a travel document, grant of a re-entry visa, will raise a strong presumption that the refugee should be considered as lawfully staying in the territory of a contracting state. It would then fall to that state to rebut the presumption by showing, for example, that the refugee was admitted for a limited time and purpose, or that he or she is in fact the responsibility of another state.[63]

[59] See also the terminology of residence used in paras. 6 and 11 of the Schedule.

[60] UN doc. E/AC.32/SR.42, 11 ff.; Goodwin-Gill, *Movement of Persons* 251-4.

[61] UN doc. E/AC.32/SR.42, p. 15.

[62] In its reservation to arts. 23 and 24, Canada states that it interprets 'lawfully staying' as referring only to refugees admitted for permanent residence; refugees admitted for temporary residence are to be accorded the same treatment with respect to those articles as is accorded to visitors generally.

[63] Cf. the approach adopted in the bilateral agreements cited above, n. 42. The Protocol to the 1962 Switzerland-Federal Republic of Germany agreement, for example, while discounting periods of stay for educational, medical, or convalescence purposes, deems authorization of establishment to arise, '*lorsque le réfugié a obtenu une autorisation de séjour illimitée ou lorsqu'il peut justifier d'une résidence régulière de trois ans ...*'. The agreements in question deal with transfer of responsibility *between states*, and no such period of elapsed residence is required for the refugee seeking to invoke the benefit of Convention articles *vis-à-vis* his or her country of asylum.

## 2. Refugees as the beneficiaries of other instruments, including regional agreements

Refugees also benefit from a wide variety of other international agreements, many of which have been cited in the preceding chapters. Others of relevance are referred to in the following note.[64]

The variety of instruments affecting refugees does not permit very many useful generalizations. How refugees are defined will often differ from agreement to agreement, although the criteria of the Convention and the Protocol tend to feature as the basic definition, often developed and expanded in the light of regional conditions. The criteria of entitlement will also necessarily vary,

[64] Instruments of universal or potentially universal application include: the 1966 Human Rights Covenants; the 1949 Geneva Convention relative to the Protection of Civilian Persons in time of War (75 UNTS 287, arts. 26, 44, 70) and Protocol 1 thereto, adopted in 1977 (arts. 73, 74, and 85; text in vol. iii, *Official Records of the Diplomatic Conference on the Reaffirmation and Development of International Humanitarian Law applicable in Armed Conflicts*, Geneva, 1974-77); conventions dealing with the safety of life at sea, incuding art. 11, 1910 Brussels Convention for the Unification of Certain Rules of Law relating to Assistance and Salvage at Sea; art. 12, 1958 Geneva Convention on the High Seas; Regulations 10 and 15, 1960 International Convention on the Safety of Life at Sea; 1979 International Convention on Maritime Search and Rescue, art. I and annexe, paras. 2.1.1, 2.1.10, and 5.3.3.8; International Labour Organization conventions, including Convention no. 118 concerning Equality of Treatment of Nationals and Non-Nationals in Social Security, 1962 (art. 1 and 10(1)), Convention no. 97 concerning Migration for Employment, 1949, annexe II, art. 11. Specific aspects of the refugee problem have been the subject of instruments such as the 1957 refugee seamen agreement and the 1973 protocol thereto, or of protocols annexed to agreements such as the 1971 revision of the Universal Copyright Convention; such protocols derive from art. 14, common to both the 1951 Convention relating to the Status of Refugees and the 1954 Convention relating to the Status of Stateless Persons, and a like protocol has also been proposed for consideration by the Diplomatic Conference on the Revision of the 1883 Paris Convention for the Protection of Industrial Property.

On a regional level, refugees and asylum-seekers may gain from the provisions and supervisory machinery established by the American and European Conventions on Human Rights or, in Latin America, from the complex network governing aspects of diplomatic and territorial asylum (1889 Montevideo Treaty on International Penal Law; 1928 Havana Convention on Asylum; 1933 Montevideo Convention on Political Asylum; 1940 Montevideo Treaty on International Penal Law (revising that of 1889); 1954 Caracas Convention on Territorial Asylum; 1954 Caracas Convention on Diplomatic Asylum). In Africa, the 1969 OAU Convention may apply, while in Europe a large number of arrangements have been concluded under the auspices of the Council of Europe (see, for example, the 1959 European agreement on the abolition of visas for refugees (ETS no. 31; its object is visa-free travel between contracting states for refugees holding CTDs issued by, and residing in, any contracting state; it is limited to visits not exceeding three months, undertaken otherwise than for employment); refugees and stateless persons resident in contracting states may also be equated with nationals, for the purpose of according them a certain standard of treatment (see, for example, arts. 1(o), (p), 2, 4, 1972 European Convention on Social Security: ETS no. 78; also EEC Regulation 1408/71, arts. 1, 2; Goodwin-Gill, *Movement of Persons* 172-3).

depending on the nature of the right claimed. In the case of non-extradition, for example, it is status as a refugee which counts, whereas in claims to equality of treatment in matters such as social security, the applicant may be required additionally to satisfy the criterion of residence or habitual residence in a contracting state.

Chapter VIII

# PROTECTION IN MUNICIPAL LAW

Whether a state takes steps to protect refugees within its jurisdiction and if so, which steps, are matters very much in the realm
of sovereign discretion. For states parties to the Convention and
Protocol, however, the outer limits of that discretion are confined
by the principle of effectiveness of obligations, and the measures
it adopts will be judged by the international standard of reasonable
efficacy and efficient implementation. Legislative incorporation
may not itself be expressly called for, but effective implementation
requires, at least, some form of procedure whereby refugees can
be identified, and some measure of protection against laws of
general application governing admission, residence, and removal.
State practice understandably reveals widely divergent methods
of implementation, from which it is difficult to extract any easy
formula for determining adequacy and sufficiency. The effectiveness of formal measures depends not only upon the overall efficacy
of a state's internal administrative and judicial system, but also
upon the particular problems with which that system is faced.
Procedures designed for the individual asylum-seeker may fail to
absorb, let alone survive, a mass influx; the needs of the latter,
moreover, will often differ radically, requiring less sophisticated,
often purely material solutions, at least in the short term.

A potentially useful distinction is that between refugee status,
on the one hand, and the legal consequences which flow from that
status, on the other hand; the latter may include an entitlement to
residence formally recognized by municipal law or simply eligibility for consideration under a discretionary power only distantly
confined by international law. In practice, that distinction is often
difficult to preserve, particularly where status is itself the criterion
for residence and where normal residence requirements—relating,
for example, to character or potential for assimilation—may filter
back to influence the decision whether someone is a refugee. Similarly, the mere fact that a state treats refugees separately from
others will not be conclusive evidence of effective protection. A
refugee enjoys fundamental human rights common to citizens and

foreign nationals; where these are generally assured, where due process of law is acknowledged, and where measures of appeal and judicial review permit examination of the merits and the legality of administrative decisions, then the refugee also may be sufficiently protected.

The object of the present chapter is to illustrate, therefore, the variety of the methods chosen by states to protect refugees, with particular reference to definition of the class; procedures for determination of refugee status and criteria for the grant of residence; and limitations on expulsion and *refoulement*.

## 1. Definition of refugees

States' differing approaches to the problem of definition have already been mentioned.[1] The criteria of the 1951 Convention are commonly adopted, with additional provision often made for others who, while not refugees in the strict sense, may yet be considered as having valid reasons for equivalent treatment. The practice in extradition laws of recognizing the 'political offender' as someone worthy of exceptional treatment has also been noted. Similar jurisdictions may employ similar concepts of political offence, but the act of characterization is dominated by municipal law considerations. Although it is not concerned with political offences as such,[2] international law is directly concerned with the treatment anticipated for the returned offender. Increasingly states' laws are adopting the criterion of liability to persecution or prejudice as the underlying rationale, the international standard precluding return.

## 2. Procedures for the determination of refugee status and the criteria for the grant of residence

The basic refugee definition, both in international law and in the form adopted by municipal systems, is highly individualistic. It supposes a dispassionate case-by-case examination of subjective and objective elements, which may well prove impractical in the face of large numbers, although they too require the benefit of

---

[1] See above, ch. I, s. 6.

[2] Save in so far as recent international agreements have had the declared object and purpose of *excluding* certain offences from the political offence exception; see above, ch. III, s. 4(1).

certain minimum standards.[3] For asylum-seekers generally, the very existence of procedures for the determination of status can guarantee both *non-refoulement* and treatment in accordance with the relevant international instruments. At its major session on protection in 1977, the Executive Committee of the High Commissioner's Programme expressed the hope that all states parties to the Convention and Protocol would establish such procedures and also give favourable consideration to UNHCR participation. The Committee further recommended basic procedural requirements, designed at such a level of generality as to be capable of adoption by most states.[4] Seven procedures are described below in detail and in the light of their adequacy and effectiveness; they have been selected on the basis of the writer's personal experience. Twenty-eight others are described summarily, on the basis of information provided by states themselves to UNHCR and transmitted to the Executive Committee.

## (1) AUSTRALIA

### (a) *Legal background*

Neither the 1951 Convention nor the 1967 Protocol has been expressly incorporated into Australian municipal law. The entry of refugees falls, therefore, within the broad discretionary provisions of the Migration Act 1958, as amended.[5] The responsible authority is the Minister for Immigration and Ethnic Affairs; a more or less parallel competence to grant 'political asylum' resides in the Minister for Foreign Affairs, but it is rarely exercised independently.[6] Following a 'regularization of status programme' in

---

[3] See report of the 1979 Arusha Conference, recommendations on the term 'refugee' and determination of refugee status: UN doc. A/AC.96/INF/158, at 9 (1979).

[4] See further below, ch. VIII, s. 4.

[5] Migration Act 1958 (no. 62 of 1958; amended by no. 87 of 1964, no. 10 of 1966, nos. 16 and 216 of 1973, nos. 37 and 91 of 1976, nos. 117 and 118 of 1979, and no. 89 of 1980). In 1980, the Immigration (Unauthorized Arrivals) Act was enacted. One of its objectives is to prevent and punish the act of carrying to Australia large numbers of asylum-seekers in boats specially fitted out for that purpose, as has frequently happened in South East Asia. Provision is made for penalties up to $100,000 and ten years imprisonment. The Act is also capable of applying to those who, having rescued refugees at sea, arrive at an Australian first port of call; it is understood, however, that prosecutorial discretion would be exercised favourably on behalf of ships' masters responsible for purely humanitarian actions. The Act was proclaimed and entered into force on 30 Sept. 1981, shortly before a bogus refugee boat carrying illegal immigrants arrived in Darwin. Those on board, though originally from Vietnam, had been lawfully resident in Hong Kong and Taiwan; they were subsequently deported to those countries.

[6] According to amendments introduced in 1980, the grant of territorial asylum in Australia 'by instrument under the hand of a Minister' is one of the limited circumstances in which residence may be accorded to a person after entry. See also following note.

1979-80, legislation was enacted to restrict the discretion of the Minister to grant amnesties by limiting the circumstances in which the status of permanent resident may be accorded to a person after entry. The eligible categories include persons granted 'territorial asylum' in Australia, and holders of temporary entry permits which are in force, whom the Minister by instrument in writing determines to have the status of refugee within the meaning of the Convention and Protocol. Also included are cases involving strong compassionate or humanitarian grounds.[7]

In May 1977, the Minister for Immigration and Ethnic Affairs announced the creation of a standing inter-departmental committee to evaluate claims to refugee status under the Convention, and to make appropriate recommendations. Later the same year, inter-departmental discussions, in which UNHCR participated, resulted in the establishment of the Determination of Refugee Status (DORS) Committee and in agreement on procedural rules.[8] The Committee began assessing applications for refugee status in 1978, and now meets regularly in Canberra. The determination and advice of the DORS Committee do not have the force of law, but in practice those recognized as refugees by the Minister, on the recommendation of the Committee, have generally been accorded residence in Australia, without limit as to time. In a few cases, recognized refugees were initially kept on temporary entry permits, generally pending confirmation of good behaviour.

(b) *Procedure*

Application for refugee status may be made on arrival at a port of entry, or after entry, either during the currency of any temporary permission to remain or after its expiry, or after the initiation of deportation machinery. Under guidelines established in 1977, every applicant first completes an application form setting out personal particulars and the basis of the claim; he or she is then interviewed, that interview is transcribed, acknowledged as accurate by signature of the applicant, and referred to the DORS Committee. Interviews are generally conducted in each state by officers of the Department of Immigration and Ethnic Affairs, while the Committee hitherto has always sat in Canberra. Appli-

---

[7] Migration Amendment Act (no. 2) 1980 (no. 175 of 1980), s. 4, inserting new s. 6A in the principal Act.

[8] Confirmed by cabinet decisions of 24 May 1977 and 16 Mar. 1978.

cants are interviewed where necessary with the aid of interpreters, they are entitled to be accompanied by a legal adviser of their choice, and they are informed of the address of UNHCR and their freedom to contact that Office.

The DORS Committee itself is chaired by an official from the Department of Immigration and Ethnic Affairs, with other members from the Department of Foreign Affairs, the Attorney-General's Department, and the Department of Prime Minister and Cabinet. The UNHCR representative in Australia is also entitled to attend meetings of the DORS Committee in an observer capacity, and to make known the views of the Office. The Committee, which is required to apply the Convention and Protocol definition of a refugee, considers applications on the basis of the interview report and any other information submitted by the applicant, government departments, or UNHCR. The applicant does not usually appear in person, which may cause problems on occasion where the decision turns on credibility. In a High Court decision in 1982, however, it was held that an applicant for refugee status has no right or legitimate expectation upon which to found an entitlement to be accorded that degree of natural justice which would permit appearance before and direct representation to the Committee. The Court also noted in passing that, 'to seek to apply anything like the full content of the maxim *audi alteram partem* to cases before the Committee, which may have to consider a wide range of confidential information about conditions overseas and whose conclusions might, if made public, affect good relations with other countries, might well stultify its operations and would not serve the best interests of applicants...'.[9]

Decisions within the Committee are by majority vote (with the chair holding a casting vote in the event of a tie), and the Committee may accept, reject, or defer an application for further inquiries. In addition, it may recommend that an applicant whose claim to refugee status is rejected, should nevertheless be considered for temporary or permanent residence in Australia on humanitarian or compassionate grounds. The Minister for Immigration and Ethnic Affairs retains overall responsibility and may therefore accept or reject the Committee's recommendation. Moreover, the question of residence for those accepted or rejected

---

[9] *Simsek* v. *Minister for Immigration and Ethnic Affairs*, 40 ALR 61 (High Court of Australia, 1982). In a very few cases, where decisions were required as a matter of urgency, applicants have in fact been called before the committee.

is not itself decided by the Committee, although a favourable recommendation on refugee status creates a strong presumption that residence will follow.

In practice, the procedure by in-depth interview and verbatim transcription proved on occasion to be cumbersome and time-consuming. In 1982, therefore, a revised application form was developed by the Committee, in which the onus of showing a good claim to refugee status was shifted more onto the applicant. A shortened interview format was also used to establish the core issues relating to the circumstances of departure from the country of origin and the reasons for unwillingness or inability to return.[10]

In 1981, the Committee discussed the question of admissibility of applications, with a view to dealing more quickly with manifestly ill-founded and incompatible applications. The necessity for maintaining effective procedural guarantees for all applicants was acknowledged, and given that the Minister retained the final power of decision in each case, it was considered inappropriate for the Committee itself summarily to reject applications on the basis of their inadmissibility. Nevertheless, decision-making could be facilitated by agreement on certain substantive bases for rejection and it was generally agreed that applications might be considered *incompatible* with the Convention and Protocol, where (1) the applicant holds dual or multiple nationality and no claim to persecution or lack of protection is made in respect of those other states with which he or she is linked; (2) the applicant has found protection elsewhere or falls within Article 1D or 1E of the Convention; (3) the applicant falls within Article 1F of the Convention; (4) the applicant having been convicted of a particularly serious crime in Australia constitutes a danger to the community; and (5) the applicant constitutes a danger to the security of Australia. Alternatively, applications might be considered *manifestly ill-founded* where (1) the information provided by the applicant discloses no appearance of a claim to a well-founded fear of persecution; or (2) the allegations made by the applicant, even if substantiated, would not bring him or her within Article 1 of the Convention.[11] Where a decision to reject a case on the above grounds is based on a preliminary interview only, it requires unanimity and the concurrence of the UNHCR representative.

---

[10] At the time of writing, Dec 1982, a pilot study was being made of the revised application process.

[11] Cf. the comparable jurisprudence of the European Commission and the European Court of Human Rights: Jacobs, *The European Convention on Human Rights* (1975) 222 ff.

Where any Committee member or UNHCR so requests, the application is deferred for full investigation.

## (c) *Appeal*

There is at present no right of appeal against an adverse decision of the DORS Committee, and the only formal provision in this regard empowers the Minister to remit for reconsideration any case in which new information is received. However, certain classes of claimants to refugee status may raise the issue in court. The Administrative Appeals Tribunal Act of 1975 introduced a limited right of appeal against deportation on behalf of aliens convicted of crimes and of immigrants in certain other specified cases, but this does not extend to one who wishes to challenge removal from the country following illegal entry or on becoming a prohibited immigrant.[12]

In a 1979 judgment, the Administrative Appeals Tribunal expressly considered relevant provisions of the 1951 Convention on expulsion and *refoulement*, although these are not formally part of Australian law.[13] As the appellant lost on the merits of the case, the extent to which an applicant for refugee status is able to rely successfully on the Convention and Protocol remains undecided. While the 1975 Act generally permits appeal on the *merits* of administrative decisions, so that the Tribunal effectively determines what is 'the right or preferred decision in the circumstances',[14] in the case of deportation decisions it is empowered only to affirm the decision 'or remit the matter for reconsideration in accordance with any recommendations' it may make.[15] Further possibilities of judicial review are raised by the entry into force in October 1980 of the Administrative Decisions (Judicial Review) Act 1977.[16] This statute codifies and extends the grounds for review of the legality of administrative action, vesting jurisdiction generally in the Federal Court of Australia, and instituting a single remedy, the order of review.[17] It is already clear, however, that

---

[12] The right of appeal is available, under the Schedule to the Act, to persons subject to deportation orders made under sections 12 and 13 of the Migration Act 1958.

[13] *Ceskovic* v. *Minister for Immigration and Ethnic Affairs*, 27 Mar. 1979, affirmed 27 ALR 423 (Federal Court of Australia).

[14] Pearce, *The Administrative Law Service* (1979) at para. 109 and generally. The Convention and the Protocol, as evidence of Australia's international obligations, would thus constitute 'relevant material' to assist the Tribunal in reaching the appropriate decision.

[15] Administrative Appeals Tribunal Act 1975, Schedule, para. 22(3).

[16] No. 59 of 1977.

[17] Administrative Decisions (Judicial Review) Act 1977, ss. 3(1), 5.

certain types of decision to which refugees may be liable (for example, deportation orders made against prohibited immigrants) may still be beyond the range of effective review.[18]

## (2) BELGIUM

### (a) *Legal background*

The legal basis for determining refugee status is found in a series of enactments adopting the 1951 Convention and 1967 Protocol, and establishing the conditions of entry, residence, and establishment of foreign nationals in Belgium.[19] Article 3 of the 1953 law appoints the Minister of Foreign Affairs as the sole authority to determine refugee status, but also provides that the Minister may delegate that competence to the international authority entrusted by the United Nations with protecting refugees.[20] This power has been duly exercised in favour of the UNHCR representative in Belgium.[21]

### (b) *Procedure*

All applications for refugee status are first examined by the Ministry of Justice with a view to determining their admissibility: applications must be made without delay (within forty-eight hours of entry, or within two weeks of the change of circumstances in the country of origin which is alleged to give rise to a fear of persecution on return) and Belgium must be the country of first asylum.[22] Admissible cases are referred to the UNHCR office in

---

[18] In *Capello* v. *Minister for Immigration and Ethnic Affairs* (3 Dec. 1980), the Federal Court of Australia confirmed that the power to deport under s. 18 of the Migration Act is not subject to an obligation to observe the rules of natural justice. The duty to give reasons, moreover, was fulfilled by the statement that the person to be deported was a prohibited immigrant. See also Simsek's case, above, n. 9 and accompanying text.

[19] Law of 26 June 1953, adopting the 1951 Convention: *Moniteur* 4 Oct. 1953, (1953) *Pasinomie* 723; ministerial decree of 22 Feb. 1954: *Moniteur* 18 Apr. 1954; royal decree of 18 June 1964: *Moniteur* 30 June 1964, (1964) *Pasinomie* 777, amending the royal decree of 25 Mar. 1961: *Moniteur* 25 Apr. 1961, (1961) *Pasinomie* 386, relating to the conditions of entry, residence, and establishment of foreign nationals in Belgium; royal decree of 21 Dec. 1965: *Moniteur* 31 Dec. 1965, (1965) *Pasinomie* 1526, as amended by decree of 11 July 1969: *Moniteur* 14 Aug. 1969, (1969) *Pasinomie* 1244, also relating to the conditions of entry, residence, and establishment of foreign nationals in Belgium; law of 27 Feb. 1969: *Moniteur* 3 May 1969, (1969) *Pasinomie* 110, approving the 1967 Protocol. See also the new law on foreigners of 15 Dec. 1980: *Moniteur* 31 Dec. 1980.

[20] Law of 26 June 1953, (1953) *Pasinomie* 723, art. 5.

[21] Ministerial decree of 22 Feb. 1954: *Moniteur* 18 Apr. 1954. For earlier precedents, see above, ch. VI, s. 1.

[22] Law of 28 Mar. 1952, art. 3: *Moniteur* 30 Mar. 1952, (1952) *Pasinomie* 209, as amended by Law of 30 Apr. 1964: *Moniteur* 30 June 1964, (1964) *Pasinomie* 543.

Brussels, where asylum-seekers are interviewed and complete a detailed application form. If the application is considered manifestly ill-founded, the Ministry of Justice may initially decide to proceed no further with the case. If this initial decision is contested, and in all other cases, the UNHCR representative will then decide the issue of refugee status. If recognition is accorded, the UNHCR branch office will issue a certificate attesting thereto. The decision on recognition is directly effective in Belgium law, and the recognized refugee is granted residence in consequence.

### (c) *Appeal*

While no formal right of appeal is accorded by Belgium law, in practice any asylum-seeker whose application has been rejected may request UNHCR to review the decision. Cases are reopened (1) if new facts or evidence are adduced which, had they been known during the first examination of the case, would have led to a favourable decision, or (2) if it appears that an error or misunderstanding has occurred. The appellant is permitted to remain in the country pending review of the case.

### (3) FRANCE

### (a) *Legal background*

The legal bases for the determination of refugee status and for the grant of residence in France are the 1958 Constitution, the Preamble of which includes a statement of the principle of asylum, and a series of operating laws and administrative decrees.[23]

The competent authority for determining refugee status is the *Office français de protection des réfugiés et apatrides* (*OFPRA*), attached to the Minister of Foreign Affairs, but with its own legal personality and financial and administrative autonomy.[24] The Director of *OFPRA* is assisted by a Council which approves the budget and the accounts of the office, advises generally on administration and on determination of refugee status, and proposes to the government any measures aimed at improving the situation of refugees. It is chaired by a representative of the Minister of Foreign Affairs

---

[23] Law no. 52-893 concerning the creation of the French Office for the Protection of Refugees and Stateless Persons (*OFPRA*) of 25 July 1952: (1952) *Journal Officiel* (*JO*) 7642; (1952) Dalloz, *Législation* (*DL*) 284; Decree no. 53-377 relating to *OFPRA*, 2 May 1953: (1953) *JO* 4029; (1953) *DL* 158; Law no. 70-1076 authorizing accession to the 1967 Protocol, 25 Nov. 1970: (1970) *JO* 10851; (1970) Dalloz-Sirey, *Législation*, 308.

[24] Law no. 52-893, art. 2; Decree no. 53-377, arts. 1, 2.

and comprises representatives of the Ministers of Justice, the Interior, Finance, Labour, and Health and a representative of voluntary organizations dealing with refugees. The UNHCR representative attends the council meetings and is entitled to present observations and proposals.[25] *OFPRA* provides legal and administrative protection to refugees and stateless persons and ensures the execution of international agreements on the protection of refugees. It determines and certifies the refugee status of any applicant who meets the definition of refugee in the Convention or Protocol, or who falls within the Mandate of UNHCR; it cooperates with the latter and is subject to its supervision (*est soumis à sa surveillance*) in accordance with international agreements.[26]

An applicant refused recognition has a right to appeal to the Appeals Commission (*Commission des Recours*), composed of a member of the French Council of State (*Conseil d'État*), who acts as president, a representative of UNHCR and a representative appointed by the *OFPRA* Council.[27]

## (b) *Procedure*

Applications for refugee status may be made initially at the local police authority (*préfecture de police*) at the time of request for residence. Circular no. 74-378 from the Minister of the Interior to the prefects of *départements* recalls the 'rules concerning the role of frontier officials when faced with an alien requesting asylum', and emphasizes that 'there is of course no question of sending a refugee back to the country from which he has had to flee'.[28] Some latitude on refusal of entry exists where the refugee does not come directly from a country of persecution and can be returned to another state without risk of being sent on to danger. Otherwise, however, frontier officials must refer those seeking asylum to the *préfecture* of the locality where they wish to reside, and issue them a safe-conduct if they are without proper documentation.

The role of the *préfecture* is largely formal. On receipt of the application for residence and recognition as a refugee, the asylum-seeker is issued a provisional permit or a written acknowledgement (*récépissé de demande de carte de séjour*) by the *préfecture*, both of which may be valid for one to three months and are renewable.

---

[25] Law no. 52-893, art. 3; Decree no. 53-377, arts. 9-14.

[26] Law no. 52-893, art. 2.

[27] Law no. 52-893, art. 5; Decree no. 53-377, art. 15.

[28] The circular is published in the report on political rights and position of aliens. European Consultative Assembly, 28th Session, doc. 3834, at 20 (1976).

The asylum-seeker is then referred to *OFPRA*, where formal application for recognition as a refugee is made. It is the responsibility
of the asylum-seeker to ensure the completion of his or her case by
providing photographs, photocopy of temporary residence permit
if held, passport or other travel documents, any papers relating to
the circumstances of departure from the country of origin, and
any supplementary information requested by *OFPRA*. An interview with *OFPRA* usually takes place only if the asylum-seeker so
requests.

From the date on which the case file is completed, the law allows
a maximum period of four months for decision. If nothing has
been heard by then, the ayslum-seeker may take this as an implicit
rejection and enter an appeal. When the decision is positive, the
asylum-seeker is issued a *certificat de réfugié*, valid generally for
three years and renewable.[29] In the event of a negative decision or
where no decision is given within four months, the asylum-seeker
has one month within which to appeal.[30]

## (c) *Appeal*

The *Commission des Recours* has two functions:[31] to decide on appeals
against refusal to recognize the status of refugee, and to advise on
the application to refugees of measures such as expulsion and
*assignation à résidence* in the light of Articles 31, 32, and 33 of the
1951 Convention.[32] In the first case the right must be exercised
within one month and in the second within one week.[33] The basic
procedure for appeals is set out in Decree no. 53-377. Hearings
are in public, although closed sessions can be required. Three
parties may be present before the *Commission des Recours*: a rapporteur, the appellant and his or her representative, and a repre-
senta' ,ve of the Director of *OFPRA*.[34] The rapporteur is provided

---

[29] Decree no. 53-377, art. 3. The certificate is formal proof of refugee status, establishing the applicant's claim to the protection of *OFPRA* and to a Convention Travel Document, and is an essential prerequisite in an application for residence.

[30] Law no. 52-893, art. 5.

[31] Decree no. 53-377, arts. 15-29.

[32] Such advisory jurisdiction is in keeping with French administrative law generally,
which concedes to the executive authorities an area of discretion beyond the control of
rule or statute. See, for example, Expulsion of Aliens, 24 Oct. 1952, (1952) Sirey, *Recueil
des Arrêts du Conseil d'État*, 467 (commenting on what constitutes a threat to *ordre public*
under art. 23 of ordinance no. 45-2658, 2 Nov. 1945: (1945) *JO* 7225; (1946) *DL* 24).

[33] Decree no. 53-377, art. 20; law. no. 52-893, art. 5. Petitioners are entitled to have
counsel present and there is no charge for the petition: Decree no. 53-377, art. 17.

[34] Decree no. 53-377, art. 23. The rapporteur is an *auditeur* or *maître des requêtes* of the
*Conseil de'État*, appointed by the president of the *Commission des Recours* to study the case
and present it to the commission, either with or without recommendation.

with copies of the appellant's grounds of appeal and annexes (the *recours*) and the observations of *OFPRA*. After the rapporteur states the case, with or without a recommendation, the appellant, alone or through counsel, presents his or her claim. The commission commonly questions appellants, and also has the power to ask for supplementary inquiries. The *OFPRA* representative may also present the views of that office to the commission, which will generally reserve its decision. The decision itself must be given in public and must be reasoned.[35] The decision (or, in the case of a request, the advisory opinion) and its reasons are then communicated to the appellant and *OFPRA* (or the Ministry of the Interior). If the decision recognizes the appellant's refugee status, *OFPRA* is required to issue immediately a *certificat de réfugié*.

Recognition as a refugee does not automatically entail the right to residence. Application for a residence permit must again be made to the local *préfecture de police*, and may be refused in certain circumstances. Previously, the issue of the ordinary resident's permit was conditional upon the applicant having either a work permit or a place as a student (and funds for support during the course of study). Until the refugee was established in employment or as a student, the provisional residence permit or *récépissé* was usually extended for periods of three months at a time. However, it was announced in 1980 that the issue of a *certificat de réfugié* will result in the issue of a work permit without further formalities.[36]

The discretion of the authorities generally to refuse residence or to impose other administrative sanctions on refugees is closely circumscribed. Circular no. 74-378 emphasizes that such cases will be exceptional, and that any decision to refuse residence should be submitted to the Minister of the Interior.[37] Likewise, any proposal to expel must be referred and, as has been noted above, the refugee concerned has the right of appeal by an expedited procedure to the *Commission des Recours*, which in turn will give an advisory opinion as to whether the measures in question should be maintained.[38]

---

[35] Decree no. 53-377, art. 25.

[36] See the statement of the French representative at the 31st Session of the Executive Committee: UN doc. A/AC.96/SR.316, para. 33 (1980).

[37] Even if asylum is denied, the circular concludes that the applicant should be allowed time to find a favourable host country, since there can be no question of returning him or her to a country of origin. If the refugee does not depart after having been denied residence, continued presence may be authorized by residence permits valid for three months only, accompanied by *assignation à résidence*. See Ordinance no. 45-2658, art. 27.

[38] Law no. 52-893, art. 5; Decree no. 53-377, arts. 27-29.

## (4) FEDERAL REPUBLIC OF GERMANY

### (a) *Legal background*

The legal bases for the determination of refugee status and the grant of asylum are the 1949 Federal Constitution,[39] the 1965 Aliens Law (*AuslG*), and, in particular, the 1982 Asylum Procedure Law (*AsylVfG*).[40] The latest revision is intended to speed up processing; it also cuts back the opportunities for judicial review and provides for prompt departure or removal of rejected applicants.

The competent authority for the determination of refugee status is the Federal Agency for the Recognition of Foreign Refugees (*Bundesamt für die Anerkennung ausländischer Flüchtlinge*).[41] The *Bundesamt*, established under *AuslG* Article 29 is continued by the 1982 *AsylVfG* and its Director is appointed by the Federal Minister of the Interior. The Director is responsible for orderly administration and, while the Minister may make regulations governing the asylum procedure, the decision maker, a single official of senior rank, is not bound by directives.[42] Proceedings are not public, but may be attended by federal and state (*Land*) representatives, by UNHCR, and by the Special Representative for Refugee Questions of the Council of Europe.[43] The federal interest is represented by the federal commissioner for asylum affairs (*Bundesbeauftragter für Asylangelegenheiten*), who is appointed by the Minister of the Interior and who must be qualified for judicial or other high administrative office. The commissioner is entitled to participate in the proceedings and before the administrative courts, and has the right to challenge decisions of the *Bundesamt*.[44]

---

[39] Art. 16(2) of the Constitution provides that the politically persecuted enjoy the right of asylum. ('*Politisch Verfolgte geniessen Asylrecht.*')

[40] *AuslG*, 28 Apr. 1965: 1965 *BGBl* 1, 353; *AsylVfG*, 16 July 1982: 1982 *BGBl* 1, 946. Opportunities for appeal and review originally built into the asylum process led to large-scale abuse by those seeking to remain in the Federal Republic for economic reasons, and amendments to combat this were introduced progressively from 1977 onwards, culminating in a thorough revision in 1982. See summary of procedure and amending legislation in Goodwin-Gill, (1982) *Michigan Yearbook of International Legal Studies*, 291 at 312-14, and sources cited.

[41] The asylum procedure is not applicable to so-called homeless foreigners (covered by other laws) or to refugees accepted for resettlement: *AsylVfG*, art 1(2). Art. 1 of the 1980 law on measures for refugees accepted in the context of humanitarian assistance (*Gesetz über Massnahmen für in Rahmen humanitärer Hilfsaktionen aufgenommene Flüchtlinge*: 1980 *BGBl* 1, 1057) declares that refugees admitted under special programmes shall enjoy the benefit and status accorded by Convention arts. 2-34.

[42] *AsylVfG*, art. 4.

[43] Ibid. art. 12(5).

[44] Ibid. art. 5.

(b) *Procedure*

In the words of the law, there is deemed to be an application for asylum when it may be concluded from written, oral, or otherwise expressed intentions that protection from political persecution is sought.[45] The applicant must appear personally either before the border police or the local aliens authority to explain the reasons for his or her fear and to provide relevant information relating to residence, travel, and other asylum applications. A written record is made containing the essential elements of the case, and applicants may be represented and accompanied by an interpreter of their choosing. The application is then forwarded to the *Bundesamt* unless it is inadmissible on the ground of protection elsewhere, or if it is a renewed application which discloses no new grounds. In such cases the applicant is obliged to depart at once, unless entitled to remain independently of the asylum application.[46] An application will also be forwarded to the *Bundesamt* where the applicant fails to appear in person without reasonable excuse, and such non-co-operation may be taken into account at the moment of decision.

The Federal Agency, the single official referred to above, examines each case and is obliged to hear the applicant in person, although this requirement may be met by appearance at the initial asylum application. Representation and interpreters are again allowed. Personal appearance can also be dispensed with if the issues are clear and the conditions exist for a positive decision, or if the applicant fails to appear without sufficient excuse. In the latter case, one month is allowed for written submissions, but thereafter the *Bundesamt* may proceed to decide, taking account of the applicant's lack of co-operation.[47]

Applicants are permitted to remain throughout the proceedings, but must reside within the jurisdiction of the competent aliens authority, and they may be subject to area or other restrictions

---

[45] Ibid. art. 7(1). An application is inadmissable if it is clear that protection has been found in another state (defined in art. 2; see also above, ch. III, s. 4(2)); such protection will be presumed where the applicant holds a Convention Travel Document issued by another state: art. 7(3). Deportation orders made in consequence of inadmissibility are subject to judicial review; if this is successful, the asylum application is forwarded to the *Bundesamt*: art. 10.

[46] *AsylVfG*, art 10(1). Immediate departure is also required in the case of applicants whose cases are rejected by the *Bundesamt* as manifestly ill-founded (*offensichtlich unbegründet*): art. 11. Otherwise applicants may reside for the duration of the proceedings, unless deportable on serious grounds of public order or safety: art. 19.

[47] *AsylVfG*, art. 12.

and have no claim to reside in any particular area which they may desire.[48]

If the applicant is recognized as *Asylberechtigter* (a person entitled to asylum), an unrestricted residence permit will be issued by the competent aliens authority. Recognition is binding in all save extradition proceedings and those recognized enjoy the status provided for under the 1951 Convention.[49] It may be revoked if accorded on the basis of false statements or concealment of material facts; it may also lapse or be revoked for the other reasons set out in Article 1C of the Convention.[50]

### (c) *Appeal*

Where an application is declined, the *Bundesamt* at once advises the competent authority, and in all cases the decision must be in writing, reasoned, and communicated to the parties. There is no appeal, but the decision is open to review by the Administrative Court (*Verwaltungsgericht*) competent for the applicant's place of residence. Where an asylum application has been rejected, the aliens authority will advise the applicant that he or she must leave, set a time-limit for departure and notify liability to expulsion in the event of non-compliance.[51] If the applicant seeks to challenge both the *Bundesamt's* decision on asylum and that of the aliens authority on residence, the two actions will be joined and determined in one proceeding. Moreover, a Chamber of the Court may direct the case to one of its members, sitting as a single judge, if the issues of fact and law disclose no particular difficulty and if matters of constitutional law are not involved.[52] Parties may now appeal from a final judgment of the Administrative Court only where they are given leave by that court or by the Higher Administrative Court (*Oberverwaltungsgericht*). This will only be given if constitutional law issues are involved, or the judgment distinguishes decisions of superior courts and rests on that distinction,

---

[48] Ibid. arts. 19, 20, 22. The constitutional right to liberty and security of the person (*körperliche Unversehrtheit*) is consequently amended: art. 37. Applicants throughout are obliged to ensure that communications reach them, whether from the *Bundesamt*, the aliens authority, or any competent court, and must immediately advise any changes of address: art. 17.

[49] *AsylVfG*, arts, 3, 18. *AuslG*, art. 44, previously distinguished between Convention refugees and other refugees recognized under art. 16(2) of the Constitution; the latter were to enjoy Convention status, apart from the benefit of arts. 27 and 28.

[50] *AsylVfG*, art 16. Revocation is decided in a procedure similar to that for recognition.

[51] *AsylVfG*, art 28.

[52] Ibid. arts. 30, 31. Cf. decision of the Federal Constitutional Court (*Bundesverfassungsgericht*), 2 July 1980: (1980) *NJW* 2641.

or there are procedural errors. Leave to seek review is excluded absolutely where the Administrative Court has rejected the proceedings as manifestly ill-founded.[53]

The concept of *Asylberechtigter* does not embrace every refugee within the meaning of the Convention and, as noted above, it excludes those who have found protection in another state. While such an exception is sufficient and acceptable for the purpose of justifying a refusal to grant asylum (in the sense of residence), clearly it may not be relevant in deportation proceedings. Accordingly, *AuslG* Article 14 applies the benefit of *non-refoulement* to all refugees within the meaning of the Convention.

## (5) NEW ZEALAND

### (a) *Legal background*

New Zealand has ratified both the Convention and the Protocol, but neither instrument has been formally incorporated into local law. As is frequently the case, questions of refugee status and asylum fall to be considered in the context of immigration law and the general law relating to administrative and judicial remedies.

The principal statute is the Immigration Act 1964,[54] decisions under which are subject to review in accordance with the Judicature Amendment Acts 1972 and 1977.[55] In 1978 the Interdepartmental Committee on Refugees (ICOR) was established, which makes recommendations to the Minister of Foreign Affairs and the Minister of Immigration, who are jointly responsible for final decisions. The composition of ICOR and procedure before it were set out in a 1978 circular letter from the Ministry of Foreign Affairs and revised in 1981. ICOR is chaired by a representative of that Ministry[56] and may include representatives from the Department of Labour and Immigration, the Department of Internal Affairs, the Police Department, and the Security Intelligence Service.[57] The UNHCR representative for New Zealand is entitled to attend as observer and to submit the views of the Office.

---

[53] *AsylVfG*, art. 32.

[54] Amended by no. 158 of 1976, no. 98 of 1977, and no. 9 of 1978.

[55] New Zealand Statutes, 1972, vol. 2; ibid. 1977, vol. 1.

[56] In practice, ICOR is chaired by the Head of the Legal Division.

[57] Actual membership fluctuates, depending on the type of case before ICOR, and whether it has ramifications beyond the interests of foreign affairs and immigration.

## (b) *Procedure*

Applicants for refugee status are referred to the Ministry of Foreign Affairs, where they are required to complete a form setting out personal details and a brief account of their claim to refugee status. The form includes the address of the UNHCR Representative and advises applicants that they may contact the representative if they so wish. The Ministry makes a first determination whether the application potentially falls within the terms of the 1951 Convention and the 1967 Protocol. Applicants who pass through the pre-screening then appear personally before ICOR where they may be accompanied by counsel of their choice. Personal appearance is practicable in view of the generally low number of applications each year (averaging 10 in 1979-81). They are invited to present their case in their own words and to reply to such questions as may be asked by individual members of the Committee or by the UNHCR representative. The Committee then considers the case in camera and makes its recommendation to the Ministers for final decision. An individual recognized as a refugee is advised in writing by the Ministry of Foreign Affairs. He or she will also be notified of such term of residence as may be granted by the Department of Labour and Immigration, which in practice is generally without any time limit.

## (c) *Appeal*

No formal right of appeal is provided in respect of a negative determination of refugee status, although the grounds for such decision can be reviewed in the same way as other administrative acts.[58] ICOR itself may also reconsider previously rejected applications, where new evidence is brought to its attention.

On the initiation of deportation machinery, an asylum-seeker has recourse to either of two review procedures, the one before the Minister of Immigration,[59] the other before the Deportation Review Tribunal. Section 20A of the Immigration Act 1964 (an amendment introduced in 1977)[60] empowers the Minister to withhold deportation if satisfied that 'because of exceptional circumstances of a humanitarian nature', such action could be unduly harsh or unjust. A further amendment the following year made

---

[58] Under the Judicature Amendment Acts 1972 and 1977, such decisions may be reviewed by the Administrative Division of the High Court.

[59] Immigration Act 1964, s. 20A (inserted by no. 98 of 1977).

[60] Immigration Act 1977 (no. 98), s. 6.

similar provision with regard to appeals before the Deportation Review Tribunal.[61] Such provisions clearly allow a re-examination of all the elements upon which a claim to refugee status might be based.[62]

## (6) UNITED KINGDOM

### (a) *Legal background*

Neither the 1951 Convention nor the 1967 Protocol are incorporated in United Kingdom law, and the entry, residence, and removal of foreign nationals is subject to control under the Immigration Act 1971.[63] The immigration rules implementing the Act, however, do acknowledge a class of persons who should be admitted, allowed to remain, or not deported on account of a well-founded fear of persecution.

### (b) *Procedure*

At a port of entry, asylum claims may be made by those with and those without visas. A visa national may claim asylum immediately upon arrival, or the intention not to return to the country of origin may emerge in the course of questioning by the immigration officer. Generally, from an immigration law perspective, the fact that the applicant resorted to misrepresentation in order to secure a visa is sufficient ground for refusal of admission. However, recent changes in the immigration rules stress that the immigration officer should refer any case which appears to fall within the asylum provisions to the central authority, the Home Office, for decision, regardless of the grounds which may justify exclusion.[64]

---

[61] Immigration Act 1964, ss. 22C and 22D (introduced by no. 9 of 1978). The Deportation Review Tribunal is competent to consider the cases of persons ordered to be deported under s. 22(1), i.e. generally, those convicted of certain offences or recommended for deportation by a court. Appeals on questions of law are permitted from the Tribunal to the Supreme Court: s. 22F. The Supreme Court itself (Administrative Division) is competent to hear appeals by those ordered to be deported under s. 22(3), i.e. generally, those associated with or believed to be associated with terrorism: s. 22G. No appeal is possible in the case of those ordered to leave New Zealand by the Governor-General by Order-in-Council, the Minister having certified that their continued presence constitutes a threat to national security.

[62] An unsuccessful applicant may finally petition the Governor-General to stay deportation in the exercise of prerogative powers.

[63] Generally on United Kingdom immigration law, see Goodwin-Gill, *International Law and the Movement of Persons between States* (1978) 97-122, 243-51, 269-74.

[64] See Statement of Changes in Immigration Rules, House of Commons Paper no. 394 (HC 394) paras. 16, 64 (1980). See also the statement of the United Kingdom representative, Dr Paul Weis, at the 31st Session of the Executive Committee: UN doc. A/AC.96/SR.322, para. 43 (1980).

Every visa national in possession of a valid visa also has a right of appeal against refusal of entry exercisable in the United Kingdom,[65] and notice of appeals involving claims to asylum is in practice given to the UNHCR branch office in London. The critical factor separating the non-visa national from the visa national who seeks asylum lies in the character of their rights of appeal. In the case of non-visa nationals, such right may be exercised *only after they have left the country*.[66] Immigration law and practice indicate the port of embarkation as the 'normal' destination of those refused entry.[67] For the asylum-seeker this may be the country of origin or some transit state, and again only the visa national may appeal against destination while still in the United Kingdom.[68] A fear of persecution may also be raised after admission, either in the course of an application for an extension of permission to stay in the United Kingdom, or as a ground of objection to deportation. Asylum-seekers are interviewed by Home Office officials or immigration officers; but the interview report is not submitted to the asylum-seeker for comment or correction. Decisions on refugee status are taken at a senior level within the Home Office and those recognized are usually given a (renewable) stay for twelve months, with permission to work, and a formal letter attesting to the recognition of refugee status.[69]

While refugee status may be raised on appeal against deportation,[70] the right of appeal is limited; there is also no right of appeal where a deportation order is made following the recommendation of a court upon conviction. The recommendation itself may be appealed against as a part of the sentence, but a superior court has ruled that the decision to order deportation is solely at the discretion of the Secretary of State, not for the court which either recommends deportation or hears an appeal against such recommendation.[71] There is also no right of appeal

---

[65] The term 'visa national' is used here also to include certain classes of Commonwealth citizens who may require so-called 'entry clearances'. See generally, Goodwin-Gill, *Movement of Persons,* 106-7.

[66] Immigration Act 1971, s. 13(3).

[67] HC 394, para. 77; Immigration Act 1971, Sched. 2, para. 8.

[68] Immigration Act 1971, ss. 13(3), 17.

[69] See UN doc. A/AC.96/SR.302, para. 16 (statement by the British representative to the 29th Session of the Executive Committee in 1978, indicating intent to begin issuing letters confirming recognition of refugee status).

[70] Immigration Act 1971, s. 3(5), (6).

[71] *Ali* v. *Immigration Appeal Tribunal: Ali* v. *Secretary of State* [1973] Imm. AR 19, 33; cf. *R.* v. *Zausmer* (1911) Cr. App. Rep. 41 in respect of the situation under the Aliens Act 1905.

exercisable within the United Kingdom by illegal entrants; they are liable to detention and summary removal.[72]

## (c) *Appeal*

Within the above-mentioned limitations, an asylum-seeker refused an extension of stay may appeal provided that both the application and the Home Office decision are made while the applicant still had permission to be in the country and that notice of intention to appeal is given within fourteen days of the negative decision. A refugee or asylum-seeker may appeal against a deportation order provided notice is given in time. A refugee lawfully in the United Kingdom has no right of appeal, however, if ordered to be deported on grounds of national security or if deportation is declared to be in the interests of relations between the United Kingdom and any other country, or for reasons of a political nature.[73] 'Representations' may be made to a non-statutory advisory panel, but the case against the refugee will not necessarily be disclosed.[74]

All appeals, whether involving refugees, aliens or Commonwealth citizens, are generally heard first by immigration appeals adjudicators. From their decisions, appeal lies to the Immigration Appeal Tribunal, and decisions of the latter are subject to judicial review in the superior courts by way of application for orders of *certiorari* and mandamus. According to the rules of procedure, the representative of UNHCR in the United Kingdom may elect to be treated as a party to any appeal in which the appellant is or claims to be a refugee,[75] and, as noted above, the UNHCR branch office is advised of all asylum appeals.

United Kingdom immigration law is of general application and, in common with that of many other states, makes no special pro-

---

[72] Immigration Act 1971, ss. 4(2), 16(1), (2): Sched. 2, para. 9.

[73] Ibid. s. 13(5); Goodwin-Gill, *Movement of Persons*, 247-8.

[74] While it remains open to the refugee to make 'representations' to the Home Secretary regarding his or her fear of persecution, neither this option nor the special procedure for political and security cases can be considered as satisfying the requirements of due process of law. Cf. the following observation of the European Comission on Human Rights in application 7729/76 (*Agee* v. *United Kingdom*): 'The Commission does not consider that the right to make representations to the advisory panel (a body with no power to decide the matter) or to the Home Secretary (the authority responsible for the decision) can be seen as effective and sufficient remedies which the applicant is required to exhaust under Article 26 of the [European] Convention [on Human Rights].' Art. 26 provides: 'The Commission may only deal with the matter after all domestic remedies have been exhausted, according to the generally recognized rules of international law ...'

[75] Immigration Appeals (Procedure) Rules 1972, arts. 7(3), 17(3).

vision for refugees. The immigration rules, while recognizing that claimants to refugee status require somewhat different treatment, are of doubtful legal standing, more like rules of practice than of law.[76] In the absence of legal guarantees, the opportunities for effective judicial review are correspondingly reduced and the law must be supplemented by administrative discretion, both to avoid the application of the general law (i.e. to prevent prosecution, removal, or detention) and to secure those benefits called for by the Convention and Protocol; in such circumstances, the local role of UNHCR may be that much more acute.

## (7) UNITED STATES OF AMERICA

### (a) *Legal background*

Radical changes in the legal regime governing the admission of refugees and the processing of asylum-seekers were effected in the United States with the enactment of the 1980 Refugee Act and the subsequent establishment of an asylum procedure.[77] For the first time, United States legislation now expressly incorporates the refugee definition of the Convention and Protocol; it also makes provision for annual intakes of refugees from among groups of specific humanitarian interest to the United States.[78] Further substantial amendments to the law were still before Congress in December 1982 and consideration was also being given to proposed revisions of the procedural regulations introduced in June 1980. A considerable backlog of applications nevertheless remained to be considered under existing arrangements.[79]

Jurisdiction to determine asylum requests is vested with the INS district director having responsibility for the particular port of entry or area of residence of the applicant; or, if exclusion of deportation proceedings have been commenced, with the

[76] See Wade, *Administrative Law* (4th. ed. 1977) 837 and cases cited.

[77] Refugee Act 1980: 94 Stat. 102. Interim regulations on refugee and asylum procedures were established under that act in June 1980: 45 *Fed. Reg.* 37, 392, to be codified in 8 CFR 207.1-7, 208.1-15, 209, 1-21, 245-1, 245-4. See also Martin, 'The Refugee Act of 1980: its Past and its Future' (1982) *Michigan Yearbook of International Legal Studies,* 91.

[78] Refugee Act 1980, s. 201(a) and (b), amending and adding to Immigration and Nationality Act (INA), s. 101(a). The law distinguishes between *refugees,* who are screened overseas and accepted for resettlement, and those granted *asylum* after making application when physically present in the US or at a border or port of entry.

[79] The Simpson/Mazzoli Bill (HR 5782, HR 6514/S 2222) was preferred by Congress to the earlier Omnibus Immigration Control Act (HR 4832/S 1765) introduced at the request of the Reagan administration in Oct. 1981. The proposed new legislation is intended principally to curb illegal immigration, but also aims to streamline asylum, exclusion and deportation procedures, in particular, by virtually cutting out all possibility for appeal or judicial review.

immigration judge.[80] The criterion for the grant of asylum is qualification as a refugee within the meaning of the Act, subject to
exceptions in respect of those who, broadly speaking, are excluded
from the Convention or come within the permissible grounds of
derogation from the principle of *non-refoulement*.[81]

## (b) *Procedure*

The regulations provide for the completion and filing of applications, and for examination in person of the applicant.[82] It is also
formally declared that the burden is on the applicant to establish
his or her claim to refugee status,[83] while the district director is
empowered to 'approve or deny the asylum application in the
exercise of discretion.'[84] Where asylum is approved, the status
lasts for one year, and its continuation is subject to annual review
until such time as 'eligibility for asylum' ends or the individual is
approved for adjustment to the status of permanent resident.[85]
Before making a decision, the district director is required in all
cases to request an advisory opinion from the Bureau of Human
Rights and Humanitarian Affairs (BHRHA) of the Department
of State. In exclusion or deportation hearings the immigration
judge need not request such opinion where one has already been
obtained in proceedings before the district director, but may seek
one if it is felt that it would materially assist adjudication, in view

[80] 8 CFR 208.1. Initially an applicant whose asylum claim was rejected by the district
director could renew the application before an immigration judge on the commencement
of exclusion or deportation proceedings. The proposed final rule (8 CFR 208.1) allows
for single determination only. Under the Simpson/Mazzoli Bill jurisdiction to determine
asylum claims would be exercised by administrative law judges, specifically designated for
that purpose by the United States Immigration Board 'as having special training in international relations and international law.'

[81] INA, s. 208(a)(4), as introduced by the 1980 Act. Specifically excluded from asylum
are those who have 'ordered, incited, assisted or otherwise participated' in the persecution
of others: INA, s. 243(h); see also INA, s. 212(a) (23), (27), (29), (33), which excludes from
adjustment of status to permanent resident asylees who are security risks, Nazi col-
laborators, or convicted of trafficking in narcotics.

[82] 8 CFR 208.2, 208.3, 208.6. In non-frivolous cases, employment may be permitted
by the district director in the exercise of discretion: ibid., 208.4.

[83] Ibid. 208.5. Revised final rules will provide for confidentiality and closed hearings,
unless otherwise requested by the applicant.

[84] Ibid. 208.8. Decisions must be in writing. Revised final rules will provide that the
district director may decide the clearly approvable or frivolous case on the record of the
proceeding and all evidence submitted by the applicant.

[85] 8 CFR 208.8(e); 208.15(a). Annual numerical limitations restrict opportunities for
change of status; see Refugee Act 1980, section 201(b), adding new section 209(b) to the
Immigration and Nationality Act 1952. See also 8 CFR 209.2(a), (b); certain waivers of
inadmissibility are available.

of a change of circumstances.[86] Where BHRHA opinions are obtained, then they form part of the record unless classified under Executive Order no.12356. In turn, if they form part or all of the basis for the immigration judge's decision, then the applicant is entitled to 'inspect, explain, or rebut' the opinion. In circumstances where non-record evidence is permitted, applicants are to be advised whether it relates to them personally, or concerns political, social, or other conditions in a specified country.[87]

No provision is made for involvement of UNHCR in the asylum process, although this has been requested with the support of numbers of concerned organizations and individuals. In past years, certain classes of cases were referred to UNHCR for its views by the Department of State, but the latest proposed amendments tend to reduce that Department's involvement in the procedure. It remains to be seen how much weight will be given to such UNHCR opinions as may be expressed in individual cases in the future.

According to INA section 208(b), asylum may be terminated if the individual ceases to be a refugee by reason of changed circumstances in the country of origin or falls within the exceptions to *non-refoulement* statutorily incorporated in INA section 243(h); these permit the *refoulement* of those found to have persecuted others, or who come within Articles 1F(b) or 33(2) of the Convention, or who are regarded as a danger to the security of the United States.

### (c) *Appeal*

No appeal lies from denial of asylum by the district director, but under the interim regulations it was possible to renew an application before an immigration judge in exclusion or deportation proceedings.[88] An asylum-seeker may nevertheless request relief from deportation under INA section 243(h), revised and strengthened by the 1980 Refugee Act. This provision makes mandatory the withholding of deportation or return to a country where it is determined that the alien's life or freedom would be threatened on account of race, religion, nationality, social group or political

---

[86] Ibid. 208.7. Under revised final rules the district director will no longer be required to seek opinions in clearly approvable or frivolous cases.
[87] 8 CFR 208.8, 208.10.
[88] Ibid. see above, note 80.

opinion.[89] The decisions of immigration judges in exclusion and deportation proceedings may also be appealed to the Board of Immigration Appeals and the process of decision and review remains subject to the supervisory jurisdiction of the superior courts.[90]

Under the statutory amendments being considered in 1982, the decisions of administrative law judges in asylum cases could be appealed to a newly constituted Immigration Board where they might be reviewed 'solely upon the administrative record, ... and the findings of fact in the judge's order, if supported by substantial evidence on the record considered as a whole, shall be conclusive'.[91] The Board's final decisions would bind all administrative law judges, immigration and consular officials.[92] Both the alien and the immigration officer in charge at the port where the hearing is held would be entitled to appeal the administrative law judge's decision to the Board.[93]

The most far-reaching of the 1982 amendments are those cutting back the opportunities for judicial review. A series of provisions declares that no court shall review final orders of exclusion or orders respecting asylum, the reopening or reconsideration of asylum applications, or denial of relief from deportation under section 243(h). The one exception maintains 'the right of habeas corpus under the Constitution'.[94] Earlier asylum procedures, and their administration in practice, were widely criticized by courts and commentators.[95] The latest revisions, however, seriously detract from established principles of due process of law and, if they are enacted, it remains to be seen whether the courts will be

---

[89] Proposed final rules provide that, where an applicant has already been denied asylum by the district director, then only evidence relating to changed circumstances in the country of alleged persecution occurring after the denial of asylum will be considered.

[90] Goodwin-Gill, *Movement of Persons,* 266-9, 274-5.

[91] Simpson/Mazzoli Bill (above, note 79), s. 107(b)(1), (4).

[92] Ibid. s. 107(b)(5). This latter may well affect the administration overseas of the refugee resettlement provisions of the INA, although consular decisions are generally non-reviewable; see Goodwin-Gill, *Movement of Persons* 123-35 at 128-9.

[93] Simpson/Mazzoli Bill, s. 236(b).

[94] Ibid. ss 106(a)(4)(B), 106(b)(1), (2), (3).

[95] See judicial criticism in *Pierre* v. *US* 547 F.2d 1281 (Ct. of Appeals, 1977); *Sannon* v. *US* 460 F.Supp. 458 (D. Ct. 1978); *Haitian Refugee Centre* v. *Civiletti* 503 F.Supp. 442 (D. Ct. 1980), modified and affirmed *sub nom. Haitian Refugee Centre* v. *Smith* (Ct. of Appeals, 1982).

inclined to exercise any substantive control through the limited review power left to them.[96]

## 3. Summary of procedures in other selected states[97]

### (1) ALGERIA

The legal basis for the determination of refugee status is Decree no. 63-274 establishing the modalities of application of the 1951 Convention;[98] the competent authority is the *Bureau pour la Protection des Réfugiés et Apatrides*, established by the above-mentioned decree, under the Ministry of Foreign Affairs. Appeals against negative decisions of the *Bureau* may be brought within 30 days to the *Commission de Recours*, also established by the above-mentioned decree, composed of the Ministers of Justice, Foreign Affairs, Labour, and the Interior, or their representatives, and the UNHCR representative in Algeria. Decisions of the *Commission de Recours* are final. In addition to being a member of the *Commission de Recours*, the UNHCR representative in Algeria is entitled to assist applicants for refugee status in presenting their cases. The *Bureau* is authorized to issue certificates of refugee status to persons recognized as refugees.

### (2) AUSTRIA

The legal basis for the determination of refugee status is the Federal Law of 7 March 1968 concerning the Right of Residence of Refugees according to the 1951 Refugee Convention, as amended by the Federal Law of 27 November 1974;[99] the competent authority is the Head of the Government of the *Land* (*Landeshauptmann*) in which the application for refugee status is made. This competence of the *Landeshauptmann* is at present exercised by the Director of Security (*Sicherheitsdirektor*) of the respective *Land*,

---

[96] Although US courts have been ready to maintain procedural standards, they have been less than willing to review decisions on their merits and to determine for themselves, for example, whether an applicant was likely to be persecuted in his or her country of origin.

[97] The information in the following section was provided by Governments to UNHCR and is reproduced in UN doc. A/AC.96/INF.152/Rev. 3 (7 Sept. 1981), *Note on Procedures for the Determination of Refugee Status under International Instruments*, submitted by the High Commissioner to the 32nd Session of the Executive Committee. In some cases, the information has been updated in the light of discussions between the author and officials of the countries concerned.

[98] *JO* 30 July 1963.

[99] *BGBl Nr.* 126/1968; *BGBl Nr.* 796/1974.

who is a federal official responsible to the Ministry of the Interior. Appeals against negative decisions can be made in the first instance to the Ministry of the Interior and thereafter in certain cases to the Administrative Court. Pursuant to the above-mentioned legislation, the UNHCR representative in Austria is informed of all applications for refugee status and may give opinions before a decision is taken, either at first instance or on appeal to the Federal Ministry of the Interior. The UNHCR representative is also entitled to contact applicants for refugee status during the procedure. Certificates of refugee status under Article 27 of the 1951 Convention are issued by the local authorities to those recognized as refugees.

## (3) BENIN

The legal basis for the determination of refugee status is Decree no. 75-153 of 16 July 1975, concerning the National Refugee Commission, and Ordinance no. 75-41 of 16 July 1975 concerning the Status of Refugees.[100] Decisions on refugee status are taken by the National Refugee Commission, composed of a representative each of the Ministries of Foreign Affairs and Co-operation (chair), of Justice and Legislation, of the Interior and Security, and Public Health and Social Affairs, appointed by the President of the Republic upon recommendation of the Ministry concerned. No provision is made for appeals against decisions of the National Refugee Commission. The UNHCR representative may be invited to attend the meetings of the National Refugee Commission as an observer, and refugee identity cards are issued to those who are recognized.

## (4) BOTSWANA

The legal basis for the determination of refugee status is the Refugee (Recognition and Control) Act of 1967 as amended by the Act of 19 December 1970.[101] Applicants appear before one of the three Refugee Advisory Committees set up in Gaborone, Francistown, and Lobatse. The Committee makes an initial determination of refugee status and submits its report to the Minister of State for final decision. The cases of recognized refugees are reviewed at six-monthly intervals. On review, the general welfare of the refugee and any change of status are examined. Rejected applicants have no right of appeal to a higher authority, but an indi-

---

[100] *JO* 15 Nov. 1975; 1 Oct. 1975.
[101] *Government Gazette*, no. 8 of 1967; no. 22, 1970.

vidual case may be reconsidered by the Advisory Committee at the request of the applicant. The UNHCR representative in Botswana may also recommend the reopening of a case, and attends the meetings of the Refugee Advisory Committee in Gabarone as an observer and meetings of the other Refugee Advisory Committees as appropriate. Where a person is recognized as a refugee, the Minister of Public Service instructs the Immigration Department to issue a residence permit.

## (5) CANADA

The legal basis for the determination of refugee status is the Immigration Act 1976, appeals are governed by the Immigration Appeal Board Act 1978,[102] and the competent authority on the issue of refugee status is the Minister for Employment and Immigration. Applicants are interviewed under oath by a senior immigration officer and may be represented by counsel. A transcript of the interview proceedings is examined by the Refugee Status Advisory Committee (RSAC), which makes a recommendation to the Minister, who decides on refugee status. The Committee is composed of representatives of the Employment and Immigration Commission and the Department of External Affairs, and three prominent Canadian citizens representing the public interest.

Where an applicant is rejected by the RSAC, the case goes to the Special Review Committee established by the Minister for Employment and Immigration to decide whether rejected applicants should be permitted to remain in Canada on humanitarian or compassionate grounds. A recommendation on such grounds may also be made by the RSAC. In the case of a negative decision by the Minister, the applicant may request the Immigration Appeal Board, an independent court of record, to redetermine the claim to refugee status. If the Board decides against the applicant, an appeal to the Federal Court of Canada (Appeals Division) is possible on any question of law, and a further appeal may be made to the Supreme Court of Canada. All immigration enforcement action, if the claimant is illegally in Canada, is delayed pending a final decision. The UNHCR representative in Canada is an observer member of the Refugee Status Advisory Committee and participates in its meetings. A person recognized as a refugee

---

[102] The *Canada Gazette*, part iii, vol. 2, no. 8; ibid., part II, vol. 112, no. 5.

is granted the status of a permanent resident (landed immigrant) and is entitled to receive a Convention Travel Document.[103]

## (6) COSTA RICA

The legal bases for the determination of refugee status are Executive Decree no. 10685-S of 26 April 1979, Executive Decree no. 11950-S of 10 October 1980 and Administrative Decision of the National Council of Migration, (Extraordinary meeting no. 037-81-cm of 25 May 1981); the competent authority is the Ministry of Public Security which deals with refugee matters through the National Council of Migration. An applicant rejected by the National Council of Migration may submit his or her case for review to the same Council. Where the review is also negative, an appeal can be made to the Minister of Public Security, and thereafter a further appeal lies under the General Administrative Law of Costa Rica. The President of the National Council of Migration maintains permanent contact with UNHCR in regard to the determination of refugee status. UNHCR is informed of all decisions taken by the Ministry of Public Security, and may also participate and submit its opinion in the review and appeal proceedings. A person recognized as a refugee is issued with a refugee identity card by the Ministry of Public Security.

## (7) DENMARK

The legal basis for the determination of refugee status is the Consolidated Act on the Entry of Aliens into Denmark of 1 July 1973;[104] the competent authority for final determinations is the

---

[103] The Canadian procedure was thoroughly reviewed by the Task Force on Immigration Practices and Procedures established in 1980; see *The Refugee Status Determination Process* (Nov. 1981). As a result, liberal and comprehensive guidelines were announced for the RSAC on refugee definition and assessment of credibility. Among others, these formally recognize that in case of doubt the applicant shall receive the benefit of the doubt; that inconsistency, misrepresentation, or concealment should be disregarded if immaterial to the claim, and that late application is not necessarily incompatible with credibility. On the refugee definition, the guidelines acknowledge that persecution may comprise deprivation of means of livelihood or of work commensurate with training or qualifications; relegation to substandard dwellings; surveillance or pressure to inform; lack of protection by government agencies; or fear of becoming a victim of government terrorist activities. Also, an individual need not be singled out for persecution, so that claims should not be rejected because large numbers of others are similarly affected; and immigration or 'flood-gates' considerations are not relevant to determining the issue of refugee status. See *New Refugee Status Advisory Committee Guidelines on Refugee Definition and Assessment of Credibility* announced on 20 Feb. 1982 by the Minister of Employment and Immigration to the National Symposium on Refugee Determination, Toronto.

[104] Proclamation (*Bekendtøgrelse*) no. 344, 22 June 1973.

Ministry of Justice. Applications for refugee status are first submitted to the local police authority, which, after a preliminary screening, refers cases to the Chief of Aliens Police. The latter makes a recommendation to the Ministry of Justice, and if negative, the case is referred to the Danish Refugee Council—a non-governmental institution—which then expresses its views before a final decision is taken. No provision is made for appeal against negative decisions, but the Ministry of Justice may reconsider a case if new elements are brought forward. UNHCR has no specific role in the procedure for determining refugee status, but does have a co-operation agreement with the Danish Refugee Council which, in appropriate cases, conveys the views of UNHCR to the Danish authorities. An applicant recognized as a refugee is informed of this fact by a letter from the Ministry of Justice.

## (8) DJIBOUTI

The legal bases for the determination of refugee status are Ordinance no. 77053/P.R./A.E. of 9 November 1977 concerning Refugee Status in the Territory of the Republic of Djibouti and Decree no. 77054/P.R./A.E. of 9 November 1977 concerning the Creation of the National Refugee Eligibility Commission;[105] the competent authority is the President of the Republic, who is also the Head of Government. Applications are first addressed to the National Police Department (*Direction de la Police Nationale*) which, after security clearance, transmits them to the Secretariat of the National Refugee Eligibility Commission. The Commission— which is composed of a representative of the President of the Republic (chair), a representative each of the Ministries of Foreign Affairs, Justice, Interior, and Public Health, and a representative of the National Committee for Assistance to Refugees—examines each application and makes recommendations to the President of the Republic who takes the final decision. There is no provision for appeal. The UNHCR representative in Djibouti attends meetings of the National Refugee Eligibility Commission in an observer capacity, and recognized refugees are issued with a refugee identity card by the Ministry of the Interior.

## (9) GABON

The legal basis for the determination of refugee status is Ordinance no. 64/76/PR of 2 October 1976 creating the *Délégation Générale aux Réfugiés*, the competent authority, which is attached to

---

[105] *JO* 1977, 118, 121.

the Office of the President of the Republic. There is no provision for appeal in the case of a negative decision by the *Délégation Générale aux Réfugiés*, and there is no specific role for UNHCR in the procedure for determining refugee status; there is an informal understanding that UNHCR will be consulted with regard to difficult cases. In accordance with Article 2 of the above-mentioned ordinance, the *Délégation Générale aux Réfugiés* issues to refugees all the necessary documents, including a refugee identity card, which enables them to benefit from national as well as international legal provisions established on behalf of refugees.

### (10) GREECE

The legal bases for the determination of refugee status are Inter-Ministerial Decree no. 5401/1.166958, signed by the Ministers of Foreign Affairs and Public Order on 10 May 1977 as modified by Decree no. 5401/1-374659(2) of 8 November 1977;[106] the competent authority is the Aliens Department of the National Security Service. Where applications are rejected, an appeal can be made to the Minister of Public Order. Before making a final decision the Minister is required to seek the opinion of an advisory committee composed of the Legal Counsel of the Ministry of Foreign Affairs (chair), Alternate Legal Counsel of the Ministry of Public Order, a representative of the Ministry of Foreign Affairs and a senior officer of the Security Service of the Ministry of Public Order. The applicant and the UNHCR representative in Greece may attend meetings of the committee. The Minister may also authorize a re-examination of a case if new facts are presented. In addition to participating in the meetings of the advisory committee, the UNHCR representative in Greece is informed of every application for refugee status, and is also entitled to see the applicant and to receive a copy of all decisions. Persons granted refugee status are issued with a refugee identity card by the Aliens Department of the National Security Service.

### (11) ITALY

The legal bases for the determination of refugee status are an Exchange of Notes between the Italian Ministry of Foreign Affairs and the Office of the United Nations High Commissioner for Refugees of 22 July 1952 concerning the establishment of the Joint Eligibility Commission, and a co-operation agreement between

---

[106] *Official Gazette,* 28 May 1977, part 2, no. 500; 8 Nov. 1977, part 2, no. 1115.

the Italian Government and UNHCR of 2 April 1952 annexed to the Law of 15 December 1954.[107] The competent authority for determining refugee status is the Joint Eligibility Commission, composed of one representative each of the Ministry of Foreign Affairs, the Ministry of the Interior, and a representative of the Italian office of the United Nations High Commissioner for Refugees. The representatives of the Italian Government and of UNHCR have equal voting rights. The representative of the Ministry of Foreign Affairs and the UNHCR representative alternate in the chair, with a casting vote in cases of disagreement. The Joint Eligibility Commission meets in Latina or in Rome. Applications by persons who have resided in Italy for less than six months are dealt with by the Commission in Latina, and those by persons in Italy for a longer period by that in Rome.

As Italy opted for the alternative provision that geographically limits the application of the Convention and the Protocol, cases other than those resulting from 'events occurring in Europe' are not referred to the Joint Eligibility Commission. If, however, the person concerned is certified by the UNHCR representative in Italy to fall within the mandate of the High Commissioner, he or she may be permitted to remain in Italy pending resettlement. In the case of certain groups of non-European refugees admitted to Italy, the Italian Government, despite the geographical limitations decided to grant refugee status under the 1951 Convention and the 1967 Protocol. Decisions of the Joint Eligibility Commission are not subject to appeal, but a case may be reviewed on the basis of new elements. Such review is normally undertaken by the Joint Eligibility Commission meeting in Rome. Persons recognized as refugees are issued with a certificate of refugee status by the Commission.

## (12) LESOTHO

The legal basis for the determination of refugee status is the Aliens (Control) Act no. 16 of 1966 and the fourth schedule to that Act;[108] the competent authority is the Ministry of the Interior. Before taking a decision the Minister seeks the advice of the Inter-Ministerial National Refugee Committee, which is responsible for the regulation and screening of asylum requests. The Committee is composed of a representative of the Ministry of the Interior (chair),

---

[107] *Gazetta Ufficiale della Repubblica Italiana*, no. 19 of 25 Jan. 1955.
[108] *Laws of Lesotho* xi.52. At the date of writing a new Refugee Bill was under consideration for possible entry into force in Feb. 1983.

the Ministry of Foreign Affairs and a representative of the Immigration and Aliens Department of the Police Department. In the case of a negative decision by the Minister of the Interior, the applicant for refugee status may appeal to the Lesotho High Court. There is no specific role for UNHCR in the procedure. Identity papers are not normally issued to refugees, but Convention Travel Documents are issued to recognized refugees for travel abroad.

## (13) LUXEMBOURG

The legal basis for the determination of refugee status is the Law of 20 May 1953 approving the 1951 Convention;[109] the competent authority is the Ministry of Foreign Affairs. An application can be made directly to the Ministry of Foreign Affairs or to the UNHCR correspondent in Luxembourg, who transmits it to the Ministry. The latter refers the case to the Ministry of Justice for advice before taking a final decision. There is no provision for an appeal against a negative decision by the Ministry of Foreign Affairs, but the UNHCR correspondent in Luxembourg may request a review on the basis of new elements. The UNHCR correspondent also maintains regular contact with the Luxembourg authorities in regard to questions concerning the determination of refugee status and to individual applications. In the case of a positive decision, the Ministry of Foreign Affairs informs the UNHCR correspondent in Luxembourg, who then issues a certificate of refugee status.

## (14) MOROCCO

The legal bases for the determination of refugee status are Decree no. 2-2-57-1256 of 29 August 1957, amended by Decree no. 2-70-647 of 8 October 1970, establishing the modalities of application of the 1951 Convention.[110] Refugee status is determined by the *Bureau des Réfugiés et Apatrides* set up by the 1957 Decree, under the Ministry of Foreign Affairs. A negative decision by the *Bureau* may be appealed within 30 days to an appeals Commission (*Commission des Recours*) composed of the Minister of Foreign Affairs, or representative (chair), the Minister of Justice, or representative, and the UNHCR representative in Morocco. The decision of the Appeals Commission is final. Recourse has not so far been had to this appeals procedure, and applications for refu-

---

[109] *Memorial* no. 37, 16 June 1953.
[110] *Bulletin Officiel* 6 Sept. 1957; 28 Apr. 1971.

gee status are reconsidered at the request of the UNHCR representative. The UNHCR representative assists asylum-seekers in presenting their applications to the *Bureau*, and certificates of refugee status are issued to persons recognized as refugees.

## (15) THE NETHERLANDS

The legal bases for the determination of refugee status are the Aliens Law of 13 January 1965, a Royal Decree of 19 September 1966, regulations of 22 September 1966, the Administrative Law Review Act of 1978 and a circular letter from the Ministry of Justice dated 21 February 1974;[111] the competent authority is the Ministry of Justice, which takes a decision in agreement with the Ministry of Foreign Affairs. If a claim for refugee status is rejected, the applicant can request review by the Minister of Justice, who is required to seek the opinion of the Advisory Committee for Aliens Affairs. An applicant rejected in the review procedure can submit a final appeal to the Judicial Division of the Council of State. The UNHCR representative in the Netherlands, or one designated by the representative for this purpose, may submit opinions in review cases referred to the Advisory Committee and on cases in which a final appeal has been made to the Council of State. The UNHCR representative is also consulted by the Advisory Committee in cases of proposed expulsion of refugees. An applicant recognized as a refugee is issued with a residence permit for an indefinite period indicating refugee status and may obtain a Convention Travel Document upon request.

## (16) NORWAY

The legal basis for the determination of refugee status is the 1956 Aliens Act.[112] The competent authority is the Aliens Division of the Ministry of Justice. In the first instance any asylum-seeker applies to the local Aliens Police, which forwards the application together with the interview transcript and other related documents to the State Aliens Office. The State Aliens Office transmits the asylum request with its recommendation to the Aliens Division of the Ministry of Justice, which decides on refugee status. The

---

[111] Respectively, *Official Gazette (Staatscourant)* nos. 40, 1965; 387, 1966; 188, 1966, and *AJZ* 3934/E.2522-A-276. A revised version of the circular letter was due to enter into effect on 1 Feb. 1983.

[112] *Norwegian Law, etc., selected for the Foreign Service*, (Royal Ministry of Foreign Affairs), rev. ed. 1 June 1972, ch. vii, A-2-3.

Ministry of Foreign Affairs and/or the Norwegian Refugee Council are consulted by the Aliens Division where this is considered necessary. In the case of a negative decision, the asylum-seeker may request a review of the application by the Aliens Division. If it does not revise its earlier decision, an appeal may be made to the King in Council for final decision. UNHCR has no special role in the procedure. A recognized refugee is issued, upon request, with a Convention Travel Document by the State Aliens Office.

## (17) PORTUGAL

The legal bases for the determination of refugee status are Law no. 38/80 on the Right of Asylum and Refugee Status[113] and Implementing Decree no. 15/81 of 9 April 1981. The competent authorities are the Minister of Internal Administration and the Minister of Justice who decide after having heard the Consultative Commission for Refugees (CRR). The CRR is composed of the representatives of the Ministries of Defence, Internal Administration, Foreign Affairs, Justice, Labour, and Social Affairs. A representative of UNHCR may attend meetings. In the case of a negative decision, the asylum-seeker can appeal, within a month, to the Supreme Administrative Tribunal. In addition to attending CRR meetings, the UNHCR representative has access to individual files of asylum-seekers and is also informed of the decisions taken. Recognized refugees are entitled to be issued with an identity card, certifying their refugee status.

## (18) SENEGAL

The legal bases for the determination of refugee status are Law no. 68-27 of 24 July 1968, establishing the status of refugees, Law no. 57-109 of 20 December 1975 and Decree no. 78-484 of 5 June 1978 relating to the Refugee Commission provided for in Article 3 of Law no. 68-27 of 24 July 1968.[114] Refugee status is determined by the Head of State upon the recommendation of a commission composed of the Attorney-General of the Supreme Court, (chair), one representative each of the Ministry of Foreign Affairs, the Ministry of the Interior and the Ministry of Social Affairs. There is currently no formal provision for review or appeal, although an application may be re-opened. The UNHCR representative in Senegal attends the meetings of the commission as an observer

---

[113] *Diario da Republica* 1 Aug. 1980.
[114] Respectively, *JO* 17 Aug. 1968; 22 Jan. 1976; 17 June 1978.

and may present views on each case. Refugee identity cards are issued to those recognized.

## (19) SOMALIA

The legal basis for the determination of refugee status is Presiential Decree of the Somali Democratic Republic no. 47 of 15 July 1979 (Means of Implementing the Recognition of Refugee Agreements);[115] the competent authority is the Committee for Refugee Acceptance, which decides on applications for, as well as loss of, refugee status. The Decree provides for an appeal, in the case of a negative decision, to the Justice Committee in the Office of the President, which also decides on appeals against measures taken on the basis of Articles 31, 32, and 33 of the 1951 Convention. The decision of the Justice Committee is final. The UNHCR representative is an ex-officio member of the Committee for Refugee Acceptance, and persons recognized as refugees are issued with a Convention Travel Document.

## (20) SPAIN

The legal basis for the determination of refugee status is the Ordinance of 16 May 1979 regulating provisionally the recognition of refugee status in Spain;[116] the competent authority in the first instance is the State Security Directorate (*Dirección de la Seguridad del Estado, Comisaría General de Documentación*). Applications are addressed to the State Security Directorate or to the Higher State Police Offices (*Jefaturas Superiores*) or to the Provincial Police Commissariats (*Comisarías Provinciales de Policia*). Upon receipt of the application, the State Security Directorate, before taking a decision, requests the views of the Ministry of Foreign Affairs and the UNHCR representative in Spain. In cases where there is a discrepancy between the proposed decision of the State Security Directorate and the views of the Ministry of Foreign Affairs or those of the UNHCR representative, the decision is taken by the Minister of the Interior. A decision is also taken by the Minister of the Interior where 45 days have elapsed without any decision having been taken. In the case of rejection, an appeal may be made under Spanish administrative law. A further application can also be made if there are new elements which substantially modify the information upon which the previous negative decision was based.

---

[115] *Official Bulletin* 15 Oct. 1979.
[116] *Boletin Oficial del Estado* no. 124, 13105, pp. 11485-6, 24 May 1979.

The UNHCR representative in Spain is consulted before a decision is taken on refugee status, and recognized refugees are issued with refugee identity cards.

## (21) SWAZILAND

The legal basis for the determination of refugee status is the Refugee (Control) Order of 1978;[117] the competent authority is the Deputy Prime Minister. On arrival in the country the applicant reports either to the Police, or to the Office of the Deputy Prime Minister, or to the UNHCR representative in Swaziland. The office in question takes down relevant particulars and transmits them to the others. The application is then referred to the Political Asylum Committee, composed of Permanent Secretaries of the Ministries of Justice, Education, and Foreign Affairs, the Commissioner of Prisons, the Commissioner of Police, the Chief Immigration Officer, and the Head of the Criminal Investigation Department. The Committee, chaired by the Permanent Secretary of the Office of the Deputy Prime Minister, makes a recommendation to the Deputy Prime Minister, who takes the final decision on refugee status. There is no provision for appeal; the role of UNHCR is advisory, and the UNHCR representative in Swaziland may be invited to attend meetings of the Political Asylum Committee. Applicants recognized as refugees are issued with a residence permit and may also obtain a Convention Travel Document for travel abroad.

## (22) SWEDEN

The legal basis for the determination of refugee status is the Aliens Law of 5 June 1980;[118] the competent authority is the National Immigration and Naturalization Board. Applications are addressed in the first instance to the local police authority which refers them to the Board. If the police authority considers an application to be manifestly untrue or without foundation, it may take an initial negative decision but is still required to report the case to the Board. If the latter finds that the application is not manifestly untrue or without foundation, it is required to take over the application for consideration, in which case the negative decision of the police authority is treated as void. The Board may also decide to take over an application in other cases if it considers this appropriate, for example, for humanitarian reasons. An

---

[117] *Government Gazette* no. 5, 1978.
[118] *Utlänningslagen: Svensk Författnignssamling* 1980 no. 376.

appeal against a negative decision of the Board can be lodged with the Government, but there is no provision for UNHCR participation in the determination procedure. Persons recognized as refugees may, upon request, obtain a written 'declaration of refugee status'. They may also apply for a Convention Travel Document. Persons who, at the time of entry into force of the Law,[119] had the right of permanent residence in Sweden, cannot obtain a 'declaration of refugee status', but may apply for a Convention Travel Document.

## (23) SWITZERLAND

The legal bases for the determination of refugee status are the Federal Constitution of 19 May 1974, Article 69 *ter*, the Law on Asylum of 5 October 1979[120] and the Ordinance on Asylum of 12 November 1980; the competent authority in the first instance is the Federal Office of Police, a division of the Federal Department of Justice and Police in Berne. Applications are normally submitted to the aliens police authority of the canton in which the applicant is staying and are then referred to the Federal Office of Police. Where the Federal Office of Police rejects a case, the applicant may appeal to the Federal Department of Justice and Police and thereafter to Federal Council (Government). UNHCR maintains regular contact with the competent Swiss authorities in regard to determination of refugee status, and pursuant to the above-mentioned law is consulted in cases of doubt. A person recognized as a refugee in Switzerland is informed of this fact in a letter from the Federal Office of Police and is also issued with a residence permit by the competent aliens police authority of the canton.

## (24) TUNISIA

The legal basis for the determination of refugee status is the Decree of 2 June 1955 concerning the publication of the 1951 Convention;[121] the competent authority is the Ministry of the Interior. Applicants normally apply to the UNHCR representative in Tunisia for a certificate that they are refugees within the mandate of the High Commissioner and, on the basis of this certificate, are recognized by the competent authorities as refugees. A person

---

[119] 1 July 1980.
[120] *Loi sur l'asile du 5 octobre* 1979: FF 1979 II 977.
[121] *JO* 14 June 1955.

recognized as a refugee receives from the Ministry of the Interior an endorsement on his or her aliens identity card.

## (25) UNITED REPUBLIC OF TANZANIA

The legal basis for the determination of refugee status is the Refugee (Control) Act of 1965; the competent authority is the Minister for Home Affairs.

In October 1982 a Refugee Eligibility committee was established by the Minister and began operating. Applicants appear personally to present their case and are questioned by committee members drawn from the Ministries of Home Affairs, Justice, Foreign Affairs, Immigration, the President's Office and the Prime Minister's Office. In addition, two representatives of UNHCR may be present. The committee makes a recommendation to the Principal Secretary of the Ministry of Home Affairs who may either confirm the decision or refer it back for reconsideration in the light of his or her own stated views. An appeal may also be made to the Minister, who can either remit the case to the committee or take an independent decision.

As at December 1982, new legislation was in contemplation which would incorporate the existing procedure and provide a legal right of appeal. It was also intended to adopt both the 1951 Convention and the 1969 OAU Convention.

## (26) YUGOSLAVIA

The legal basis for the determination of refugee status is the Law on the Movement and Stay of Foreigners in Yugoslavia of 8 February 1973.[122] Applications are referred by the local police authorities to the Federal Secretariat for Internal Affairs which is competent to approve and to withdraw refugee status. There is no explicit provision for appeals against negative decisions, but, in accordance with Yugoslav law, a rejected applicant may submit a request for a reconsideration of the decision to the Federal Secretary for Internal Affairs. There also exists a Federal Co-ordinating Committee for the Protection of Refugees, composed of representatives of the Federal Secretariats for Foreign Affairs, for Labour, for Social Welfare and Health, and for Internal Affairs, which, as an advisory body, may discuss refugee matters including determination of status. The UNHCR honorary representative in Yugoslavia attends the meetings of the Committee in an advisory

---

[122] *Official Gazette* of the Socialist Federal Republic of Yugoslavia no. 6, 1973.

capacity. Applicants recognized as refugees are issued with a refugee identity card.

## (27) ZAIRE

The legal bases for the determination of refugee status are the Ordinance-Law no. 67-302 of 2 August 1967, amended by Law 67-478 of 19 November 1967, and Ordinance-Law no. 67-483 of 30 November 1967;[123] the competent authority is the *Département de l'Administration du Territoire*. Applications are made to the local office of the *Département*, which examines the application and determines refugee status. However, an applicant in Bukavu or Kinshasa applies to the UNHCR regional office in Kinshasa, which examines the request and sends its recommendations to the *Département*, which takes the final decision. There is no provision for appeal in the case of a negative decision by the *Département*, and the role of UNHCR in the procedure for the determination of refugee status is advisory. As at December 1982, commissions for the determination of refugee status were on the point of being established. An applicant recognized as a refugee is issued with a refugee identity document by the Immigration Service.

## (28) ZAMBIA

The legal bases for the determination of refugee status are the Refugees (Control) Act of 4 September 1970 and the Refugee (Control) (Declaration of Refugees) (no. 2) Order 1971.[124] Applications are referred to the Committee for the Determination of Refugee Status composed of the Refugee Commissioner, Ministry of Home Affairs (chair), and two other representatives (Principal and Secretary) of the Ministry of Home Affairs, a representative each of the President's Office (Special Branch), Immigration Headquarters, the Regional Immigration Department, Lusaka, the Police Department, the Passport and Citizenship Office and a representative of UNHCR. After an initial determination of refugee status and a recommendation thereon, the Committee refers the applications to the Minister of Home Affairs for final decision. There is no appeal against negative decisions, but a rejected applicant may request the Minister for reconsideration. The UNHCR representative in Zambia attends the meetings of the Committee as observer, and is entitled to question the

---

[123] *Moniteur Congolais* no. 22, 15 Nov. 1967; no. 23, 1 Dec. 1967.
[124] *Government Gazette,* Act no. 40 1970; Statutory Instrument no. 240 1971.

applicant and to record dissenting opinions. An applicant recognized as a refugee may, upon request, be issued with a Convention Travel Document.

## 3.  Refugee status procedures and the role of UNHCR

Formal procedures for the determination of refugee status clearly go far towards securing the effective internal implementation and application of the 1951 Convention and the 1967 Protocol. In adopting the UNHCR Statute in 1950, the General Assembly urged Governments to co-operate with the High Commissioner not only by becoming parties to international conventions, but also by taking the necessary steps of implementation. In succeeding years the General Assembly has repeated this call, inviting states in particular to improve the legal status of refugees residing in their territory. The object and purpose of the 1951 Convention, protection and assurance of fundamental rights and freedoms for refugees without discrimination, likewise argue for effective internal implementation. At its session in 1977, the Executive Committee of the High Commissioner's Programme elaborated this approach, not only urging Governments to establish formal procedures,[125] but also recommending the following basic procedural requirements:[126]

(1) The competent official (e.g. immigration officer or border police officer) to whom applicants address themselves at the border or in the territory of a contracting state, should have clear instructions for dealing with cases which might come within the purview of the relevant international instruments. The official should be required to act in accordance with the principle of *non-refoulement* and to refer such cases to a higher authority.

(2) Applicants should receive the necessary guidance as to the procedure to be followed.

[125] UN doc. A/AC.96/549, para. 36. See also Council of Europe Recommendation no. R(81) 16 on the harmonization of national procedures relating to asylum, adopted by the Committee of Ministers on 5 Nov. 1981. The recommended principles expand considerably on the minimum requirements proposed by the Executive Committee.

[126] UN doc. A/AC.96/549, para. 53.6(d), (e). The Executive Committee followed up on its 1977 conclusions in 1982, but states were not generally prepared to accept stricter procedural requirements. Concern was also expressed about the need to safeguard procedures in the face of manifestly unfounded and abusive applications: UN doc A/AC.96/615, paras. 65-6, 70(4) (Report of the 33rd Session of the Executive Committee).

(3) There should be a clearly identified authority—wherever possible a single central authority—with responsibility for examining requests for refugee status and taking a decision in the first instance.

(4) Applicants should be given the necessary facilities, including the services of competent interpreters for submitting their case to the authorities concerned. Applicants should also be given the opportunity, of which they should be duly informed, to contact a representative of UNHCR.

(5) Applicants recognized as refugees should be informed accordingly and issued with documentation certifying refugee status.

(6) Applicants not recognized should be given a reasonable time to appeal for a formal reconsideration of the decision, either to the same or a different authority, whether administrative or judicial, according to the prevailing system.

(7) Applicants should be permitted to remain in the country pending decisions on the initial request by the competent authority referred to in paragraph (3) above, unless it has been established by that authority that the request is clearly abusive. They should also be permitted to remain in the country while an appeal to a higher administrative authority or to the courts is pending.

Participation by UNHCR in the determination of refugee status derives sensibly from its supervisory role and from the obligation of states parties to co-operate with the Office, and it allows UNHCR to monitor closely matters of status and of the entry and removal of asylum-seekers. The procedures themselves will differ, necessarily, in the light of states' own administrative and judicial framework; so too will the nature and degree of involvement of UNHCR. The fundamental issue, however, remains the same— identifying those who should benefit from recognition of their refugee status, and ensuring, so far as is practical, consistent and generous interpretations of essentially international criteria.

As noted above, Belgium has a unique arrangement, for it is the local UNHCR representative who determines refugee status. In Australia, Canada, and many other countries, UNHCR has an observer role. In France, the determining authority is formally subject to the supervision of UNHCR, while the local representative is also a full voting member of the *Commission des Recours*. In the Federal Republic of Germany, the law provides expressly for asylum-seekers to have the opportunity to contact UNHCR and, although prescribing closed sessions generally for the recognition process, declares that the UNHCR representative shall be entitled to attend. In the United Kingdom, UNHCR may elect to be a party to proceedings before the immigration appeal authorities, while in the United States, UNHCR's advisory capacity remains *ad hoc*. In many other states, UNHCR's role may be even less formal. Where no procedure as such exists, or where UNHCR maintains no presence, the Office nevertheless holds a watching brief in all matters affecting refugees; should there arise cause for concern, then appropriate interventions will be made.

In the procedures of the thirty-five states described above, UNHCR involvement falls, roughly speaking, into the following categories: (1) no formal role—eight states; (2) observer on advisory committee or similar body—three states; (4) UNHCR determines status—three states (including one state in which decisions are jointly taken); (5) UNHCR is informed of cases or its views may be sought or given or it may be invited to attend decision-making bodies—nine states. Considered broadly, UNHCR's role in such procedures is to contribute to the effective identification of bona fide refugees. This entails: (1) offering an assessment of the applicant's credibility in the light of the claim and of conditions known to exist in his or her country of origin;[127] (2) providing information on the treatment of similar cases or similar legal points in other jurisdictions; (3) representing the international community's interest by providing its interpretation of fundamental concepts, such as 'well-founded fear', and persecution; and (4) promoting a liberal application of humanitarian instruments (which includes giving the benefit of the doubt in appropriate cases), as well as a generous policy on asylum. Evidently, the burden is on the applicant to establish his or her case, but given the practical problems as well as the trauma which a person in flight may face, a corresponding duty rests also upon those charged with ascertaining and evaluating the relevant facts. Providing international protection may thus include helping those unable, for one reason or another, to help themselves, in order to ensure

---

[127] UNHCR's duty to provide international protection to refugees also requires that it provide information known to it regarding conditions in an asylum-seeker's country of origin, at least if such information is critical for the determination of refugee status. Care is obviously needed, however, in providing such information, particularly if UNHCR is at the same time involved in protecting and assisting refugees from elsewhere in that same country.

that no bona fide refugee is returned to a place in which life or freedom may be endangered.

## 4. The status and rights of the refugee in municipal law: some observations

A fully comprehensive survey of the status and rights of refugees in municipal law is beyond the scope of this work. The following is therefore intended to sketch the situation by reference to selected countries, and to highlight the areas requiring attention if an effective system of protection is to be maintained.

### (1) TREATIES

A first distinction exists between those states which have and those which have not ratified the relevant international instruments. For certain states parties, the very act of ratification may cause the treaty to have internal effect, so that it can be relied upon at law by the refugee who seeks to establish status or to secure a particular advantage or standard of treatment.[128] Even in such countries, however, specific measures of incorporation may be appropriate, particularly in procedural matters.[129] In other states, including many with a common law tradition, specific legislation is essential if the concept of refugee status is to have any legal content, and if standards of treatment are to be legally enforceable, rather than dependent upon executive discretion.

### (2) REFUGEES AND ASYLUM—SEEKERS ADMITTED OR ALLOWED TO REMAIN ON A TEMPORARY BASIS

The divorce between refugee status, on the one hand, and asylum in the sense of a lasting solution, on the other hand, has been analysed above; states are bound by one consequence of refugee status, *non-refoulement*, but retain discretion in the grant of asylum. Between the obligation and the liberty, refugees may yet find themselves in a limbo of varying degrees of legal and administrative security.

---

[128] See, for example, art. 65 of the Constitution of the Netherlands, under which self-executing treaties have the force of law as from their publication, taking precedence over existing statutes and those which follow. See also arts. 25 and 59, Constitution of the Federal Republic of Germany; arts. 53 and 55, 1958 Constitution of France.

[129] See, for example, the laws of France and the Federal Republic of Germany, cited above; see also Austria, *Bundesgesetz vom 7. März 1968 über die Aufenthaltsberechtigung von Flüchtlingen im Sinne der Konvention über die Rechtsstellung der Flüchtlinge* (Federal law on the right of residence of Convention refugees) *BGBl Nr.* 126/1968; *Änderungsgesetz vom 27. November 1974* (Amending law), *BGBl Nr.* 796/1974.

Many states in practice allow or tolerate the presence of asylum-seekers pending the conclusion of procedures for the determination of status. The 1980 Portuguese law on asylum, for example, provides not only for the issue of temporary residence permits, but also for those in process to be treated, for the duration of the proceedings, as if they had in fact been granted asylum.[130] The Federal Administrative Court of the Federal Republic of Germany ruled in 1981 that residence permits, rather than toleration permits (*Duldung*), were required to be issued to asylum-seekers.[131] Swiss law likewise permits residence pending decision, although departure to a third country can be required, if possible and reasonable in the circumstances.[132] Temporary residence, again under varying conditions, may also be granted to asylum-seekers pending resettlement elsewhere. Italy, which maintains the geographical limitation to its obligations under the Convention and Protocol, is also a country of first refuge for many refugees in transit.[133] The refugee status of such persons is determined by the UNHCR office in Rome, which then seeks 'sojourn permits' of two to three months duration from the Ministry of the Interior; these often require renewal where emigration processing is delayed. A similar situation prevails in Greece with regard to asylum-seekers from Iraq and Iran who may be granted renewable six-months residence permits pending resettlement. Legislation introduced in Hong Kong in 1981 went so far as to *define* a Vietnamese refugee as a person who '(a) was previously resident in Vietnam; and (b) is permitted to remain in Hong Kong as a refugee pending his re-settlement elsewhere'.[134] The law also provided for sanctions to encourage onward movement by making it a condition of stay that an offer of resettlement elsewhere should not be refused 'with-

---

[130] Art. 16, Law no. 38/80 of 1 Aug. 1980 (*Lei no. 38/80 de 1 de Agosto, Direito de asile e Estatuto de Refugiado: 1 Serie N⁰ 176-1-8-1980*).

[131] *BVerwG* 1 C 168.79 (19 May 1981); the Court expressly noted that art. 16(2) of the Constitution 'also protects the asylum-seeker'. Cf. *AuslG*, art. 17(1).

[132] For example, if the person in question has resided some time in such country or if close relatives or friends reside there: art. 19(1), *loi sur l'asile du 5 Octobre 1979* (FF 1979 II 977). Cf. art. 5, Austria, *Bundesgesetz* (above, n. 129).

[133] This category includes, in particular, Jews from the Soviet Union. Although they leave the USSR with visas valid for Israel, many in fact seek resettlement in other countries, such as Australia, Canada, and the United States, making residence in Italy necessary pending processing.

[134] Immigration Amendment Ordinance 1981 (no. 35/81) s. 2; Mushkat, 'Hong Kong as a country of temporary refuge: an interim analysis', 12 *Hong Kong LJ* 157 (1982).

out reasonable excuse'.[135] Possible penalties included detention and a prohibition on employment.

Hong Kong initially encouraged refugees to take local employment, but other countries in the recent periods of recession have not been so liberal. Owing to the abuse to which the asylum procedure was subject, the Federal Republic of Germany prohibited employment by asylum-seekers for two years (one year in the case of those from Eastern Europe). Other states, including Switzerland and the United States, made the grant of permission to work in the interim period a matter of discretion.[136]

## (3) REFUGEE STATUS AND THE GRANT OF 'ASYLUM'

In many countries, formal recognition of refugee status is the practical precursor to the grant of asylum in the sense of lawful residence. On occasion, asylum follows as a matter of legal right[137] or of administrative practice. In other cases, however, it is clear that even recognized refugees are, openly or tacitly, expected to move on to other countries.[138] Where asylum in the sense of residence does follow, then the precise standards of treatment to be accorded will again depend upon the standing of the relevant international treaties in the local law and upon the provisions of any incorporating legislation. In Australia and in the United Kingdom, refugees recognized and allowed to remain are treated in the same context as migrants or resident aliens, any higher standard of treatment (for example, regarding travel documents) being left to discretionary decisions by the executive branch. Under Portuguese law, a refugee enjoys the rights and is liable to the duties of aliens resident in Portugal, in so far as these are not inconsistent with the Convention and the Protocol.[139] Swiss law

---

[135] Ibid. s. 3 (adding new s. 13A(3) to the principal ordinance). Further amendments in 1982, intended to discourage further arrivals, prescribed wide powers of detention and removal of Vietnamese arriving after 2 July of that year: Immigration Amendment Ordinance 1982 (no. 42/82), s. 7.

[136] Switzerland, art. 21, *loi sur l'asile* (above, n. 132): *'En règle générale, une autorisation d'exercer une activité lucrative dépendante est délivrée au requérant s'il en a besoin pour subvenir à son entretien.'*

[137] Austria, *Bundesgesetz*, art. 7(1) (above, n. 129): *'Der Flüchtling ist zum Aufenthalt im Bundesgebiet berechtigt.'* Federal Republic of Germany, above, s. 2(4); Portugal, art. 1, Law no. 38/80 (above, n. 130): *'E garantido o direito de asilo aos eestrangeiros e aos apatridas perseguidos ...'.*

[138] This is so particularly with regard to refugees in Austria and Greece, even though recognition of their status may entitle them formally to remain.

[139] Art. 5, Law no 38/80 (above, n. 130).

is to similar effect,[140] as is that of the Federal Republic of Germany.[141] The right to work is a natural concomitant of asylum in the sense of residence, and may also be laid down by law.[142]

(4) PROTECTION AGAINST EXTRADITION, EXPULSION, AND *REFOULEMENT*

The relation between the protection of refugees and the non-extradition of political offenders shows a growing concordance between the two practices, though with qualifications on the part of certain states.[143] Protection against expulsion and *refoulement* may be secured by law indirectly (for example, where deportation appeals tribunals are empowered to take all relevant factors into account); or directly, by express restrictions upon the permissible grounds of expulsion and choice of destination. Thus, in the Federal Republic of Germany lawfully resident refugees may be expelled only for serious reasons of public safety and order,[144] while the principle of *non-refoulement* is expressly incorporated with regard to any foreign national whose life or freedom would be threatened in the sense of Article 33 of the Convention.[145] Portuguese and Swiss law contain very similar provisions.[146]

## 5. Termination of refugee status and the principle of acquired rights

The justification for refugee status may come to an end in a variety of circumstances, without the individual at the same time constituting a threat to the security of the state of asylum. The question then arises whether that state, in the exercise of its discretion generally over the conditions of residence of foreign nationals, is entitled to require the former refugee to leave its territory. As a matter of law, and at first glance, this aspect of sovereign competence cannot be doubted. In practice, however, it is common to find that, once asylum is granted, the issue of refugee status is

---

[140] Arts. 24 and 25, *loi sur l'asile* (above, n. 132).

[141] *AuslG*, art. 44.

[142] Switzerland, art. 27, *loi sur l'asile* (above, n. 132).

[143] See above, ch. IV, s. 2(2). The law of Portugal provides that the grant of asylum precludes the grant of any application for the extradition of the refugee based on the circumstances by reason of which asylum is granted: art. 7(1), Law no. 38/80 (above, n. 130).

[144] *AuslG*, art. 11(2): '*schwerwiegenden Gründen der öffentlichen Sicherheit und Ordnung*'.

[145] Ibid. art. 14(1).

[146] Portugal, arts. 12 and 13, Law no. 38/80 (above, n. 130); Switzerland, arts. 43 and 45, *loi sur l'asile* (above, n. 132).

reviewed only if, by their own actions, refugees render themselves liable to deportation (for example, by engaging in criminal activity). Where refugee status ceases in other cases, then the individual becomes subject to the ordinary law governing the residence of foreign nationals. The corollary is that he or she is entitled to the same standards of treatment, including the right not to be arbitrarily expelled. This right, it has been argued elsewhere, entails not only that decisions on expulsion be in accordance with law, but that the foreign national's 'legitimate expectations' be taken into account, including such 'acquired rights' as may derive from long residence and establishment, business, marriage, and local integration.[147]

[147] See Goodwin-Gill, *Movement of Persons,* 178-9, 230, 255-61, 294.

# PART FOUR

## CONCLUSIONS

# Chapter IX

# THE REFUGEE IN
# INTERNATIONAL LAW

The legal framework within which the refugee is located remains characterized, on the one hand, by the principle of state sovereignty and the related principles of territorial supremacy and self-preservation; and, on the other hand, by competing humanitarian principles deriving from general international law (including the purposes and principles of the United Nations) and from treaty. The sum of developments over the last half-century, and particularly since 1945, is that significant limitations now confine and structure states' apparently absolute or near absolute discretion not only over the entry of foreign nationals, but also over the treatment of local citizens. Refugee law remains an incomplete legal regime of protection, imperfectly covering what ought to be a situation of exception—the breakdown of the 'normal' relationship between citizen and state. It exists to meet the problems posed by the expulsion, directly or indirectly caused, of citizens, considered as those connected by the internationally relevant social fact of attachment to the body politic. Refugee law goes some way to alleviate, if not to resolve the plight of those affected by breaches of human rights standards or by the collapse of an existing social order in the wake of revolution, civil strife, or aggression. International protection remains incomplete, in so far as refugees and asylum-seekers may still be denied even temporary refuge, safe return to their homes, or compensation.

It is a moot point, to what extent further development of the principles of international solidarity and equitable burden-sharing would fill the gaps in the existing system. Concentration on these issues, moreover, may detract from that other and higher objective which is the recognition for everyone of 'the right to belong—or alternatively to move in an orderly fashion to seek work, decent living conditions and freedom from strife'.[1]

---

[1] Sadruddin Aga Khan, *Study on Human Rights and Mass Exoduses*: UN doc. E/CN.4/1503, para. 9.

## 1. The status of refugees summarized

There is now abundant evidence that 'refugees' are a class known to, and occupying a special position in general international law. The definition and basic characteristics of that class are to be found in treaties dating from the time of the League of Nations, and in the constituent documents of international protection agencies. The standing of that legal definition has been consolidated and confirmed beyond the limit of *inter se* relations by state practice, both as regards the admission and treatment of refugees, and in the light of views expressed in resolutions adopted in appropriate international forums.

### (1) REFUGEE STATUS

The core elements in general international law define a refugee as a person outside his or her country of origin, who is unable or unwilling to return there owing to a well-founded fear of being persecuted on grounds of race, religion, nationality, social group, or political opinion. Apart from the 1969 OAU Convention, no international instrument has formally expanded this basic definition, either for UNHCR or for states parties to the Convention and Protocol. State and international organization practice, however, now also acknowledges, at least for certain purposes, the inclusion of a broader class. The latter, who may be described together with the former as 'refugees and displaced persons of concern to the international community', comprises others who, having left their country of origin, are without or unable to avail themselves of the protection of the government of that country. Relevant factors in classifying 'displaced persons' will be 'external aggression, occupation, foreign domination or events seriously disturbing public order' in all or part of the country of origin.[2]

None of the UN General Assembly's resolutions approving UNHCR action on behalf of those outside the Statute sufficiently and clearly declares that the Office's mandate is being extended, or that new or greater obligations are being imposed on states. Given the status of such resolutions as recommendations only, their terms require analysis in the context of the voting on adoption and, in particular, the actual behaviour of states. In practice, such resolutions are adopted by consensus and there are few, if

[2] Art. I(2), 1969 OAU Convention; see also UN doc. A/AC.96/601, report of the Executive Committee, 32nd Session, 1981.

any, recorded objections to the expanded definition.[3] Such reservations as have been made are generally concerned with objecting to the status of various individuals or groups, or with disputing the legal consequences of acknowledging the broader class. State practice in admission and treatment also tends not to distinguish between refugees and displaced persons, at least in respect to initial reception. Standards of treatment after entry may vary, however, as may the choice of lasting solutions.[4]

## (2) DECISIONS ON REFUGEE STATUS

The existence of an international legal definition of refugees raises the question of the opposability of determinations of refugee status by UNHCR and individual states. UNHCR is the agency charged with protection of refugees and is alone competent to decide who comes within its jurisdiction under the Statute or any relevant General Assembly resolution. In view of the acquiescence of states in UNHCR's protection function, its determinations of status are in principle binding on states. The very definition of refugees, however, incorporates areas of appreciation, so that in practice UNHCR's position on individuals and groups may be exposed to challenge. Nevertheless, as has been noticed in another context,[5] UNHCR's opinions must be considered by objecting states in good faith and a refusal to accept its determinations requires substantial justification.[6]

The 'international character' of refugee status was expressly recognized by the Executive Committee at its 29th Session in 1978, after considering the extra-territorial effect of determinations.[7] The Committee noted that, *inter alia*, states parties to the

[3] See above, ch. I, ss. 3, 7; ch. IV, s. 4; Schwebel, 'The Effect of Resolutions of the U.N. General Assembly on Customary International Law' *ASIL Procs.* 73rd Annual Meeting, 301-9 (1979).

[4] In 1981, Thailand introduced a policy and practice of 'humane deterrence' in which it was supported by a number of Western countries. All Laotians entering Thailand after 1 Jan. 1981 and all Vietnamese arriving after 31 Aug. 1981 were consigned to so-called closed camps (Ban Na Pho and Sikhiu) and were declared ineligible for resettlement in third states. This policy was largely contemporaneous with expressions of doubt in various quarters whether individuals then leaving Indo-China were genuine refugees or economic migrants. Sikhiu was finally opened in January 1983 for the resettlement processing of those detained.

[5] See above, ch. VI, s. 1(2).

[6] UNHCR's decisions on refugee status, although possessing an international character, do not have the same binding character as, say, the 'housekeeping' or technical resolutions of international organizations, which may directly create obligations for member states.

[7] See UNHCR's background note: UN doc. EC/SCP/9.

Convention and Protocol undertake to recognize and accept for visa purposes CTDs issued by other states,[8] and that in certain circumstances refugees resident in one contracting state may exercise rights in another.[9] It considered that the purpose of the Convention and Protocol implied that refugee status determined by one contracting state would be recognized also by other contracting states. Determinations, moreover, should only be questioned in exceptional cases, for example, fraud or where refugee status might have terminated.[10]

Neither the Convention nor the Protocol in fact makes any express provision for extra-territorial effect. The undertaking to 'recognize the validity' of travel documents issued under Article 28 is arguably limited to their validity for visa, identity, and returnability purposes. However, just as a passport is generally accepted as prima-facie proof of nationality,[11] so as a matter of comity if not obligation, ought the CTD to be accepted as evidence that the holder possesses the international legal status of refugee. State practice either for or against the Executive Committee's recommendations is sparse, and the occasions on which one state will challenge another's determinations are likely to be rare. A refugee who has offended the law can generally be deported to the state which issued the travel document. A more acute problem arises, however, where the extradition is sought of a refugee recognized in one state but physically present in another. Where the requesting state is the country of origin, the protecting or asylum state may justifiably object to the potential *refoulement* of 'its' refugee.[12] In such a case the refusal to accept the latter's determination of status, followed by extradition of the refugee, constitutes a putative wrong to the protecting state.

---

[8] 1951 Convention, Schedule, para. 7.

[9] See, for example, arts. 14 and 16(3).

[10] See report of the Executive Committee: UN doc. A/AC.96/559, para. 68.2. The committee also accepted that a decision by one state *not* to recognize refugee status does not preclude another state from examining a new request by the person concerned.

[11] Goodwin-Gill, *International Law and the Movement of Persons between States* (1978) 45-9.

[12] Cf. 1 BVR 654/79 (decision of the *Bundesverfassungsgericht* 17 Nov. 1979) in which the Federal Constitutional Court of the Federal Republic of Germany, in an extradition case, expressed the view that recognition of refugee status by another state should be given due weight as evidence indicating that the person requested was a political persecutee within the meaning of the Constitution.

## (3) *NON-REFOULEMENT* AND ITS RELATION TO SOLUTIONS

The international legal status of the refugee necessarily imports certain legal consequences for states, the most important of which is the obligation of states to respect the principle of *non-refoulement* through time. There are recognized exceptions to the principle deriving from the threat which an individual refugee may pose to the community or the security of the state of refuge. It also has to be acknowledged that, simply by coming in large numbers, asylum-seekers have the potential to constitute a like threat. In view of the existence of machinery of response, however, it is doubtful whether the size of an influx would alone justify breach of the principle.

In practice, the (legal) obligation to respect the principle of *non-refoulement* through time, though independent and peremptory, may be difficult to isolate from the (political) options which govern the availability of solutions. To the ultimate objective of permanent solutions to refugee problems, there are two basic alternatives, voluntary repatriation, or assimilation in new national communities, with the latter encompassing either integration in the country of first refuge or resettlement in a third state. The availability of a lasting solution necessarily depends upon political factors, including the conditions which gave rise to the refugee's flight, while for any solution to be ultimately satisfactory, some account must also be taken of the wishes of the individual,[13] for example, in the light of connections which he or she may have with one or another state.

### (a) *Voluntary repatriation*

The situation of the refugee is anomalous. Voluntary repatriation has thus been recognized as the most desirable solution, and it was one of the principal objectives of the International Refugee Organization after the Second World War. The General Assembly, when establishing UNHCR, similarly called upon Governments to assist in the promotion of voluntary repatriation, which was declared to be one of UNHCR's principal functions.[14] Successive resolutions have stressed the importance of this

---

[13] A number of General Assembly resolutions have referred to the need to pursue permanent solutions through voluntary repatriation, resettlement, or integration on a purely humanitarian basis and in accordance with the freely expressed wishes of the individuals themselves; see GA Resolutions 1285(XII), 5 Dec. 1958, 1502(XV), 5 Dec. 1960, and 2294(XXII), 11 Dec. 1967.

[14] GA Res. 428(V), para. 2(d); annexe, paras. 1, 8(c), 9.

solution, both generally and in relation to specific situations. The temporary nature of the refugees' predicament has also frequently been acknowledged, particularly in the case of those fleeing internal disorder resulting from independence struggles.[15] When ten million fled East Pakistan during the war of secession, voluntary repatriation was acknowledged as the only satisfactory solution.[16] Clearly, the attainment of independence becomes the sufficient condition or 'change of circumstances', both removing the cause of flight and permitting return.

Repatriation may itself cause serious problems; for this reason, the General Assembly has increasingly authorized UNHCR involvement in rehabilitation and reintegration programmes,[17] and a fund for durable solutions was at one time proposed, to assist developing countries to resettle and integrate refugees.[18] In 1980, the Executive Committee adopted a series of conclusions on voluntary repatriation, proposed by the Sub-Committee of the Whole on International Protection.[19] It emphasized the essentially voluntary character of repatriation, and the importance of refugees being provided with the necessary information regarding conditions in their country of origin. Formal guarantees for the safety of those returning were also recommended.

Although the subject of resolution and debate, voluntary repatriation has not figured to any great extent in international instruments. Article V of the 1969 OAU Convention is one exception,[20] while some potential for development lies in the putative human right to return to, or not to be arbitrarily deprived of the right to

---

[15] See, for example, GA Resolutions 1500(XV), 5 Dec. 1960, and 1672(XVI), 18 Dec. 1961, regarding refugees from Algeria in Tunisia and Morocco; 1671(XVI), 18 Dec. 1961 regarding refugees from Angola; and 2040(XX), 7 Dec. 1965, regarding African refugees generally.

[16] GA Res. 2790(XXVI), 6 Dec. 1971.

[17] See GA Resolutions 2956(XXVII), 12 Dec. 1972; 3143(XXVIII), 14 Dec. 1973, 3271(XXIX), 10 Dec. 1974, 3454(XXX), 9 Dec. 1975, 31/35, 30 Nov. 1976, 33/26, 29 Nov. 1978, 34/60, 29 Nov. 1979, and 35/41, 25 Nov. 1980.

[18] See UN doc. A/AC.96/569 and summary of debate in the Executive Committee: A/AC.96/SR.312, paras. 48-9; (30th Session, 1979); A/AC.96/SR.322, paras. 66-73; SR.323, paras. 14-36 (31st Session, 1980). Concern was expressed that UNHCR might, through the fund, become involved in developmental activities better left to other international agencies; see A/AC.96/SR.305, para. 16 and SR.319, para. 25 (statements by the Netherlands representative in 1979 and 1980).

[19] See UN docs. A/AC.96/588 (report of the Executive Committee), para. 48(3); A/AC.96/586 (report of the Subcommittee) paras. 17-29.

[20] At the Arusha Conference on the Situation of Refugees in Africa, held in 1979, all African governments were called upon to consider making official public declarations of amnesty to their nationals in exile, so as to encourage, with appropriate guarantees, their voluntary repatriation; see UN doc. A/AC.96/INF.158, 14.

return to, one's own country. This is proclaimed in Article 13(2) of the Universal Declaration of Human Rights and has been incorporated in a number of universal and regional conventions.[21] It is debatable, however, whether the individual right in question has established itself apart from the treaty context. The duty to admit nationals is most usually considered as an obligation between states, being the corollary of the right to expel *foreign* nationals.[22] Recent state practice, moreover, indicates that countries of origin are often less than enthusiastic about the return of those who have fled. Thus, when it sought UNHCR assistance with repatriation in 1975, the Provisional Revolutionary Government of South Vietnam emphasized that authorization for return fell within the government's sovereign rights, and that each case would need to be examined.[23] Similarly, in 1974, the Government of Chile enacted a law to prohibit the return of Chileans on various grounds, for example, where it considered the person a danger to the state. A 1978 amnesty left generally unchanged the legal situation of Chilean exiles wishing to repatriate.[24]

In 1980 and 1981, however, the General Assembly began to develop initiatives on co-operation to avert new flows of refugees. These not only reaffirmed 'the right of refugees to return to their homes in their homelands', but also the right of those not wishing to return to receive adequate compensation.[25] Whether the former right will develop substance remains to be seen, but in the present state of the law, the right to compensation is little more than a

---

[21] See art. 5(d), 1966 Convention on the Elimination of All Forms of Racial Discrimination; art. 12, 1966 Covenant on Civil and Political Rights; arts. 2, 3, Fourth Protocol, 1950 European Convention on Human Rights.

[22] See Goodwin-Gill, *Movement of Persons*, 11-21, 136-7, 201-5; Ingles, *Study of Discrimination in respect of the Right of Everyone to leave any Country, including his own, and to return to his Country*, UN doc. E/CN.4/Sub.2/229/Rev. 1 (1964), *passim*.

[23] See UN doc. A/AC.96/521, para. 105 (Observer for the Democratic Republic of Vietnam).

[24] See UN doc. A/33/331, para. 433; also E/CN.4/1310, paras. 129-38 (Study of Reported Violations of Human Rights in Chile, Feb. 1979).

[25] GA Resolutions 35/124 of 11 Dec. 1980; 36/148 of 16 Dec. 1981. See also Radley, 'The Palestinian Refugees: The Right to return in International Law' 72 *AJIL* 586-614 (1978). He notes the General Assembly's initial espousal of return or compensation in the alternative (GA Res. 194(III), 11 Dec. 1948), the subsequent move to the terminology of self-determination, rather than repatriation (e.g. GA Res. 2535B(XXIV), 10 Dec. 1969), and later avoidance altogether of the term 'refugee' (e.g. GA Res. 3236(XXIX), 22 Nov. 1974). He calls attention (at 611) to the 'uniqueness of the Palestinian claim [which] is that it finds little support in international law, since the protection of refugees has been invariably perceived as a problem of asylum and *non-refoulement*, not of repatriation'.

pious ideal. The subject of damages for the expulsion of foreign nationals is itself controversial,[26] and there are very few precedents for the compensation of refugees.[27]

Voluntary repatriation will continue as the preferred solution to refugee problems, but its success will depend both on political factors, including the clearly expressed wish of the country of origin that the refugees should return, and on the personal choice of the refugees themselves. An amnesty or change of circumstances may indicate, of course, that the basis for a claim to refugee status has been removed, and it will be for the state of refuge to decide whether this is a sufficient or necessary reason for requiring the individual to quit national territory. This may be justified, for example, where the period of refuge has been relatively short. In other cases, however, the former refugee should benefit from standards generally applicable to resident aliens, including respect for any 'acquired right of residence' deriving from lengthy stay, integration, and local connections, establishment of business, marriage, and so forth.

/ (b) *Local integration*

Although there is no obligation to accord to refugees asylum in the sense of a local, lasting solution, state practice is replete with examples of generosity in that regard. In many countries, recognition as a refugee by the national authorities is both a necessary and a sufficient condition for the grant of residence, together with standards of treatment (including the right to work) equal and often superior to those required under the 1951 Convention. States have even been prepared to offer a durable local solution to large numbers of refugees, sometimes as a prelude to voluntary repatriation, but often also on an indefinite basis, resulting finally in the attainment of full integration and naturalization in the host community. The success of local integration schemes will naturally be enhanced by international assistance, reflecting the responsibility of the international community at large to lighten the social, political, and economic problems faced by receiving states.

---

[26] Goodwin-Gill, *Movement of Persons*, 278-80.

[27] The indemnification of the victims of Nazi persecution by the Government of the Federal Republic of Germany is a relevant precedent. See also the payment by the Government of Uganda, through UNHCR, of compensation to 'Asians of undetermined nationality' expelled in 1972; Goodwin-Gill, 216, n. 1.

### (c) *Resettlement in third states*

The refugee crises in Indo-China, in Latin America, and in Europe, underlined the necessity for states on occasion to go beyond measures of economic assistance and to offer opportunities for resettlement. This least preferred option may be dictated by a variety of factors, including political, economic, and ethnic pressures on the state of first admission and concern for the security of the refugees themselves. Recent debate has revealed different perceptions among states regarding the desirability of different responses to refugee problems. Broadly, these demonstrate either (a) an emphasis on regional responsibility and local integration;[28] or (b) an emphasis on global responsibility and a broadening of the resettlement burden;[29] or (c) a resistance to local integration, for various reasons, with a corresponding emphasis on resettlement.[30] Certain states have also expressly accepted responsibility, as countries of first admission, to accept for local integration a proportion of asylum-seekers, provided that other states lighten the burden by offering appropriate resettlement opportunities.[31]

Not surprisingly, the self-same reasons which may be advanced against resettlement by certain states (for example, their physical, demographic, and socio-economic limitations, together with the potential for cultural shock and problems of adjustment for resettled refugees) may also be advanced by other states unwilling to accept refugees for local integration.[32] Economic and social problems caused by large numbers of refugees, particularly in developing countries,[33] as well as political and security factors,

---

[28] See, for example, the various views expressed in the Executive Committee in 1978 by Turkey: UN doc. A/AC.96/SR.294, para. 7; the Netherlands, ibid. SR.295, paras. 2,4; Sweden, ibid. paras. 11, 12; UNHCR, ibid. SR.297, para. 34 and SR.299, paras. 9, 13; and in 1980 by Colombia, ibid. SR.317, para. 64 and Tanzania, ibid. paras. 49-51.

[29] See the views expressed in 1978 and 1979 by Norway: UN docs. A/AC.96/SR.294, para 15 and SR.306, para, 2; by Canada: ibid. SR.295, para. 38 and SR.305, para. 46; in 1978, by France: ibid. SR.296, para. 21 and Botswana: ibid. SR.302, para. 14; in 1979, by the USA: ibid. SR.305, para. 29 and Italy: ibid. SR.307, para. 48.

[30] See the views expressed in 1978 by Malaysia: UN doc. A/AC.96/SR.295, para. 43; the Philippines: ibid. SR.296, para. 4; and Thailand: ibid. SR.296, para. 81; in 1979, Malaysia: ibid. SR.306, para. 81; Djibouti: ibid. SR.307, para. 63; Indonesia: ibid. SR.308, para. 42; and in 1980, by Thailand: ibid. SR.317, para. 11; and Djibouti: ibid. SR.319, para. 54.

[31] This view has been expressed by Australia and adopted in regard to refugees disembarked on its shores after rescue at sea.

[32] See, for example, the views expressed by the Netherlands: UN doc. A/AC.96. SR.295, para. 2 and by UNHCR: ibid. SR.299, para. 13 (1978). On problems of adjustment faced by resettled refugees, see *Refugees: News from UNHCR* no. 4, July/Aug. 1981.

[33] Developed countries may also face a numbers problem; see statements by Austria: UN doc. A/AC.96/SR.296, para. 1 (1978); SR.300, para. 29 (1979) and SR. 325, paras. 46-7 (1980); and by Italy: ibid. SR.307, para. 48 (1979).

may militate against local acceptance.[34] Save in the most general sense, no coherent, practical theory of response can yet be raised upon the emerging principles of international solidarity and equitable burden-sharing.

### (d)  *International protection*

In view of developments in conventional and general international law, it is no longer correct to view the refugee as *res nullius* and unprotected. In many respects, refugees enjoy a legal standing superior to that of citizens in their own country. The existence of the class of refugees not only imports legal consequences for states in regard to *non-refoulement* and standards of treatment,[35] but also an entitlement to exercise protection on behalf of refugees. UNHCR is the agency principally entrusted with this function, as the representative of the international community, but other states also may have a protecting role, even though their material interests are not engaged. The fundamental rights of refugees are firmly entrenched in general international law, while questions of their standard of treatment (for example, after admission and pending a solution) either are covered by treaty or are affected by norms developing under the pressure of recent state practice. Refugees themselves now benefit from the existence of supervisory machinery in some ways similar to that established under treaties such as the European Convention on Human Rights, although it may not possess the same degree of effectiveness in the field of investigation, adjudication and enforcement.

[34] These factors have been stressed repeatedly by first-refuge countries; see statements by Djibouti: UN doc. A/AC.96/SR.307, para. 63 (1979) and SR.319, para. 54 (1980); Malaysia: ibid. SR.306, para. 81 (1979) and Indonesia: ibid. SR.308, para. 42 (1979). The settlement problems of refugees may be further exacerbated by the break-up of families. Family unity and the right to respect for family life and to protection of the family have long been recognized in human rights instruments (e.g. art. 16(3), Universal Declaration of Human Rights; arts. 17 and 23, 1966 Covenant on Civil and Political Rights; art. 8, European Convention on Human Rights) and the special plight of the refugee family was acknowledged in Recommendation B of the Final Act of the 1951 Convention. The Indo-China refugee problem also highlighted the need for resettlement countries to take account of traditional extended family relationships. Incorporating recognition of such relationships in resettlement programmes can in turn cause problems, as where other migrant groups perceive themselves disadvantaged by comparison. See UN docs. A/AC.96/599, paras. 26-36; A/AC.96/601, paras. 54, 57(4). On UNHCR's activities in promoting family reunion, see *Note on International Protection:* UN doc. A/AC.96/538, annexe, 5-9 (28th Session of the Executive Committee, 1977).

[35] Cf. *Filartiga* v. *Peña-Irala* 630 F.2d 876 (Ct. of Appeals, 1980), in which the Federal Appeals Court held that the District Court had subject-matter jurisdiction in an action between two Paraguayan nationals for wrongful death by torture. Blum and Steinhardt, 'Federal Jurisdiction over International Human Rights Claims: The Alien Tort Claims Act after *Filartiga* v. *Peña-Irala*' 22 *Harv. ILJ* 53-113 (1981).

## 2. The grant of asylum

States remain under no obligation to grant to refugees asylum in the sense of lasting protection against the exercise of jurisdiction by another state and an opportunity to integrate themselves indefinitely in the state of refuge. States' discretion in this matter, however, is substantially circumscribed by the normative effect of the principle of *non-refoulement*, which does require a measure of protection of refugees through time. It is self-evident that protection within a state 'implies only the normal exercise of territorial sovereignty'.[36] Save in so far as it does not trespass upon a state's other obligations under international law, the sovereign act comprising the beneficial exercise of territorial jurisdiction is entitled to respect by all other states, including the country of origin of the refugees.

General Assembly resolutions and those of regional organizations have stressed time and again that the grant of asylum 'is a peaceful and humanitarian act and that, as such, it cannot be regarded as unfriendly by any other State'.[37] This principle has also been reiterated in regional treaty arrangements.[38] At the same time it has been recognized that the grant of asylum imports the continuing responsibility of the state 'not to allow knowingly its territory to be used for acts contrary to the rights of other States'.[39] The state granting asylum becomes, as it were, under a duty to take reasonable care to ensure that its hospitality is not abused to the detriment of other states. Again, this general issue has been the subject of recommendation and specific undertakings.

Article 4 of the 1967 Declaration on Territorial Asylum requires states not to permit those granted asylum 'to engage in activities contrary to the purposes and principles of the United Nations'. The Preamble to the 1969 OAU Convention announces a distinction between the refugee in search of a peaceful and normal life and one who flees solely for the purpose of 'fomenting subversion'. The latter's activities are to be discouraged. Article II (6) calls for the settlement of refugees at a reasonable distance

---

[36] *Asylum* case ICJ Rep. 1950, 266, at 274.

[37] Preamble, 1967 Declaration on Territorial Asylum; see also para. 3, Council of Europe, 1977 Declaration on Territorial Asylum.

[38] See, for example, art. II(2), 1969 OAU Convention; art. 1, 1954 Caracas Convention on Territorial Asylum.

[39] *Corfu Channel* case, ICJ Rep. 1949, 4, 22; *Alabama* arbitration (1872), Moore, *Arbitrations*, 653.

from the frontier of their country of origin. Article III expressly calls upon refugees to refrain from subversive activities, and requires states to prohibit refugees from attacking member states 'by any activity likely to cause tension ... and in particular by use of arms, through the press, or by radio'. The 1954 Caracas Convention on Territorial Asylum recognizes that the exercise of 'freedom of expression of thought' by refugees shall not ground a complaint by a third state, save in the case of 'systematic propaganda through which they incite to the use of force or violence against the government of the complaining state'.[40] Similarly, no state has the right to request restriction of refugees' freedom of assembly and association, unless that freedom is being exercised for the purpose of 'fomenting the use of force or violence against the government of the soliciting State'.[41]

The provisions of these treaties may lend some colour to the general principles of international law which lie at the basis of state responsibility for the activities of those granted asylum in its territory, namely, that states shall refrain in their international relations from the threat or use of force; and shall not intervene in matters within the domestic jurisdiction of any state.[42]

## 3. Issues of state responsibility

The study of refugee law invites consideration not only of states' obligations with regard to admission and treatment after entry, but also of the potential responsibility in international law of the state whose conduct or omissions cause an outflow. In the early 1980s, two initiatives, by Canada and the Federal Republic of Germany, drew attention to the refugee problem as a whole, including causes, effects, and consequences, and laid the foundations for future efforts to avert crises.[43] A principle of responsibility for 'creating' refugees is easy to state, but more precise formulation of the underlying rights and duties remains prob-

---

[40] Art. 7.

[41] Art. 8. See also art. 9, providing that, on request, an asylum state shall watch over or intern at a reasonable distance from the frontier, 'notorious leaders' of subversive movements and those inclined to join them. Cf. art. 18, 1954 Caracas Convention on Diplomatic Asylum.

[42] See the elaboration of these principles in the Declaration on Principles of International Law concerning Friendly Relations and Co-operation among States in accordance with the Charter of the United Nations, annexe to GA Res. 2625(XXV), 24 Oct. 1970.

[43] See further below, s. 4.

lematic. Writing in 1939, Jennings posited liability on the repercussions which a refugee exodus has on the material interests of third states. In his view, conduct resulting in 'the flooding of other States with refugee populations' was illegal, '… *a fortiori* where the refugees are compelled to enter the country of refuge in a destitute condition'.[44] The doctrine of abuse of rights was adduced in answer to any argument that a state's treatment of its nationals was not governed by international law. The duty to receive back nationals could not be avoided by denationalization, and a state could not 'evade the duty by the creation of internal conditions which make it impossible for a humanitarian government to insist on … return … Otherwise the duty to receive back is bereft of all real significance.'[45]

With developments since 1939, the bases for the liability of source countries now lie not so much in the doctrine of abuse of rights, as in the breach of original obligations regarding human rights and fundamental freedoms. Legal theory nevertheless remains incomplete, in view of the lack of any clearly correlative rights in favour of a subject of international law competent to exercise protection and of the uncertain legal consequences which follow where breach of the obligations in question leads to a refugee exodus. States are under a duty to co-operate with one another in accordance with the UN Charter,[46] but the method of application of this principle in a given refugee case requires care. The promotion of 'orderly departure programmes', as an example of co-operation, supposes a degree of recognition of the right to leave one's country *and* to enter another which is not generally and currently justified by state practice.[47] Moreover, little is likely

[44] Jennings, 'Some International Law Aspects of the Refugee Question' 20 *BYIL* 98, 111 (1939).

[45] Ibid. 112-3: 'Domestic rights must be subject to the principle *sic utere tuo ut alienum non laedas*. And for a state to employ these rights with the avowed purpose of saddling other states with unwanted sections of its population is as clear an abuse of right as can be imagined.'

[46] Above, n. 42.

[47] The Director of the Intergovernmental Committee established by the 1938 Evian Conference was charged with undertaking 'negotiations to improve the present conditions of exodus (of refugees from Germany and Austria) and to replace them by orderly emigration'. Orderly departure was also proposed as an alternative to the departure of refugees from Vietnam by boat. An agreement on the outlines of such a scheme was reached between UNHCR and the Socialist Republic of Vietnam in 1979; receiving countries began to participate only after some hesitation, but the number of departures, particularly for family reunion, increased towards the end of 1981 and in 1982.

to be gained by attempting to elaborate principles of reparation for loss suffered by receiving states.[48]

This area of potential state responsibility remains to be developed. A more complete regime might incorporate the delinquent state's obligation to remedy its conduct or omissions, as well as its obligations of reparation, *restitutio in integrum* and satisfaction. Established rules of international law nevertheless do permit the conclusion that states are bound by a general principle not to create refugee outflows and to co-operate with other states in the resolution of such problems as may emerge.

First, by analogy with the rule enunciated in the *Corfu Channel* case, responsibility may be attributed whenever a state, within whose territory substantial transboundary harm is generated, has knowledge or means of knowledge of the harm and the opportunity to act.[49] Secondly, even if at a somewhat high level of generality, states do now owe to the international community the duty to accord to their nationals a certain standard of treatment in the matter of human rights. Thirdly, a state owes to other states at large (and to particular states after entry), the duty to re-admit its nationals. Fourthly, a state, in the exercise of its domestic rights is bound by the principle *sic utere tuo ut alienum non laedas*. Finally, as noted above, states are bound by the principle of co-operation.

A *rule* to the effect that 'states shall not create refugees' is too general and incomplete. An ambulatory principle does operate, however, which obliges states to exercise care in their domestic affairs in the light of other states' legal interests,[50] and to co-operate in the solution of refugee problems. Such co-operation would include facilitating both the voluntary return of nationals abroad and, in agreement with other states, the processes of orderly departure and family reunion.

---

[48] Cf. Brownlie, *Principles of Public International Law* (3rd ed. 1979) 520, who suggests that expulsion (of aliens) which causes specific loss to the national state receiving groups without adequate notice would ground a claim for indemnity as for incomplete privilege. Such a claim would in principle be stronger where the expulsion is unlawful *ab initio*, as in the case of nationals.

[49] Cf. Stockholm Declaration: 'States have ... the responsibility to ensure that activities within their jurisdiction or control do not cause damage to the environment of other States or of areas beyond the limits of national jurisdiction.' Report of the UN Conference on the Human Environment: UN doc. A/CONF.48/14/Rev.1 and Corr.1, Principle 21, 5. To compare the flow of refugees with the flow of, for example, noxious fumes may appear invidious; the basic issue, however, is the responsibility which derives from the fact of control over territory.

[50] Cf. International Law Commission, 'International Liability for Injurious Consequences arising out of acts not prohibited by international law': UN doc. A/36/10, 337 ff. (1981).

## 4. Measures to avert and to resolve refugee crises

The situation of the refugee is a situation of exception which falls to be resolved in the context of competing principles of responsibility affecting both source and receiving states. Problems ought to be capable of resolution on the basis of the principle of co-operation elaborated above and in the light of certain self-evident premises. Thus, the enjoyment of human rights and fundamental freedoms is conditioned, in part at least, upon the opportunity of individuals and groups to participate in and benefit from the nation and body politic. The responsibility of states, in turn, springs from the fact of control over a territory and its inhabitants. *A priori*, individuals and groups ought to be free to enjoy human rights in the territory with which they are connected by the internationally relevant social fact of attachment. The right to seek asylum and the benefits due to refugees, including *non-refoulement* and a certain standard of treatment, may therefore be seen as a consequence of the breakdown of the norm.

Recent experience has once again emphasized the inadequacy of the existing legal framework to cope satisfactorily with refugee crises, particularly where large numbers are involved. In 1980, the UN Commission on Human Rights, expressing concern that large exoduses were frequently the result of human rights violations, called for a report by the Secretary-General.[51] The following year, the Commission decided to appoint a Special Rapporteur to study the question of human rights and mass exoduses;[52] Sadruddin Aga Khan, a former High Commissioner for Refugees, was named to this post in April 1981. In this same period the General Assembly, on an initiative of the Federal Republic of Germany in the Special Political Committee, considered the question of international co-operation to avert new flows of refugees and to facilitate their return.[53] Debate in 1980 revealed considerable opposition to the initiative,[54] although a measure of

---

[51] Commission on Human Rights, Res. 30(XXXVI) of 11 Mar. 1980: UN doc. E/1980/13, 191. See also UN doc. E/CN.4/1440; GA Res. 35/196, 15 Dec. 1980 (adopted without a vote) endorsing the Commission's initiative and requesting its recommendations for further action.

[52] Commission on Human Rights, Res. 28(XXXVII), 11 Mar. 1981.

[53] GA Res. 35/124, 11 Dec. 1980, adopted by 105 votes for, 16 against, and 14 abstentions.

[54] Special Political Committee, agenda item 122, summary records: UN doc. A/SPC/35/SR.43 *et seq.*

consensus was achieved the following year.[55] On that occasion the General Assembly decided to establish a seventeen member group of governmental experts to review all aspects of the refugee problem, with a view to developing appropriate means of co-operation. The Group of Experts was instructed to take due account of the right of refugees to return, or to adequate compensation in the alternative, and of the principle of non-intervention in the internal affairs of states.

There is clear complementarity between the work of the Commission on Human Rights and that developed within the General Assembly. In his report, the Special Rapporteur noted that people uproot themselves for a variety of reasons,[56] such as war, repression, and economic factors, including the 'pull factor' exercised by conditions in more developed countries. Those who leave tend to be 'written off' by their country of origin, resulting in the necessity of large-scale international relief operations involving that country only infrequently. Problems of co-ordination of relief may further exacerbate the problem of outflows, especially where it is concentrated in states of refuge, while political constraints can hamper assisting and protecting agencies by restricting their competence to deal with problems as a whole, including their causes.[57] The Special Rapporteur therefore proposed a number of measures, including updating refugee, nationality, and labour law in the context of a New International Humanitarian Order.[58] He also suggested a reappraisal of the economic needs of developing countries in relation to possible causes, standardization of international aid criteria and measures to prevent duplication, simultaneous approaches to source and receiving countries, and the introduction of effective census and early warning systems. Finally, he recommended the appointment of a Special Representative for Humanitarian Questions, whose work might be facilitated by a corps of 'humanitarian observers' to monitor situations and contribute, by their presence, to a de-escalation of

[55] GA Res. 36/148, 16 Dec. 1981; report of the Special Political Committee: UN doc. A/36/790; summary records: UN doc. A/SPC/36/SR.40 *et seq.*

[56] *Study on Human Rights and Mass Exoduses*: UN doc. E/CN.4/1503. In the form in which it was originally issued, this study included three useful annexes of case studies summarizing mass movements in the previous decade. These provoked considerable controversy and were subsequently withdrawn. The annexes were later published as a special study in *Transnational Perspectives* (1982).

[57] Ibid. paras. 114-40.

[58] See GA Res. 36/136, 14 Dec. 1981 requesting the Secretary-General to seek the views of governments regarding the proposal for a New International Humanitarian Order; also GA Res. 37/186, 17 Dec. 1982 and GA Res. 37/201, 18 Dec. 1982.

tension. The Special Representative's task would be to forewarn, to monitor, to de-politicize humanitarian situations, to carry out functions barred to other agencies because of institutional or mandatory constraints, and to act as an intermediary of good-will.[59]

In developing its parallel initiative, the Federal Republic of Germany proposed, *inter alia,* ten general guidelines for the prevention of new flows.[60] These recognized the political dimension to cross-frontier movements and their potentially destabilizing effect, as well as the concern of the international community as a whole. Preventive action should take account of states' duty to co-operate with one another, to settle their disputes peacefully and not to interfere in matters within the domestic jurisdiction of other states. Moreover, states ought not, by threat or use of force or by administrative or other matters, directly or indirectly compel their nationals to flee. At the same time, the 'internationally recognized right' of individuals to leave any country, including their own, and to return to their country should be maintained. On a practical level, the Federal Republic suggested the establishment of a special body under Article 22 of the UN Charter to promote the objective of international co-operation.

These recent initiatives may in due course galvanize the political will which is necessary if the legal deficiencies of the existing regime are to be remedied. Large scale refugee flows affect dramatically the material interests of receiving states and there is some potential for more frequent resolution of such problems on the basis of the principle of voluntary repatriation. The situation of the individual refugee in fear of persecution, however, is often qualitatively different; the solution to his or her plight is likely to continue to depend upon the effective implementation of the principles of international law including, in particular, the development in the municipal law context, of guarantees in respect of *non-refoulement* and asylum.

[59] At its Mar. 1982 session, the Commission on Human Rights requested the Secretary-General to transmit the study to the General Assembly and to bring it to the attention of the Group of Governmental Experts. It also requested the Special Rapporteur to remain available for consultations with the Group.

[60] Report of the Secretary-General: UN doc. A/36/582, 18, 21-5. The General Assembly decided in 1982 to enlarge the group of experts from seventeen to twenty-four members: GA Res. 37/121, 16 Dec. 1982.

# ANNEXES

# I. Constitution of the International Refugee Organization 1946—Extract

## 18 UNTS 3

## ANNEX 1: DEFINITIONS

### General Principles

1. The following general principles constitute an integral part of the definitions as laid down in Parts I and II of this Annex.

(a) The main object of the Organization will be to bring about a rapid and positive solution of the problem of bona fide refugees and displaced persons, which shall be just and equitable to all concerned.

(b) The main task concerning displaced persons is to encourage and assist in every way possible their early return to their countries of origin, having regard to the principles laid down in paragraph (c) (ii) of the resolution adopted by the General Assembly of the United Nations on 12 February 1946 regarding the problem of refugees ...

(c) As laid down in the resolution adopted by the Economic and Social Council on 16 February 1946, no international assistance should be given to traitors, quislings and war criminals, and nothing should be done to prevent in any way their surrender and punishment.

(d) It should be the concern of the Organization to ensure that its assistance is not exploited in order to encourage subversive or hostile activities directed against the Government of any of the United Nations.

(e) It should be the concern of the Organization to ensure that its assistance is not exploited by persons in the case of whom it is clear that they are unwilling to return to their countries of origin because they prefer idleness to facing the hardships of helping in the reconstruction of their countries, or by persons who intend to settle in other countries for purely economic reasons, thus qualifying as emigrants.

(f) On the other hand it should equally be the concern of the Organization to ensure that no *bona fide* and deserving refugee or displaced person is deprived of such assistance as it may be in a position to offer.

(g) The Organization should endeavour to carry out its functions in such a way as to avoid disturbing friendly relations between nations. In the pursuit of this objective, the Organization should exercise special care in cases in which the re-establishment or resettlement of refugees or displaced persons might be contemplated, either in countries contiguous to their respective countries of origin or in non-self-governing countries. The Organization should give due weight, among other factors, to any evidence of genuine apprehension and concern felt in regard to such plans, in the former case, by the country of origin of the persons involved, or, in the latter case, by the indigenous population of the non-self-governing country in question.

2. To ensure the impartial and equitable application of the above principles and of the terms of the definition which follows, some special system of semi-judicial machinery should be created, with appropriate constitution, procedure and terms of reference.

*Part I: Refugees and Displaced Persons within the Meaning of the Resolution adopted by the Economic and Social Council of the United Nations on 16 February 1946*

Section A—Definition of Refugees

1. Subject to the provisions of sections C and D and of Part II of this Annex, the term 'refugee' applies to a person who has left, or who is outside of, his country of nationality or of former habitual residence, and who, whether or not he had retained his nationality, belongs to one of the following categories:

(a) victims of the nazi or fascist regimes or of regimes which took part on their side in the second world war, or of the quisling or similar regimes which assisted them against the United Nations, whether enjoying international status as refugees or not;

(b) Spanish Republicans and other victims of the Falangist regime in Spain, whether enjoying international status as refugees or not;

(c) persons who were considered 'refugees' before the outbreak of the second world war, for reasons of race, religion, nationality or political opinion.

2. Subject to the provisions of sections C and D and of Part II of this Annex regarding the exclusion of certain categories of persons, including war criminals, quislings and traitors, from the benefits of the Organization, the term 'refugee' also applies to a person, other than a displaced person as defined in section B of this Annex, who is outside of his country of nationality or former habitual residence, and who, as a result of events subsequent to the outbreak of the second world war, is unable or unwilling to avail himself of the protection of the Government of his country of nationality or former nationality.

3. Subject to the provisions of Section D and of Part II of this Annex, the term 'refugee' also applies to persons who, having resided in Germany or Austria, and being of Jewish origin or foreigners or stateless persons, were victims of nazi persecution and were detained in, or were obliged to flee from, and were subsequently returned to, one of those

countries as a result of enemy action, or of war circumstances, and have not yet been firmly resettled therein.

4. The term 'refugee' also applies to unaccompanied children who are war orphans or whose parents have disappeared, and who are outside their countries of origin. Such children, 16 years of age or under, shall be given all possible priority assistance, including, normally, assistance in repatriation in the case of those whose nationality can be determined.

### Section B—Definition of Displaced Persons

The term 'displaced person' applies to a person who, as a result of the actions of the authorities of the regimes mentioned in Part I, Section A, paragraph 1(a) of this Annex has been deported from, or has been obliged to leave his country of nationality or of former habitual residence, such as persons who were compelled to undertake forced labour or who were deported for racial, religious or political reasons. Displaced persons will only fall within the mandate of the Organization subject to the provisions of sections C and D of Part I and to the provisions of Part II of this Annex. If the reasons for their displacement have ceased to exist, they should be repatriated as soon as possible in accordance with Article 2, paragraph 1(a) of this Constitution, and subject to the provision of paragraph (c), sub-paragraphs (ii) and (iii) of the General Assembly resolution of 12 February 1946 regarding the problem of refugees ...

### Section C—Conditions under which 'Refugees' and 'Displaced Persons' will become the Concern of the Organization

1. In the case of all the above categories except those mentioned in section A, paragraphs 1(b) and 3 of this Annex, persons will become the concern of the Organization in the sense of the resolution adopted by the Economic and Social Council on 16 February 1946 if they can be repatriated, and the help of the Organization is required in order to provide for their repatriation, or if they have definitely, in complete freedom and after receiving full knowledge of the facts, including adequate information from the Governments of their countries of nationality or former habitual residence, expressed valid objections to returning to those countries.

(a) The following shall be considered as valid objections:

(i) Persecution, or fear, based on reasonable grounds of persecution because of race, religion, nationality or political opinions, provided these opinions are not in conflict with the principles of the United Nations, as laid down in the Preamble of the Charter of the United Nations;

(ii) objections of a political nature judged by the Organization to be 'valid', as contemplated in paragraph 8(a)[1] of the Report of the Third Committee of the General Assembly as adopted by the Assembly on 12 February 1946;

(iii) in the case of persons falling within the category mentioned in section A, paragraphs 1(a) and 1(c) compelling family reasons arising out of previous persecution, or, compelling reasons of infirmity or illness.

(b) The following shall normally be considered 'adequate information': information regarding conditions in the countries of nationality of the refugees and displaced persons concerned, communicated to them directly by representatives of the Governments of these countries, who shall be given every facility for visiting camps and assembly centres of refugees and displaced persons in order to place such information before them.

2. In the case of all refugees falling within the terms of section A, paragraph 1(b) of this Annex, persons will become the concern of the Organization in the sense of the resolution adopted by the Economic and Social Council of the United Nations on 16 February 1946, so long as the Falangist regime in Spain continues. Should that regime be replaced by a democratic regime they will have to produce valid objections against returning to Spain corresponding to those indicated in paragraph 1(a) of this section.

### Section D—Circumstances in which Refugees and Displaced Persons will cease to be the Concern of the Organization

Refugees or displaced persons will cease to be the concern of the Organization:

(a) when they have returned to the countries of their nationality in United Nations territory, unless their former habitual residence to which they wish to return is outside the country of nationality; or

(b) when they have acquired a new nationality; or

(c) when they have, in the determination of the Organization become otherwise firmly established; or

(d) when they have unreasonably refused to accept the proposals of the Organization for their re-establishment or repatriation; or

(e) when they are making no substantial effort towards earning their living when it is possible for them to do so, or when they are exploiting the assistance of the Organization.

---

[1] Paragraph 8(a): 'In answering the representative of Belgium, the Chairman stated that it was implied that the international body would judge what were or what were not, "valid objections"; and that such objections clearly might be of a political nature.'

*Part II: Persons who will not be the Concern of the Organization*

1. War criminals, quislings and traitors.

2. Any other persons who can be shown:

(a) to have assisted the enemy in persecuting civil populations of countries, Members of the United Nations; or

(b) to have voluntarily assisted the enemy forces since the outbreak of the second world war in their operations against the United Nations.[2]

3. Ordinary criminals who are extraditable by treaty.

4. Persons of German ethnic origin, whether German nationals or members of German minorities in other countries, who:

(a) have been or may be transferred to Germany from other countries;

(b) have been, during the second world war, evacuated from Germany to other countries;

(c) have fled from, or into, Germany, or from their places of residence into countries other than Germany in order to avoid falling into the hands of Allied armies.

5. Persons who are in receipt of financial support and protection from their country of nationality, unless their country of nationality requests international assistance for them.

6. Persons who, since the end of hostilities in the second world war:

(a) have participated in any organization having as one of its purposes the overthrow by armed force of the Government of their country of origin, being a Member of the United Nations; or the overthrow by armed force of the Government of any other Member of the United Nations, or have participated in any terrorist organization;

(b) have become leaders of movements hostile to the Government of their country of origin, being a Member of the United Nations, or sponsors of movements encouraging refugees not to return to their country of origin;

(c) at the time of application for assistance, are in the military or civil service of a foreign State.

---

[2] Mere continuance of normal and peaceful duties, not performed with the specific purpose of aiding the enemy against the Allies or against the civil population of territory in enemy occupation, shall not be considered to constitute 'voluntary assistance'. Nor shall acts of general humanity, such as care of wounded or dying, be so considered except in cases where help of this nature given to enemy nationals could equally well have been given to Allied nationals and was purposely withheld from them.

# II. Universal Declaration of Human Rights 1948—Extract

*[Adopted by the United Nations General Assembly on 10 December 1948]*

[UN Doc. A/811]

### Article 13

(1) Everyone has the right to freedom of movement and residence within the borders of each State.
(2) Everyone has the right to leave any country, including his own, and to return to his country.

### Article 14

(1) Everyone has the right to seek and to enjoy in other countries asylum from persecution.
(2) This right may not be invoked in the case of prosecutions genuinely arising from non-political crimes or from acts contrary to the purposes and principles of the United Nations.

### Article 15

(1) Everyone has the right to a nationality.
(2) No one shall be arbitrarily deprived of his nationality nor denied the right to change his nationality.

# III. Statute of the Office of the United Nations High Commissioner for Refugees

## GENERAL ASSEMBLY RESOLUTION 428(V) OF 14 DECEMBER 1950

*The General Assembly,*

In view of its resolution 319 A(IV) of 3 December 1949,

1. Adopts the annex to the present resolution, being the Statute of the Office of the United Nations High Commissioner for Refugees;

2. Calls upon Governments to co-operate with the United Nations High Commissioner for Refugees in the performance of his functions concerning refugees falling under the competence of his Office, especially by:

(a) Becoming parties to international conventions providing for the protection of refugees, and taking the necessary steps of implementation under such conventions;

(b) Entering into special agreements with the High Commissioner for the execution of measures calculated to improve the situation of refugees and to reduce the number requiring protection;

(c) Admitting refugees to their territories, not excluding those in the most destitute categories;

(d) Assisting the High Commissioner in his efforts to promote the voluntary repatriation of refugees;

(e) Promoting the assimilation of refugees, especially by facilitating their naturalization;

(f) Providing refugees with travel and other documents such as would normally be provided to other aliens by their national authorities, especially documents which would facilitate their resettlement.

(g) Permitting refugees to transfer their assets and especially those necessary for their resettlement;

(h) Providing the High Commissioner with information concerning the number and condition of refugees, and laws and regulations concerning them;

3. Requests the Secretary-General to transmit the present resolution, together with the annex attached thereto, also to States non-members of the United Nations, with a view to obtaining their co-operation in its implementation.

# ANNEX: STATUTE OF THE OFFICE OF THE UNITED NATIONS HIGH COMMISSIONER FOR REFUGEES

## Chapter I. General Provisions

1. The United Nations High Commissioner for Refugees, acting under the authority of the General Assembly, shall assume the function of providing international protection, under the auspices of the United Nations, to refugees who fall within the scope of the present Statute and of seeking permanent solutions for the problem of refugees by assisting Governments and, subject to the approval of the Governments concerned, private organizations to facilitate the voluntary repatriation of such refugees, or their assimilation within new national communities.

In the exercise of his functions, more particularly when difficulties arise, and for instance with regard to any controversy concerning the international status of these persons, the High Commissioner shall request the opinion of the advisory committee on refugees if it is created.

2. The work of the High Commissioner shall be of an entirely non-political character; it shall be humanitarian and social and shall relate, as a rule, to groups and categories of refugees.

3. The High Commissioner shall follow policy directives given him by the General Assembly or the Economic and Social Council.

4. The Economic and Social Council may decide, after hearing the views of the High Commissioner on the subject, to establish an advisory committee on refugees, which shall consist of representatives of States Members and States non-members of the United Nations, to be selected by the Council on the basis of their demonstrated interest in and devotion to the solution of the refugee problem.

5. The General Assembly shall review, not later than at its eighth regular session, the arrangements for the Office of the High Commissioner with a view to determining whether the Office should be continued beyond 31 December 1953.

## Chapter II. Functions of the High Commissioner

6. The competence of the High Commissioner shall extend to:

A (i) Any person who has been considered a refugee under the Arrangements of 12 May 1926 and of 30 June 1928 or under the Conventions of 28 October 1933 and 10 February 1938, the Protocol of 14 September 1939 or the Constitution of the International Refugee Organization.

(ii) Any person who, as a result of the events occurring before 1 January 1951 and owing to well-founded fear of being persecuted for reasons of race, religion, nationality or political opinion, is outside the country of his nationality and is unable or, owing to such fear or for reasons other than personal convenience, is unwilling to avail himself of the protection of that country; or who, not having a nationality and being outside the country of his former habitual residence, is unable or, owing to such fear or for reasons other than personal convenience, is unwilling to return to it.

Decisions as to eligibility taken by the International Refugee Organization during the period of its activities shall not prevent the status of refugee being accorded to persons who fulfil the conditions of the present paragraph;

The competence of the High Commissioner shall cease to apply to any person defined in section A above if:

(a) He has voluntarily reavailed himself of the protection of the country of his nationality; or

(b) Having lost his nationality, he has voluntarily reacquired it; or

(c) He has acquired a new nationality, and enjoys the protection of the country of his new nationality; or

(d) He has voluntarily re-established himself in the country which he left or outside which he remained owing to fear of persecution; or

(e) He can no longer, because the circumstances in connexion with which he has been recognized as a refugee have ceased to exist, claim grounds other than those of personal convenience for continuing to refuse to avail himself of the protection of the country of his nationality. Reasons of a purely economic character may not be invoked; or

(f) Being a person who has no nationality, he can no longer, because the circumstances in connexion with which he has been recognized as a refugee have ceased to exist and he is able to return to the country of his former habitual residence, claim grounds other than those of personal conveneince for continuing to refuse to return to that country;

B. Any other person who is outside the country of his nationality, or if he has no nationality, the country of his former habitual residence, because he has or had well-founded fear of persecution by reason of his race, religion, nationality or political opinion and is unable or, because of such fear, is unwilling to avail himself of the protection of the government of the country of his nationality, or, if he has no nationality, to return to the country of his former habitual residence.

7. Provided that the competence of the High Commissioner as defined in paragraph 6 above shall not extend to a person:

(a) Who is a national of more than one country unless he satisfies the provisions of the preceding paragraph in relation to each of the countries of which he is a national; or

(b) Who is recognized by the competent authorities of the country in which he has taken residence as having the rights and obligations which are attached to the possession of the nationality of that country; or

(c) Who continues to receive from other organs or agencies of the United Nations protection or assistance; or

(d) In respect of whom there are serious reasons for considering that he has committed a crime covered by the provisions of treaties of extradition or a crime mentioned in article VI of the London Charter of the International Military Tribunal or by the provisions of article 14, paragraph 2, of the Universal Declaration of Human Rights.

8. The High Commissioner shall provide for the protection of refugees falling under the competence of his Office by:

(a) Promoting the conclusion and ratification of international conventions for the protection of refugees, supervising their application and proposing amendments thereto;

(b) Promoting through special agreements with Governments the execution of any measures calculated to improve the situation of refugees and to reduce the number requiring protection;

(c) Assisting governmental and private efforts to promote voluntary repatriation or assimilation within new national communities;

(d) Promoting the admission of refugees not excluding those in the most destitute categories, to the territories of States;

(e) Endeavouring to obtain permission for refugees to transfer their assets and especially those necessary for their resettlement;

(f) Obtaining from Governments information concerning the number and conditions of refugees in their territories and the laws and regulations concerning them;

(g) Keeping in close touch with the Governments and inter-governmental organizations concerned;

(h) Establishing contact in such manner as he may think best with private organizations dealing with refugee questions;

(i) Facilitating the co-ordination of the efforts of private organizations concerned with the welfare of refugees.

9. The High Commissioner shall engage in such additional activities, including repatriation and resettlement, as the General Assembly may determine, within the limits of the resources placed at his disposal.

10. The High Commissioner shall administer any funds, public or private, which he receives for assistance to refugees, and shall distribute them among the private and, as appropriate, public agencies which he deems best qualified to administer such assistance.

The High Commissioner may reject any offers which he does not consider appropriate or which cannot be utilized.

The High Commissioner shall not appeal to Governments for funds or make a general appeal, without the prior approval of the General Assembly.

The High Commissioner shall include in his annual report a statement of his activities in this field.

11. The High Commissioner shall be entitled to present his views before the General Assembly, the Economic and Social Council and their subsidiary bodies.

The High Commissioner shall report annually to the General Assembly through the Economic and Social Council; his report shall be considered as a separate item on the agenda of the General Assembly.

12. The High Commissioner may invite the co-operation of the various specialized agencies.

### *Chapter III. Organization and Finances*

13. The High Commissioner shall be elected by the General Assembly on the nomination of the Secretary-General. The terms of appointment of the High Commissioner shall be proposed by the Secretary-General and approved by the General Assembly. The High Commissioner shall be elected for a term of three years, from 1 January 1951.

14. The High Commissioner shall appoint, for the same term, a Deputy High Commissioner of a nationality other than his own.

15. (a) Within the limits of the budgetary appropriations provided, the staff of the Office of the High Commissioner shall be appointed by the High Commissioner and shall be responsible to him in the exercise of their functions.

(b) Such staff shall be chosen from persons devoted to the purposes of the Office of the High Commissioner.

(c) Their conditions of employment shall be those provided under the staff regulations adopted by the General Asembly and the rules promulgated thereunder by the Secretary-General.

(d) Provision may also be made to permit the employment of personnel without compensation.

16. The High Commissioner shall consult the Government of the countries of residence of refugees as to the need for appointing representatives therein. In any country recognizing such need, there may be appointed a representative approved by the Government of that country. Subject to the foregoing, the same representative may serve in more than one country.

17. The High Commissioner and the Secretary-General shall make appropriate arrangements for liaison and consultation on matters of mutual interest.

18. The Secretary-General shall provide the High Commissioner with all necessary facilities within budgetary limitations.

19. The Office of the High Commissioner shall be located in Geneva, Switzerland.

20. The Office of the High Commissioner shall be financed under the budget of the United Nations. Unless the General Assembly subsequently decides otherwise, no expenditure other than administrative expenditures relating to the functioning of the Office of the High Commissioner shall be borne on the budget of the United Nations and all other expenditures relating to the activities of the High Commissioner shall be financed by voluntary contributions.

21. The administration of the Office of the High Commissioner shall be subject to the Financial Regulations of the United Nations and to the financial rules promulgated thereunder by the Secretary-General.

22. Transactions relating to the High Commissioner's funds shall be subject to audit by the United Nations Board of Auditors, provided that the Board may accept audited accounts from the agencies to which funds have been allocated. Administrative arrangements for the custody of such funds and their allocation shall be agreed between the High Commissioner and the Secretary-General in accordance with the Financial Regulations of the United Nations and rules promulgated thereunder by the Secretary-General.

# IV. 1951 Convention relating to the Status of Refugees

Text: 189 UNTS 150

## FINAL ACT OF THE UNITED NATIONS CONFERENCE OF PLENIPOTENTIARIES ON THE STATUS OF REFUGEES AND STATELESS PERSONS

*I*

The General Assembly of the United Nations, by Resolution 429(V) of 14 December 1950, decided to convene in Geneva a Conference of Plenipotentiaries to complete the drafting of, and to sign, a Convention relating to the Status of Refugees and a Protocol relating to the Status of Stateless Persons.

The Conference met at the European Office of the United Nations in Geneva from 2 to 25 July 1951.

The Governments of the following twenty-six States were represented by delegates who all submitted satisfactory credentials or other communications of appointment authorizing them to participate in the Conference:

| | |
|---|---|
| Australia | Italy |
| Austria | Luxembourg |
| Belgium | Monaco |
| Brazil | Netherlands |
| Canada | Norway |
| Colombia | Sweden |
| Denmark | Switzerland (the Swiss delegation |
| Egypt | also represented Liechtenstein) |
| France | Turkey |
| Federal Republic of Germany | United Kingdom of Great Britain |
| Greece | and Northern Ireland |
| Holy See | United States of America |
| Iraq | Venezuela |
| Israel | Yugoslavia |

The Governments of the following two States were represented by observers:
Cuba
Iran

Pursuant to the request of the General Assembly, the United Nations High Commissioner for Refugees participated, without the right to vote, in the deliberations of the Conference.

The International Labour Organization and the International Refugee Organization were represented at the Conference without the right to vote.

The Conference invited a representative of the Council of Europe to be represented at the Conference without the right to vote.

Representatives of the following Non-Governmental Organizations in consultative relationship with the Economic and Social Council were also present as observers:

*Category A*
International Confederation of Free Trade Unions
International Federation of Christian Trade Unions
Inter-Parliamentary Union

*Category B*
Agudas Israel World Organization
Caritas Internationalis
Catholic International Union for Social Service
Commission of the Churches on International Affairs
Consultative Council of Jewish Organizations
Co-ordinating Board of Jewish Organizations
Friends' World Committee for Consultation
International Association of Penal Law
International Bureau for the Unification of Penal Law
International Committee of the Red Cross
International Council of Women
International Federation of Friends of Young Women
International League for the Rights of Man
International Social Service
International Union for Child Welfare
International Union of Catholic Women's Leagues
Pax Romana
Women's International League for Peace and Freedom
World Jewish Congress
World Union for Progressive Judaism
World Young Women's Christian Association

*Register*
International Relief Committee for Intellectual Workers
League of Red Cross Societies
Standing Conference of Voluntary Agencies
World Association of Girl Guides and Girl Scouts
World University Service

Representatives of Non-Governmental Organizations which have been granted consultative status by the Economic and Social Council as well as those entered by the Secretary-General on the Register referred to in Resolution 288 B (X) of the Economic and Social Council, paragraph 17, had under the rules of procedure adopted by the Conference the right to submit written or oral statements to the Conference.

The Conference elected Mr. Knud Larsen, of Denmark, as President, and Mr. A. Herment, of Belgium, and Mr. Talat Miras, of Turkey, as Vice-Presidents.

At its second meeting, the Conference, acting on a proposal of the representative of Egypt, unanimously decided to address an invitation to the Holy See to designate a plenipotentiary representaive to participate in its work. A representative of the Holy See took his place at the Conference on 10 July 1951.

The Conference adopted as its agenda the Provisional Agenda drawn up by the Secretary-General (A/CONF.2/2/Rev.1). It also adopted the Provisional Rules of Procedure drawn up by the Secretary-General, with the addition of a provision which authorized a representative of the Council of Europe to be present at the Conference without the right to vote and to submit proposals (A/CONF.2/3/Rev.1).

In accordance with the Rules of Procedure of the Conference, the President and Vice-Presidents examined the credentials of representatives and on 17 July 1951 reported to the Conference the results of such examination, the Conference adopting the report.

The Conference used as the basis of its discussions the draft Convention relating to the Status of Refugees and the draft Protocol relating to the Status of Stateless Persons prepared by the *ad hoc* Committee on Refugees and Stateless Persons at its second session held in Geneva from 14 to 25 August 1950, with the exception of the preamble and article 1 (Definition of the term 'refugee') of the draft Convention. The text of the preamble before the Conference was that which was adopted by the Economic and Social Council on 11 August 1950 in Resolution 319 B II (XI). The text of article 1 before the Conference was that recommended by the General Assembly on 14 December 1950 and contained in the Annex to Resolution 429 (V). The latter was a modification of the text as it had been adopted by the Economic and Social Council in Resolution 319 B II (XI).[1]

The Conference adopted the Convention relating to the Status of Refugees in two readings. Prior to its second reading it established a Style Committee composed of the President and the representatives of Belgium, France, Israel, Italy, the United Kingdom of Great Britain and Northern Ireland and the United States of America, together with the High Commissioner for Refugees, which elected as its Chairman

---

[1] The texts referred to in the paragraph above are contained in document A/CONF.2/1.

Mr. G. Warren, of the United States of America. The Style Committee re-drafted the text which had been adopted by the Conference on first reading, particularly from the point of view of language and of concordance between the English and French texts.

The Convention was adopted on 25 July by 24 votes to none with no abstentions and opened for signature at the European Office of the United Nations from 28 July to 31 August 1951. It will be re-opened for signature at the permanent headquarters of the United Nations in New York from 17 September 1951 to 31 December 1952.

The English and French texts of the Convention, which are equally authentic, are appended to this Final Act.

## II

The Conference decided, by 17 votes to 3 with 3 abstentions, that the titles of the chapters and of the articles of the Convention are included for practical purposes and do not constitute an element of interpretation.

## III

With respect to the draft Protocol relating to the Status of Stateless Persons, the Conference adopted the following resolution:

'*The Conference,*

'*Having Considered* the draft Protocol relating to the Status of Stateless Persons,

'*Considering* that the subject still requires more detailed study,

'*Decides* not to take a decision on the subject at the present Conference and refers the draft Protocol back to the appropriate organs of the United Nations for further study.'

## IV

The Conference adopted unanimously the following recommendations:

### A

'*The Conference,*

'*Considering* that the issue and recognition of travel documents is necessary to facilitate the movement of refugees, and in particular their resettlement,

'*Urges* Governments which are parties to the Inter-Governmental Agreement on Refugee Travel Documents signed in London on 15 October 1946, or which recognize travel documents issued in accordance with the Agreement, to continue to issue or to recognize such travel documents, and to extend the issue of such documents to refugees as defined in article 1 of the Convention relating to the Status of Refugees or to recognize the travel documents so issued to such persons, until they shall have undertaken obligations under article 28 of the said Convention.'

## B

'*The Conference*,
*Considering* that the unity of the family, the natural and fundamental group unit of society, is an essential right of the refugee, and that such unity is constantly threatened, and

*Noting* with satisfaction that, according to the official commentary of the *ad hoc* Committee on Statelessness and Related Problems (E/1618, p. 40) the rights granted to a refugee are extended to members of his family,

'*Recommends* Governments to take the necessary measures for the protection of the refugee's family, especially with a view to:

'(1) Ensuring that the unity of the refugee's family is maintained particularly in cases where the head of the family has fulfilled the necessary conditions for admission to a particular country,

'(2) The protection of refugees who are minors, in particular unaccompanied children and girls, with special reference to guardianship and adoption.'

## C

'*The Conference*,
'*Considering* that, in the moral, legal and material spheres, refugees need the help of suitable welfare services, especially that of appropriate non-governmental organizations.

'*Recommends* Governments and inter-governmental bodies to facilitate, encourage and sustain the efforts of properly qualified organizations.'

## D

'*The Conference*,
'*Considering* that many persons still leave their country of origin for reasons of persecution and are entitled to special protection on account of their position,

'*Recommends* that Governments continue to receive refugees in their territories and that they act in concert in a true spirit of international co-operation in order that these refugees may find asylum and the possibility of resettlement.'

## E

'*The Conference*,
'*Expresses* the hope that the Convention relating to the Status of

Refugees will have value as an example exceeding its contractual scope and that all nations will be guided by it in granting so far as possible to persons in their territory as refugees and who would not be covered by the terms of the Convention, the treatment for which it provides.'

*In Witness Whereof* the President, Vice-Presidents and the Executive Secretary of the Conference have signed this Final Act.

*Done* at Geneva this twenty-eighth day of July one thousand nine hundred and fifty-one in a single copy in the English and French languages, each text being equally authentic. Translations of this Final Act into Chinese, Russian and Spanish will be prepared by the Secretary-General of the United Nations, who will, on request, send copies thereof to each of the Governments invited to attend the Conference.

The President of the Conference: Knud Larsen
The Vice-Presidents of the Conference: A. Herment. Talat Miras
The Executive Secretary of the Conference: John P. Humphrey


CONVENTION RELATING TO THE STATUS OF REFUGEES

*Preamble*

The High Contracting Parties
*Considering* that the Charter of the United Nations and the Universal Declaration of Human Rights approved on 10 December 1948 by the General Assembly have affirmed the principle that human beings shall enjoy fundamental rights and freedoms without discrimination.

*Considering* that the United Nations has, on various occasions, manifested its profound concern for refugees and endeavoured to assure refugees the widest possible exercise of these fundamental rights and freedoms,

*Considering* that it is desirable to revise and consolidate previous international agreements relating to the status of refugees and to extend the scope of and the protection accorded by such instruments by means of a new agreement,

*Considering* that the grant of asylum may place unduly heavy burdens on certain countries, and that a satisfactory solution of a problem of which the United Nations has recognized the international scope and nature cannot therefore be achieved without international co-operation.

*Expressing* the wish that all States, recognizing the social and humanitarian nature of the problem of refugees, will do everything within their power to prevent this problem from becoming a cause of tension between States,

*Noting* that the United Nations High Commissioner for Refugees is charged with the task of supervising international conventions providing for the protection of refugees, and recognizing that the effective co-ordination of measures taken to deal with this problem will depend upon the co-operation of States with the High Commissioner,

*Have agreed as follows*:

## Chapter 1. General Provisions

### Article 1. Definition of the Term 'Refugee'

A. For the purposes of the present Convention, the term 'refugee' shall apply to any person who:

(1) Has been considered a refugee under the Arrangements of 12 May 1926 and 30 June 1928 or under the Conventions of 28 October 1933 and 10 February 1938, the Protocol of 14 September 1939 or the Constitution of the International Refugee Organization;

Decisions of non-eligibility taken by the International Refugee Organization during the period of its activities shall not prevent the status of refugee being accorded to persons who fulfil the conditions of paragraph 2 of this section;

(2) As a result of events occurring before 1 January 1951 and owing to well-founded fear of being persecuted for reasons of race, religion, nationality, membership of a particular social group or political opinion, is outside the country of his nationality and is unable or, owing to such fear, is unwilling to avail himself of the protection of that country; or who, not having a nationality and being outside the country of his former habitual residence as a result of such events, is unable or, owing to such fear, is unwilling to return to it.

In the case of a person who has more than one nationality, the term 'the country of his nationality' shall mean each of the countries of which he is a national, and a person shall not be deemed to be lacking the protection of the country of his nationality if, without any valid reason based on well-founded fear, he has not availed himself of the protection of one of the countries of which he is a national.

B.(1) For the purposes of this Convention, the words 'events occurring before 1 January 1951' in Article 1, Section A, shall be understood to mean either

(*a*) 'events occurring in Europe before 1 January 1951'; or

(*b*) 'events occurring in Europe or elsewhere before 1 January 1951', and each Contracting State shall make a declaration at the time of signature, ratification or accession, specifying which of these meanings it applies for the purpose of its obligations under this Convention.

(2) Any Contracting State which has adopted alternative (*a*) may at any time extend its obligations by adopting alternative (*b*) by means of a notification addressed to the Secretary-General of the United Nations.

C. This Convention shall cease to apply to any person falling under the terms of section A if:

(1) He has voluntarily re-availed himself of the protection of the country of his nationality; or

(2) Having lost his nationality, he has voluntarily re-acquired it, or

(3) He has acquired a new nationality, and enjoys the protection of the country of his new nationality; or

(4) He has voluntarily re-established himself in the country which he left or outside which he remained owing to fear of persecution; or

(5) He can no longer, because the circumstances in connexion with which he has been recognized as a refugee have ceased to exist, continue to refuse to avail himself of the protection of the country of his nationality;

Provided that this paragraph shall not apply to a refugee falling under section A(1) of this Article who is able to invoke compelling reasons arising out of previous persecution for refusing to avail himself of the protection of the country of nationality;

(6) Being a person who has no nationality he is, because the circumstances in connexion with which he has been recognized as a refugee have ceased to exist, able to return to the country of his former habitual residence;

Provided that this paragraph shall not apply to a refugee falling under section A(1) of this Article who is able to invoke compelling reasons arising out of previous persecution for refusing to return to the country of his former habitual residence.

D. This Convention shall not apply to persons who are at present receiving from organs or agencies of the United Nations other than the United Nations High Commissioner for Refugees protection or assistance.

When such protection or assistance has ceased for any reason, without the position of such persons being definitively settled in accordance with the relevant resolutions adopted by the General Assembly of the United Nations, these persons shall *ipso facto* be entitled to the benefits of this Convention.

E. This Convention shall not apply to a person who is recognized by the competent authorities of the country in which he has taken residence as having the rights and obligations which are attached to the possession of the nationality of that country.

F. The provisions of this Convention shall not apply to any person with respect to whom there are serious reasons for considering that:

(*a*) he has committed a crime against peace, a war crime, or a crime against humanity, as defined in the international instruments drawn up to make provision in respect of such crimes;

(*b*) he has committed a serious non-political crime outside the country of refuge prior to his admission to that country as a refugee;

(*c*) he has been guilty of acts contrary to the purposes and principles of the United Nations.

## Article 2. General Obligations

Every refugee has duties to the country in which he finds himself, which require in particular that he conform to its laws and regulations as well as to measures taken for the maintenance of public order.

## Article 3. Non-discrimination

The Contracting States shall apply the provisions of this Convention to refugees without discrimination as to race, religion or country of origin.

## Article 4. Religion

The Contracting States shall accord to refugees within their territories treatment at least as favourable as that accorded to their nationals with respect to freedom to practise their religion and freedom as regards the religious education of their children.

## Article 5. Rights Granted Apart from this Convention

Nothing in this Convention shall be deemed to impair any rights and benefits granted by a Contracting State to refugees apart from this Convention.

## Article 6. The Term 'in the Same Circumstances'

For the purpose of this Convention, the term 'in the same circumstances' implies that any requirements (including requirements as to length and conditions of sojourn or residence) which the particular individual would have to fulfil for the enjoyment of the right in question, if he were not a refugee, must be fulfilled by him, with the exception of requirements which by their nature a refugee is incapable of fulfilling.

## Article 7. Exemption from Reciprocity

1. Except where this Convention contains more favourable provisions, a Contracting State shall accord to refugees the same treatment as is accorded to aliens generally.

2. After a period the three years' residence, all refugees shall enjoy exemption from legislative reciprocity in the territory of the Contracting States.

3. Each Contracting State shall continue to accord to refugees the rights and benefits to which they were already entitled, in the absence of reciprocity, at the date of entry into force of this Convention for that State.

4. The Contracting States shall consider favourably the possibility of according to refugees, in the absence of reciprocity, rights and benefits beyond those to which they are entitled according to paragraphs 2 and 3, and to extending exemption from reciprocity to refugees who do not fulfil the conditions provided for in paragraphs 2 and 3.

5. The provisions of paragraphs 2 and 3 apply both to the rights and benefits referred to in Articles 13, 18, 19, 21 and 22 of this Convention and to rights and benefits for which this Convention does not provide.

### Article 8. Exemption from Exceptional Measures

With regard to exceptional measures which may be taken against the person, property or interests of nationals of a foreign State, the Contracting States shall not apply such measures to a refugee who is formally a national of the said State solely on account of such nationality. Contracting States which, under their legislation, are prevented from applying the general principle expressed in this Article, shall, in appropriate cases, grant exemptions in favour of such refugees.

### Article 9. Provisional Measures

Nothing in this Convention shall prevent a Contracting State, in time of war or other grave and exceptional circumstances, from taking provisionally measures which it considers to be essential to the national security in the case of a particular person, pending a determination by the Contracting State that that person is in fact a refugee and that the continuance of such measures is necessary in his case in the interests of national security.

### Article 10. Continuity of Residence

1. Where a refugee has been forcibly displaced during the Second World War and removed to the territory of a Contracting State, and is resident there, the period of such enforced sojourn shall be considered to have been lawful residence within that territory.

2. Where a refugee has been forcibly displaced during the Second World War from the territory of a Contracting State and has, prior to the date of entry into force of this Convention, returned there for the purpose of taking up residence, the period of residence before and after such enforced displacement shall be regarded as one uninterrupted period for any purposes for which uninterrupted residence is required.

### Article 11. Refugee Seamen

In the case of refugees regularly serving as crew members on board a ship flying the flag of a Contracting State, that State shall give sympathetic consideration to their establishment on its territory and the issue of travel documents to them or their temporary admission to its territory particularly with a view to facilitating their establishment in another country.

## Chapter II. Juridical Status

### Article 12. Personal Status

1. The personal status of a refugee shall be governed by the law of the country of his domicile or, if he has no domicile, by the law of the country of his residence.

2. Rights previously acquired by a refugee and dependent on personal status, more particularly rights attaching to marriage, shall be respected by a Contracting State, subject to compliance, if this be necessary, with the formalities required by the law of that State, provided that the right in question is one which would have been recognized by the law of that State had he not become a refugee.

### Article 13. Movable and Immovable Property

The Contracting States shall accord to a refugee treatment as favourable as possible and, in any event, not less favourable than that accorded to aliens generally in the same circumstances, as regards the acquisition of movable and immovable property and other rights pertaining thereto, and to leases and other contracts relating to movable and immovable property.

### Article 14. Artistic Rights and Industrial Property

In respect of the protection of industrial property, such as inventions, designs or models, trade marks, trade names, and of rights in literary, artistic and scientific works, a refugee shall be accorded in the country in which he has his habitual residence the same protection as is accorded to nationals of that country. In the territory of any other Contracting State, he shall be accorded the same protection as is accorded in that territory to nationals of the country in which he has his habitual residence.

### Article 15. Right of Association

As regards non-political and non-profit-making associations and trade unions the Contracting States shall accord to refugees lawfully staying in their territory the most favourable treatment accorded to nationals of a foreign country, in the same circumstances.

### Article 16. Access to Courts

1. A refugee shall have free access to the courts of law on the territory of all Contracting States.

2. A refugee shall enjoy in the Contracting State in which he has his habitual residence the same treatment as a national in matters pertaining to access to the Courts, including legal assistance and exemption from *cautio judicatum solvi*.

3. A refugee shall be accorded in the matters referred to in paragraph 2 in countries other than that in which he has his habitual residence the treatment granted to a national of the country of his habitual residence.

## Chapter III. Gainful Employment

### Article 17. Wage-Earning Employment

1. The Contracting State shall accord to refugees lawfully staying in their territory the most favourable treatment accorded to nationals of a foreign country in the same circumstances, as regards the right to engage in wage-earning employment.

2. In any case, restrictive measures imposed on aliens or the employment of aliens for the protection of the national labour market shall not be applied to a refugee who was already exempt from them at the date of entry into force of this Convention for the Contracting State concerned, or who fulfils one of the following conditions:

(*a*) He has completed three years' residence in the country,

(*b*) He has a spouse possessing the nationality of the country of residence. A refugee may not invoke the benefits of this provision if he has abandoned his spouse,

(*c*) He has one or more children possessing the nationality of the country of residence.

3. The Contracting States shall give sympathetic consideration to assimilating the rights of all refugees with regard to wage-earning employment to those of nationals, and in particular of those refugees who have entered their territory pursuant to programmes of labour recruitment or under immigration schemes.

### Article 18. Self-Employment

The Contracting States shall accord to a refugee lawfully in their territory treatment as favourable as possible and, in any event, not less favourable than that accorded to aliens generally in the same circumstances, as regards the right to engage on his own account in agriculture, industry, handicrafts and commerce and to establish commercial and industrial companies.

### Article 19. Liberal Professions

1. Each Contracting State shall accord to refugees lawfully staying in their territory who hold diplomas recognized by the competent authori-

ties of that State, and who are desirous of practising a liberal profession, treatment as favourable as possible and, in any event, not less favourable than that accorded to aliens generally in the same circumstances.

2. The Contracting States shall use their best endeavours consistently with their laws and constitutions to secure the settlement of such refugees in the territories, other than the metropolitan territory, for whose international relations they are responsible.

## Chapter IV. Welfare

### Article 20. Rationing

Where a rationing system exists, which applies to the population at large and regulates the general distribution of products in short supply, refugees shall be accorded the same treatment as nationals.

### Article 21. Housing

As regards housing, the Contracting States, in so far as the matter is regulated by laws or regulations or is subject to the control of public authorities, shall accord to refugees lawfully staying in their territory treatment as favourable as possible and, in any event, not less favourable than that accorded to aliens generally in the same circumstances.

### Article 22. Public Education

1. The Contracting States shall accord to refugees the same treatment as is accorded to nationals with respect to elementary education.

2. The Contracting States shall accord to refugees treatment as favourable as possible, and, in any event, not less favourable than that accorded to aliens generally in the same circumstances, with respect to education other than elementary education and, in particular, as regards access to studies, the recognition of foreign school certificates, diplomas and degrees, the remission of fees and charges and the award of scholarships.

### Article 23. Public Relief

The Contracting States shall accord to refugees lawfully staying in their territory the same treatment with respect to public relief and assistance as is accorded to their nationals.

### Article 24. Labour Legislation and Social Security

1. The Contracting States shall accord to refugees lawfully staying in their territory the same treatment as is accorded to nationals in respect of the following matters:

(*a*) In so far as such matters are governed by laws or regulations or are subject to the control of administrative authorities: remuneration, including family allowances where these form part of remuneration, hours of work, overtime arrangements, holidays with pay, restrictions on home work, minimum age of employment, apprenticeship and training, women's work and the work of young persons, and the enjoyment of the benefits of collective bargaining;

(*b*) Social security (legal provisions in respect of employment injury, occupational diseases, maternity, sickness, disability, old age, death, unemployment, family responsibilities and any other contingency which, according to national laws or regulations, is covered by a social security scheme), subject to the following limitations.

(i) There may be appropriate arrangements for the maintenance of acquired rights and rights in course of acquisition;

(ii) National laws or regulations of the country of residence may prescribe special arrangements concerning benefits or portions of benefits which are payable wholly out of public funds, and concerning allowances paid to persons who do not fulfil the contribution conditions prescribed for the award of a normal pension.

2. The right to compensation for the death of a refugee resulting from employment injury or from occupational disease shall not be affected by the fact that the residence of the beneficiary is outside the territory of the Contracting State.

3. The Contracting States shall extend to refugees the benefits of agreements concluded between them, or which may be concluded between them in the future, concerning the maintenance of acquired rights and rights in the process of acquisition in regard to social security, subject only to the conditions which apply to nationals of the States signatory to the agreements in question.

4. The Contracting States will give sympathetic consideration to extending to refugees so far as possible the benefits of similar agreements which may at any time be in force between such Contracting States and non-contracting States.

## Chapter V. Administrative Measures

### Article 25. Administrative Assistance

1. When the exercise of a right by a refugee would normally require the assistance of authorities of a foreign country to whom he cannot have recourse, the Contracting States in whose territory he is residing shall arrange that such assistance be afforded to him by their own authorities or by an international authority.

2. The authority or authorities mentioned in paragraph 1 shall deliver or cause to be delivered under their supervision to refugees such docu-

ments or certifications as would normally be delivered to aliens by or through their national authorities.

3. Documents or certifications so delivered shall stand in the stead of the official instruments delivered to aliens by or through their national authorities, and shall be given credence in the absence of proof to the contrary.

4. Subject to such exceptional treatment as may be granted to indigent persons, fees may be charged for the services mentioned herein, but such fees shall be moderate and commensurate with those charged to nationals for similar services.

5. The provisions of this Article shall be without prejudice to Articles 27 and 28.

## Article 26. Freedom of Movement

Each Contracting State shall accord to refugees lawfully in its territory the right to choose their place of residence and to move freely within its territory, subject to any regulations applicable to aliens generally in the same circumstances.

## Article 27. Identity Papers

The Contracting States shall issue identity papers to any refugee in their territory who does not possess a valid travel document.

## Article 28. Travel Documents

1. The Contracting States shall issue to refugees lawfully staying in their territory travel documents for the purpose of travel outside their territory unless compelling reasons of national security or public order otherwise require, and the provisions of the Schedule to this Convention shall apply with respect to such documents. The Contracting States may issue such a travel document to any other refugee in their territory; they shall in particular give sympathetic consideration to the issue of such a travel document to refugees in their territory who are unable to obtain a travel document from the country of their lawful residence.

2. Travel documents issued to refugees under previous international agreements by parties thereto shall be recognized and treated by the Contracting States in the same way as if they had been issued pursuant to this article.

### Article 29. Fiscal Charges

1. The Contracting States shall not impose upon refugees duties, charges or taxes, of any description whatsoever, other or higher than those which are or may be levied on their nationals in similar situations.

2. Nothing in the above paragraph shall prevent the application to refugees of the laws and regulations concerning charges in respect of the issue to aliens of administrative documents including identity papers.

### Article 30. Transfer of Assets

1. A Contracting State shall, in conformity with its laws and regulations, permit refugees to transfer assets which they have brought into its territory, to another country where they have been admitted for the purposes of resettlement.

2. A Contracting State shall give sympathetic consideration to the application of refugees for permission to transfer assets wherever they may be and which are necessary for their resettlement in another country to which they have been admitted.

### Article 31. Refugees Unlawfully in the Country of Refuge

1. The Contracting States shall not impose penalties, on account of their illegal entry or presence, on refugees who, coming directly from a territory where their life or freedom was threatened in the sense of Article 1, enter or are present in their territory without authorization, provided they present themselves without delay to the authorities and show good cause for their illegal entry or presence.

2. The Contracting States shall not apply to the movements of such refugees restrictions other than those which are necessary and such restrictions shall only be applied until their status in the country is regularized or they obtain admission into another country. The Contracting States shall allow such refugees a reasonable period and all the necessary facilities to obtain admission into another country.

### Article 32. Expulsion

1. The Contracting States shall not expel a refugee lawfully in their territory save on grounds of national security or public order.

2. The expulsion of such a refugee shall be only in pursuance of a decision reached in accordance with due process of law. Except where compelling reasons of national security otherwise require, the refugee shall be allowed to submit evidence to clear himself, and to appeal to and

be represented for the purpose before competent authority or a person or persons specially designated by the competent authority.

3. The Contracting States shall allow such a refugee a reasonable period within which to seek legal admission into another country. The Contracting States reserve the right to apply during that period such internal measures as they may deem necessary.

### Article 33. Prohibition of Expulsion or Return ('Refoulement')

1. No Contracting State shall expel or return ('refouler') a refugee in any manner whatsoever to the frontiers of territories where his life or freedom would be threatened on account of his race, religion, nationality, membership of a particular social group or political opinion.

2. The benefit of the present provision may not, however, be claimed by a refugee whom there are reasonable grounds for regarding as a danger to the security of the country in which he is, or who, having been convicted by a final judgment of a particularly serious crime, constitutes a danger to the community of that country.

### Article 34. Naturalization

The Contracting States shall as far as possible facilitate the assimilation and naturalization of refugees. They shall in particular make every effort to expedite naturalization proceedings and to reduce as far as possible the charges and costs of such proceedings.

### Chapter VI. Executory and Transitory Provisions

### Article 35. Co-operation of the National Authorities with the United Nations

1. The Contracting States undertake to co-operate with the Office of the United Nations High Commissioner for Refugees, or any other agency of the United Nations which may succeed it, in the exercise of its functions, and shall in particular facilitate its duty of supervising the application of the provisions of this Convention.

2. In order to enable the Office of the High Commissioner or any other agency of the United Nations which may succeed it, to make reports to the competent organs of the United Nations, the Contracting States undertake to provide them in the appropriate form with information and statistical data requested concerning:

(*a*) the condition of refugees,

(*b*) the implementation of this Convention, and

(*c*) laws, regulations and decrees which are, or may hereafter be, in force relating to refugees.

### Article 36. Information on National Legislation

The Contracting States shall communicate to the Secretary-General of the United Nations the laws and regulations which they may adopt to ensure the application of this Convention.

### Article 37. Relation to Previous Conventions

Without prejudice to Article 28, paragraph 2, of this Convention, this Convention replaces, as between parties to it, the Arrangements of 5 July 1922, 31 May 1924, 12 May 1926, 30 June 1928 and 30 July 1935, the Conventions of 28 October 1933 and 10 February 1938, the Protocol of 14 September 1939 and the Agreement of 15 October 1946.

## *Chapter VII. Final Clauses*

### Article 38. Settlement of Disputes

Any dispute between parties to this Convention relating to its interpretation or application, which cannot be settled by other means, shall be referred to the International Court of Justice at the request of any one of the parties to the dispute.

### Article 39. Signature, Ratification and Accession

1. This Convention shall be opened for signature at Geneva on 28 July 1951 and shall thereafter be deposited with the Secretary-General of the United Nations. It shall be open for signature at the European Office of the United Nations from 28 July to 31 August 1951 and shall be re-opened for signature at the Headquarters of the United Nations from 17 September 1951 to 31 December 1952.

2. This Convention shall be open for signature on behalf of all States Members of the United Nations, and also on behalf of any other State invited to attend the Conference of Plenipotentiaries on the Status of Refugees and Stateless Persons or to which an invitation to sign will have been addressed by the General Assembly. It shall be ratified and the instruments of ratification shall be deposited with the Secretary-General of the United Nations.

3. This Convention shall be open from 28 July 1951 for accession by the States referred to in paragraph 2 of this Article. Accession shall be effected by the deposit of an instrument of accession with the Secretary-General of the United Nations.

### Article 40. Territorial Application Clause

1. Any State may, at the time of signature, ratification or accession, declare that this Convention shall extend to all or any of the territories for the international relations of which it is responsible. Such a declara-

tion shall take effect when the Convention enters into force for the State concerned.

2. At any time thereafter any such extension shall be made by notification addressed to the Secretary-General of the United Nations and shall take effect as from the ninetieth day after the day of receipt by the Secretary-General of the United Nations of this notification, or as from the date of entry into force of the Convention for the State concerned, whichever is the later.

3. With respect to those territories to which this Convention is not extended at the time of signature, ratification or accession, each State concerned shall consider the possibility of taking the necessary steps in order to extend the application of this Convention to such territories, subject, where necessary for constitutional reasons, to the consent of the governments of such territories.

### Article 41. Federal Clause

In the case of a Federal or non-unitary State, the following provisions shall apply:

(*a*) With respect to those Articles of this Convention that come within the legislative jurisdiction of the federal legislative authority, the obligations of the Federal Government shall to this extent be the same as those of Parties which are not Federal States,

(*b*) With respect to those Articles of this Convention that come within the legislative jurisdiction of constituent States, provinces or cantons which are not, under the constitutional system of the federation, bound to take legislative action, the Federal Government shall bring such Articles with a favourable recommendation to the notice of the appropriate authorities of States, provinces or cantons at the earliest possible moment.

(*c*) A Federal State Party to this Convention shall, at the request of any other Contracting State transmitted through the Secretary-General of the United Nations, supply a statement of the law and practice of the Federation and its constituent units in regard to any particular provision of the Convention showing the extent to which effect has been given to that provision by legislative or other action.

### Article 42. Reservations

1. At the time of signature, ratification or accession, any State may make reservations to articles of the Convention other than to Articles 1, 3, 4, 16 (1), 33, 36-46 inclusive.

2. Any State making a reservation in accordance with paragraph 1 of this article may at any time withdraw the reservation by a communication to that effect addressed to the Secretary-General of the United Nations.

### Article 43. Entry into Force

1. This Convention shall come into force on the ninetieth day following the day of deposit of the sixth instrument of ratification or accession.

2. For each State ratifying or acceding to the Convention after the deposit of the sixth instrument of ratification or accession, the Convention shall enter into force on the ninetieth day following the date of deposit by such State of its instrument of ratification or accession.

### Article 44. Denunciation

1. Any Contracting State may denounce this Convention at any time by a notification addressed to the Secretary-General of the United Nations.

2. Such denunciation shall take effect for the Contracting State concerned one year from the date upon which it is received by the Secretary-General of the United Nations.

3. Any State which has made a declaration or notification under Article 40 may, at any time thereafter, by a notification to the Secretary-General of the United Nations, declare that the Convention shall cease to extend to such territory one year after the date of receipt of the notification by the Secretary-General.

### Article 45. Revision

1. Any Contracting State may request revision of this Convention at any time by a notification addressed to the Secretary-General of the United Nations.

2. The General Assembly of the United Nations shall recommend the steps, if any, to be taken in respect of such request.

### Article 46. Notifications by the Secretary-General of the United Nations

The Secretary-General of the United Nations shall inform all Members of the United Nations and non-member States referred to in Article 39:

(*a*) of declarations and notifications in accordance with Section B of Article 1;

(*b*) of signatures, ratifications and accessions in accordance with Article 39;

(*c*) of declarations and notifications in accordance with Article 40;

(*d*) of reservations and withdrawals in accordance with Article 42;

(*e*) of the date on which this Convention will come into force in accordance with Article 43;

(*f*) of denunciations and notifications in accordance with Article 44;

(*g*) of requests for revision in accordance with Article 45.

IN FAITH WHEREOF the undersigned, duly authorized, have signed this Convention of behalf of their respective Governments,

DONE at Geneva, this twenty-eighth day of July, one thousand nine hundred and fifty-one, in a single copy, of which the English and French texts are equally authentic and which shall remain deposited in the archives of the United Nations, and certified true copies of which shall be delivered to all Members of the United Nations and to the non-member States referred to in Article 39.

## *Schedule*

### Paragraph 1

1. The travel document referred to in Article 28 of this Convention shall be similar to the specimen annexed hereto.

2. The document shall be made out in at least two languages, one of which shall be English or French.

### Paragraph 2

Subject to the regulations obtaining in the country of issue, children may be included in the travel document of a parent or, in exceptional circumstances, of another adult refugee.

### Paragraph 3

The fees charged for issue of the document shall not exceed the lowest scale of charges for national passports.

### Paragraph 4

Save in special or exceptional cases, the document shall be made valid for the largest possible number of countries.

### Paragraph 5

The document shall have a validity of either one or two years, at the discretion of the issuing authority.

### Paragraph 6

1. The renewal or extension of the validity of the document is a matter for the authority which issued it, so long as the holder has not established lawful residence in another territory and resides lawfully in the territory of the said authority. The issue of a new document is, under the same conditions, a matter for the authority which issued the former document.

2. Diplomatic or consular authorities, specially authorized for the purpose, shall be empowered to extend, for a period not exceeding six months, the validity of travel documents issued by their Governments.

3. The Contracting States shall give sympathetic consideration to renewing or extending the validity of travel documents or issuing new documents to refugees no longer lawfully resident in their territory who are unable to obtain a travel document from the country of their lawful residence.

### Paragraph 7

The Contracting States shall recognize the validity of the documents issued in accordance with the provisions of Article 28 of this Convention.

### Paragraph 8

The competent authorities of the country to which the refugee desires to proceed shall, if they are prepared to admit him and if a visa is required, affix a visa on the document of which he is the holder.

### Paragraph 9

1. The Contracting States undertake to issue transit visas to refugees who have obtained visas for a territory of final destination.

2. The issue of such visas may be refused on the grounds which would justify refusal of a visa to any alien.

### Paragraph 10

The fees for the issue of exit, entry or transit visas shall not exceed the lowest scale of charges for visas on foreign passports.

### Paragraph 11

When a refugee has lawfully taken up residence in the territory of another Contracting State, the responsibility for the issue of a new document, under the terms and conditions of Article 28, shall be that of the competent authority of that territory, to which the refugee shall be entitled to apply.

### Paragraph 12

The authority issuing a new document shall withdraw the old document and shall return it to the country of issue, if it is stated in the document that it should be so returned; otherwise it shall withdraw and cancel the document.

### Paragraph 13

1. Each Contracting State undertakes that the holder of a travel document issued by it in accordance with Article 28 of this Convention shall be re-admitted to its territory at any time during the period of its validity.

2. Subject to the provisions of the preceding sub-paragraph, a Contracting State may require the holder of the document to comply with such formalities as may be prescribed in regard to exit from or return to its territory.

3. The Contracting States reserve the right, in exceptional cases, or in cases where the refugee's stay is authorized for a specific period, when issuing the document, to limit the period during which the refugee may return to a period of not less than three months.

### Paragraph 14

Subject only to the terms of paragraph 13, the provisions of this Schedule in no way affect the laws and regulations governing the conditions of admission to, transit through, residence and establishment in, and departure from, the territories of the Contracting States.

### Paragraph 15

Neither the issue of the document nor the entries made thereon determine or affect the status of the holder, particularly as regards nationality.

### Paragraph 16

The issue of the document does not in any way entitle the holder to the protection of the diplomatic or consular authorities of the country of issue, and does not confer on these authorities a right of protection.

### ANNEX

#### Specimen Travel Document

The document will be in booklet form (approximately 15 × 10 centimetres).

It is recommended that it be so printed that any erasure or alteration by chemical or other means can be readily detected, and that the words 'Convention of 28 July 1951' be printed in continuous repetition on each page, in the language of the issuing country.

[The details of the Specimen Travel Document are omitted.]

# V. 1967 Protocol relating to the Status of Refugees

Text: 606 UNTS 267

*The States Parties* to the present Protocol,

*Considering* that the Convention relating to the Status of Refugees done at Geneva on 28 July 1951 (hereinafter referred to as the Convention) covers only those persons who have become refugees as a result of events occurring before 1 January 1951,

*Considering* that new refugee situations have arisen since the Convention was adopted and that the refugees concerned may therefore not fall within the scope of the Convention,

*Considering* that it is desirable that equal status should be enjoyed by all refugees covered by the definition in the Convention irrespective of the dateline 1 January 1951,

*Have agreed* as follows:

## Article I.  General Provision

1. The States Parties to the present Protocol undertake to apply articles 2 to 34 inclusive of the Convention to refugees as hereinafter defined.

2. For the purpose of the present Protocol, the term 'refugee' shall, except as regards the application of paragraph 3 of this article, mean any person within the definition of article 1 of the Convention as if the words 'As a result of events occurring before 1 January 1951 and ...' and the words '... as a result of such events', in article 1 A (2) were omitted.

3. The present Protocol shall be applied by the States Parties hereto without any geographic limitation, save that existing declarations made by States already Parties to the Convention in accordance with article 1 B (1) (*a*) of the Convention, shall, unless extended under article 1 B (2) thereof, apply also under the present Protocol.

## Article II.  Co-operation of the National Authorities with the United Nations

1. The States Parties to the present Protocol undertake to co-operate with the Office of the United Nations High Commissioner for Refugees, or any other agency of the United Nations which may succeed it, in the exercise of its functions, and shall in particular facilitate its duty of supervising the application of the provisions of the present Protocol.

2. In order to enable the Office of the High Commissioner, or any other agency of the United Nations which may succeed it, to make reports to the competent organs of the United Nations, the States Parties to the

present Protocol undertake to provide them with the information and statistical data requested, in the appropriate form, concerning

(a) The condition of refugees;

(b) The implementation of the present Protocol;

(c) Laws, regulations and decrees which are, or may hereafter be, in force relating to refugees.

### Article III. *Information on National Legislation*

The States Parties to the present Protocol shall communicate to the Secretary-General of the United Nations the laws and regulations which they may adopt to ensure the application of the present Protocol.

### Article IV. *Settlement of Disputes*

Any dispute between States Parties to the present Protocol which relates to its interpretation or application and which cannot be settled by other means shall be referred to the International Court of Justice at the request of any one of the parties to the dispute.

### Article V. *Accession*

The present Protocol shall be open for accession on behalf of all States Parties to the Convention and of any other State Member of the United Nations or member of any of the specialized agencies or to which an invitation to accede may have been addressed by the General Assembly of the United Nations. Accession shall be effected by the deposit of an instrument of accession with the Secretary-General of the United Nations.

### Article VI. *Federal Clause*

In the case of a Federal or non-unitary State, the following provisions shall apply:

(a) With respect to those articles of the Convention to be applied in accordance with article I, paragraph 1, of the present Protocol that come within the legislative jurisdiction of the federal legislative authority, the obligations of the Federal Government shall to this extent be the same as those of States Parties which are not Federal States;

(b) With respect to those articles of the Convention to be applied in accordance with article I, paragraph 1, of the present Protocol that come within the legislative jurisdiction of constituent States, provinces or cantons which are not, under the constitutional system of the federation, bound to take legislative action, the Federal Government shall bring such articles with a favourable recommendation to the notice of the appropriate authorities of States, provinces or cantons at the earliest possible moment;

(c) A Federal State Party to the present Protocol shall, at the request of any other State Party hereto transmitted through the Secretary-General of the United Nations, supply a statement of the law and practice of the Federation and its constituent units in regard to any particular provision of the Convention to be applied in accordance with article I, paragraph 1, of the present Protocol, showing the extent to which effect has been given to that provision by legislative or other action.

### *Article VII. Reservations and Declarations*

1. At the time of accession, any State may make reservations in respect of article IV of the present Protocol and in respect of the application in accordance with article I of the present Protocol of any provisions of the Convention other than those contained in articles 1, 3, 4, 16 (1) and 33 thereof, provided that in the case of a State Party to the Convention reservations made under this article shall not extend to refugees in respect of whom the Convention applies.

2. Reservations made by States Parties to the Convention in accordance with article 42 thereof shall, unless withdrawn, be applicable in relation to their obligations under the present Protocol.

3. Any State making a reservation in accordance with paragraph 1 of this article may at any time withdraw such reservation by a communication to that effect addressed to the Secretary-General of the United Nations.

4. Declarations made under article 40, paragraphs 1 and 2, of the Convention by a State Party thereto which accedes to the present Protocol shall be deemed to apply in respect of the present Protocol, unless upon accession a notification to the contrary is addressed by the State Party concerned to the Secretary-General of the United Nations. The provisions of article 40, paragraphs 2 and 3, and of article 44, paragraph 3, of the Convention shall be deemed to apply *mutatis mutandis* to the present Protocol.

### *Article VIII. Entry into Force*

1. The present Protocol shall come into force on the day of deposit of the sixth instrument of accession.

2. For each State acceding to the Protocol after the deposit of the sixth instrument of accession, the Protocol shall come into force on the date of deposit by such State of its instrument of accession.

### *Article IX. Denunciation*

1. Any State Party hereto may denounce this Protocol at any time by a notification addressed to the Secretary-General of the United Nations.

2. Such denunciation shall take effect for the State Party concerned one year from the date on which it is received by the Secretary-General of the United Nations.

### Article X. *Notifications by the Secretary-General of the United Nations*

The Secretary-General of the United Nations shall inform the States referred to in article V above of the date of entry into force, accessions, reservations and withdrawals of reservations to and denunciations of the present Protocol, and of declarations and notifications relating hereto.

### Article XI. *Deposit in the Archives of the Secretariat of the United Nations*

A copy of the present Protocol, of which the Chinese, English, French, Russian and Spanish texts are equally authentic, signed by the President of the General Assembly and by the Secretary-General of the United Nations, shall be deposited in the archives of the Secretariat of the United Nations. The Secretary-General will transmit certified copies thereof to all States Members of the United Nations and to the other States referred to in article V above.

## GENERAL ASSEMBLY RESOLUTION 2198 (XXI) OF 16 DECEMBER 1966

### *Protocol relating to the Status of Refugees*

*The General Assembly,*

*Considering* that the Convention relating to the Status of Refugees, signed at Geneva on 28 July 1951, covers only those persons who have become refugees as a result of events occurring before 1 January 1951,

*Considering* that new refugee situations have arisen since the Convention was adopted and that the refugees concerned may therefore not fall within the scope of the Convention,

*Considering* that it is desirable that equal status should be enjoyed by all refugees covered by the definition in the Convention, irrespective of the date-line of 1 January 1951,

*Taking note* of the recommendations of the Executive Committee of the Programme of the United Nations High Commissioner for Refugees that the draft Protocol relating to the Status of Refugees should be submitted to the General Assembly after consideration by the Economic and Social Council, in order that the Secretary-General might be authorized to open the Protocol for accession by Governments within the shortest possible time,

*Considering* that the Economic and Social Council, in its resolution 1186 (XLI) of 18 November 1966, took note with approval of the draft Protocol contained in the addendum to the report of the United Nations High Commissioner for Refugees and concerning measures to extend the personal scope of the Convention and transmitted the addendum to the General Assembly.

1. *Takes note* of the Protocol relating to the Status of Refugees, the text of which is contained in the addendum to the report of the United Nations High Commissioner for Refugees,

2. *Requests* the Secretary-General to transmit the text of the Protocol to the States mentioned in article V thereof, with a view to enabling them to accede to the Protocol.[1]

---

[1] The Protocol was signed by the President of the General Assembly and by the Secretary-General on 31 January 1967.

# VI. Declaration on Territorial Asylum

*Adopted by the General Assembly of the United Nations on
14 December 1967 (resolution 2312 (XXII))*

*The General Assembly,*

*Recalling* its resolutions 1839 (XVII) of 19 December 1962, 2100 (XX)
of 20 December 1965 and 2203 (XXI) of 16 December 1966 concerning
a declaration on the right of asylum,

*Considering* the work of codification to be undertaken by the International Law Commission in accordance with General Assembly resolution 1400 (XIV) of 21 November 1959,

*Adopts* the following Declaration:

## DECLARATION ON TERRITORIAL ASYLUM

*The General Assembly,*

*Noting* that the purposes proclaimed in the Charter of the United
Nations are to maintain international peace and security, to develop
friendly relations among all nations and to achieve international co-
operation in solving international problems of an economic, social,
cultural or humanitarian character and in promoting and encouraging
respect for human rights and for fundamental freedoms for all without
distinction as to race, sex, language or religion,

*Mindful* of the Universal Declaration of Human Rights, which
declares in article 14 that:

'1. Everyone has the right to seek and to enjoy in other countries
asylum from persecution.

'2. This right may not be invoked in the case of prosecutions genuinely arising from non-political crimes or from acts contrary to the purposes and principles of the United Nations'.

*Recalling* also article 13, paragraph 2, of the Universal Declaration of
Human Rights, which states:

'Everyone has the right to leave any country, including his own, and
to return to his country',

*Recognizing* that the grant of asylum by a State to persons entitled to
invoke article 14 of the Universal Declaration of Human Rights is a
peaceful and humanitarian act and that, as such, it cannot be regarded
as unfriendly by any other State,

*Recommends* that, without prejudice to existing instruments dealing
with asylum and the status of refugees and stateless persons, States
should base themselves in their practices relating to territorial asylum on
the following principles:

## *Article 1*

1. Asylum granted by a State, in the exercise of its sovereignty, to persons entitled to invoke article 14 of the Universal Declaration of Human Rights, including persons struggling against colonialism, shall be respected by all other States.

2. The right to seek and to enjoy asylum may not be invoked by any person with respect to whom there are serious reasons for considering that he has committed a crime against peace, a war crime or a crime against humanity, as defined in the international instruments drawn up to make provision in respect of such crimes.

3. It shall rest with the State granting asylum to evaluate the grounds for the grant of asylum.

## *Article 2*

1. The situation of persons referred to in article 1, paragraph 1, is, without prejudice to the sovereignty of States and the purposes and principles of the United Nations, of concern to the international community.

2. Where a State finds difficulty in granting or continuing to grant asylum, States individually or jointly or through the United Nations shall consider, in a spirit of international solidarity, appropriate measures to lighten the burden on that State.

## *Article 3*

1. No person referred to in article 1, paragraph 1, shall be subjected to measures such as rejection at the frontier or, if he has already entered the territory in which he seeks asylum, expulsion or compulsory return to any State where he may be subjected to persecution.

2. Exception may be made to the foregoing principle only for overriding reasons of national security or in order to safeguard the population, as in the case of a mass influx of persons.

3. Should a State decide in any case that exception to the principle stated in paragraph 1 of this article would be justified, it shall consider the possibility of granting to the person concerned, under such conditions as it may deem appropriate, an opportunity, whether by way of provisional asylum or otherwise, of going to another State.

## *Article 4*

States granting asylum shall not permit persons who have received asylum to engage in activities contrary to the purposes and principles of the United Nations.

# VII. Draft Convention on Territorial Asylum

## TEXT OF ARTICLES CONSIDERED AT THE UNITED NATIONS CONFERENCE ON TERRITORIAL ASYLUM HELD IN GENEVA FROM 10 JANUARY TO 4TH FEBRUARY 1977

*Note*: The Committee of the Whole approved and referred to the Drafting Committee, Article 1, Article 2, Article 3, a new Article on the Question of Family Reunion and a new Article on the Question of Activities of Asylees. The Drafting Committee only completed its examination of draft Article 1. None of the draft Articles was referred back to the Committee of the Whole for reconsideration. They were not approved by the Conference in Plenary Session. See Report of the United Nations Conference on Territorial Asylum: UN doc. A/CONF.78/12 (21 April 1977).

### Article 1. *Grant of asylum*

Each Contracting State, acting in the exercise of its sovereignty, shall endeavour in a humanitarian spirit to grant asylum in its territory to any person eligible for the benefits of this Convention.

### Additional paragraph

Asylum should not be refused by a Contracting State solely on the ground that it could be sought from another State. However, where it appears that a person requesting asylum from a Contracting State already has a connexion or close links with another State, the Contracting State may, if it appears fair and reasonable, require him first to request asylum from that State.

### Article 2

1. Each Contracting State may grant the benefits of this Convention to a person seeking asylum, if he, being faced with a definite possibility of:

(a) Persecution for reasons of race, colour, national or ethnic origin, religion, nationality, kinship, membership of a particular social group or political opinion, including the struggle against colonialism and *apartheid*, foreign occupation, alien domination and all forms of racism; or

(b) Prosecution or punishment for reasons directly related to the persecution as set forth in (a);

is unable or unwilling to return to the country of his nationality, or, if he has no nationality, the country of his former domicile or habitual residence.

2. The provisions of paragraph 1 of this article shall not apply to any person with respect to whom there are serious reasons for considering that he is still liable to prosecution or punishment for:

(a) A crime against peace, a war crime, or crime against humanity as defined in the international instruments drawn up to make provision in respect of such crimes; or

(a *bis*) Other grave crimes as defined in multilateral conventions to which a Contracting State in which he is seeking asylum is a party; or

(b) An offence which would be a serious criminal offence if committed in the Contracting State from which asylum is requested;

(c) Acts contrary to the Purposes and Principles of the United Nations.

3. The provisions of paragraph 1 of this article shall also not apply to any person requesting territorial asylum for purely economic reasons.

3 *bis*. The provisions of paragraph 1 of this article shall not apply to any person whom there are serious reasons for regarding as a threat or danger to the security of the country in which he is seeking asylum.

## *Article 3*

1. No person eligible for the benefits of this Convention in accordance with article 2, paragraph 1, subparagraphs (a) and (b), who is at the frontier seeking asylum or in the territory of a Contracting State shall be subjected by such Contracting State to measures such as rejection at the frontier, return or expulsion, which would compel him to remain in or return to a territory with respect to which he has a well-founded fear of persecution, prosecution or punishment for any of the reasons stated in Article 2.

2. The benefit of the present provision, however, may not be claimed by a person whom there are reasons for regarding as a danger to the security of the country in which he is, or who, being still liable to prosecution or punishment for, or having been convicted by a final judgement of a particularly serious crime, constitutes a danger to the community in that country or in exceptional cases, by a great number of persons whose massive influx may constitute a serious problem to the security of a Contracting State.

3. Where a Contracting State decides that an exception should be made on the basis of the preceding paragraph, it shall consider the possibility of granting to the person concerned, under such conditions as it may deem appropriate, an opportunity of going to another State.

### New Article on the Question of Activities of Asylees

1. A person enjoying the benefits of this Convention shall comply with the laws and regulations of the country granting asylum.

2. To the extent to which it is possible under their law, Contracting States granting asylum shall not permit persons enjoying the benefits of this Convention to engage in activities contrary to the Purposes and Principles of the United Nations as set forth in the Charter.

### New Article on the Question of Family Reunion

1. Each Contracting State shall, in the interest of family reunification and for humanitarian reasons, facilitate the admission to its territory of the spouse and the minor or dependent children of any person to whom it has granted the benefits of this Convention.

2. These Members of the family should, save in exceptional circumstances be given the same benefits under this Convention as that person.

# VIII. Organization of African Unity: 1969 Convention on Refugee Problems in Africa

[*Done at Addis Ababa, September 10, 1969*]

Text: UNTS No. 14,691

## OAU CONVENTION GOVERNING THE SPECIFIC ASPECTS OF REFUGEE PROBLEMS IN AFRICA

### *Preamble*

We, the Heads of State and Government assembled in the city of Addis Ababa, September 6-10, 1969

1. *Noting with concern* the constantly increasing numbers of refugees in Africa and desirous of finding ways and means of alleviating their misery and suffering as well as providing them with a better life and future,

2. *Recognizing* the need for an essentially humanitarian approach towards solving the problems of refugees,

3. *Aware*, however, that refugee problems are a source of friction among many Member States, and desirous of eliminating the source of such discord,

4. *Anxious* to make a distinction between a refugee who seeks a peaceful and normal life and a person fleeing his country for the sole purpose of fomenting subversion from outside,

5. *Determined* that the activities of such subversive elements should be discouraged, in accordance with the Declaration on the Problem of Subversion and Resolution on the Problem of Refugees adopted at Accra in 1965,

6. *Bearing* in mind that the Charter of the United Nations and the Universal Declaration of Human Rights have affirmed the principle that human beings shall enjoy fundamental rights and freedoms without discrimination,

7. *Recalling* Resolution 2312 (XXII) of 14 December 1967 of the United Nations General Assembly, relating to the Declaration on Territorial Asylum,

8. *Convinced* that all the problems of our continent must be solved in the spirit of the Charter of the Organization of African Unity and in the African context,

9. *Recognizing* that the United Nations Convention of 28 July 1951, as modified by the Protocol of 31 January 1967, constitutes the basic and universal instrument relating to the status of refugees and reflects the deep concern of States for refugees and their desire to establish common standards for their treatment,

10. *Recalling* Resolutions 26 and 104 of the OAU Assemblies of Heads of State and Government, calling upon Member States of the Organization who had not already done so to accede to the United Nations Convention of 1951 and to the Protocol of 1967 relating to the Status of Refugees, and meanwhile to apply their provisions to refugees in Africa,

11. *Convinced* that the efficiency of the measures recommended by the present Convention to solve the problem of refugees in Africa necessitates close and continuous collaboration between the Organization of African Unity and the Office of the United Nations High Commissioner for Refugees,

*HAVE AGREED* as follows:

## Article I. Definition of the term 'Refugee'

1. For the purposes of this Convention, the term 'refugee' shall mean every person who, owing to well-founded fear of being persecuted for reasons of race, religion, nationality, membership of a particular social group or political opinion, is outside the country of his nationality and is unable or, owing to such fear, is unwilling to avail himself of the protection of that country, or who, not having a nationality and being outside the country of his former habitual residence as a result of such events is unable or, owing to such fear, is unwilling to return to it.

2. The term 'refugee' shall also apply to every person who, owing to external agression, occupation, foreign domination or events seriously disturbing public order in either part or the whole of his country of origin or nationality, is compelled to leave his place of habitual residence in order to seek refuge in another place outside his country of origin or nationality.

3. In the case of a person who has several nationalities, the term 'a country of which he is a national' shall mean each of the countries of which he is a national, and a person shall not be deemed to be lacking the protection of the country of which he is a national if, without any valid reason based on well-founded fear, he has not availed himself of the protection of one of the countries of which he is a national.

4. This Convention shall cease to apply to any refugee if:

(a) he has voluntarily re-availed himself of the protection of the country of his nationality, or,

(b) having lost his nationality, he has voluntarily reacquired it, or,

(c) he has acquired a new nationality, and enjoys the protection of the country of his new nationality, or,

(d) he has voluntarily re-established himself in the country which he left or outside which he remained owing to fear of persecution, or,

(e) he can no longer, because the circumstances in connection with which he was recognized as a refugee have ceased to exist, continue to refuse to avail himself of the protection of the country of his nationality, or,

(f) he has committed a serious non-political crime outside his country of refuge after his admission to that country as a refugee, or,

(g) he has seriously infringed the purposes and objectives of this Convention.

5. The provisions of this Convention shall not apply to any person with respect to whom the country of asylum has serious reasons for consider-that:

(a) he has committed a crime against peace, a war crime, or a crime against humanity, as defined in the international instruments drawn up to make provision in respect of such crimes;

(b) he committed a serious non-political crime outside the country of refuge prior to his admission to that country as a refugee;

(c) he has been guilty of acts contrary to the purposes and principles of the Organization of African Unity;

(d) he has been guilty of acts contrary to the purposes and principles of the United Nations.

6. For the purposes of this Convention, the Contracting State of Asylum shall determine whether an applicant is a refugee.

### *Article II. Asylum*

1. Member States of the OAU shall use their best endeavours consistent with their respective legislations to receive refugees and to secure the settlement of those refugees who, for well-founded reasons, are unable or unwilling to return to their country of origin or nationality.

2. The grant of asylum to refugees is a peaceful and humanitarian act and shall not be regarded as an unfriendly act by any Member State.

3. No person shall be subjected by a Member State to measures such as rejection at the frontier, return or expulsion, which would compel him to return to or remain in a territory where his life, physical integrity or liberty would be threatened for the reasons set out in Article I, paragraphs 1 and 2.

4. Where a Member State finds difficulty in continuing to grant asylum to refugees, such Member State may appeal directly to other Member States and through the OAU, and such other Member States shall in the

spirit of African solidarity and international co-operation take appropriate measures to lighten the burden of the Member State granting asylum.

5. Where a refugee has not received the right to reside in any country of asylum, he may be granted temporary residence in any country of asylum in which he first presented himself as a refugee pending arrangement for his resettlement in accordance with the preceeding paragraph.

6. For reasons of security, countries of asylum shall, as far as possible, settle refugees at a reasonable distance from the frontier of their country of origin.

## *Article III. Prohibition of Subversive Activities*

1. Every refugee has duties to the country in which he finds himself, which require in particular that he conforms with its laws and regulations as well as with measures taken for the maintenance of public order. He shall also abstain from any subversive activities against any Member State of the OAU.

2. Signatory States undertake to prohibit refugees residing in their respective territories from attacking any State Member of the OAU, by any activity likely to cause tension between Member States, and in particular by use of arms, through the press, or by radio.

## *Article IV. Non-Discrimination*

Member States undertake to apply the provisions of this Convention to all refugees without discrimination as to race, religion, nationality, membership of a particular social group or political opinions.

## *Article V. Voluntary Repatriation*

1. The essentially voluntary character of repatriation shall be respected in all cases and no refugee shall be repatriated against his will.

2. The country of asylum, in collaboration with the country of origin, shall make adequate arrangements for the safe return of refugees who request repatriation.

3. The country of origin, on receiving back refugees, shall facilitate their resettlement and grant them the full rights and privileges of nationals of the country, and subject them to the same obligations.

4. Refugees who voluntarily return to their country shall in no way be penalized for having left it for any of the reasons giving rise to refugee situations. Whenever necessary, an appeal shall be made through national information media and through the Administrative Secretary-General of the OAU, inviting refugees to return home and giving assurance

that the new circumstances prevailing in their country of origin will enable them to return without risk and to take up a normal and peaceful life without fear of being disturbed or punished, and that the text of such appeal should be given to refugees and clearly explained to them by their country of asylum.

5. Refugees who freely decide to return to their homeland, as a result of such assurances or on their own initiative, shall be given every possible assistance by the country of asylum, the country of origin, voluntary agencies and international and intergovernmental organizations, to facilitate their return.

## Article VI. Travel Documents

1. Subject to Article III, Member States shall issue to refugees lawfully staying in their territories travel documents in accordance with the United Nations Convention relating to the Status of Refugees and the Schedule and Annex thereto, for the purpose of travel outside their territory, unless compelling reasons of national security or public order otherwise require. Member States may issue such a travel document to any other refugee in their territory.

2. Where an African country of second asylum accepts a refugee from a country of first asylum, the country of first asylum may be dispensed from issuing a document with a return clause.

3. Travel documents issued to refugees under previous international agreements by States Parties thereto shall be recognized and treated by Member States in the same way as if they had been issued to refugees pursuant to this Article.

## Article VII. Co-operation of the National Authorities with the Organization of African Unity

In order to enable the Administrative Secretary-General of the Organization of African Unity to make reports to the competent organs of the Organization of African Unity, Member States undertake to provide the Secretariat in the appropriate form with information and statistical data requested concerning:

(a) the condition of refugees;

(b) the implementation of this Convention, and

(c) laws, regulations and decrees which are, or may hereafter be, in force relating to refugees.

## Article VIII. Co-operation with the Office of the United Nations High Commissioner for Refugees

1. Member States shall co-operate with the Office of the United Nations High Commissioner for Refugees

2. The present Convention shall be the effective regional complement in Africa of the 1951 United Nations Convention on the Status of Refugees.

## Article IX. Settlement of Disputes

Any dispute between States signatories to this Convention relating to its interpretation or application, which cannot be settled by other means, shall be referred to the Commission for Mediation, Conciliation and Arbitration of the Organization of African Unity, at the request of any one of the Parties to the dispute.

## Article X. Signature and Ratification

1. This Convention is open for signature and accession by all Member States of the Organization of African Unity and shall be ratified by signatory States in accordance with their respective constitutional processes. The instruments of ratification shall be deposited with the Administrative Secretary-General of the Organization of African Unity.

2. The original instrument, done if possible in African languages, and in English and French, all texts being equally authentic, shall be deposited with the Administrative Secretary-General of the Organization of African Unity.

3. Any independent African State, Member of the Organization of African Unity, may at any time notify the Administrative Secretary-General of the Organization of African Unity of its accession to this Convention.

## Article XI. Entry into force

This Convention shall come into force upon deposit of instruments of ratification by one-third of the Member States of the Organization of African Unity.

## Article XII. Amendment

This Convention may be amended or revised if any member State makes a written request to the Administrative Secretary-General to that effect, provided however that the proposed amendment shall not be submitted to the Assembly of Heads of State and Government for consideration until all Member States have been duly notified of it and a period of one year has elapsed. Such an amendment shall not be effective unless approved by at least two-thirds of the Member States Parties to the present Convention.

### *Article XIII. Denunciation*

1. Any Member State Party to this Convention may denounce its provisions by a written notification to the Administrative Secretary-General.

2. At the end of one year from the date of such notification, if not withdrawn, the Convention shall cease to apply with respect to the denouncing State.

### *Article XIV*

Upon entry into force of this Convention, the Administrative Secretary-General of the OAU shall register it with the Secretary-General of the United Nations, in accordance with Article 102 of the Charter of the United Nations.

### *Article XV. Notifications by the Administrative Secretary-General of the Organization of African Unity*

The Administrative Secretary-General of the Organization of African Unity shall inform all Members of the Organization:

(a) of signatures, ratifications and accessions in accordance with Article X;

(b) of entry into force, in accordance with Article XI;

(c) of requests for amendments submitted under the terms of Article XII;

(d) of denunciations, in accordance with Article XIII.

IN WITNESS WHEREOF WE, the Heads of African State and Government, have signed this Convention.

# IX. Caracas Convention on Territorial Asylum 1954

*Signed in Caracas on March 28, 1954 at the Tenth
Inter-American Conference*

Entry into force: 29 December 1954, in accordance with Article 14

Text: OAS Official Records, OEA/Ser.X/1. Treaty Series 34

The Governments of the Member States of the Organization of American States, desirous of concluding a Convention regarding Territorial Asylum, have agreed to the following articles:

## Article 1

Every State has the right, in the exercise of its sovereignty, to admit into its territory such persons as it deems advisable, without, through the exercise of this right, giving rise to complaint by any other State.

## Article 2

The respect which, according to international law, is due to the jurisdictional right of each State over the inhabitants in its territory, is equally due, without any restriction whatsoever, to that which it has over persons who enter it proceeding from a State in which they are persecuted for their beliefs, opinions, or political affiliations, or for acts which may be considered as political offenses.

Any violation of sovereignty that consists of acts committed by a government or its agents in another State against the life or security of an individual, carried out on the territory of another State, may not be considered attenuated because the persecution began outside its boundaries or is due to political considerations or reasons of state.

## Article 3

No State is under the obligation to surrender to another State, or to expel from its own territory, persons persecuted for political reasons or offenses.

## Article 4

The right of extradition is not applicable in connection with persons who, in accordance with the qualifications of the solicited State, are sought for political offenses, or for common offenses committed for political ends, or when extradition is solicited for predominantly political motives.

## Article 5

The fact that a person has entered into the territorial jurisdiction of a State surreptitiously or irregularly does not affect the provisions of this Convention.

## Article 6

Without prejudice to the provisions of the following articles, no State is under the obligation to establish any distinction in its legislation, or in its regulations or administrative acts applicable to aliens, solely because of the fact that they are political asylees or refugees.

## Article 7

Freedom of expression of thought, recognized by domestic law for all inhabitants of a State, may not be ground of complaint by a third State on the basis of opinions expressed publicly against it or its government by asylees or refugees, except when these concepts constitute systematic propaganda through which they incite to the use of force or violence against the government of the complaining State.

## Article 8

No State has the right to request that another State restrict for the political asylees or refugees the freedom of assembly or assocation which the latter State's internal legislation grants to all aliens within its territory, unless such assembly or association has as its purpose fomenting the use of force or violence against the government of the soliciting State.

## Article 9

At the request of the interested State, the State that has granted refuge or asylum shall take steps to keep watch over, or to intern at a reasonable distance from its border, those political refugees or asylees who are notorious leaders of a subversive movement, as well as those against whom there is evidence that they are disposed to join it.

Determination of the reasonable distance from the border, for the purpose of internment, shall depend upon the judgment of the authorities of the State of refuge.

All expenses incurred as a result of the internment of political asylees and refugees shall be chargeable to the State that makes the request.

## Article 10

The political internees referred to in the preceding article shall advise the government of the host State whenever they wish to leave its territory. Departure therefrom will be granted, under the condition that they are not to go to the country from which they came and the interested government is to be notified.

## Article 11

In all cases in which a complaint or request is permissible in accordance with this Convention, the admissibility of evidence presented by the demanding State shall depend on the judgment of the solicited State.

## Article 12

This Convention remains open to the signature of the Member States of the Organization of American States, and shall be ratified by the signatory States in accordance with their respective constitutional procedures.

## Article 13

The original instrument, whose texts in the English, French, Portuguese, and Spanish languages are equally authentic, shall be deposited in the Pan American Union, which shall send certified copies to the governments for the purpose of ratification. The instruments of ratification shall be deposited in the Pan American Union; this organization shall notify the signatory governments of said deposit.

## Article 14

This Convention shall take effect among the States that ratify it in the order in which their respective ratifications are deposited.

## Article 15

This Convention shall remain effective indefinitely, but may be denounced by any of the signatory States by giving advance notice of one year, at the end of which period it shall cease to have effect for the denouncing State, remaining, however, in force among the remaining signatory States. The denunciation shall be forwarded to the Pan American Union which shall notify the other signatory States thereof.

# X. Caracas Convention on Diplomatic Asylum 1954

*Signed in Caracas, March 28, 1954 at the Tenth Inter-American Conference*

Entry into force: 29 December 1954, in accordance with Article 23

Text: OAS Official Records, OEA/Ser.X/1. Treaty Series 34

The Governments of the Member States of the Organization of American States, desirous of concluding a Convention on Diplomatic Asylum, have agreed to the following articles:

## *Article 1*

Asylum granted in legations, war vessels, and military camps or aircraft, to persons being sought for political reasons or for political offenses shall be respected by the territorial State in accordance with the provisions of this Convention.

For the purposes of this Convention, a legation is any seat of a regular diplomatic mission, the residence of chiefs of mission, and the premises provided by them for the dwelling places of asylees when the number of the latter exceeds the normal capacity of the buildings.

War vessels or military aircraft that may be temporarily in shipyards, arsenals, or shops for repair may not constitute a place of asylum.

## *Article 2*

Every State has the right to grant asylum; but it is not obligated to do so or to state its reasons for refusing it.

## Article 3

It is not lawful to grant asylum to persons who, at the time of requesting it, are under indictment or on trial for common offenses or have been convicted by competent regular courts and have not served the respective sentence, nor to deserters from land, sea, and air forces, save when the acts giving rise to the request for asylum, whatever the case may be, are clearly of a political nature.

Persons included in the foregoing paragraph who de facto enter a place that is suitable as an asylum shall be invited to leave or, as the case may be, shall be surrendered to the local authorities, who may not try them for political offenses committed prior to the time of the surrender.

## Article 4

It shall rest with the State granting asylum to determine the nature of the offense or the motives for the persecution.

## Article 5

Asylum may not be granted except in urgent cases and for the period of time strictly necessary for the asylee to depart from the country with the guarantees granted by the Government of the territorial State, to the end that his life, liberty, or personal integrity may not be endangered, or that the asylee's safety is ensured in some other way.

## Article 6

Urgent cases are understood to be those, among others, in which the individual is being sought by persons or mobs over whom the authorities have lost control, or by the authorities themselves, and is in danger of being deprived of his life or liberty because of political persecution and cannot, without risk, ensure his safety in any other way.

## Article 7

If a case of urgency is involved, it shall rest with the State granting asylum to determine the degree of urgency of the case.

## Article 8

The diplomatic representative, commander of a warship, military camp, or military airship, shall, as soon as possible after asylum has been granted, report the fact to the Minister of Foreign Affairs of the territorial State, or to the local administrative authority if the case arose outside the Capital.

## Article 9

The official furnishing asylum shall take into account the information furnished to him by the territorial government in forming his judgment as to the nature of the offense or the existence of related common crimes; but the decision to continue the asylum or to demand a safe-conduct for the asylee shall be respected.

## Article 10

The fact that the Government of the territorial State is not recognized by the State granting asylum shall not prejudice the application of the present Convention, and no act carried out by virtue of this Convention shall imply recognition.

## Article 11

The Government of the territorial State, may, at any time, demand that the asylee be withdrawn from the country, for which purpose the said State shall grant a safe-conduct and the guarantees stipulated in Article 5.

## Article 12

Once asylum has been granted, the State granting asylum may request that the asylee be allowed to depart for foreign territory, and the territorial State is under obligation to grant immediately, except in case of *force majeure*, the necessary guarantees, referred to in Article 5, as well as the corresponding safe-conduct.

## Article 13

In the cases referred to in the preceding articles the State granting asylum may require that the guarantees be given in writing, and may take into account, in determining the rapidity of the journey, the actual conditions of danger involved in the departure of the asylee.

The State granting asylum has the right to transfer the asylee out of the country. The territorial State may point out the preferable route for the departure of the asylee, but this does not imply determining the country of destination.

If the asylum is granted on board a warship or military airship, departure may be made therein, but complying with the previous requisite of obtaining the appropriate safe-conduct.

## Article 14

The State granting asylum cannot be held responsible for the prolongation of asylum caused by the need for obtaining the information required to determine whether or not the said asylum is proper, or whether there are circumstances that might endanger the safety of the asylee during the journey to a foreign country.

## Article 15

When, in order to transfer an asylee to another country it may be necessary to traverse the territory of a State that is a party to this Convention, transit shall be authorized by the latter, the only requisite being the presentation, through diplomatic channels, of a safe-conduct, duly countersigned and bearing a notation of his status as asylee by the diplomatic mission that granted asylum.

En route, the asylee shall be considered under the protection of the State granting asylum.

## *Article 16*

Asylees may not be landed at any point in the territorial State or at any place near thereto, except for exigencies of transportation.

## *Article 17*

Once the departure of the asylee has been carried out, the State granting asylum is not bound to settle him in its territory; but it may not return him to his country of origin, unless this is the express wish of the asylee.

If the territorial State informs the official granting asylum of its intention to request the subsequent extradition of the asylee, this shall not prejudice the application of any provision of the present Convention. In that event, the asylee shall remain in the territory of the State granting asylum until such time as the formal request for extradition is received, in accordance with the juridical principles governing that institution in the State granting asylum. Preventive surveillance over the asylee may not exceed thirty days.

Payment of the expenses incurred by such transfer and of preventive control shall devolve upon the requesting State.

## *Article 18*

The official furnishing asylum may not allow the asylee to perform acts contrary to the public peace or to interfere in the internal politics of the territorial State.

## *Article 19*

If as a consequence of rupture of diplomatic relations the diplomatic representative who granted asylum must leave the territorial State, he shall abondon it with the asylees.

If this is not possible for reasons independent of the wish of the asylees or the diplomatic representative, he must surrender them to the diplomatic mission of a third State, which is a party to this Convention, under the guarantees established in the Convention.

If this is also not possible, he shall surrender them to a State that is not a party to this Convention and that agrees to maintain the asylum. The territorial State is to respect the said asylum.

## *Article 20*

Diplomatic asylum shall not be subject to reciprocity.
Every person is under its protection, whatever his nationality.

## *Article 21*

The present Convention shall be open for signature by the Member States of the Organization of American States and shall be ratified by the signatory States in accordance with their respective constitutional procedures.

## Article 22

The original instrument, whose texts in the English, French, Spanish, and Portuguese languages are equally authentic, shall be deposited in the Pan American Union, which shall send certified copies to the governments for the purpose of ratification. The instruments of ratification shall be deposited in the Pan American Union, and the said organization shall notify the signatory governments of the said deposit.

## Article 23

The present Convention shall enter into force among the States that ratify it in the order in which their respective ratifications are deposited.

## Article 24

The present Convention shall remain in force indefinitely, but may be denounced by any of the signatory States by giving advance notice of one year, at the end of which period it shall cease to have effect for the denouncing State, remaining in force, however, among the remaining signatory States. The denunciation shall be transmitted to the Pan American Union, which shall inform the other signatory States thereof.

# XI. American Convention on Human Rights, 1969—Extract

[Text in 9 *International Legal Materials* 99, reproduced from OAS, Official Records OEA/Ser. K/xvi/1.1, doc. 65, Rev. 1, Corr. 1 of 7 January 1970]

### Article 20. Right to Nationality

1. Every person has the right to a nationality.

2. Every person has the right to the nationality of the state in whose territory he was born if he does not have the right to any other nationality.

3. No one shall be arbitrarily deprived of his nationality or of the right to change it.

### Article 22. Freedom of Movement and Residence

1. Every person lawfully in the territory of a state party has the right to move about in it and to reside in it subject to the provisions of the law.

2. Every person has the right to leave any country freely, including his own.

3. The exercise of the foregoing rights may be restricted only pursuant to a law to the extent necessary in a democratic society to prevent crime or to protect national security, public safety, public order, public morals, public health, or the rights or freedoms of others.

4. The exercise of the rights recognized in paragraph 1 may also be restricted by law in designated zones for reasons of public interest.

5. No one can be expelled from the territory of the state of which he is a national or be deprived of the right to enter it.

6. An alien lawfully in the territory of a state party to this Convention may be expelled from it only pursuant to a decision reached in accordance with law.

7. Every person has the right to seek and be granted asylum in a foreign territory, in accordance with the legislation of the state and international conventions, in the event he is being pursued for political offences or related common crimes.

8. In no case may an alien be deported or returned to a country, regardless of whether or not it is his country of origin, if in that country his right to life or personal freedom is in danger of being violated because of his race, nationality, religion, social status, or political opinions.

9. The collective expulsion of aliens is prohibited.

# XII. Council of Europe Conventions

## EUROPEAN CONVENTION ON HUMAN RIGHTS 1950—EXTRACT

Text: ETS, No. 5

### *Article 3*

No one shall be subjected to torture or to inhumane or degrading treatment or punishment.

## PROTOCOL NO. 4 1963—EXTRACT

Text: ETS, No. 46

### *Article 2*

1. Everyone lawfully within the territory of a State shall, within that territory, have the right to liberty of movement and freedom to choose his residence.

2. Everyone shall be free to leave any country, including his own.

3. No restrictions shall be placed on the exercise of these rights other than such as are in accordance with law and are necessary in a democratic society in the interests of national security or public safety, for the maintenance of *'ordre public'*, for the prevention of crime, or for the protection of the rights and freedoms of others.

4. The rights set forth in paragraph 1 may also be subject, in particular areas, to restrictions imposed in accordance with law and justified by the public interest in a democratic society.

### *Article 3*

1. No one shall be expelled, by means either of an individual or of a collective measure, from the territory of the State of which he is a national.

2. No one shall be deprived of the right to enter the territory of the State of which he is a national.

### *Article 4*

Collective expulsion of aliens is prohibited.

# EUROPEAN CONVENTION ON EXTRADITION
## 1957—EXTRACT

Text: ETS, No. 24

### *Article 3*

1. Extradition shall not be granted if the offence in respect of which it is requested is regarded by the requested Party as a political offence or as an offence connected with a political offence.

2. The same rule shall apply if the requested Party has substantial grounds for believing that a request for extradition for an ordinary criminal offence has been made for the purpose of prosecuting or punishing a person on account of his race, religion, nationality or political opinion, or if that person's position may be prejudiced for any of these reasons.

3. The taking or attempted taking of the life of a Head of State or a member of his family shall not be deemed to be a political offence for the purposes of this Convention.

4. This Article shall not affect any obligations which the Contracting Parties may have undertaken or may undertake under any other international convention of a multilateral character.

### *Article 21*

1. Transit through the territory of one of the Contracting Parties shall be granted on submission of a request by the means mentioned in Article 12, paragraph 1, provided that the offence concerned is not considered by the Party requested to grant transit as an offence of a political or purely military character having regard to Articles 3 and 4 of this Convention. ...

6. The transit of the extradited person shall not be carried out through any territory where there is reason to believe that his life or freedom may be threatened by reason of his race, religion, nationality or political opinion.

# XIII. Selected Resolutions Relating to Refugee Issues Adopted by the General Assembly of the United Nations

|  | *Title* | *Date adopted* |
|---|---|---|
| 319 (IV) | Refugees and stateless persons: Resolutions A and B | 3 December 1949 |
| 428(V) | Statute of the Office of the United Nations High Commissioner for Refugees | 14 December 1950 |
| 429(V) | Draft Convention relating to the Status of Refugees | 14 December 1950 |
| 430(V) | Problems of assistance to Refugees | 14 December 1950 |
| 538(VI) | Assistance to and protection of refugees Resolutions A and B | 2 February 1952 |
| 629(VII) | Draft Protocol relating to the Status of Stateless Persons | 6 November 1952 |
| 638(VII) | Integration of refugees | 20 December 1952 |
| 639(VII) | Report of the United Nations High Commissioner for Refugees | 20 December 1952 |
| 727(VIII) | Prolongation of the Office of the United Nations High Commissioner for Refugees | 23 October 1953 |
| 728(VIII) | Work of the Office of the United Nations High Commissioner for Refugees | 23 October 1953 |
| 832(IX) | International assistance to refugees within the mandate of the United Nations High Commissioner for Refugees | 21 October 1954 |
| 925(X) | Report of the United Nations High Commissioner for Refugees | 25 October 1955 |

| | Title | Date adopted |
|---|---|---|
| 928(X) | Ratification of, or accession to, the Convention relating to the Status of Stateless Persons | 14 December 1955 |
| 1006(ES-II) | Hungarian refugees | 9 November 1956 |
| 1039(XI) | Report of the United Nations High Commissioner for Refugees: Resolutions A and B | 23 January 1957 |
| 1129(XI) | Hungarian Refugees | 21 November 1956 |
| 1165(XII) | Prolongation of the Office of the United Nations High Commissioner for Refugees | 26 November 1957 |
| 1166(XII) | International assistance to refugees within the mandate of the United Nations High Commissioner for Refugees | 26 November 1957 |
| 1167(XII) | Chinese refugees in Hong Kong | 26 November 1957 |
| 1284(XIII) | Report of the United Nations High Commissioner for Refugees | 5 December 1958 |
| 1285(XIII) | World Refugee Year | 5 December 1958 |
| 1286(XIII) | Refugees in Morocco and Tunisia | 5 December 1958 |
| 1388(XIV) | Report of the United Nations High Commissioner for Refugees | 20 November 1959 |
| 1389(XIV) | Refugees from Algeria in Morocco and Tunisia | 20 November 1959 |
| 1390(XIV) | World Refugee Year | 20 November 1959 |
| 1499(XV) | Report of the United Nations High Commissioner for Refugees | 5 December 1960 |
| 1500(XV) | Refugees from Algeria in Morocco and Tunisia | 5 December 1960 |
| 1502(XV) | World Refugee Year | 5 December 1960 |
| 1671(XVI) | Problem raised by the situation of Angolan refugees in the Congo | 18 December 1961 |
| 1672(XVI) | Refugees from Algeria in Morocco and Tunisia | 18 December 1961 |

|  | *Title* | *Date adopted* |
|---|---|---|
| 1673(XVI) | Report of the United Nations High Commissioner for Refugees | 18 December 1961 |
| 1783(XVII) | Continuation of the Office of the United Nations High Commissioner for Refugees | 7 December 1962 |
| 1784(XVII) | The Problem of Chinese Refugees in Hong Kong | 7 December 1962 |
| 1958(XVIII) | Membership of the Executive Committee of the High Commissioner's Programme | 12 December 1963 |
| 1959(XVIII) | Report of the United Nations High Commissioner for Refugees | 12 December 1963 |
| 2039(XX) | Reports of the United Nations High Commissioner for Refugees | 7 December 1965 |
| 2040(XX) | Assistance to Refugees in Africa | 7 December 1965 |
| 2197(XXI) | Report of the United Nations High Commissioner for Refugees | 16 December 1966 |
| 2198(XXI) | Protocol relating to the Status of Refugees | 16 December 1966 |
| 2294(XXII) | Continuation of the Office of the United Nations High Commissioner for Refugees | 11 December 1967 |
| 2312(XXII) | Declaration on Territorial Asylum | 14 December 1967 |
| 2399(XXIII) | Report of the United Nations High Commissioner for Refugees | 6 December 1968 |
| 2594(XXIV) | Report of the United Nations High Commissioner for Refugees | 16 December 1969 |
| 2650(XXV) | Report of the United Nations High Commissioner for Refugees | 30 November 1970 |
| 2789(XXVI) | Report of the United Nations High Commissioner for Refugees | 6 December 1971 |

| | *Title* | *Date adopted* |
|---|---|---|
| 2790(XXVI) | United Nations assistance to East Pakistan refugees through the United Nations focal point and United Nations humanitarian assistance to East Pakistan | 6 December 1971 |
| 2956(XXVII) | Report of the United Nations High Commissioner for Refugees | 12 December 1972 |
| 2957(XXVII) | Continuation of the Office of the United Nations High Commissioner for Refugees | 12 December 1972 |
| 2958(XXVII) | Assistance to Sudanese refugees returning from abroad | 12 December 1972 |
| 3143(XXVIII) | Report of the United Nations High Commissioner for Refugees | 14 December 1973 |
| 3271(XXIX) | Report of the United Nations High Commissioner for Refugees | 10 December 1974 |
| 3272(XXIX) | Elaboration of a draft Convention on Territorial Asylum | 10 December 1974 |
| 3274(XXIX) | Question of the establishment, in accordance with the Convention on the Reduction of Statelessness, of a body to which persons claiming the benefit of the Convention may apply | 10 December 1974 |
| 3454(XXX) | Report of the United Nations High Commissioner for Refugees | 9 December 1975 |
| 3455(XXX) | Humanitarian assistance to the Indo-Chinese displaced persons | 9 December 1975 |
| 3456(XXX) | Elaboration of a draft Convention on Territorial Asylum | 9 December 1975 |
| 31/35 | Report of the United Nations High Commissioner for Refugees | 30 November 1976 |
| 31/36 | Question of the establishment, in accordance with the | 30 November 1976 |

|  | *Title* | *Date adopted* |
|---|---|---|
|  | Convention on the Reduction of Statelessness, of a body to which persons claiming the benefit of the Convention may apply |  |
| 31/126 | Emergency assistance for South African refugee students | 16 December 1976 |
| 32/67 | Report of the United Nations High Commissioner for Refugees | 8 December 1977 |
| 32/68 | Continuation of the Office of the United Nations High Commissioner for Refugees | 8 December 1977 |
| 32/70 | Assistance to refugees in southern Africa | 8 December 1977 |
| 32/119 | Assistance to South African student refugees | 16 December 1977 |
| 33/25 | Enlargement of the Executive Committee of the Programme of the United Nations High Commissioner for Refugees | 29 November 1978 |
| 33/26 | Report of the United Nations High Commissioner for Refugees | 29 November 1978 |
| 33/167 | Assistance to South African student refugees | 20 December 1978 |
| 34/60 | Report of the United Nations High Commissioner for Refugees | 29 November 1979 |
| 34/61 | Situation of African Refugees | 29 November 1979 |
| 34/62 | Report of the Secretary-General on the Meeting on Refugees and Displaced Persons in South East Asia | 29 November 1979 |
| 34/161 | Women refugees | 17 December 1979 |
| 34/174 | Assistance to Student Refugees from Namibia, Zimbabwe and South Africa | 17 December 1979 |
| 35/41 | Report of the United Nations High Commissioner for Refugees | 25 November 1980 |

| | *Title* | *Date adopted* |
|---|---|---|
| 35/42 | International Conference on Assistance to Refugees in Africa | 25 November 1980 |
| 35/124 | International co-operation to avert new flows of refugees | 11 December 1980 |
| 35/135 | Refugee and displaced women | 11 December 1980 |
| 35/196 | Mass exoduses | 15 December 1980 |
| 36/124 | International Conference on Assistance to Refugees in Africa | 14 December 1981 |
| 36/125 | Report of the United Nations High Commissioner for Refugees | 14 December 1981 |
| 36/136 | New international humanitarian order | 14 December 1981 |
| 36/148 | International co-operation to avert new flows of refugees | 16 December 1981 |
| 37/121 | International co-operation to avert new flows of refugees | 16 December 1982 |
| 37/186 | Human rights and mass exoduses | 17 December 1982 |
| 37/195 | Report of the United Nations High Commissioner for Refugees | 18 December 1982 |
| 37/196 | Continuation of the Office of the United Nations High Commissioner for Refugees | 18 December 1982 |
| 37/197 | International Conference on Assistance to Refugees in Africa | 18 December 1982 |
| 37/201 | New international humanitarian order | 18 December 1982 |

# XIV. List of States Parties to the 1951 Convention, the 1967 Protocol, and the 1969 OAU Convention; and of States Members of the Executive Committee of the High Commissioner's Programme (as at 31 December 1982)

## 1. STATES PARTIES TO THE 1951 CONVENTION AND/OR THE 1967 PROTOCOL

Algeria
Angola
Argentina
Australia
Austria
Belgium
Benin
Bolivia
Botswana
Brazil
Burundi
Canada
Central African
    Republic
Chad
Chile
China
Colombia
Congo
Costa Rica
Cyprus
Denmark
Djibouti
Dominican Republic
Ecuador
Egypt
Ethiopia
Fiji
Finland

France
Gabon
Gambia
Germany, Federal
    Republic
Ghana
Greece
Guinea
Guinea-Bissau
Holy See
Iceland
Iran
Ireland
Israel
Italy
Ivory Coast
Jamaica
Japan
Kenya
Lesotho
Liberia
Liechtenstein
Luxembourg
Madagascar[1]
Mali
Malta
Monaco[1]
Morocco
Netherlands

New Zealand
Nicaragua
Niger
Nigeria
Norway
Panama
Paraguay
Peru[1]
Philippines
Portugal
Rwanda
Sao Tome and
    Principe
Senegal
Seychelles
Sierra Leone
Somalia
Spain
Sudan
Suriname
Swaziland[2]
Sweden
Switzerland
Togo
Tunisia
Turkey
Uganda
United Kingdom
United Republic of
    Cameroon

[1] Party to 1951 Convention only.

United Republic of
Tanzania
United States of
America²

Upper Volta
Uruguay
Yemen
Yugoslavia

Zaïre
Zambia
Zimbabwe

² Party to 1967 Protocol only.

## 2. LIST OF STATES PARTIES TO THE 1969 OAU CONVENTION

Algeria
Benin
Burundi
Chad
Central African
Republic
Congo
Equatorial Guinea
Ethiopia

Gambia
Ghana
Guinea
Liberia
Libya
Mauritania
Morocco
Niger
Rwanda

Senegal
Seychelles
Sudan
Tanzania
Togo
Upper Volta
Zaïre
Zambia

## 3. LIST OF STATES MEMBERS OF THE EXECUTIVE COMMITTEE

Algeria
Argentina
Australia
Austria
Belgium
Brazil
Canada
China
Colombia
Denmark
Finland
France
Germany, Federal
Republic
Greece

Holy See
Iran
Israel
Italy
Japan
Lebanon
Lesotho
Madagascar
Morocco
Namibia¹
Netherlands
Nicaragua
Nigeria
Norway
Sudan

Sweden
Switzerland
Thailand
Tunisia
Turkey
Uganda
United Kingdom
United Republic of
Tanzania
United States of
America
Venezuela
Yugoslavia
Zaïre

¹ Represented by the United Nations Council for Namibia

# Select Bibliography

Aga Khan, Sadruddin. 'Legal Problems Relating to Refugees and Displaced Persons'. Hague *Recueil* (1976-I) 287.
– *Study on Human Rights and Massive Exoduses.* UN doc. E/CN.4/1503 (1981).

Aiboni, Sam Amaize. *Protection of Refugees in Africa.* Uppsala. Swedish Institute of International Law. 1978.

Amnesty International. *Annual Reports,* 1978, 1979, 1980, 1981, 1982.
—— *Guatemala—A Government Program of Political Murder.* 1981.

Bethell, N. *The Last Secret.* André Deutsch. London. 1974.

Blum, Jeffrey M. and Steinhardt, Ralph G. 'Federal Jurisdiction over International Human Rights Claims: The Alien Tort Claims Act, after *Filartiga* v. *Peña-Irala*'. 22 *Harv. ILJ* 53. 1981.

Bossuyt, M. *L'Interdiction de la Discrimination dans le Droit International des Droits de l'Homme.* Bruylant. Bruxelles. 1976.

Buzan, B. 'Negotiating by consensus: Developments in Technique at the United Nations Conference on the Law of the Sea'. 75 *AJIL* 324. 1981.

Capotorti, Francesco. *Study on the Rights of Persons Belonging to Ethnic, Religious and Linguistic Minorities.* UN doc. E/CN.4/Sub.2/384/Rev.1. 1978.

Council of Europe. *Explanatory Report on the European Agreement on Transfer of Responsibility.* Strasbourg. 1980.
—— *Supplementary Report of the Committee of Experts on Extradition to the Committee of Ministers.* CM(57) 52. 1957.
—— European Consultative Assembly. *Report on the Political Rights and Position of Aliens.* Doc. 3834. 1976.

Daes, Erica-Irene A. *Study of the Individual's Duties to the Community and the Limitations of Human Rights and Freedoms under Article 29 of the Universal Declaration of Human Rights.* UN doc. E/CN.4/Sub.2/432/Rev.1 and Add. 1-7. 1980.

Dale, W. 'UNRWA—A subsidiary organ of the United Nations'. 23 *ICLQ* 576. 1974.

D'Amato, A. 'On Consensus'. 8 *Can. YIL* 104. 1970.

Draper, G. I. A. *The Red Cross Conventions.* Stevens. London. 1958.

Elles, Baroness. *International Provisions Protecting the Human Rights of Non-Citizens.* UN doc. E/CN.4/Sub.2/392/Rev.1. 1980.

Epps, V. 'The Validity of the Political Offence Exception in Extradition Treaties in Anglo-American Jurisprudence'. 20 *Harv. ILJ* 61. 1979.

Evans, A. 'Political Refugees "not firmly resettled" as in Section 203(A)(7) of the Immigration Act 1952 as amended'. 66 *AJIL* 101. 1972.

—— 'Political Refugees and the United States Immigration Laws'. 66 *AJIL* 571. 1972.

Foreign Language Press, Hanoi. *The Hoa in Vietnam, Dossiers* I & II. 1978.

—— *Those who leave.* 1979.

—— *With Firm Steps: Southern Vietnam since Liberation 1975-1977.* 1978.

Garcia Marquez, G. 'The Vietnam Wars'. *Rolling Stone.* May 1980.

Garcia-Mora, Manuel R. *International Law and Asylum as a Human Right.* Public Affairs Press. Washington DC. 1956.

Gold, Martin E. 'Non-extradition for Political Offenses: The Communist Perspective'. 11 *Harv. ILJ* 191. 1970.

Goodwin-Gill, Guy S. *International Law and the Movement of Persons between States.* Clarendon Press. Oxford. 1978.

—— 'Entry and Exclusion of Refugees: The Obligations of States and the Protection Function of the Office of the United Nations High Commissioner for Refugees' in *Transnational Legal Problems of Refugees,* 1982 *Michigan Yearbook of International Legal Studies,* 291.

Grahl-Madsen, A. *The Status of Refugees in International Law,* vols. i and ii. Sijthoff. Leyden. 1966, 1972.

—— *Territorial Asylum,* 1980. Uppsala. Swedish Institute of International Affairs. 1979.

—— and Melander, G. (eds.). *Towards an Asylum Convention: Report of the Nansen Symposium.* IUEF. Geneva. 1976.

Grant, B. *The Boat People.* Penguin. Melbourne. 1979.

Hambro, E. *The Problem of Chinese Refugees in Hong Kong.* Sijthoff. Leyden. 1955.

Hathaway, James C. and Schelew, Michael S. 'Persecution by Economic Proscription: A New Refugee Dilemma'. 28 *Chitty's LJ* 190. 1980.

Hawthorne, L. *Refugee—The Vietnamese Experience.* Oxford University Press. Melbourne. 1982.

Henkel, J. 'Anatomie des Deutschen Asylverfahrens'. *NJW* 479. 1980.

—— 'Wege Zur Gesündung des Deutschen Asylverfahrens'. *Zeitschrift für Rechtspolitik* 67. 1980.

Holborn, Louise W. *The International Refugee Organization.* Oxford University Press. London. 1956.

—— *Refugees—A Problem of our Time. The Work of the UNHCR: 1951-1972.* 2 vols. Metuchen. Scarecrow Press. 1975.

Hyndman, P. 'An appraisal of the development of the protection afforded to refugees under international law'. 1 *Lawasia* (NS) 229. 1979-81.

Ingles, José. *Study of Discrimination in Respect of the Right of Everyone to leave any country, including his own, and to return to his country.* UN doc. E/CN.4/Sub.2/229/Rev.1. 1964.

International Commission of Jurists. *The Application in Latin America of International Declarations and Conventions relative to Asylum.* ICJ. Geneva. 1975.

Jahn, E. 'The Work of the Asian-African Legal Consultative Committee on the Legal Status of Refugees'. 27 *Zeitschrift für ausländisches öffentliches Recht und Völkerrecht* 122-38. 1967.

Jennings, R. Y. 'Some International Law Aspects of the Refugee Question'. 20 *BYIL* 98. 1939.

Johnson, D. H. N. 'Refugees, Departees and Illegal Migrants'. 9 *Sydney LR* 11. 1980.

Kimminich, O. *Der internationale Rechtsstatus des Fluchtlings.* Carl Heymans Verlag. Cologne. 1962.

—— *Asylrecht.* Luchterhand. Berlin. 1968.

Kozibrodski, L. B. *Le Droit d'Asile.* Sijthoff. Leyden. 1962.

Kunz, E. F. 'The Refugee in Flight: Kinetic Models and Forms of Displacement'. *International Migration Review* (Summer 1973) 7.

Lauterpacht, H. *International Law and Human Rights.* Stevens. London. 1950.

—— *The Development of International Law by the International Court.* Stevens. London. 1958.

Mann, F. A. 'The Enforcement of Treaties by English Courts' in *Studies in International Law*, 327. Oxford University Press. 1973.

—— 'Britain's Bill of Rights'. 94 *LQR* 512. 1978.

Martin, D. 'The Refugee Act of 1980: its Past and its Future' in *Transnational Legal Problems of Refugees*, 1982 *Michigan Yearbook of International Legal Studies*, 91.

—— 'Large-scale migrations of asylum-seekers', 76 *AJIL* 598. 1982.

Martin, Jean I. *Refugee Settlers: A Study of Displaced Persons in Australia.* Australian National University. Canberra. 1965.

Martinez Cobo, José R. *Study of the Problem of Discrimination against Indigenous Populations.* UN doc. E/CN.4/Sub 2/L. 707.

Melander, G. *Refugees in Orbit.* IUEF. Geneva. 1978.

*Michigan Yearbook of International Legal Studies* 1982: *Transnational Legal Problems of Refugees.*

Minority Rights Group. Religious Minorities in the Soviet Union. No. 1, rev. ed. 1977.

—— Selective Genocide in Burundi. No. 20. 1974.

—— Jehovah's Witnesses in Africa. No. 29. 1976.

—— The Two Irelands—the Double Minority. No. 2, rev. ed. 1979.

—— The Social Psychology of Minorities. No. 38. 1978.

—— The Biharis in Bangladesh. No. 11, rev. ed. 1977.

—— The Crimean Tatars, Volga Germans and Meskhetvans. No. 6, rev. ed. 1980.

—— What Future for the Amerindians of South America? No. 15, rev. ed. 1977.

—— The Asian Minorities of East and Central Africa. No. 4. 1971.

—— Problems of a Displaced Minority—the New Position of Africa's Asians. No. 16, rev. ed. 1978.

—— The Kurds. No. 23, rev. ed. 1981.

—— The Refugee Dilemma: International Recognition and Acceptance. No. 43, rev. ed. 1981.

—— The Namibians of South West Africa. No. 19, rev. ed. 1978.

—— The Palestinians. No. 24, rev. ed. 1979.

—— Constitutional Law and Minorities. No. 36. 1978.

Morgenstern, F. 'The Right of Asylum'. 26 *BYIL* 327. 1949.

Morse, B. 'Practice, Norms and Reform of International Rescue Operations'. Hague *Recueil* (1977-IV) 121.

McKean, W. A. 'The Meaning of Discrimination in International Law'. 44 *BYIL* 177. 1970.

McNair, Lord (Arnold Duncan McNair). 'Extradition and Exterritorial Asylum'. 28 *BYIL* 172. 1951.

Mushkat, R. 'Hong Kong as a country of temporary refuge: an interim analysis'. 12 *Hong Kong LJ* 157. 1982.

Osborne, M. 'The Indo-Chinese Refugees: Causes and Effects'. *International Affairs* (1980) 37-53.

——, Male, B., Lawrie, Q., and O'Malley, W. J. *Refugees: Four Political Case Studies*. Studies in World Affairs, no.3. Australian National University. Canberra. 1981.

Palley, C. *Constitutional Law and Minorities*. Minority Rights Group. No. 36. 1978.

Paludan, Anne. *The New Refugees in Europe*. IUEF. Geneva. 1974.

Pompe, C. A. *The Convention of 28 July 1951 and the International Protection of Refugees*: UN doc. HCR/INF/42. 1958. (Originally published in Dutch in *Rechtsgeleerd Magazyn Themis* (1956) 425-91.

Pugash, J. Z. 'The Dilemma of the Sea Refugee: Rescue without Refuge'. 18 *Harv. ILJ* 577. 1977.

Radley, K. R. 'The Palestinian Refugees: The Right to Return in International Law'. 72 *AJIL* 586. 1978.

Reale, E. 'Le Droit d'Asile'. Hague *Recueil* (1938-I) 473.

—— 'Le Problème des Passeports'. Hague *Recueil* (1934-IV) 89.

Reynolds, E. E. *Nansen*. Penguin. London. Rev. ed. 1949.

Robinson, N. *Convention relating to the Status of Refugees: A Commentary*. Institute of Jewish Affairs. New York. 1953.

Ruhashyankiko, N. *Study of the Question of the Prevention and Punishment of the Crime of Genocide*: UN doc. E/CN.4/Sub.2/416. 1978.

Schaffer, R. P. 'South-East Asian Refugees—The Australian Experience'. *Aust. YIL* (1981) 200.

Schnapp, F. E. 'Beschleunigung des Asylverfahrens'. *NJW* (1978) 1726.

Schnyder, F. 'Les Aspects Juridiques Actuels du Problème des Réfugiés'. Hague *Recueil* (1965-I) 339-450.

Schwebel, S. 'The Effect of Resolutions of the UN General Assembly on Customary International Law'. *ASIL Proceedings*, 73rd Annual Meeting, 301.

Shearer, I. *Extradition in International Law.* Manchester University Press. 1971.

Simpson, Sir J. H. *The Refugee Problem.* Royal Institute of International Affairs. Oxford University Press. London. 1939.

Sinha, S. Prakash. *Asylum and International Law.* Nijhoff. The Hague. 1971.

Stein, B. N. 'Occupational Adjustment of Refugees: The Vietnamese in the United States'. *International Migration Review* (Spring 1979) 13.

Thayer, C. 'Dilemmas of Development in Vietnam'. 75 *Current History.* No. 442. 1978.

—— 'Vietnam—Beleaguered Outpost of Socialism'. 79 *Current History.* No. 461. 1980.

Tolstoy, N. *Victims of Yalta.* Hodder & Stoughton. 1977. Rev. ed., Corgi, 1979.

Tsamenyi, M. *The Vietnamese Boat People and International Law.* Centre for the Study of Australian-Asian Relations, Griffith University, Brisbane. 1980.

United Nations. Report of the Secretary-General on the Meeting on Refugees and Displaced Persons in South-East Asia, Geneva, 20-21 July 1979, and subsequent developments. A/34/637.

—— Elimination of all Forms of Religious Intolerance. Note by the Secretary-General. A/8330. 1971.

—— A Select Bibliography on Territorial Asylum. ST/GENEVA/LIB. SER.B/Ref.9. 1977.

—— A Study on Statelessness. E/1112 & Add.1. 1949.

—— Multilateral Treaties in respect of which the Secretary-General performs depository functions: Ratifications, etc. ST/LEG/SER. D/13. 1981.

UNHCR. *A Mandate to Protect and Assist Refugees.* Geneva. 1971.

—— *Collection of International Instruments concerning Refugees.* Geneva. 2nd ed., 1979.

—— *Handbook on Procedures and Criteria for determining Refugee Status.* Geneva. 1979.

—— *Jurisprudence de la Commission de Recours des Réfugiés.* Dalloz. Paris. 1961.

Vernant, Jacques. *The Refugee in the Post-War World.* Yale Press. New Haven. 1953.

Verwey, W. D. 'The International Hostages Convention and National Liberation Movements'. 75 *AJIL* 69. 1981.

Vierdag, E. W. *The Concept of Discrimination in International Law.* Nijhoff. The Hague. 1973.

—— '"Asylum" and "Refugee" in International Law'. 24 *Neth. ILR* 287. 1971.

Viviani, Nancy. *Australian Government Policies on the Entry of Vietnamese 1975 to 1982: Record and Responsibility.* Centre for the Study of Australian-Asian Relations, Griffith University, Brisbane. 1981.

Wain, B. *'The Refused: The Agony of the Indochina Refugees'*. Simon and Schuster. New York. 1982.

Weis, P. 'The Legal Aspects of the Problems of *de facto* Refugees' in *Problems of Refugees and Exiles in Europe*. IUEF. Geneva. 1974.

—— 'The Concept of the Refugee in International Law'. *Journal du Droit International* (1960) 1.

—— 'Legal Aspects of the Convention of 28 July 1951 relating to the Status of Refugees'. 30 *BYIL* 478. 1953.

—— 'Territorial Asylum'. 6 *Indian JIL* 173. 1966.

—— 'The United Nations Declaration on Territorial Asylum'. 7 *Can YIL* 92. 1969.

—— 'Refugee Seamen'. 7 *ICLQ* 340. 1958.

—— 'The Draft United Nations Convention on Territorial Asylum'. 50 *BYIL* 151. 1980.

—— 'The 1967 Protocol relating to the Status of Refugees and some Questions of the Law of Treaties'. 42 *BYIL* 39. 1967.

—— 'The International Status of Refugees and Stateless Persons'. *Journal du Droit International* (1956) 4.

—— 'The International Protection of Refugees'. 48 *AJIL* 193. 1954.

—— 'The United Nations Convention on the Reduction of Statelessness, 1961'. 11 *ICLQ* 1073. 1962.

—— 'The Convention relating to the Status of Stateless Persons'. 10 *ICLQ* 255. 1961.

—— *Nationality and Statelessness in International Law*. Sijthoff. Leyden. 2nd ed., 1979.

Whitaker, B. (ed.). *The Fourth World: Victims of Groups Oppression*. Schocken. New York. 1973.

Williams, Sir. J. Fischer. 'Denationalization'. 8 *BYIL* 45. 1927.

Wydryzynski, C. J. 'Refugees and the Immigration Act'. 25 *McGill LJ* 154. 1979.

De Zayas, Alfred M. *Die Anglo-Americaner und Die Vertreibung der Deutschen*. 1977. (Published in English as *Nemesis at Potsdam: the Anglo-Americans and the Expulsion of the Germans*. 1977.)

—— 'International Law and Mass Population Transfers'. 16 *Harv. ILJ* 207. 1975.

# INDEX